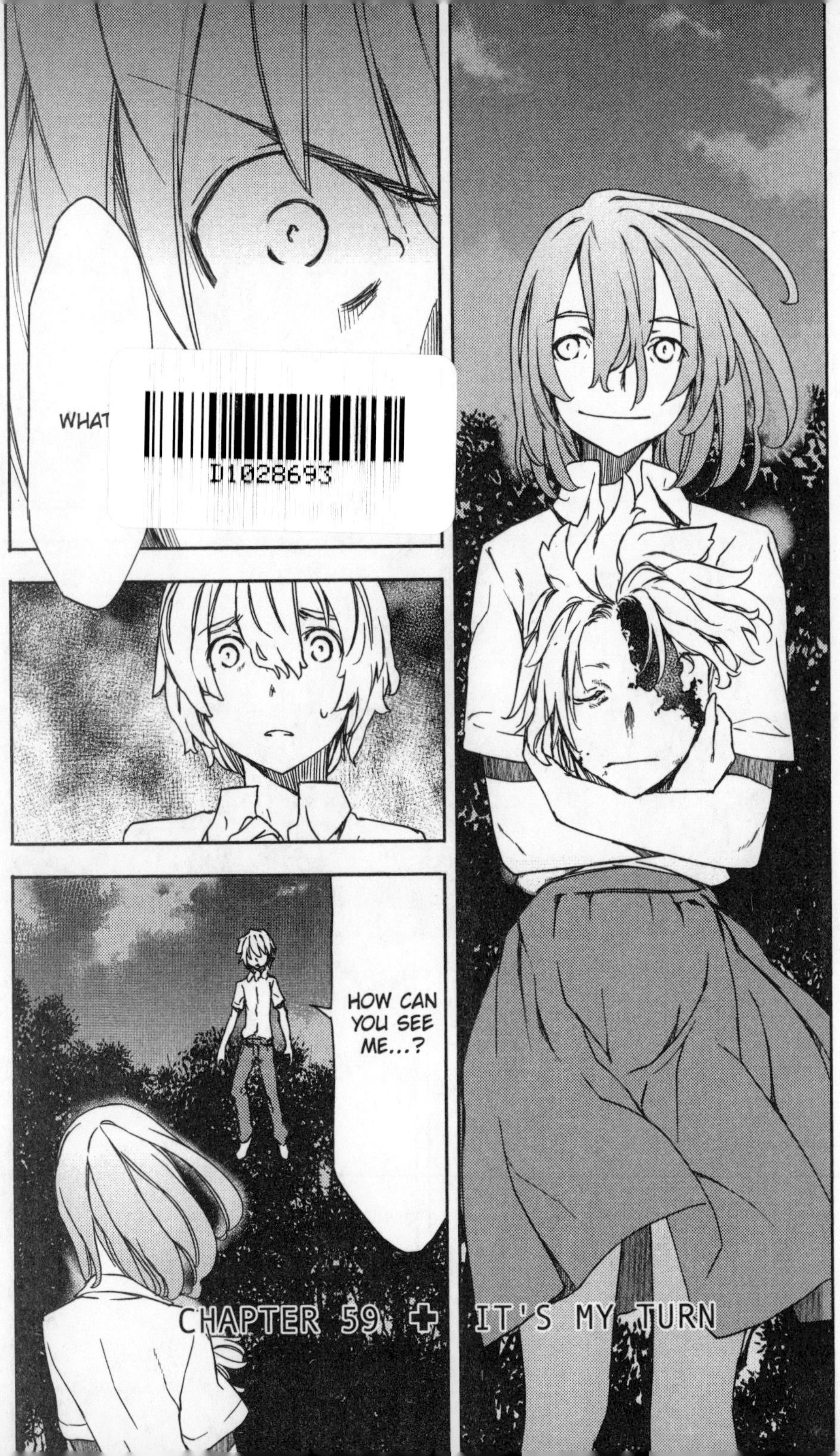
WHAT
HOW CAN YOU SEE ME...?
CHAPTER 59 ✚ IT'S MY TURN

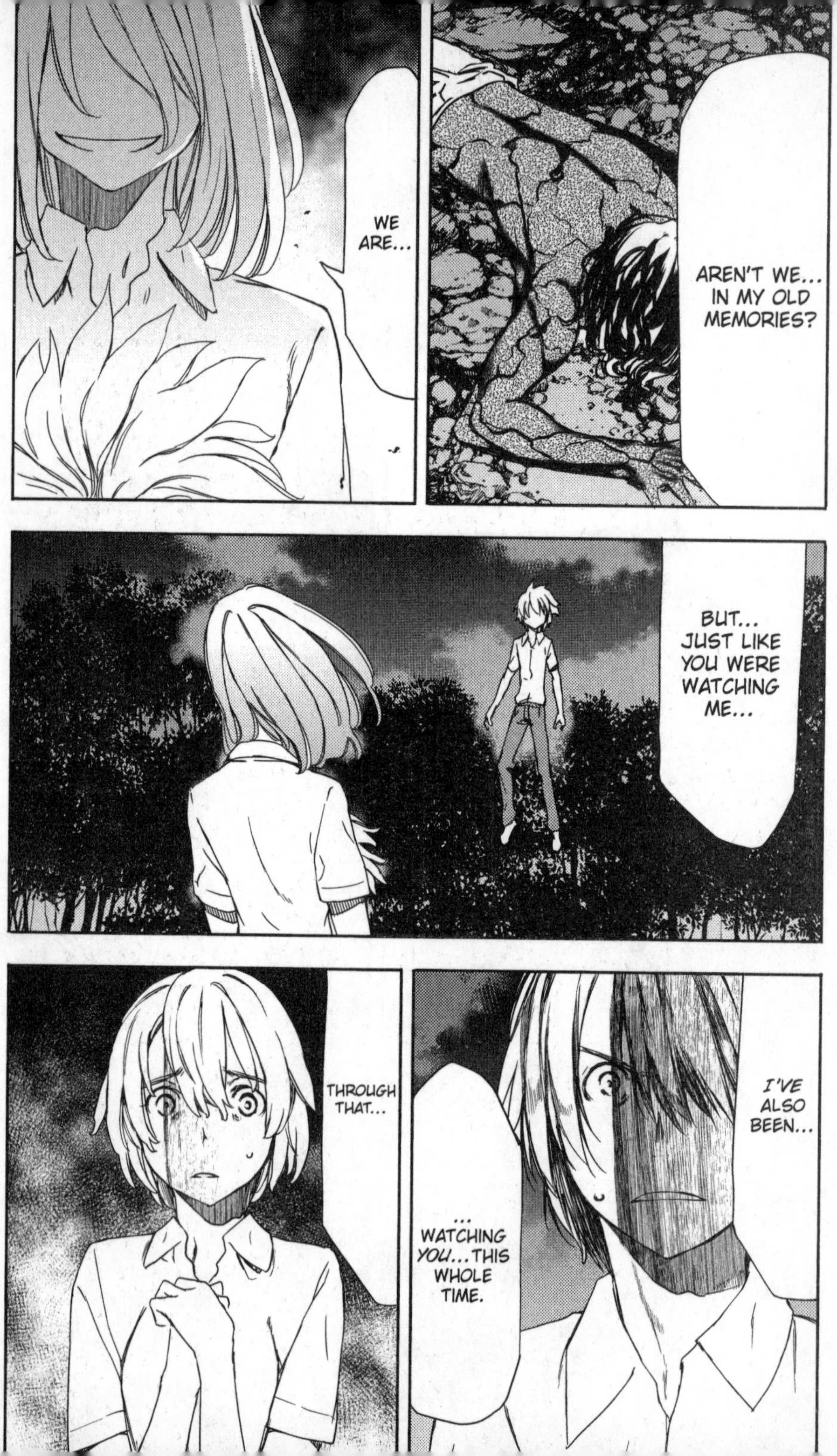
WE ARE...
AREN'T WE... IN MY OLD MEMORIES?
BUT... JUST LIKE YOU WERE WATCHING ME...
THROUGH THAT...
I'VE ALSO BEEN...
... WATCHING YOU... THIS WHOLE TIME.

...GIRL YOU'RE WITH.

GLEIPNIR vol. 10

SUN TAKEDA

CONTENTS

CHAPTER 59 ✚ It's My Turn.....................001

CHAPTER 60 ✚ Claire.........................033

CHAPTER 61 ✚ To Hope and Suffer...........067

CHAPTER 62 ✚ What I Want to Protect.....101

CHAPTER 63 ✚ A Gushing Force.............137

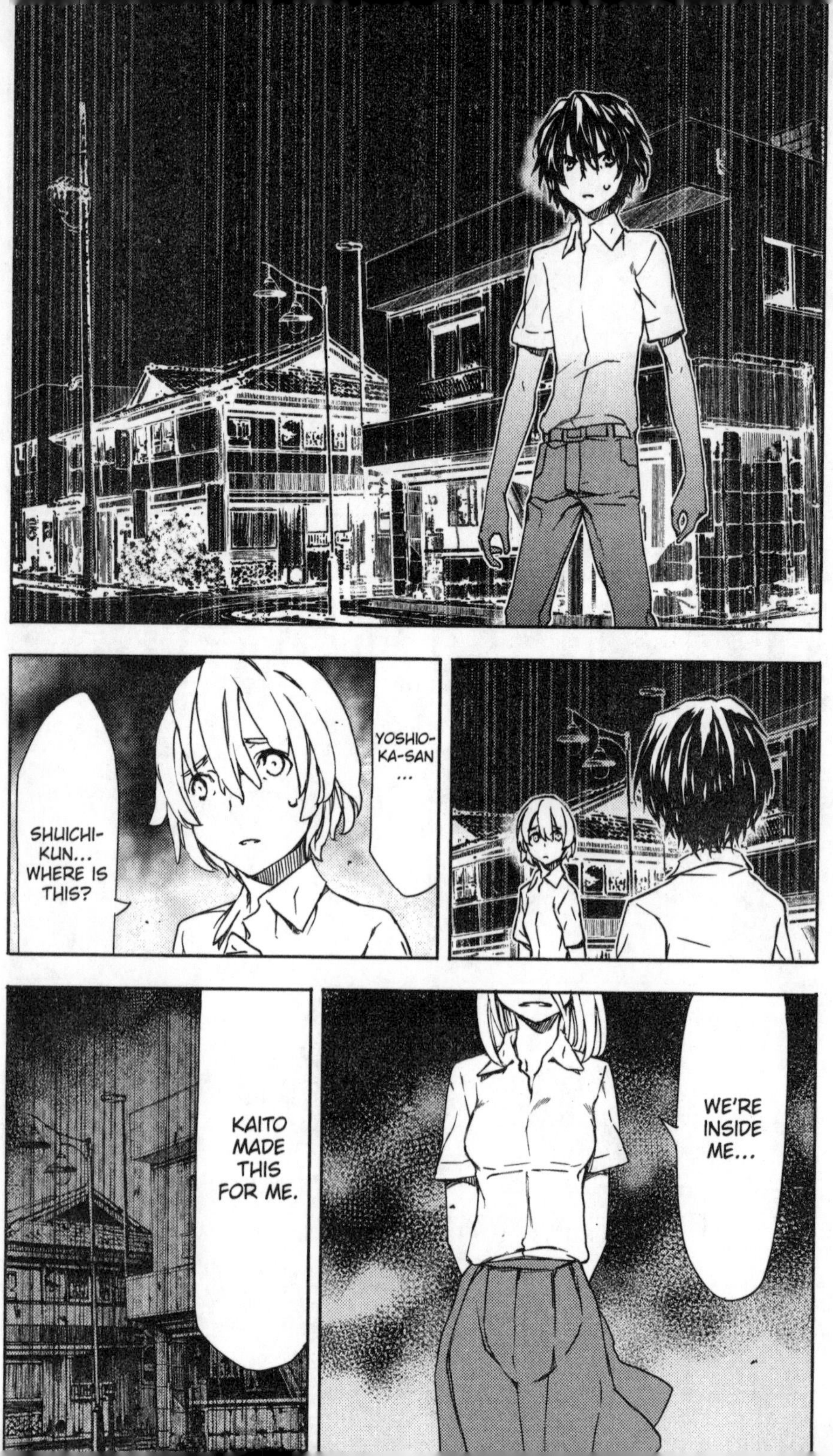
YOSHIOKA-SAN...
SHUICHI-KUN... WHERE IS THIS?
WE'RE INSIDE ME...
KAITO MADE THIS FOR ME.

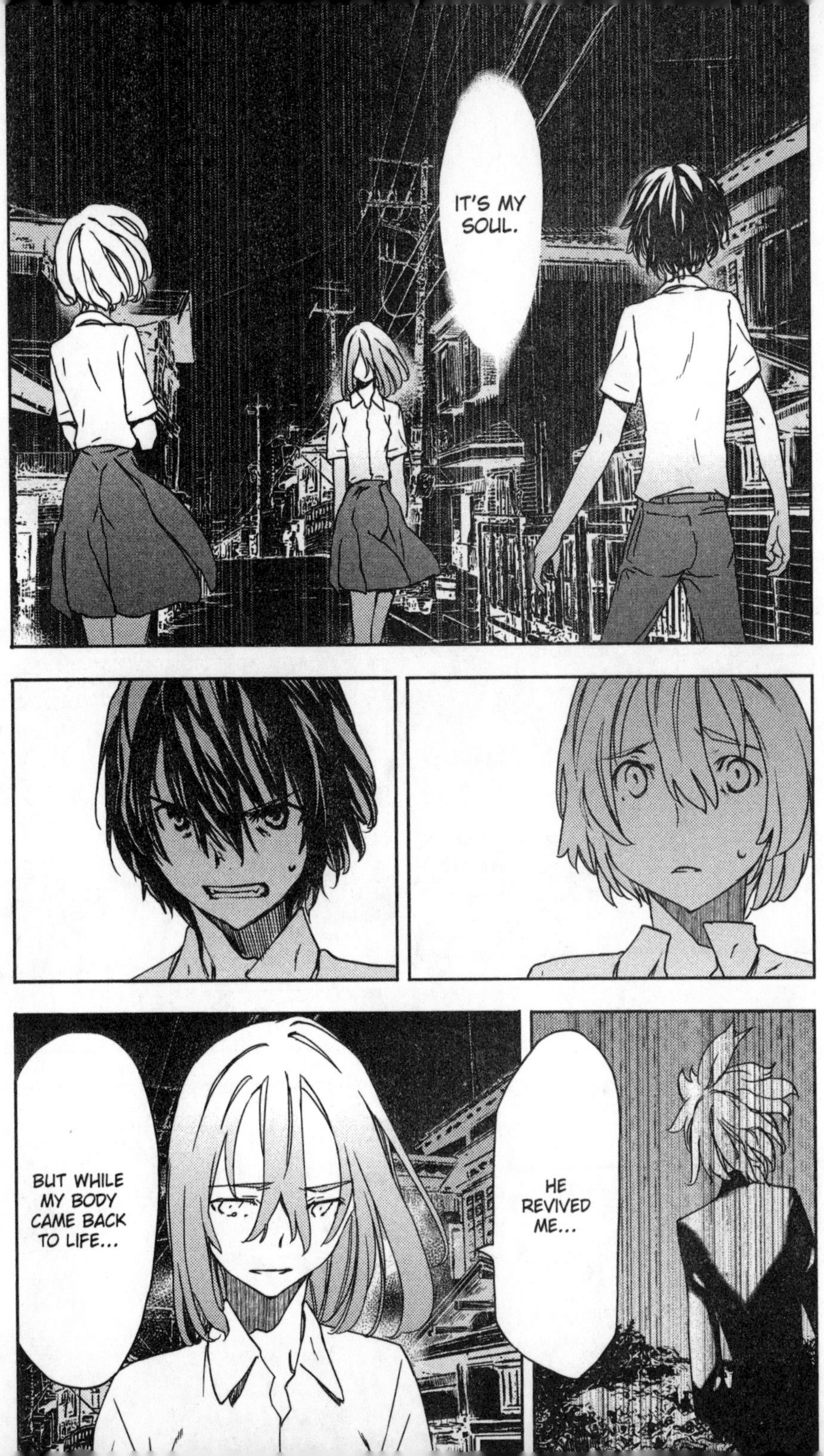
IT'S MY SOUL.
HE REVIVED ME...
BUT WHILE MY BODY CAME BACK TO LIFE...

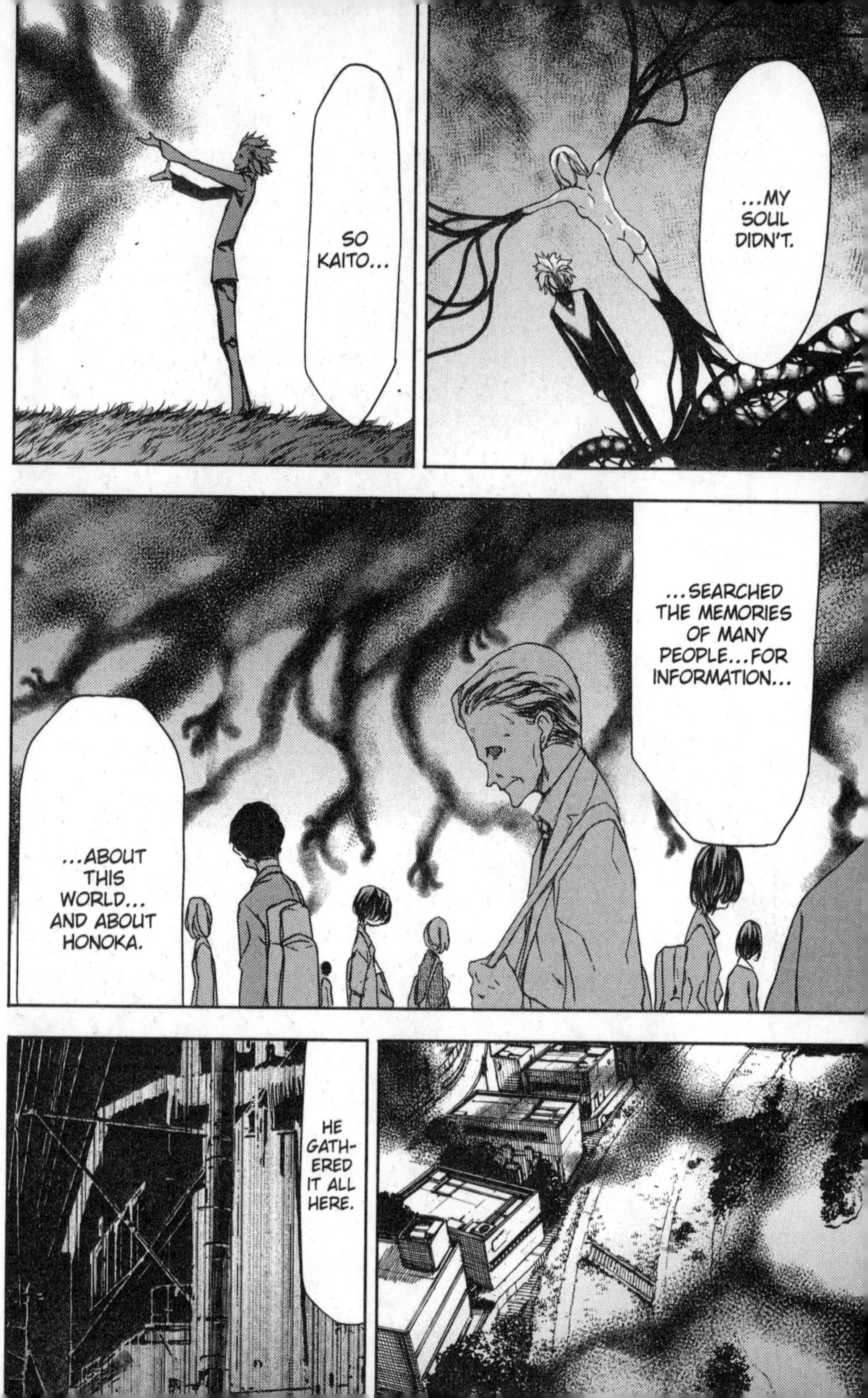
...MY SOUL DIDN'T.
SO KAITO...
...SEARCHED THE MEMORIES OF MANY PEOPLE...FOR INFORMATION...
...ABOUT THIS WORLD... AND ABOUT HONOKA.
HE GATH-ERED IT ALL HERE.

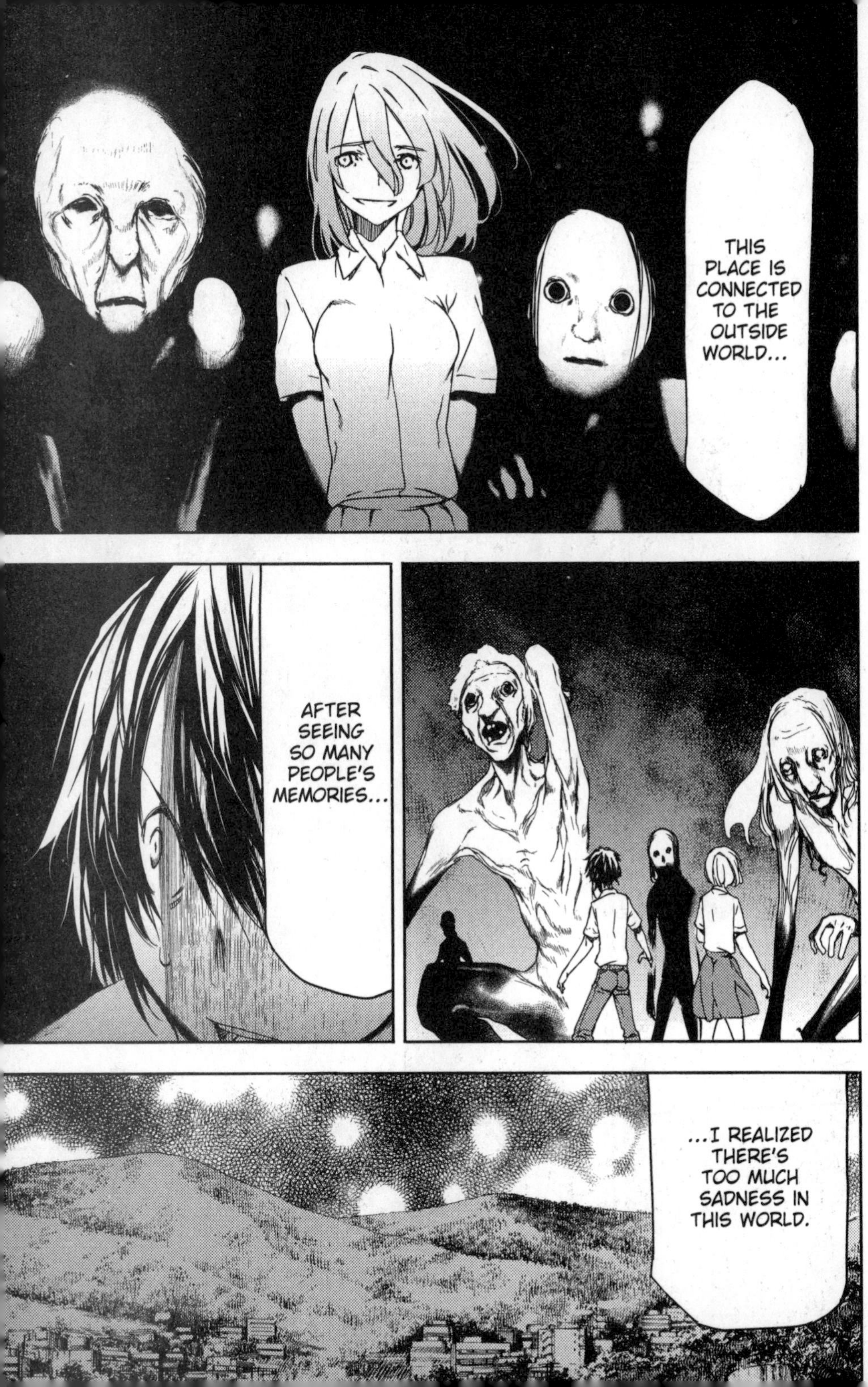
THIS PLACE IS CONNECTED TO THE OUTSIDE WORLD...
AFTER SEEING SO MANY PEOPLE'S MEMORIES...
...I REALIZED THERE'S TOO MUCH SADNESS IN THIS WORLD.

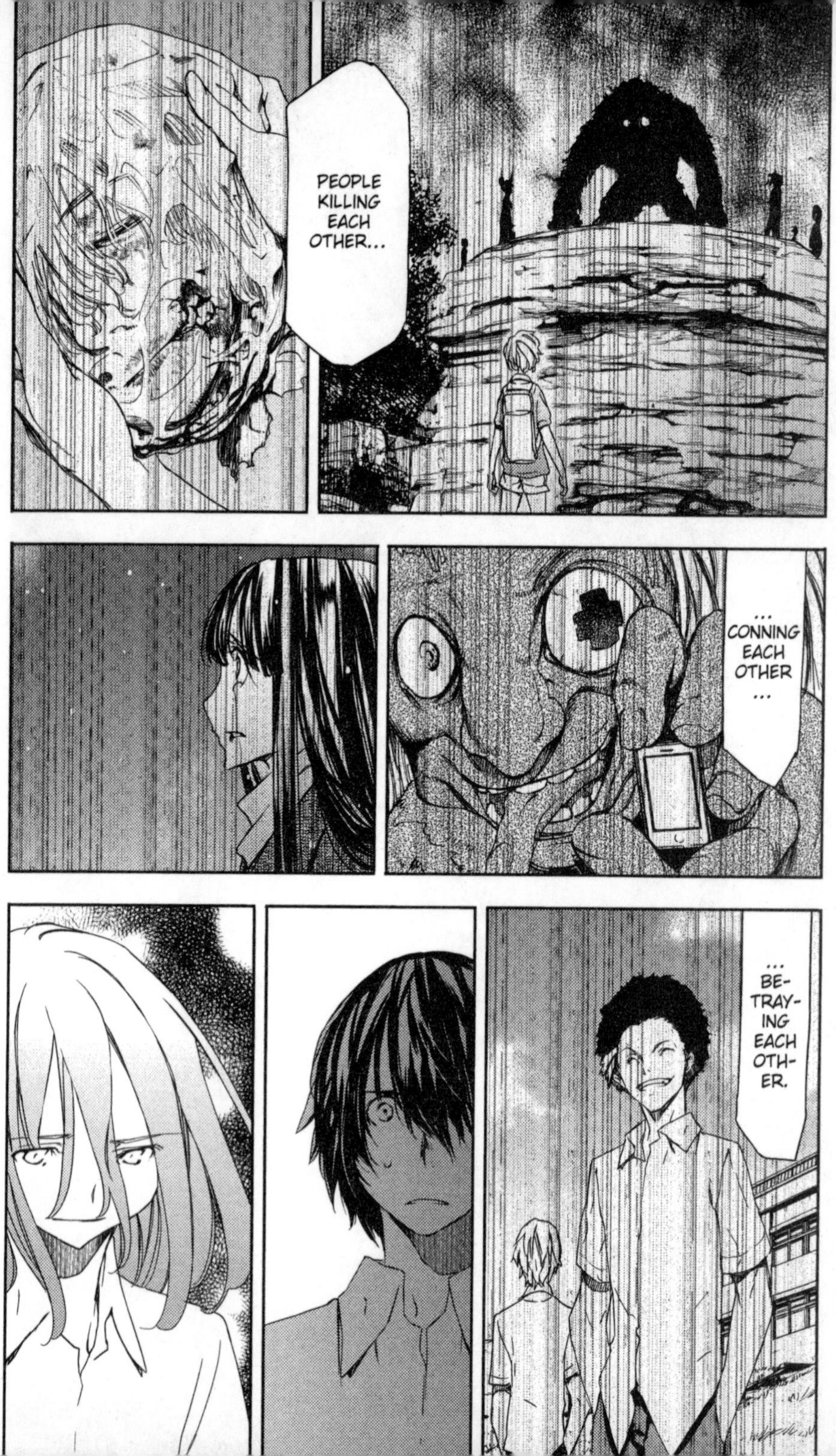
PEOPLE KILLING EACH OTHER...
...CONNING EACH OTHER...
...BE-TRAY-ING EACH OTH-ER.

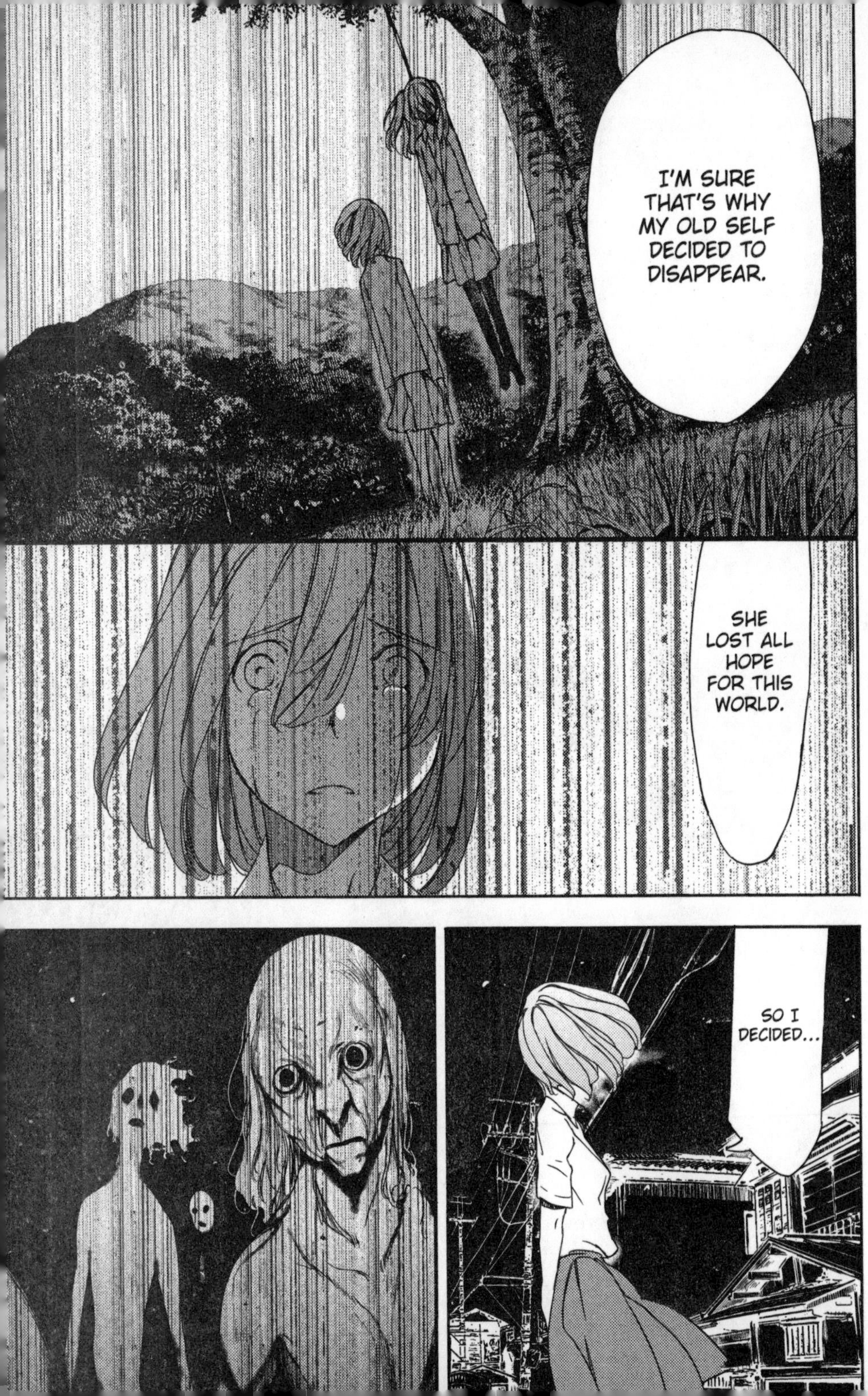
I'M SURE THAT'S WHY MY OLD SELF DECIDED TO DISAPPEAR.
SHE LOST ALL HOPE FOR THIS WORLD.
SO I DECIDED...

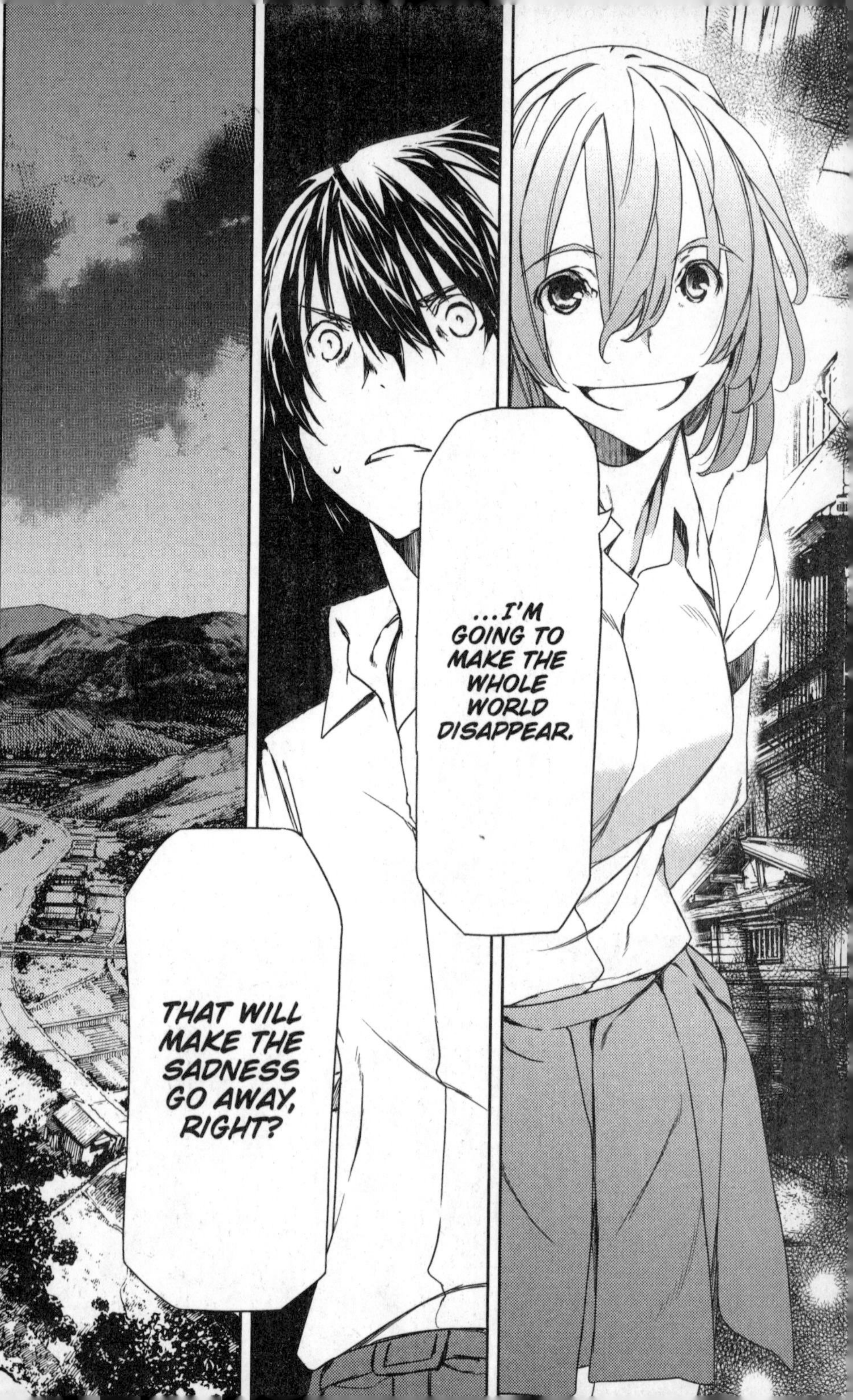
...I'M GOING TO MAKE THE WHOLE WORLD DISAPPEAR.
THAT WILL MAKE THE SADNESS GO AWAY, RIGHT?

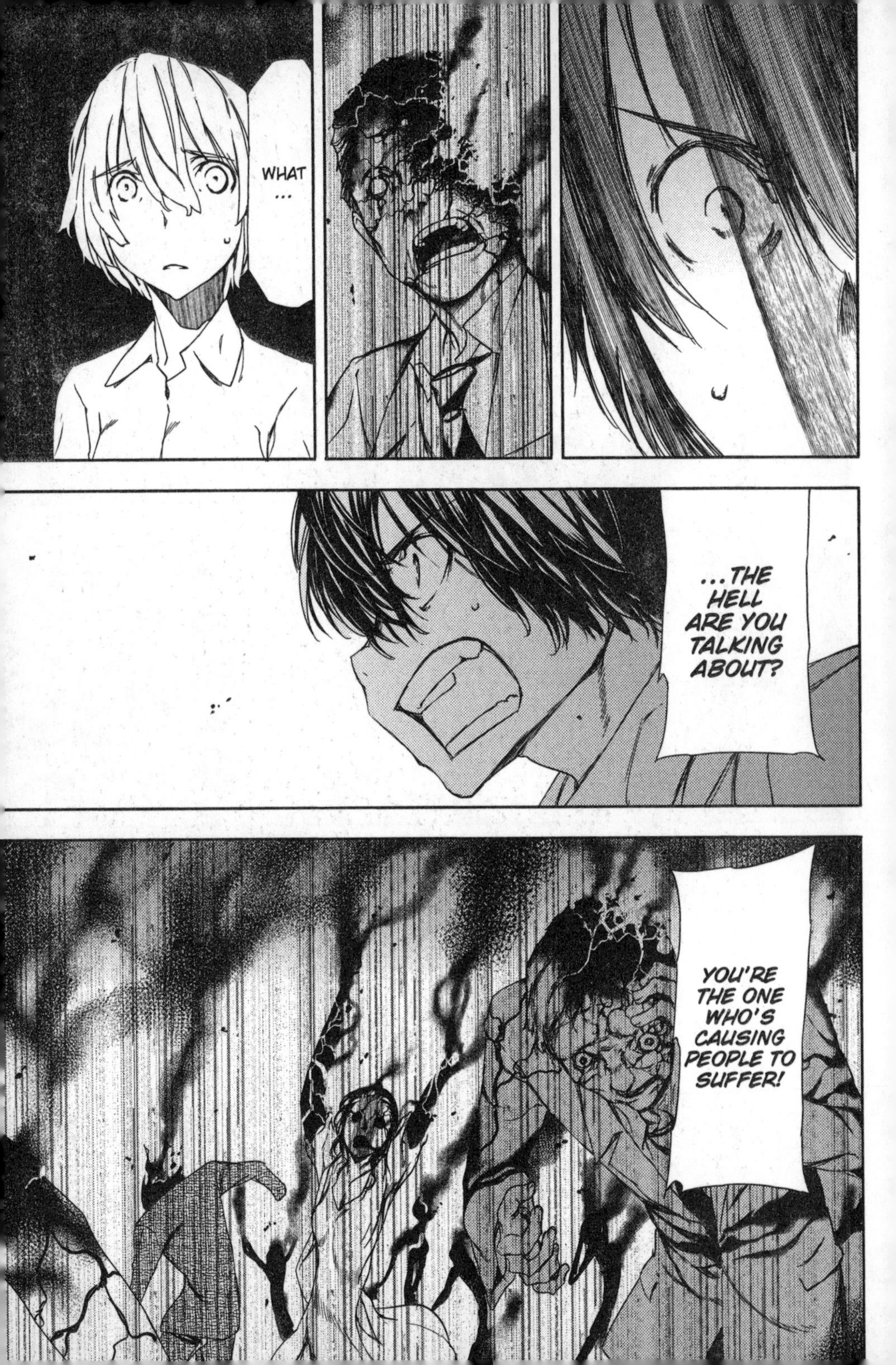
WHAT ...
...THE HELL ARE YOU TALKING ABOUT?
YOU'RE THE ONE WHO'S CAUSING PEOPLE TO SUFFER!

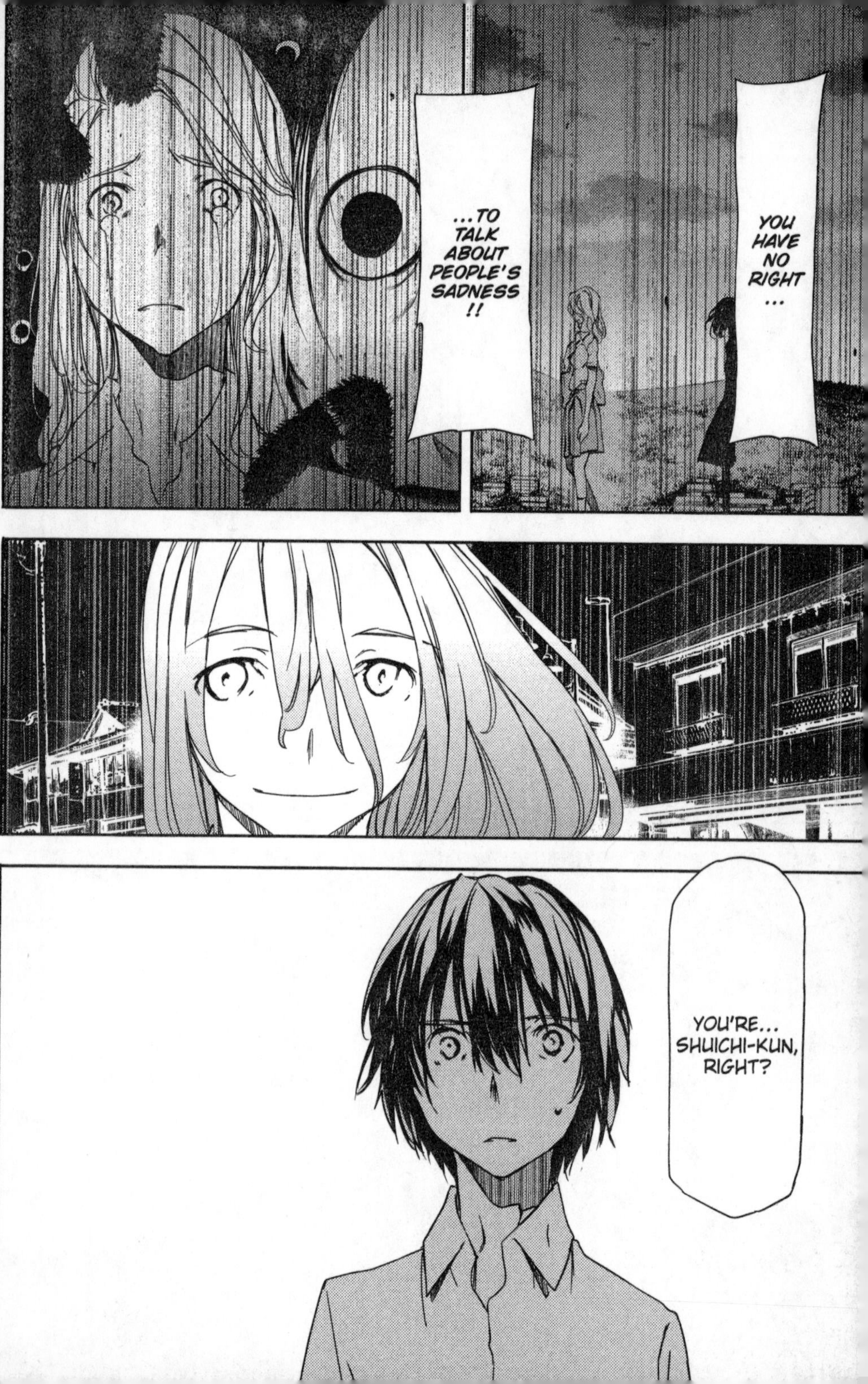
YOU HAVE NO RIGHT ...
...TO TALK ABOUT PEOPLE'S SADNESS !!
YOU'RE... SHUICHI-KUN, RIGHT?

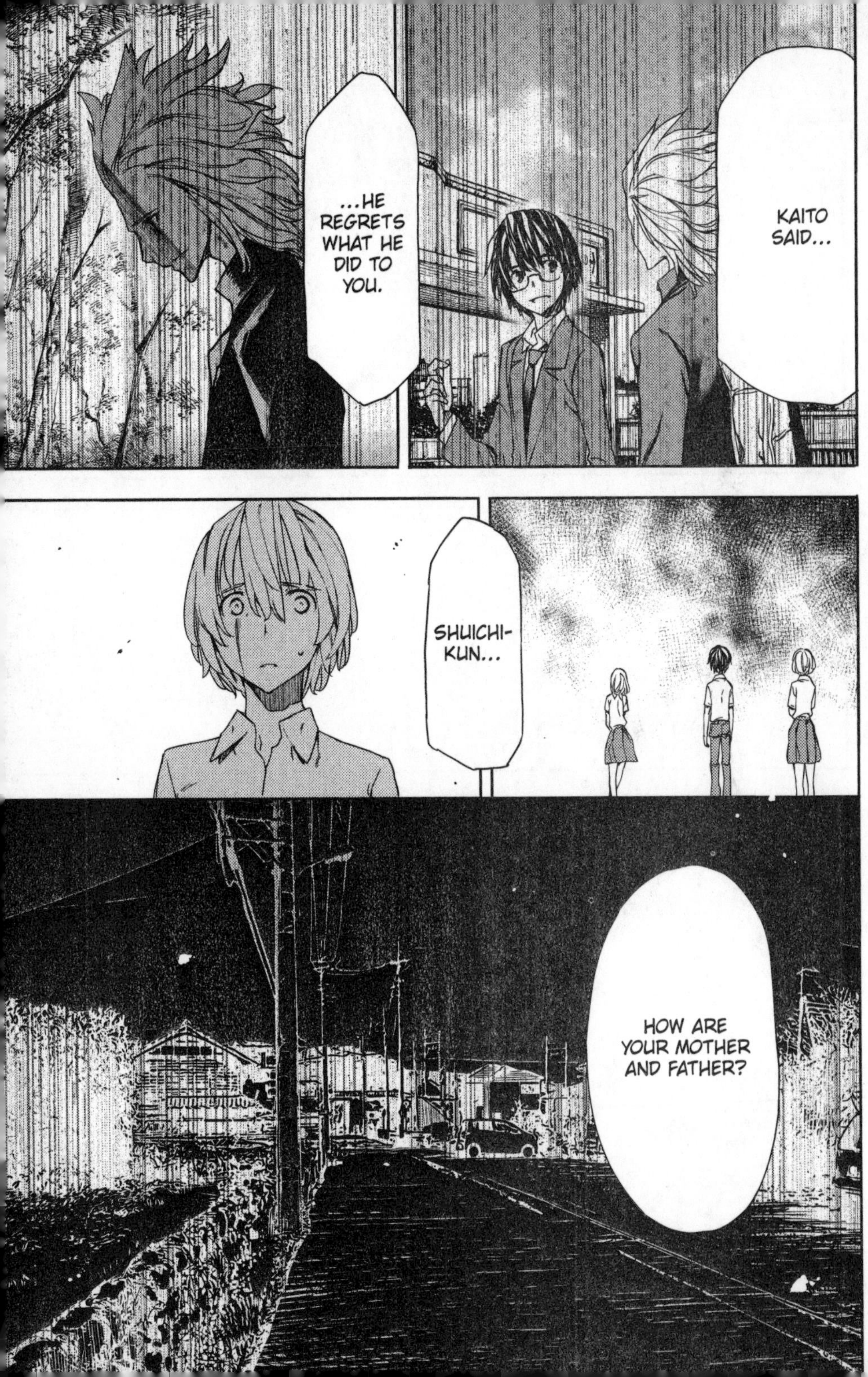
KAITO SAID...
...HE REGRETS WHAT HE DID TO YOU.
SHUICHI-KUN...
HOW ARE YOUR MOTHER AND FATHER?

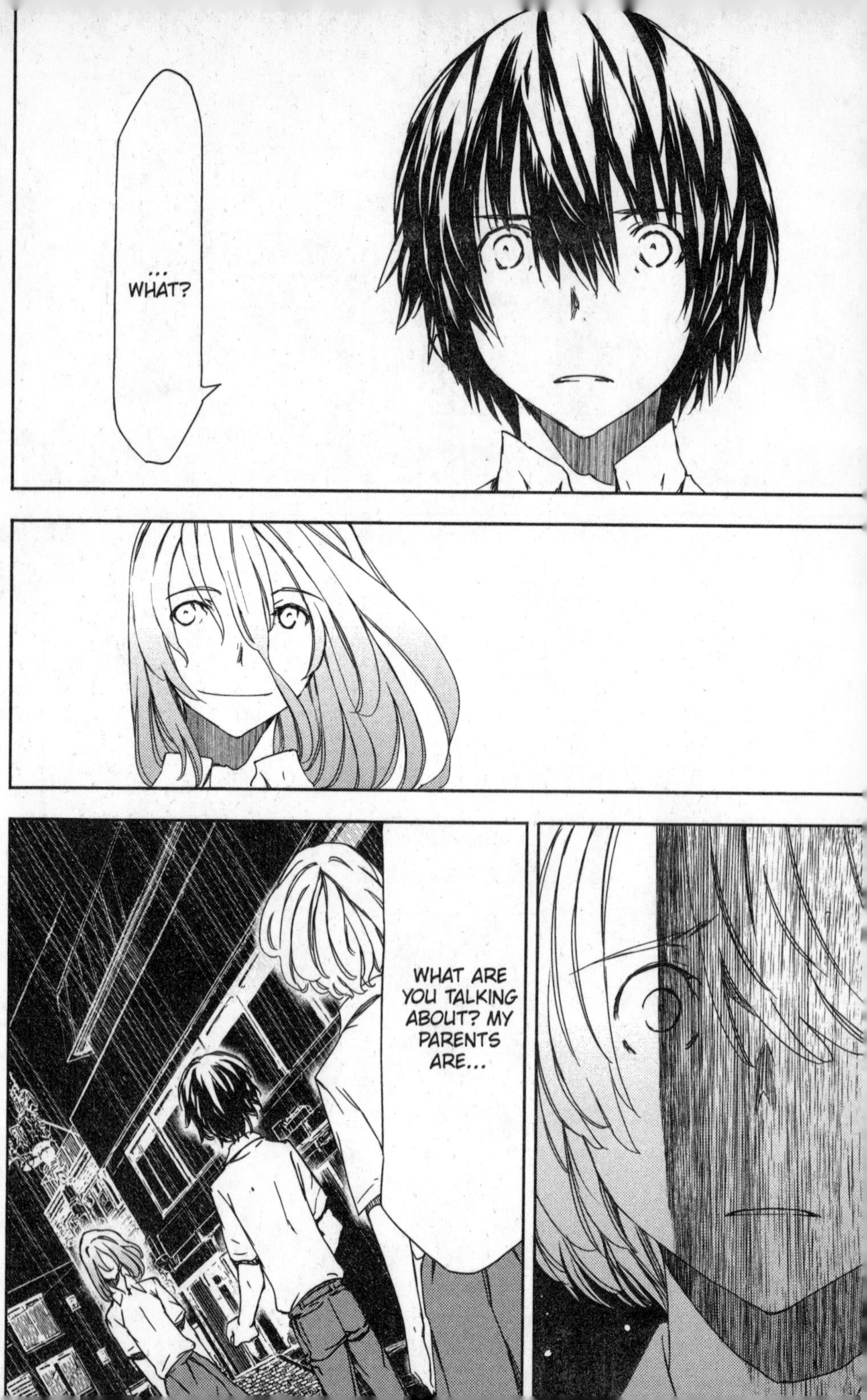
...
WHAT?
WHAT ARE YOU TALKING ABOUT? MY PARENTS ARE...

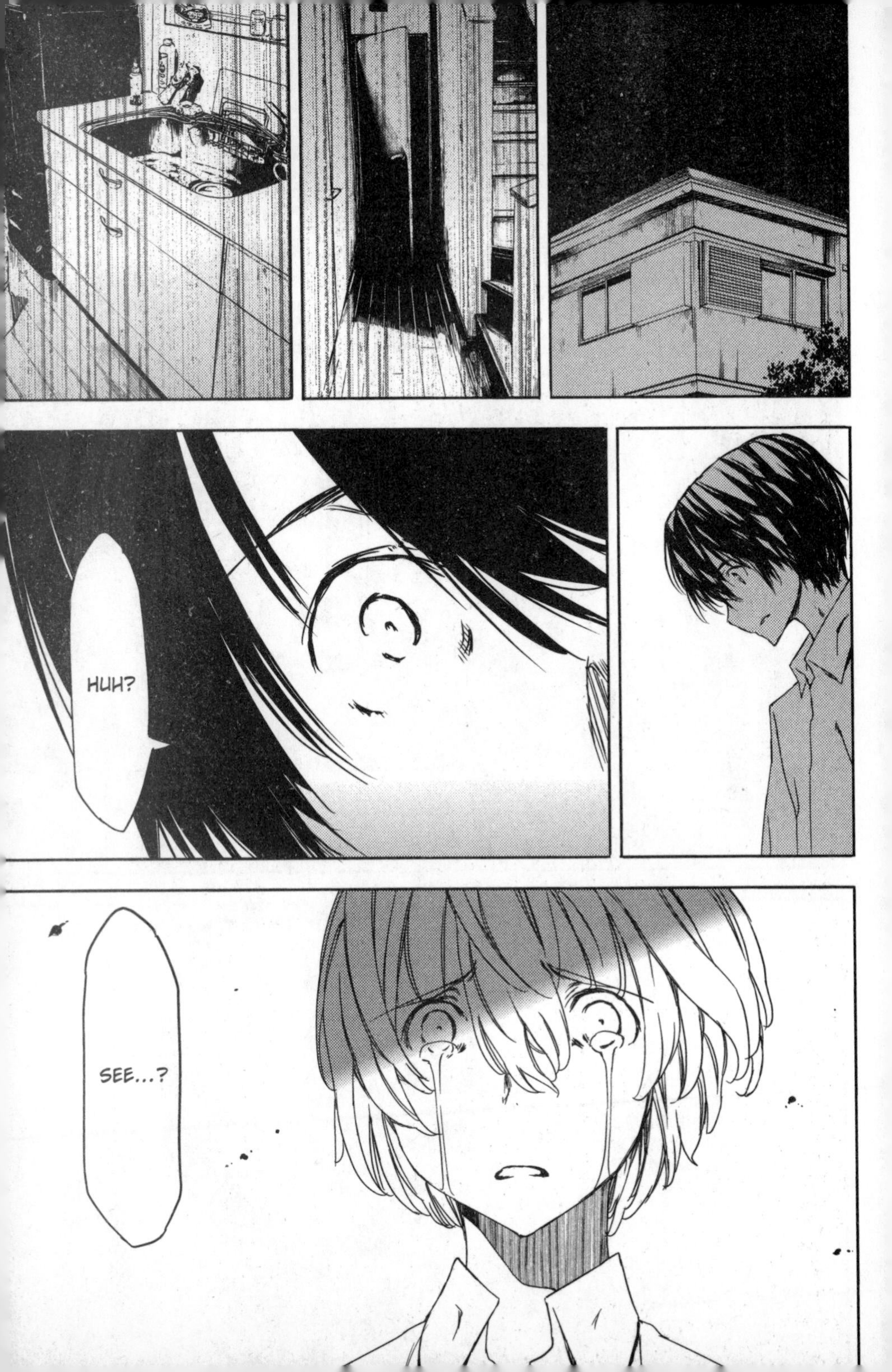
HUH?
SEE...?

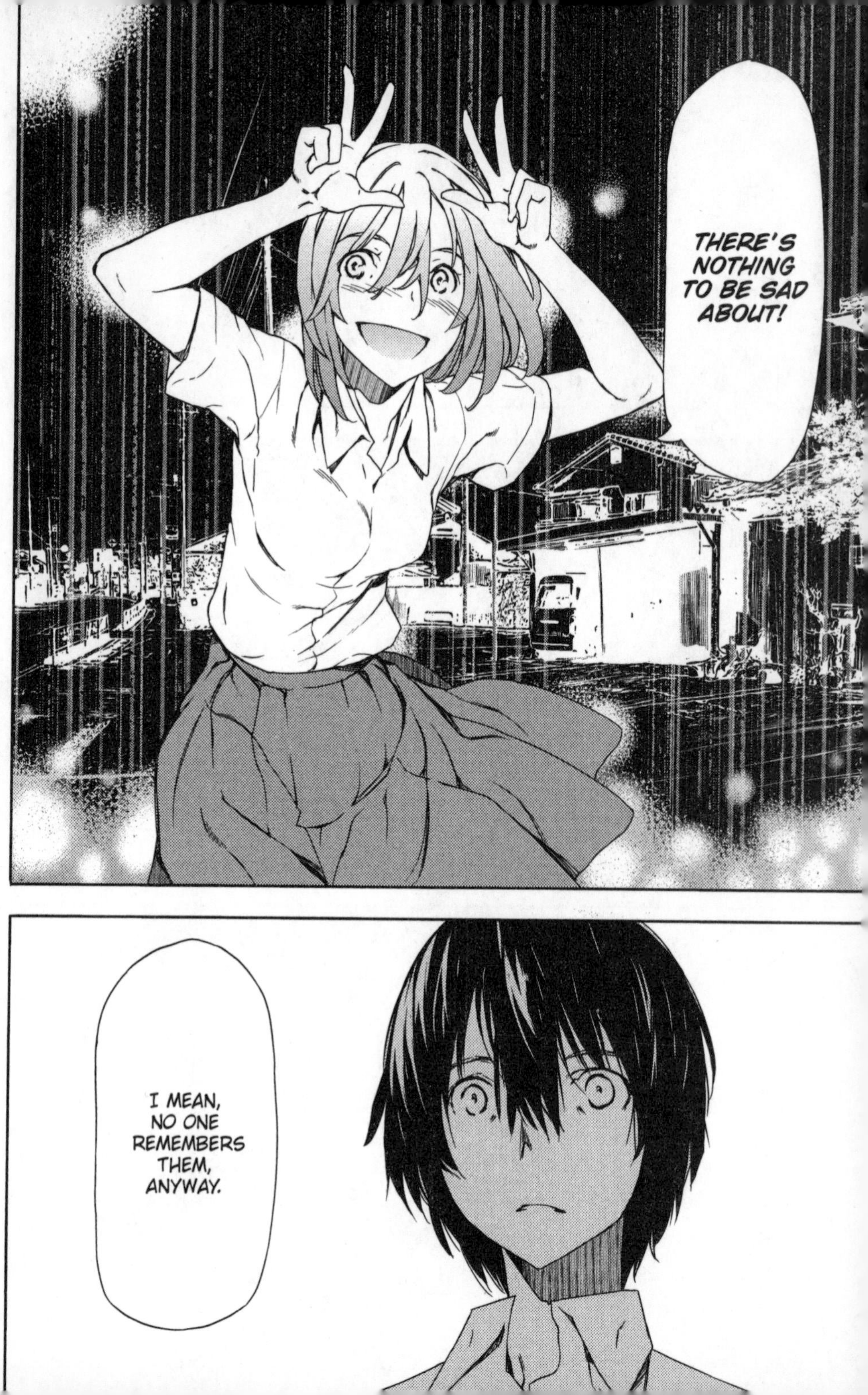
THERE'S NOTHING TO BE SAD ABOUT!
I MEAN, NO ONE REMEMBERS THEM, ANYWAY.

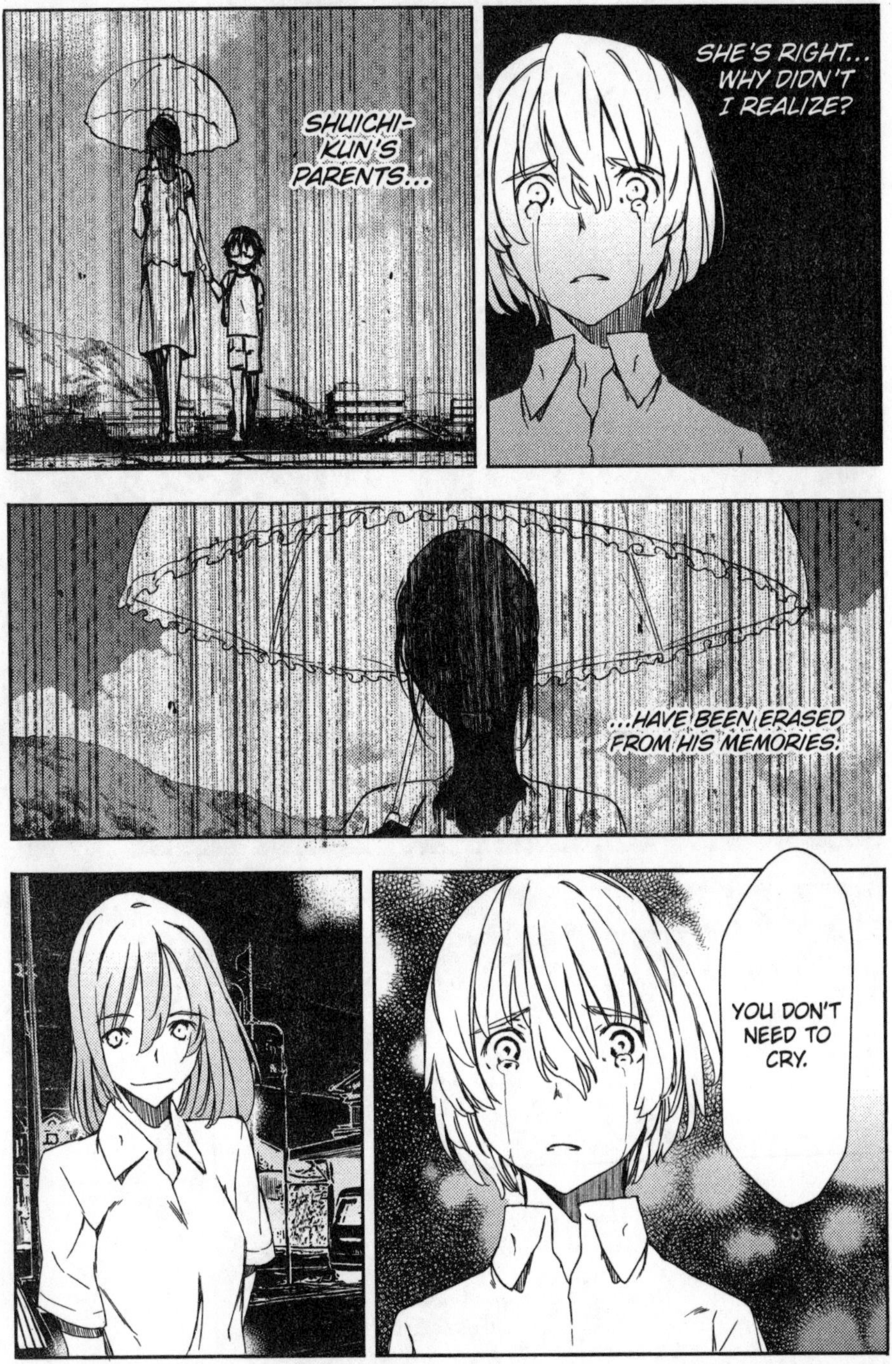
SHE'S RIGHT... WHY DIDN'T I REALIZE?
SHUICHI-KUN'S PARENTS...
...HAVE BEEN ERASED FROM HIS MEMORIES.
YOU DON'T NEED TO CRY.

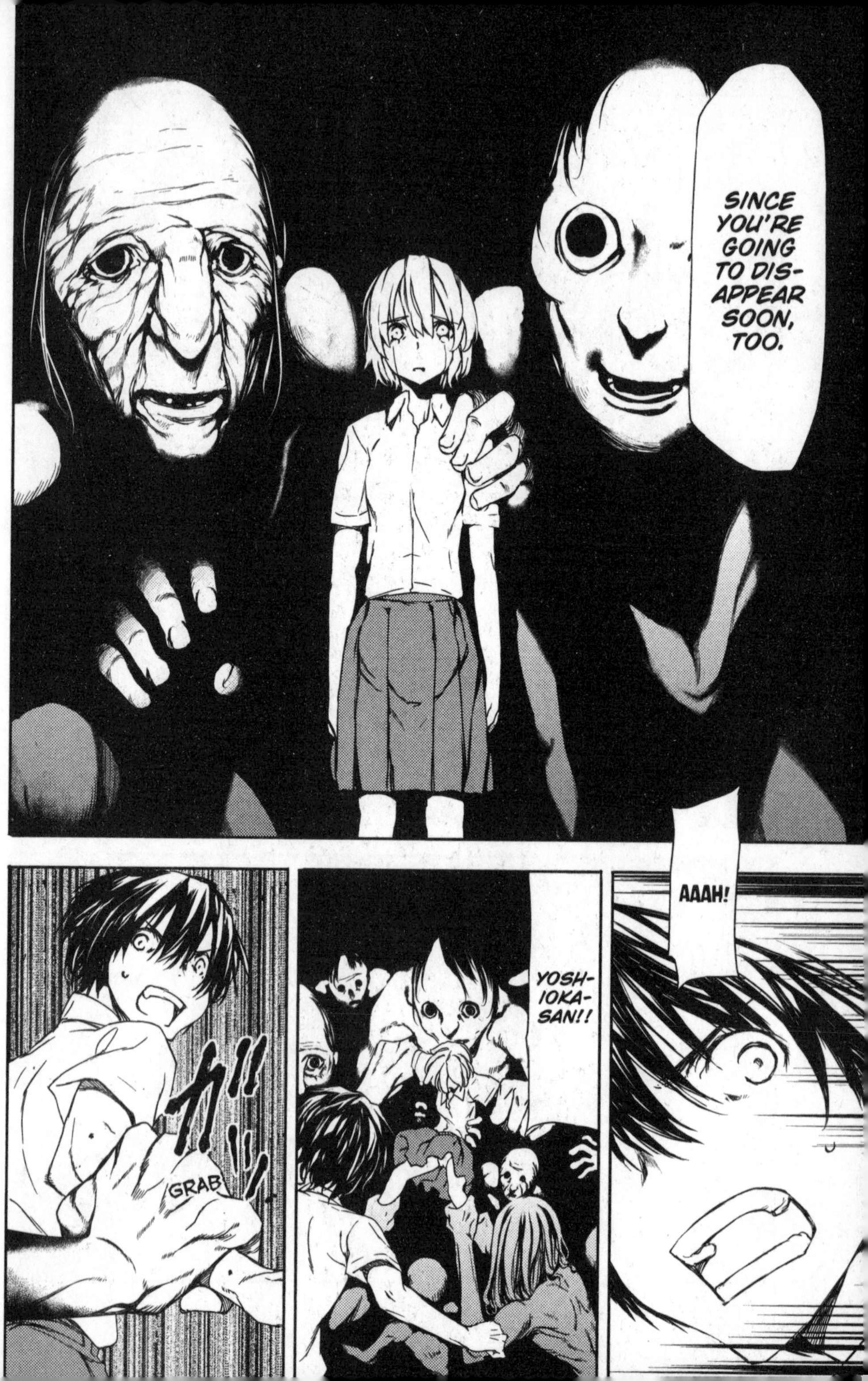
SINCE YOU'RE GOING TO DIS-APPEAR SOON, TOO.
AAAH!
YOSH-IOKA-SAN!!
GRAB

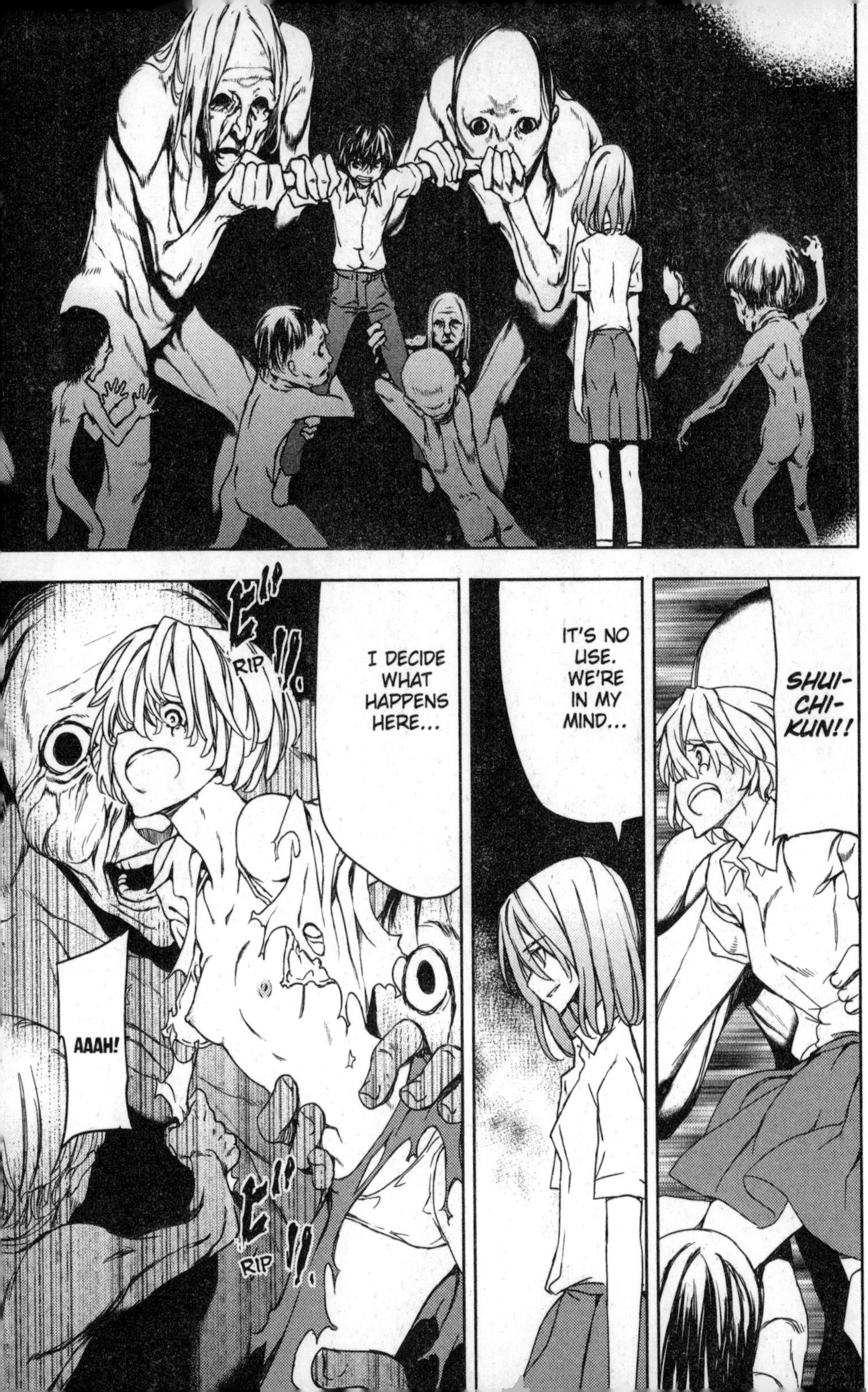
SHUICHI-KUN!!
IT'S NO USE. WE'RE IN MY MIND...
I DECIDE WHAT HAPPENS HERE...
RIP
AAAH!
RIP

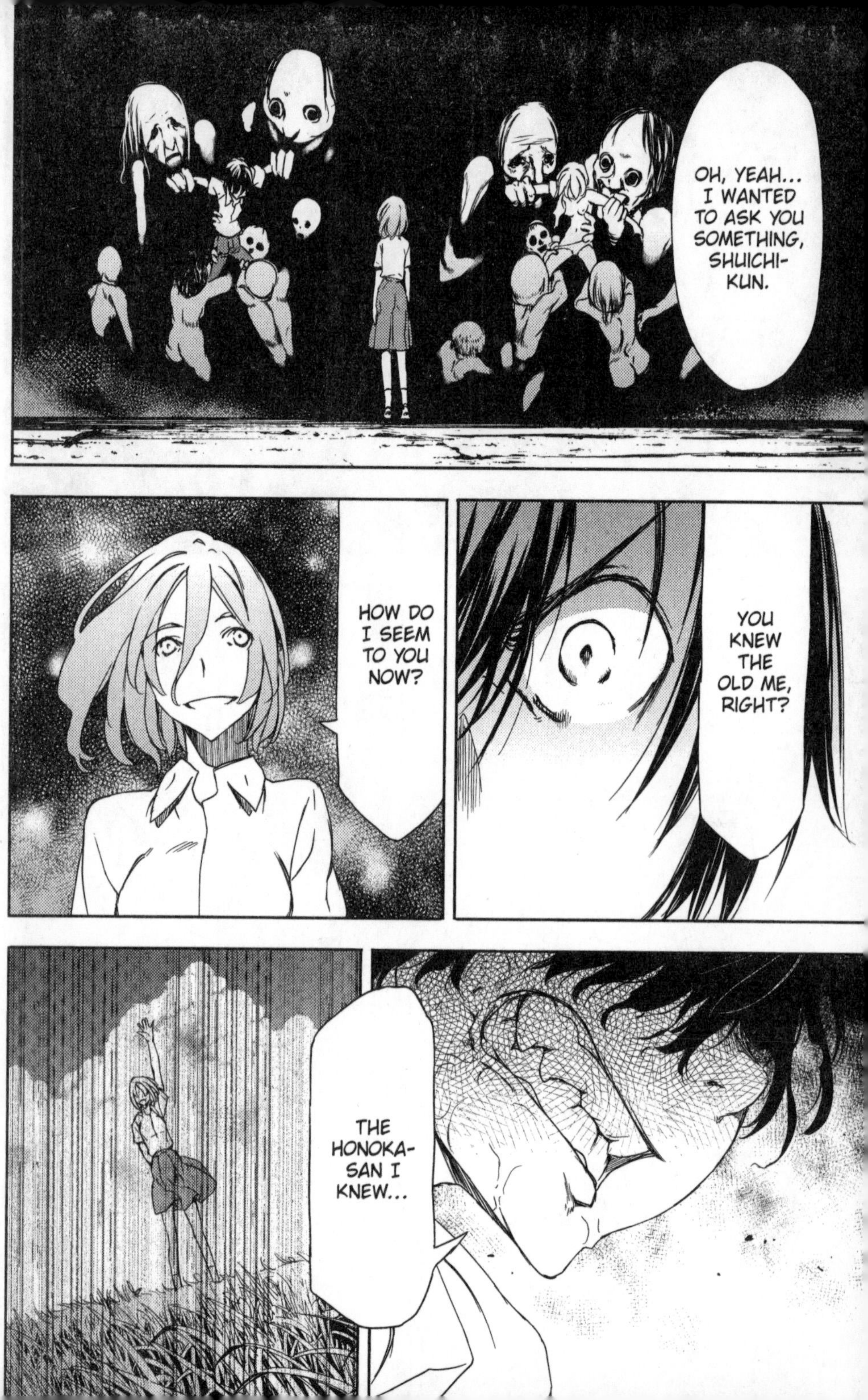
OH, YEAH... I WANTED TO ASK YOU SOMETHING, SHUICHI-KUN.
YOU KNEW THE OLD ME, RIGHT?
HOW DO I SEEM TO YOU NOW?
THE HONOKA-SAN I KNEW...

...WASN'T SOME MONSTER LIKE YOU.

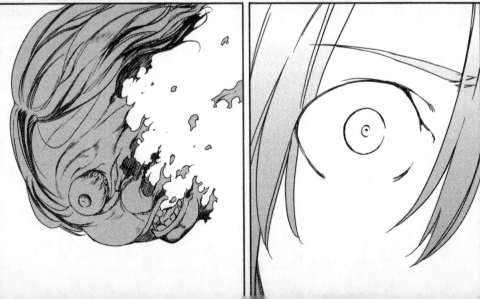

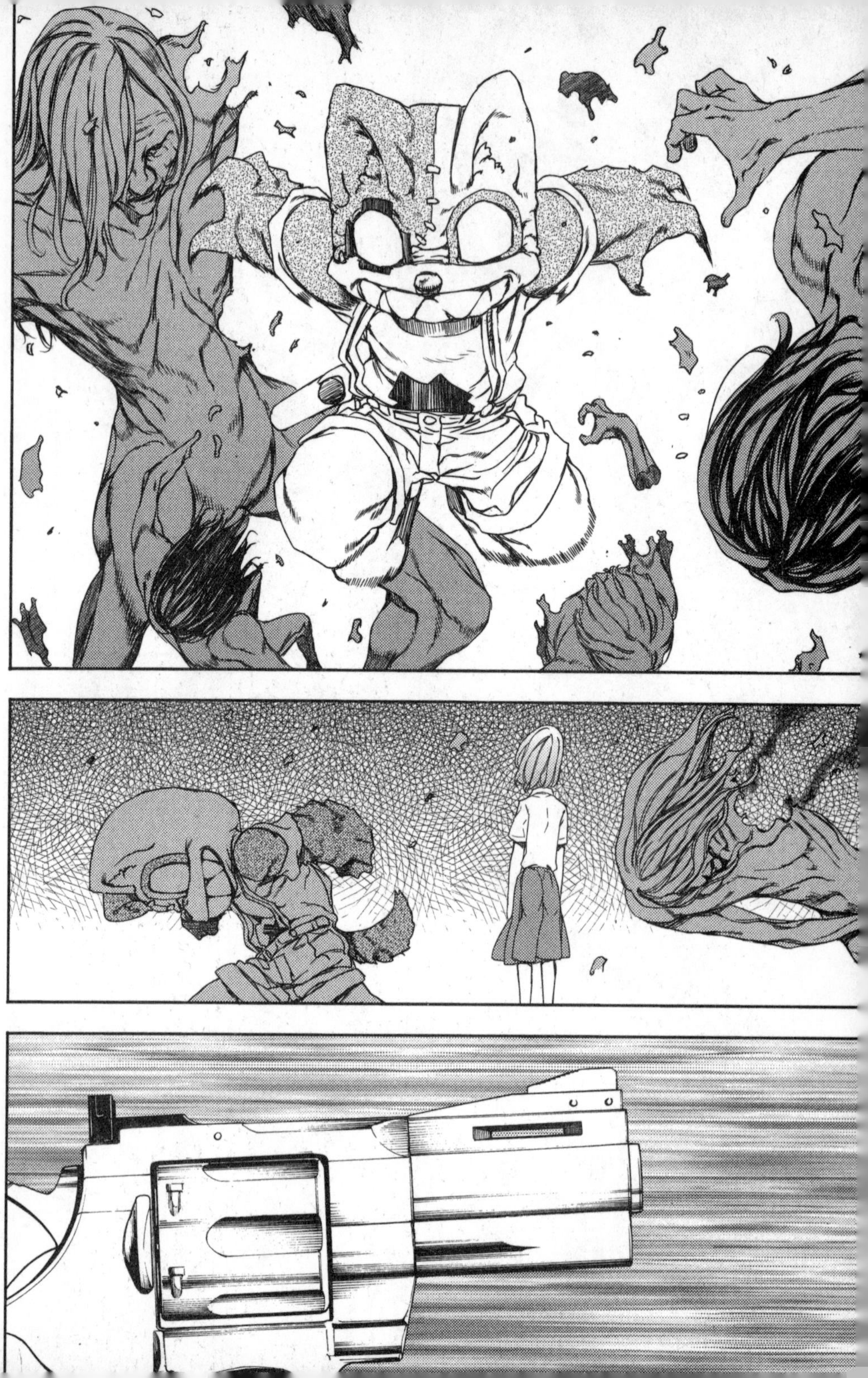

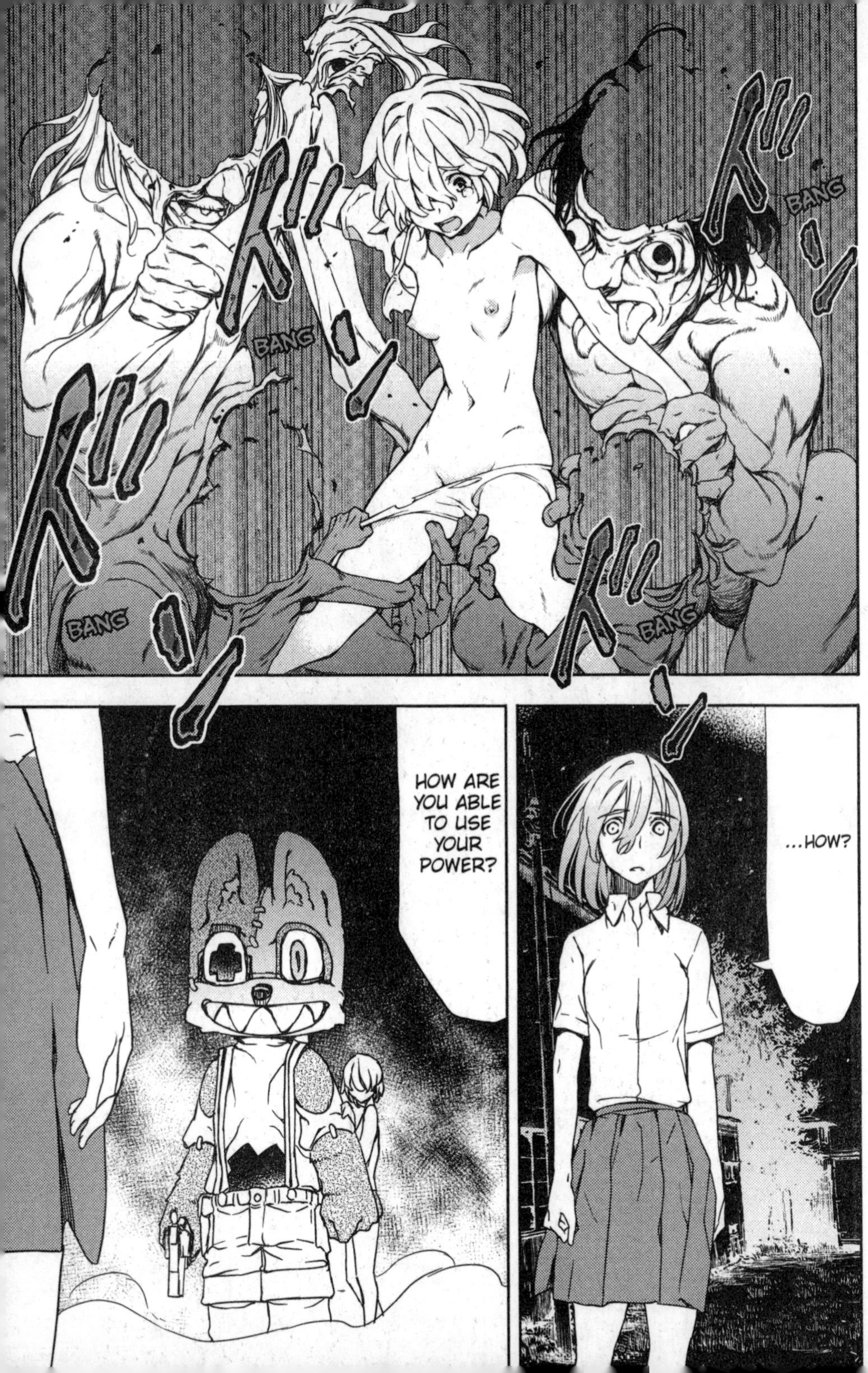
BANG
BANG
BANG
BANG
...HOW?
HOW ARE YOU ABLE TO USE YOUR POWER?

WE'RE IN MY...

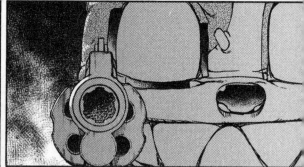

YOU'RE FASCINATING.

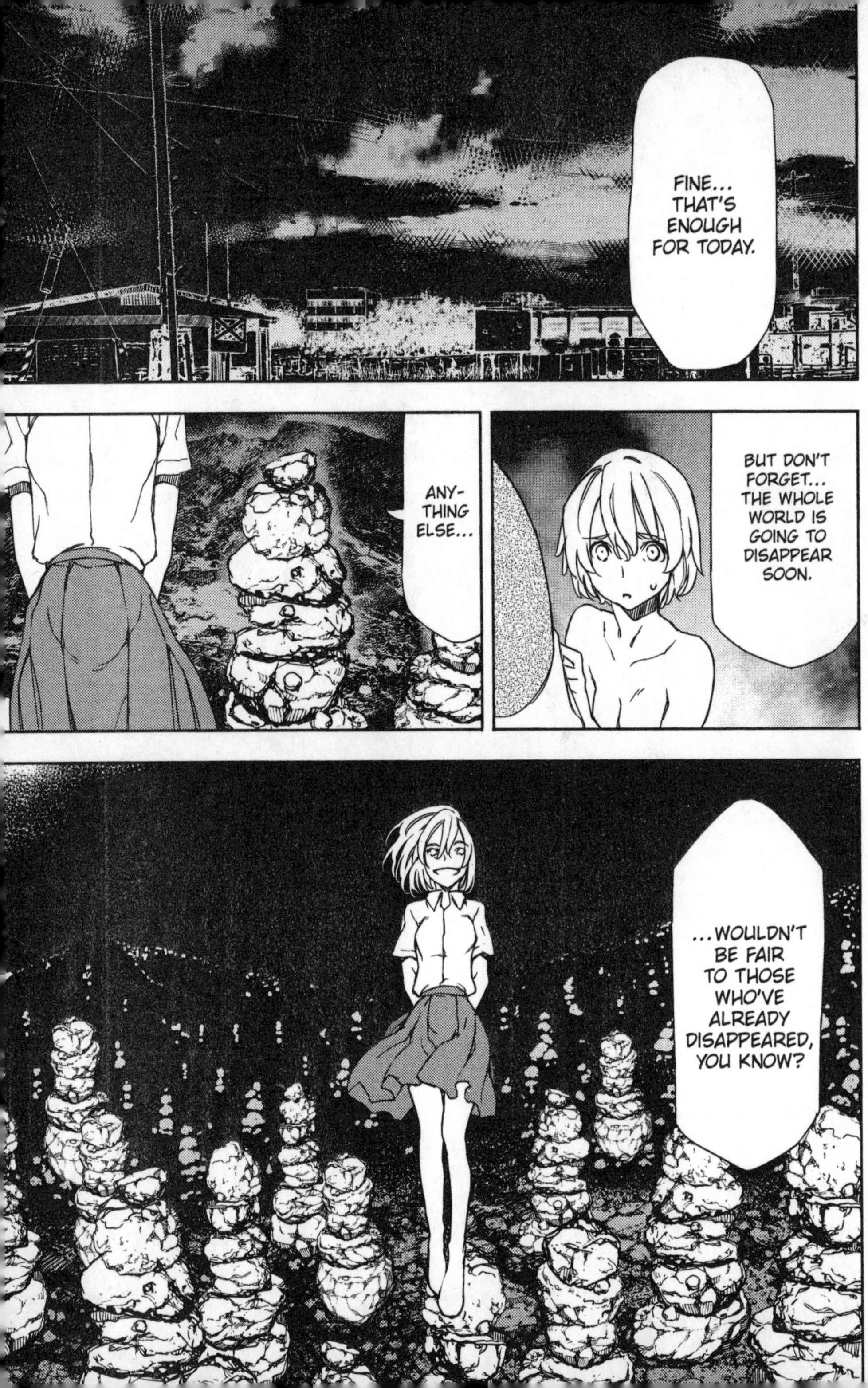
FINE... THAT'S ENOUGH FOR TODAY.
BUT DON'T FORGET... THE WHOLE WORLD IS GOING TO DISAPPEAR SOON.
ANY-THING ELSE...
...WOULDN'T BE FAIR TO THOSE WHO'VE ALREADY DISAPPEARED, YOU KNOW?

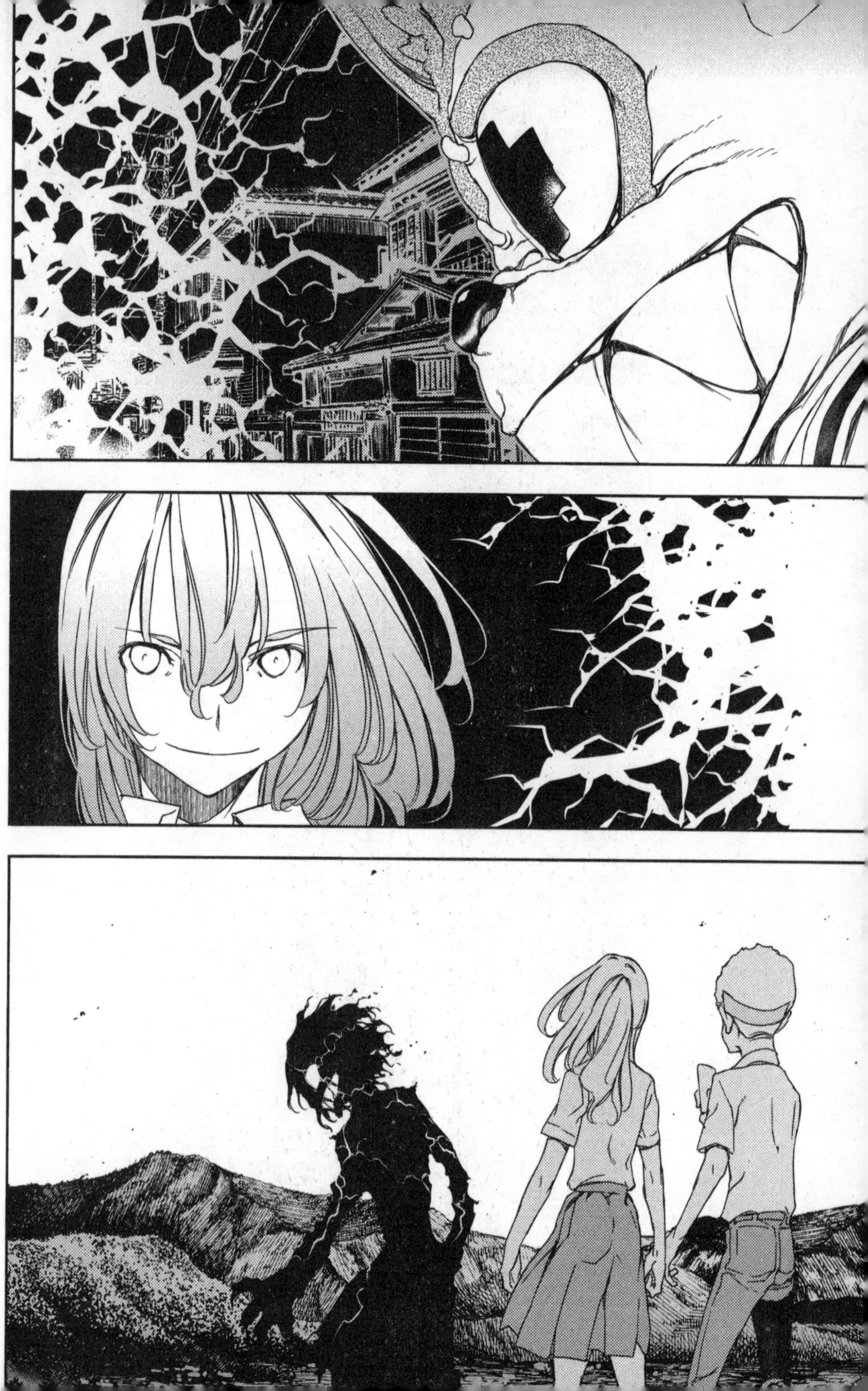

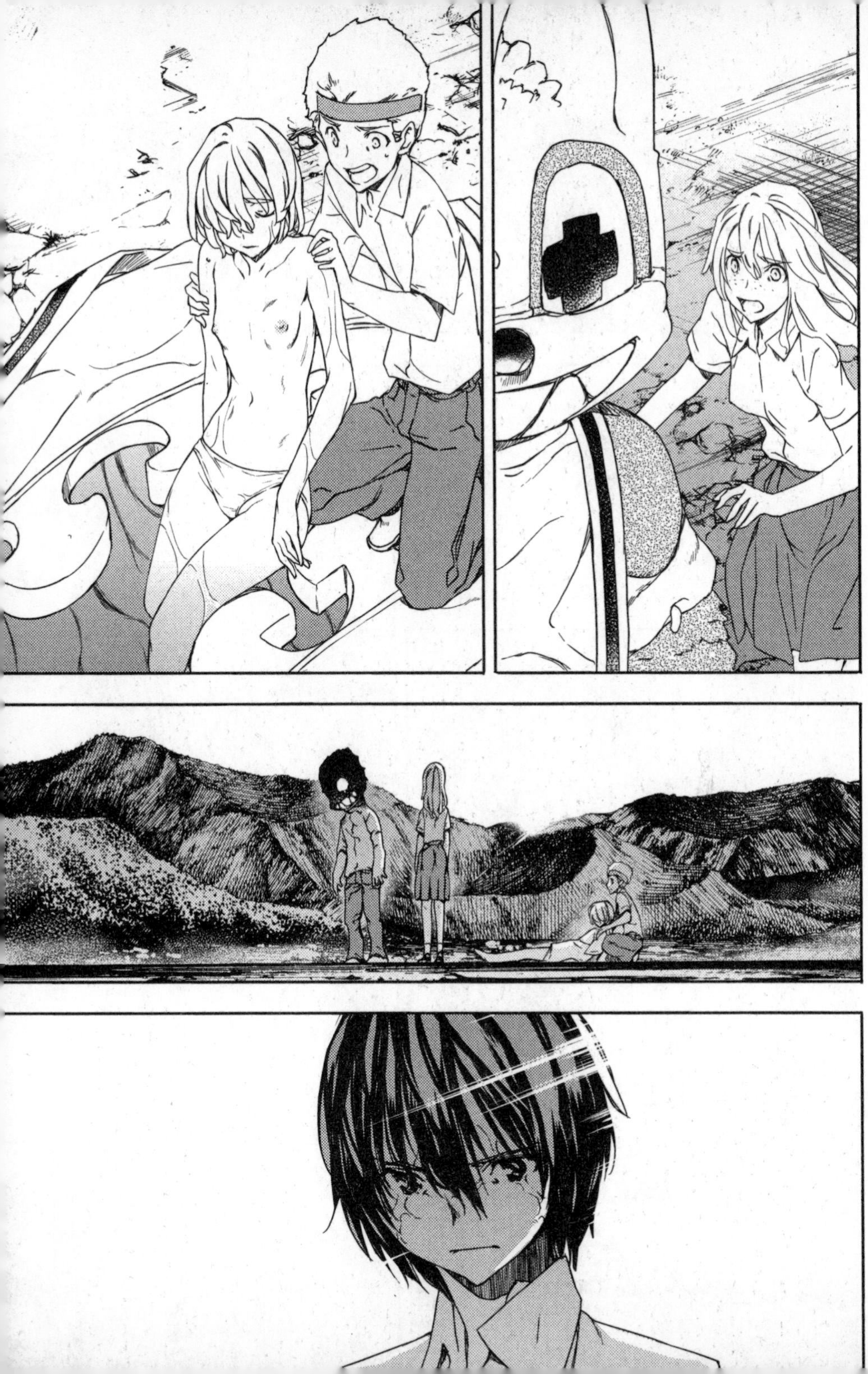

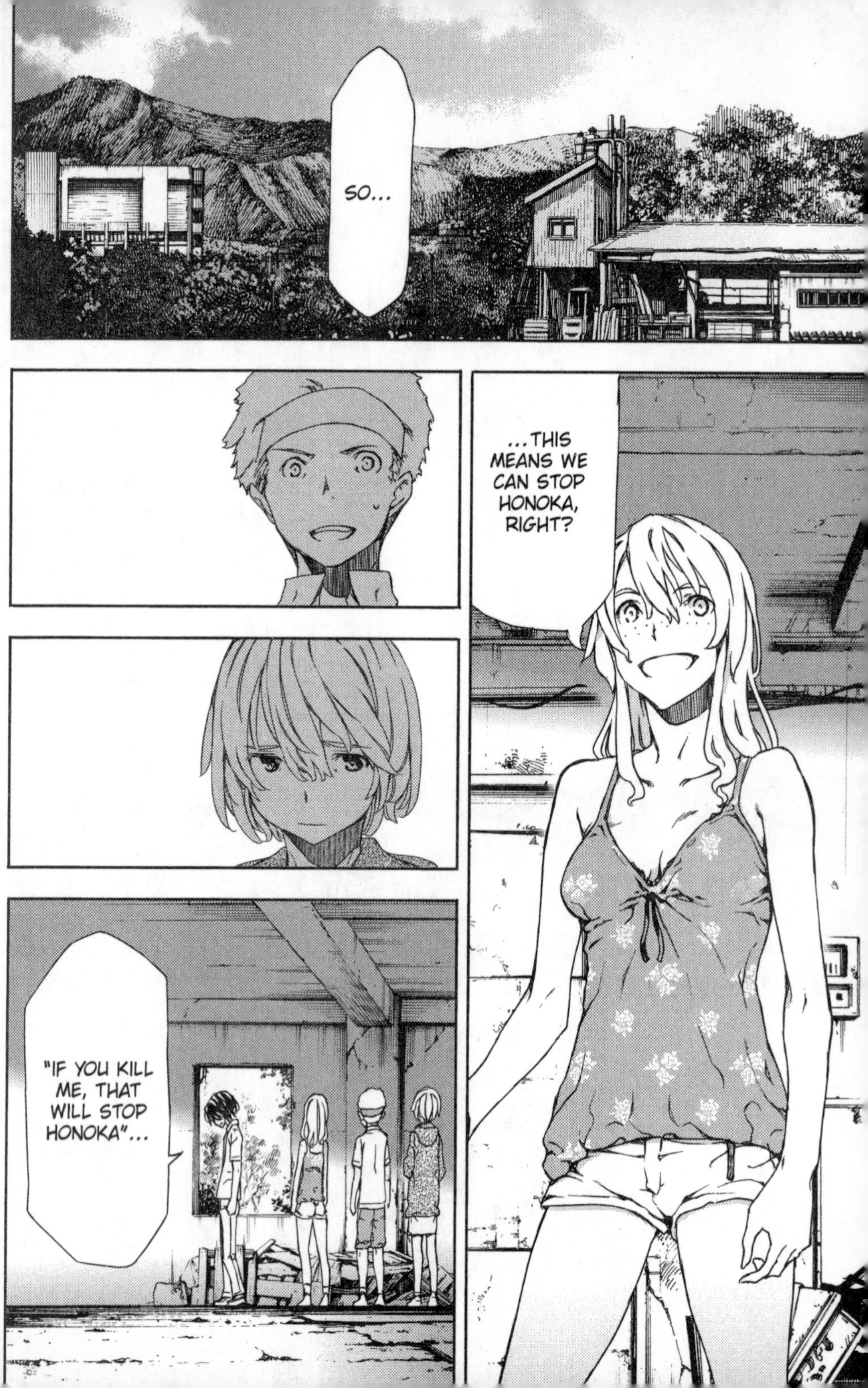
SO...
...THIS MEANS WE CAN STOP HONOKA, RIGHT?
"IF YOU KILL ME, THAT WILL STOP HONOKA"...

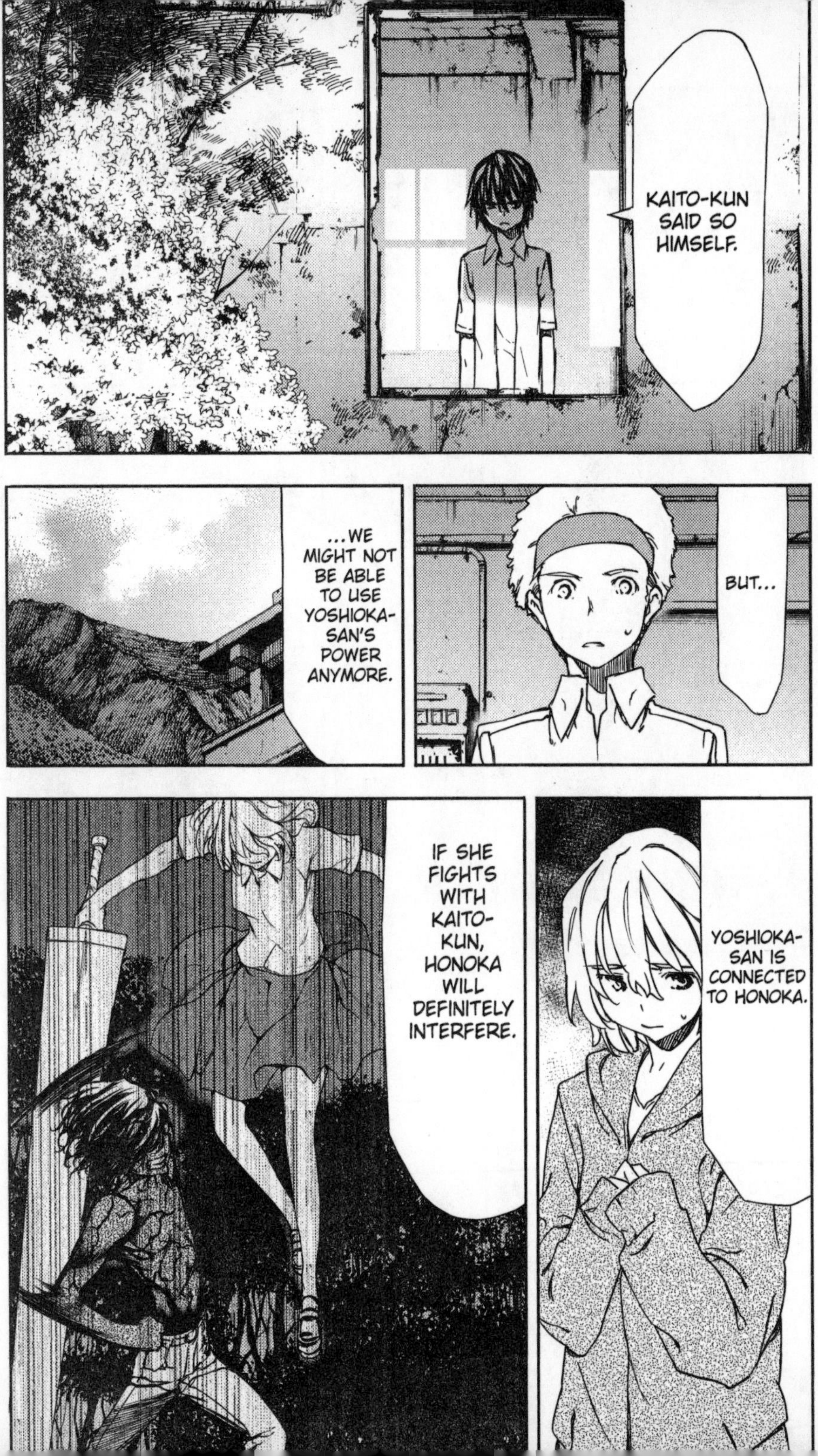
KAITO-KUN SAID SO HIMSELF.
BUT...
...WE MIGHT NOT BE ABLE TO USE YOSHIOKA-SAN'S POWER ANYMORE.
YOSHIOKA-SAN IS CONNECTED TO HONOKA.
IF SHE FIGHTS WITH KAITO-KUN, HONOKA WILL DEFINITELY INTERFERE.

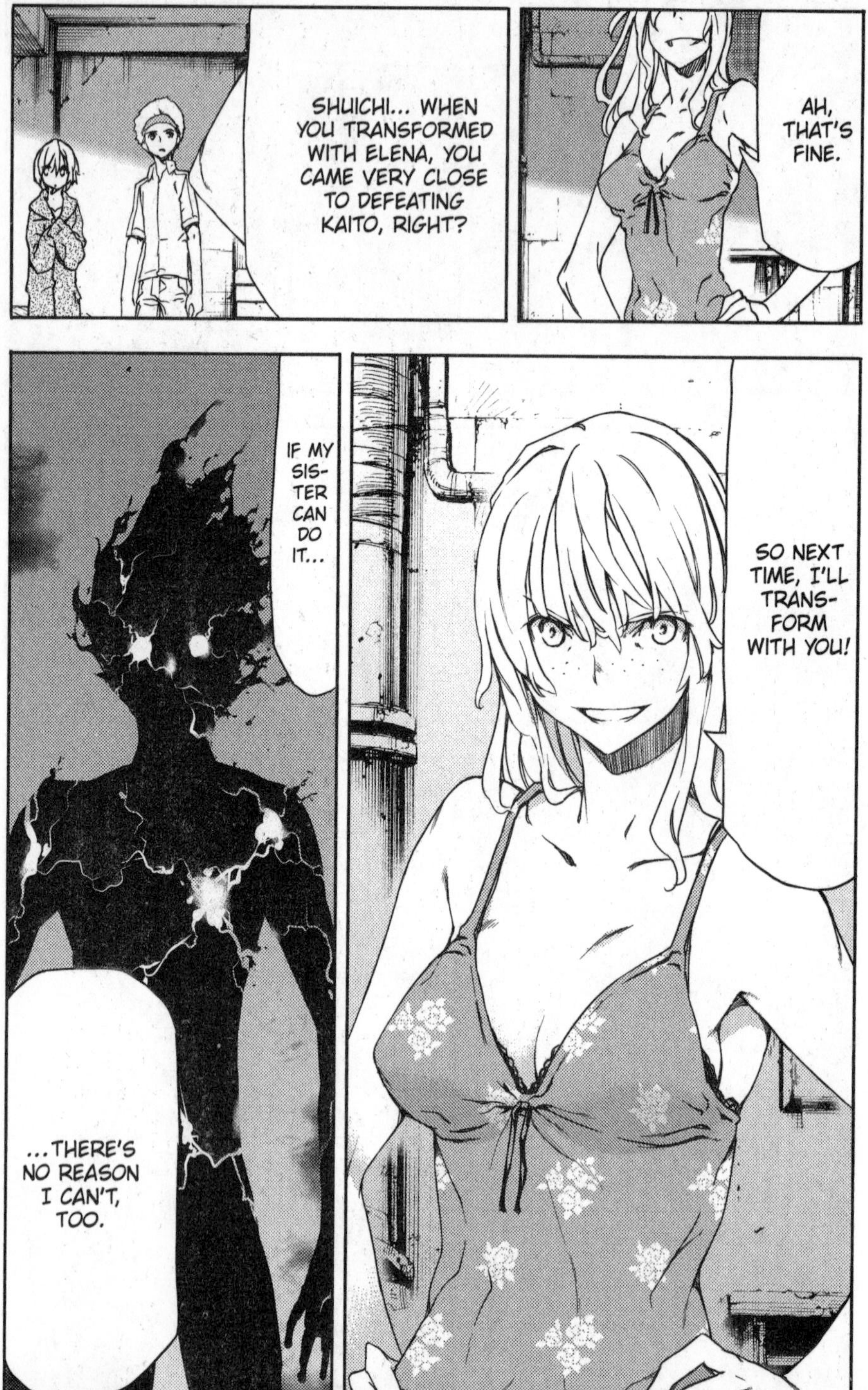
AH, THAT'S FINE.
SHUICHI... WHEN YOU TRANSFORMED WITH ELENA, YOU CAME VERY CLOSE TO DEFEATING KAITO, RIGHT?
SO NEXT TIME, I'LL TRANS-FORM WITH YOU!
IF MY SIS-TER CAN DO IT...
...THERE'S NO REASON I CAN'T, TOO.

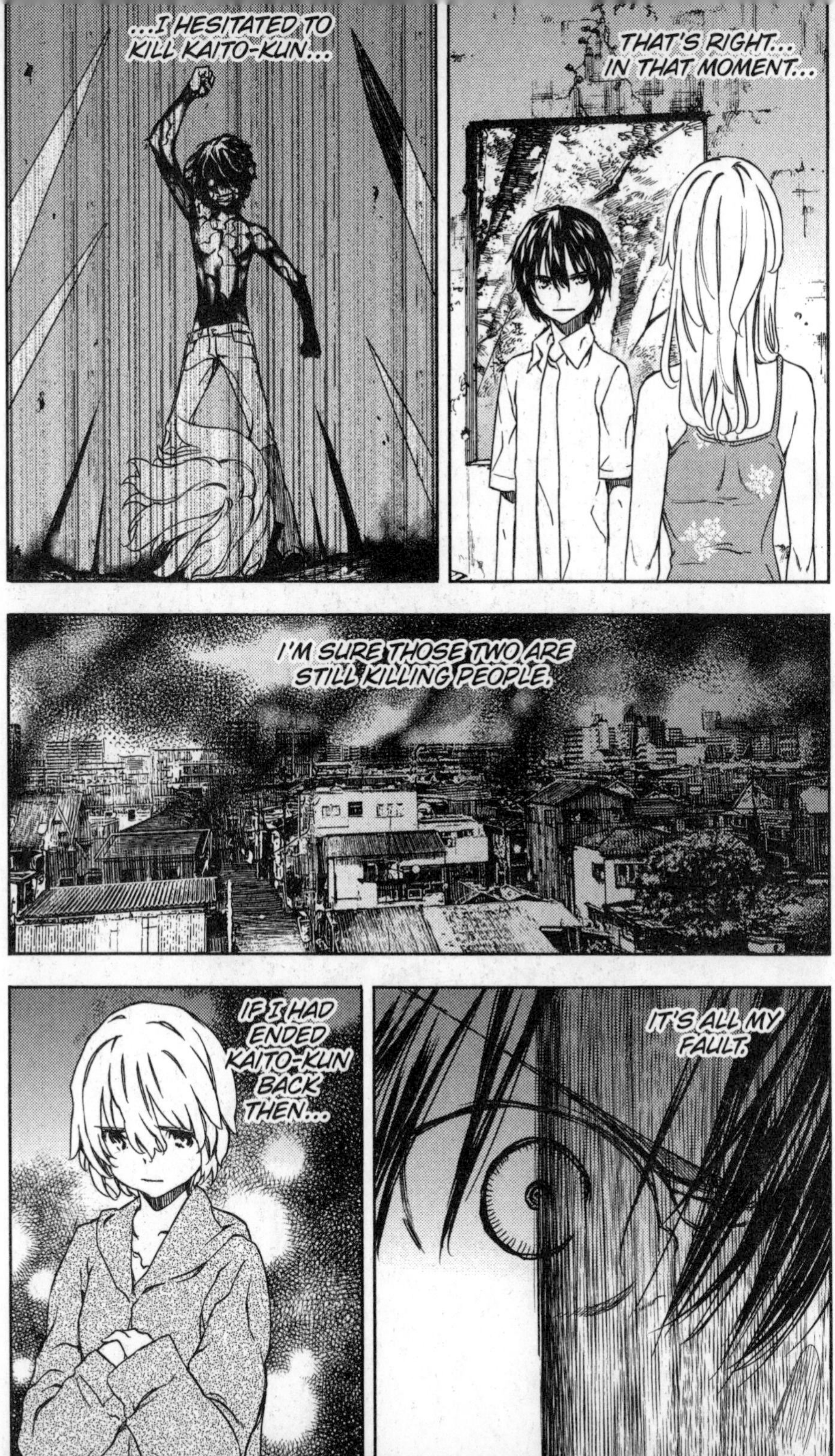
THAT'S RIGHT... IN THAT MOMENT...
...I HESITATED TO KILL KAITO-KUN...
I'M SURE THOSE TWO ARE STILL KILLING PEOPLE.
IT'S ALL MY FAULT.
IF I HAD ENDED KAITO-KUN BACK THEN...

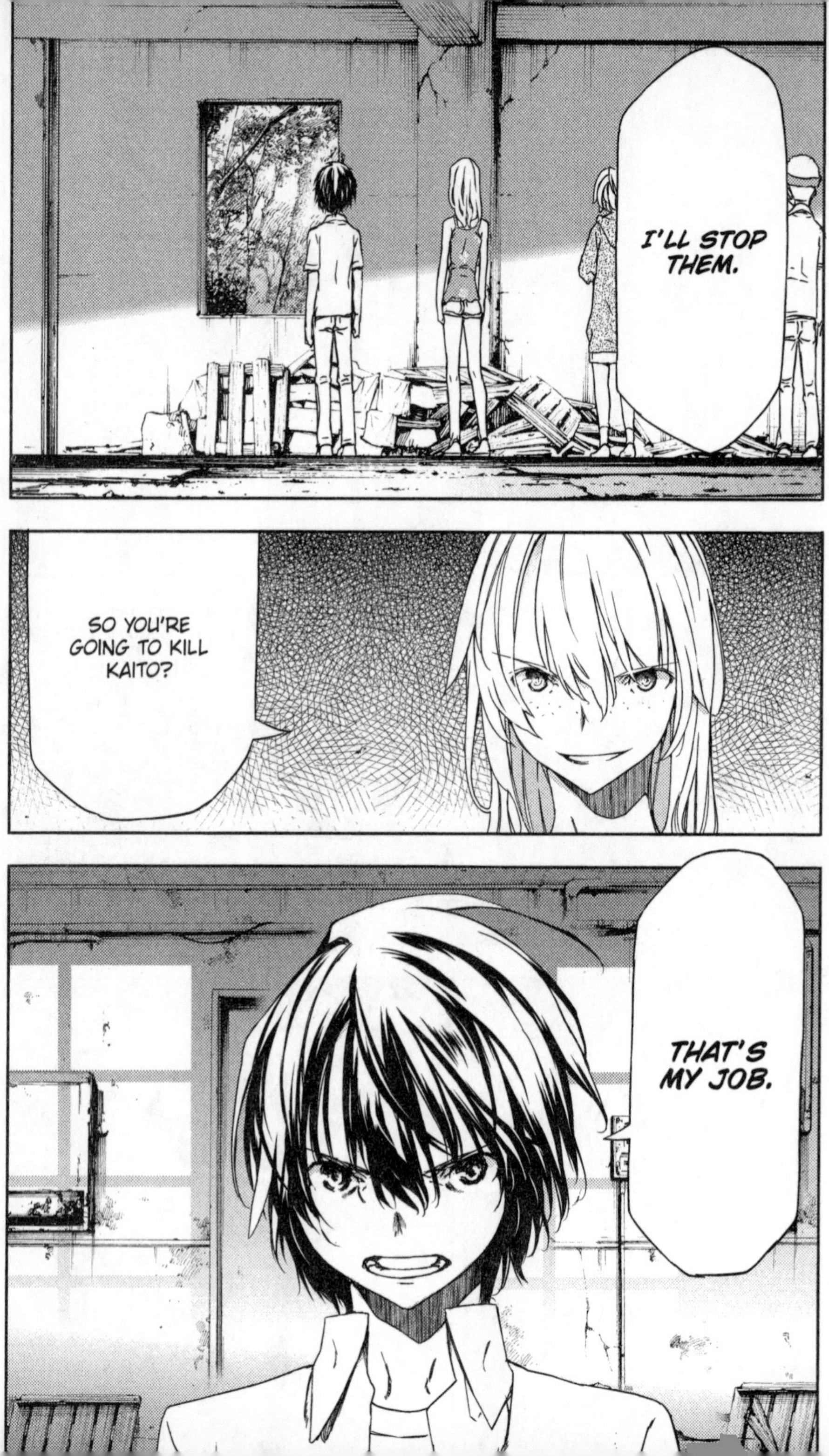
I'LL STOP THEM.
SO YOU'RE GOING TO KILL KAITO?
THAT'S MY JOB.

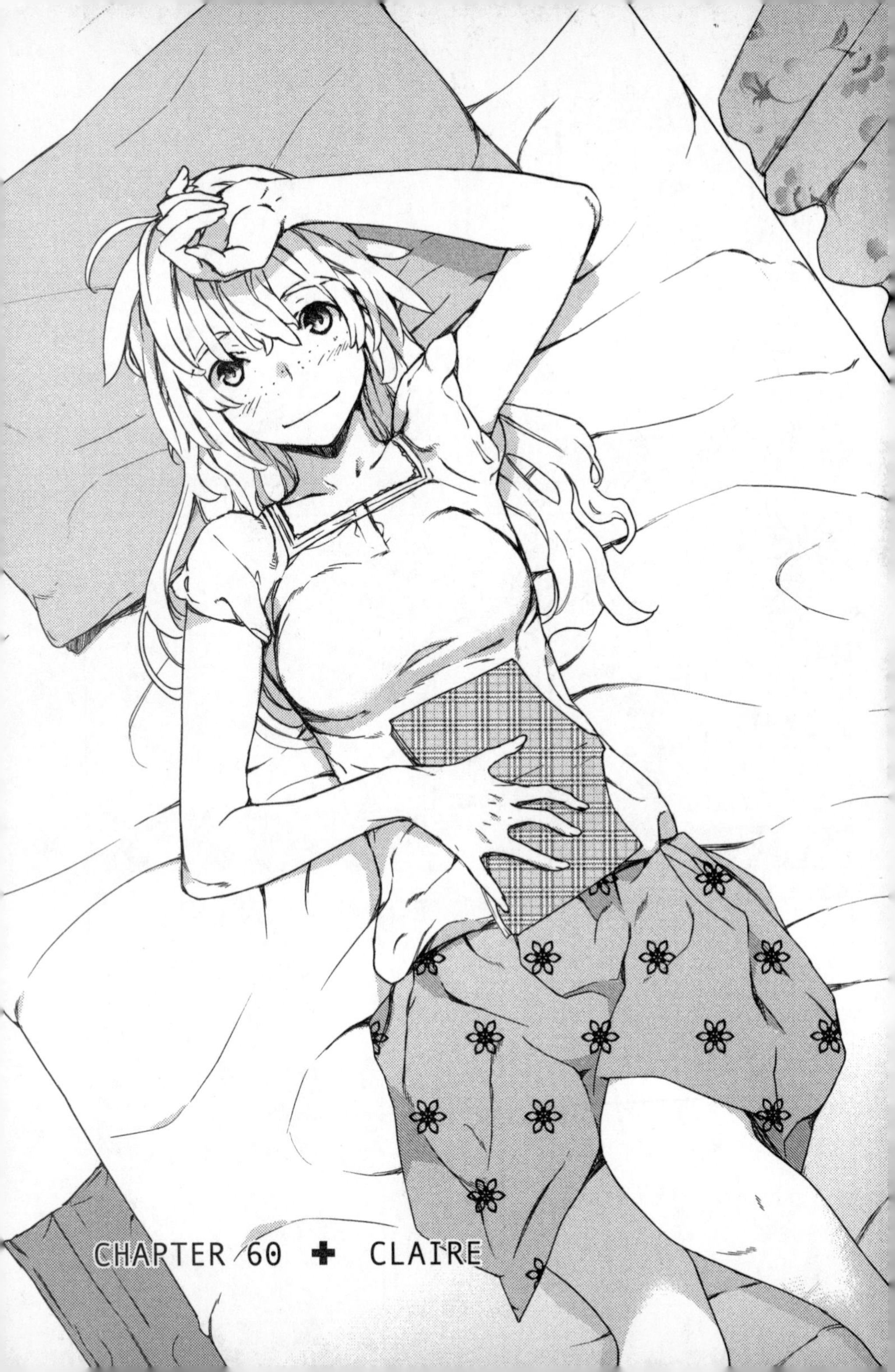
CHAPTER 60 ✚ CLAIRE

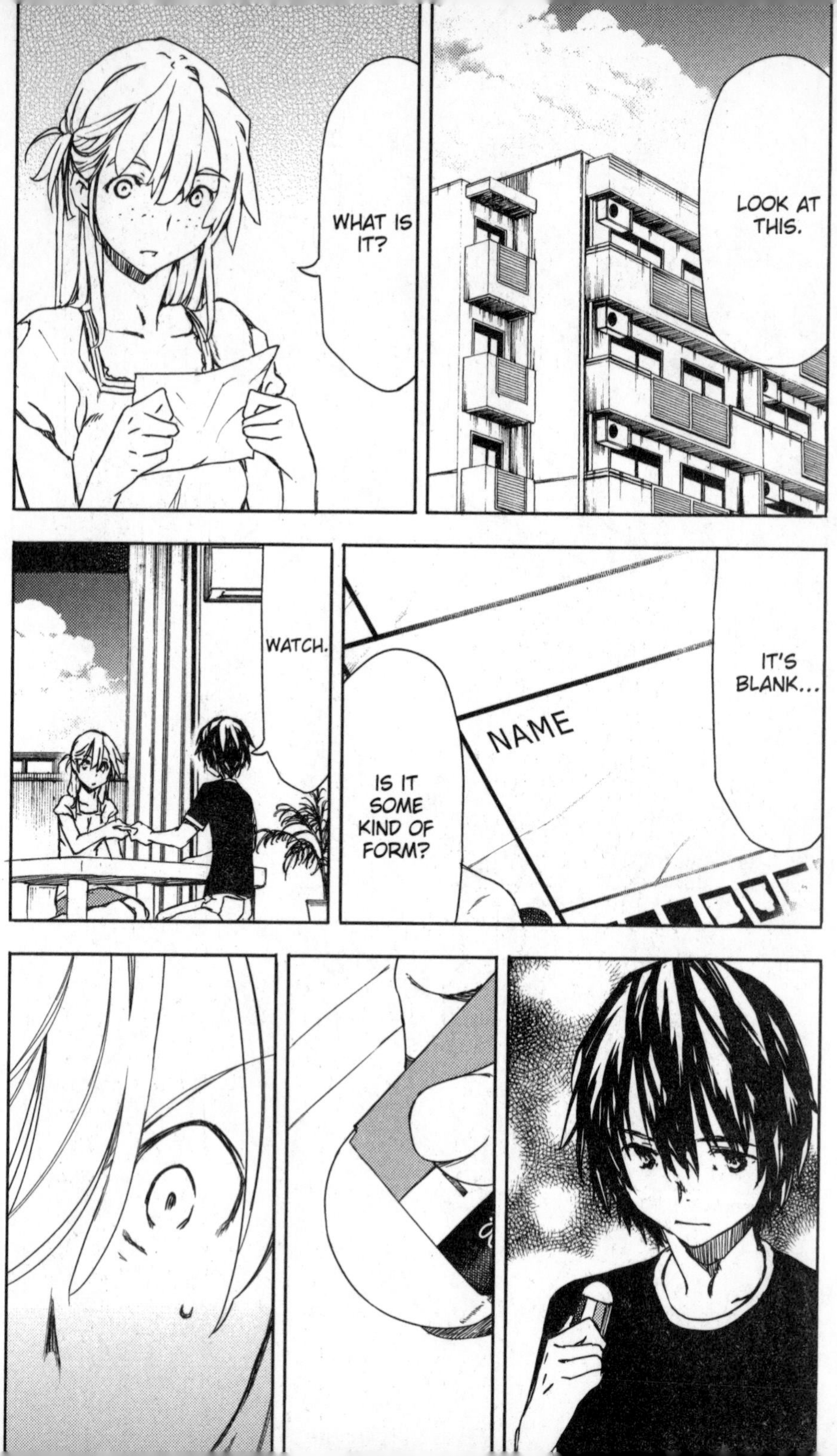
LOOK AT THIS.
WHAT IS IT?
IT'S BLANK...
NAME
IS IT SOME KIND OF FORM?
WATCH.

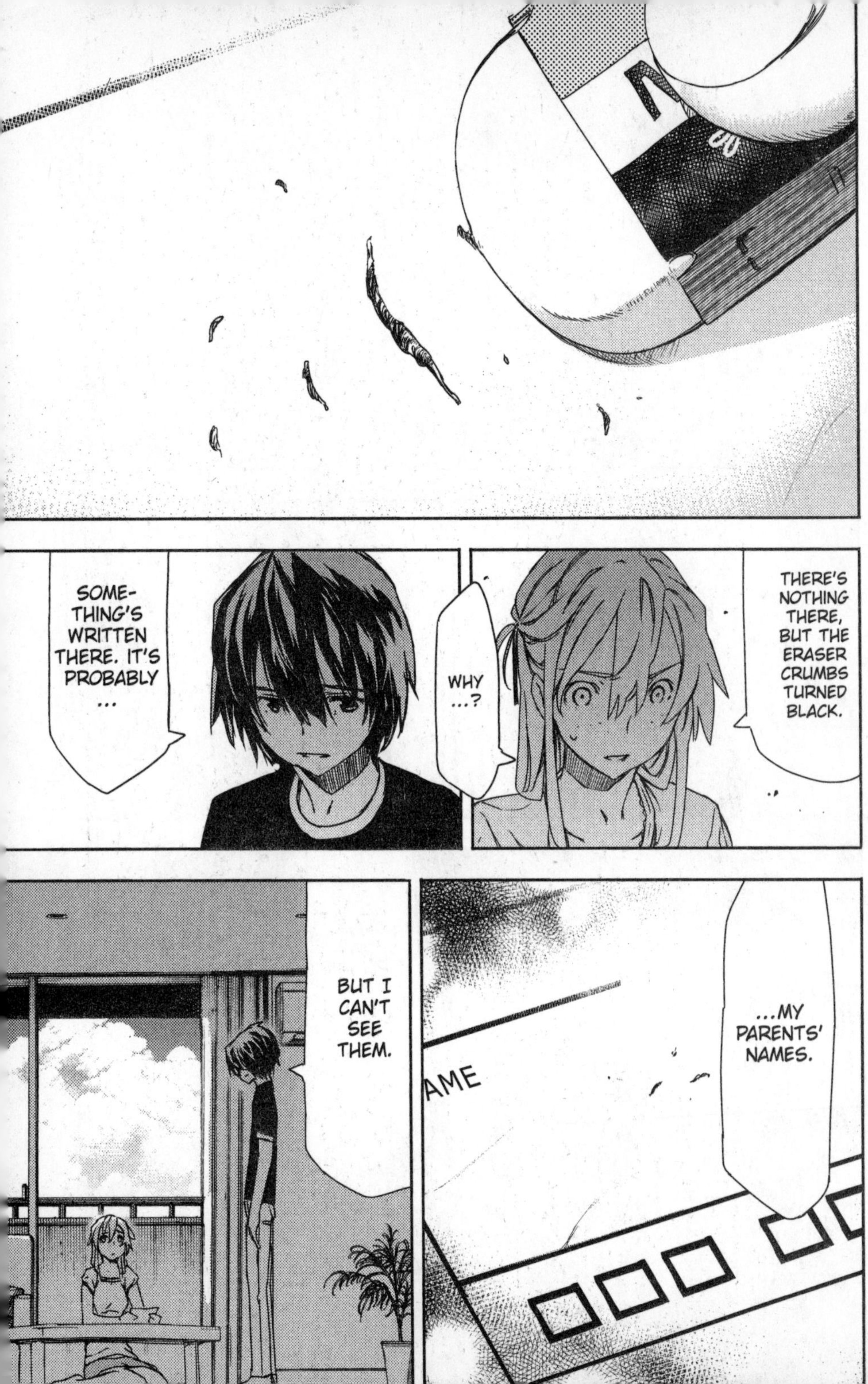
THERE'S NOTHING THERE, BUT THE ERASER CRUMBS TURNED BLACK.
WHY ...?
SOME-THING'S WRITTEN THERE. IT'S PROBABLY ...
...MY PARENTS' NAMES.
AME
BUT I CAN'T SEE THEM.

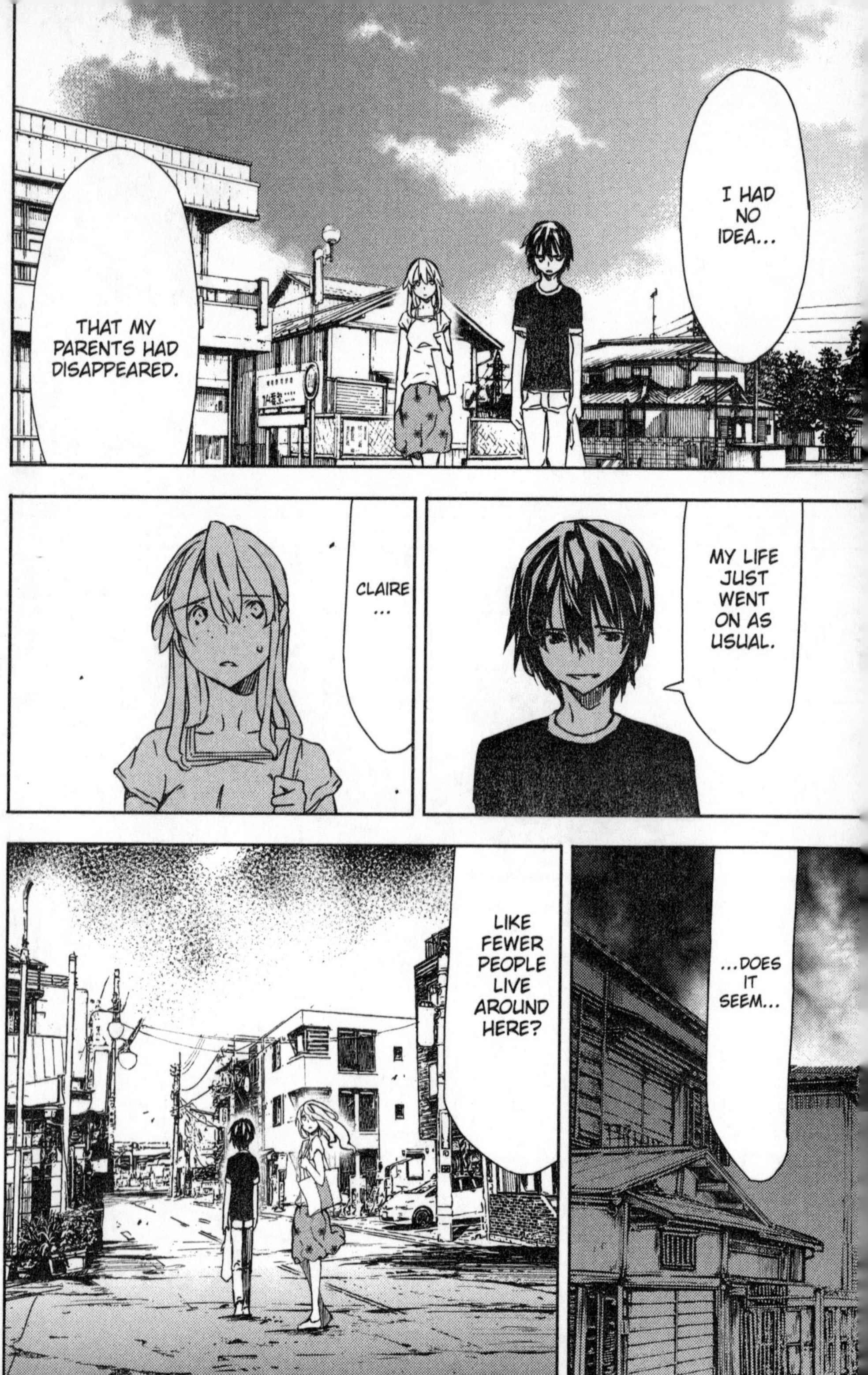
I HAD NO IDEA...
THAT MY PARENTS HAD DISAPPEARED.
MY LIFE JUST WENT ON AS USUAL.
CLAIRE...
...DOES IT SEEM...
LIKE FEWER PEOPLE LIVE AROUND HERE?

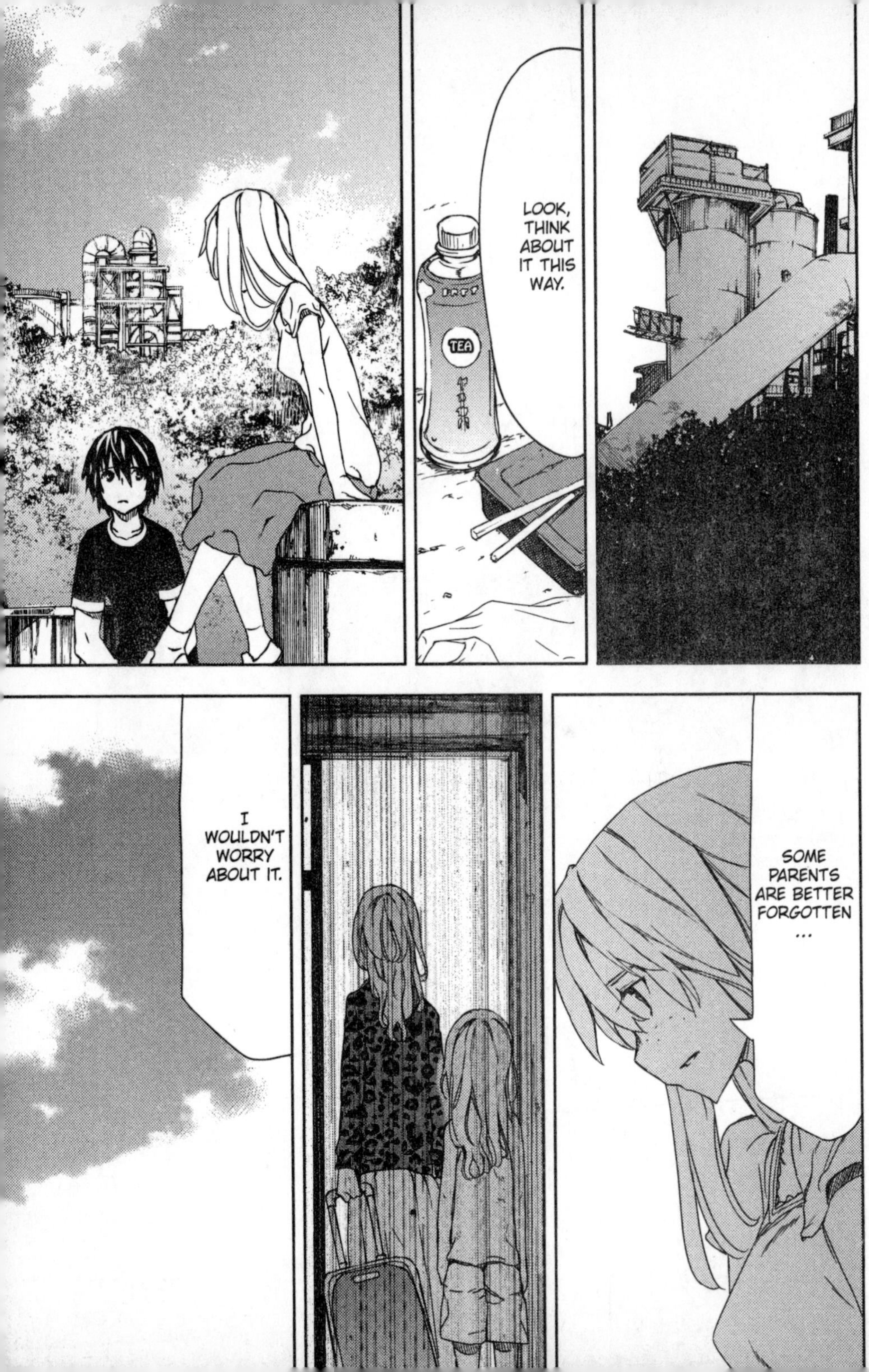
LOOK, THINK ABOUT IT THIS WAY.
TEA
SOME PARENTS ARE BETTER FORGOTTEN ...
I WOULDN'T WORRY ABOUT IT.

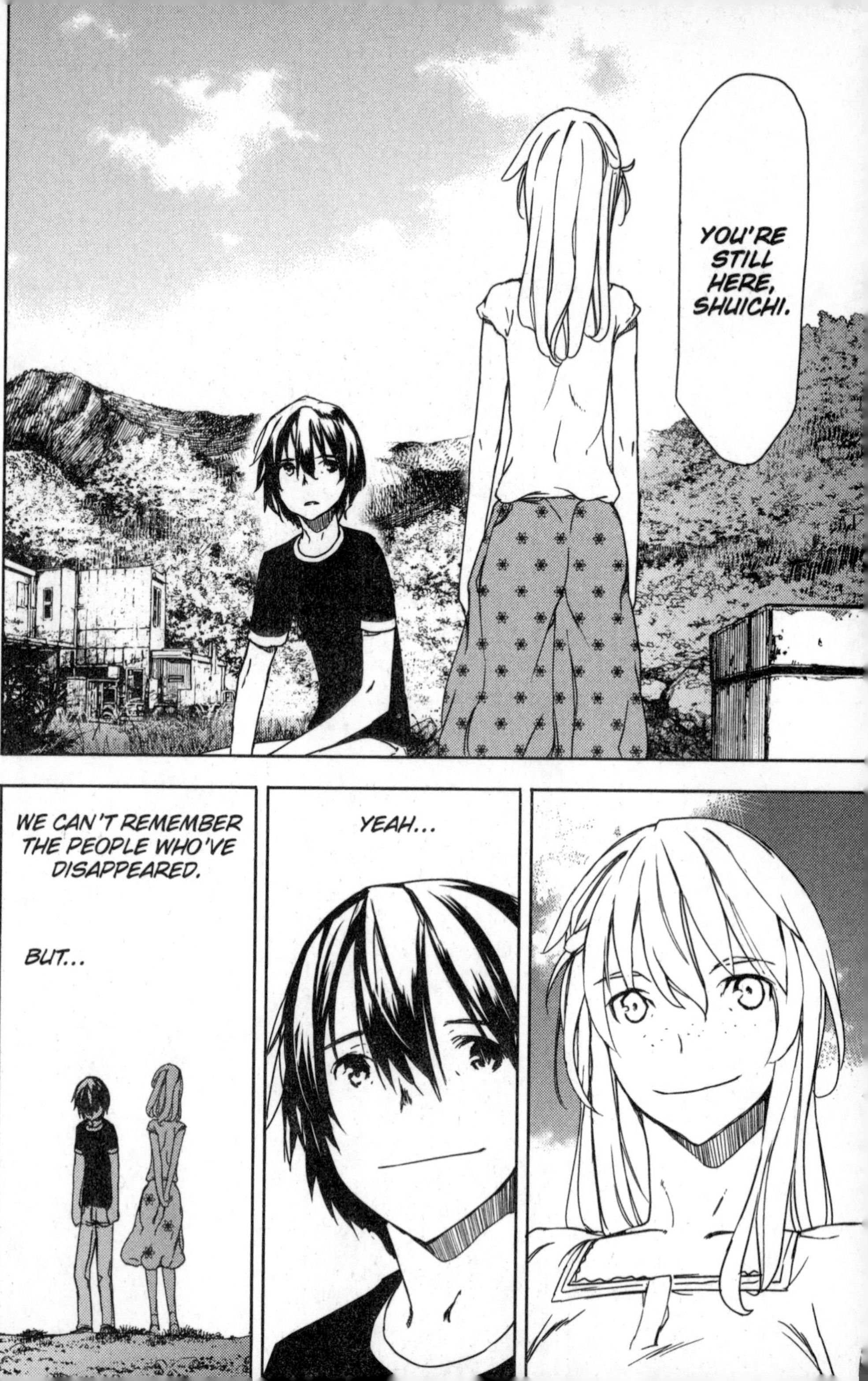
YOU'RE STILL HERE, SHUICHI.
YEAH...
WE CAN'T REMEMBER THE PEOPLE WHO'VE DISAPPEARED.
BUT...

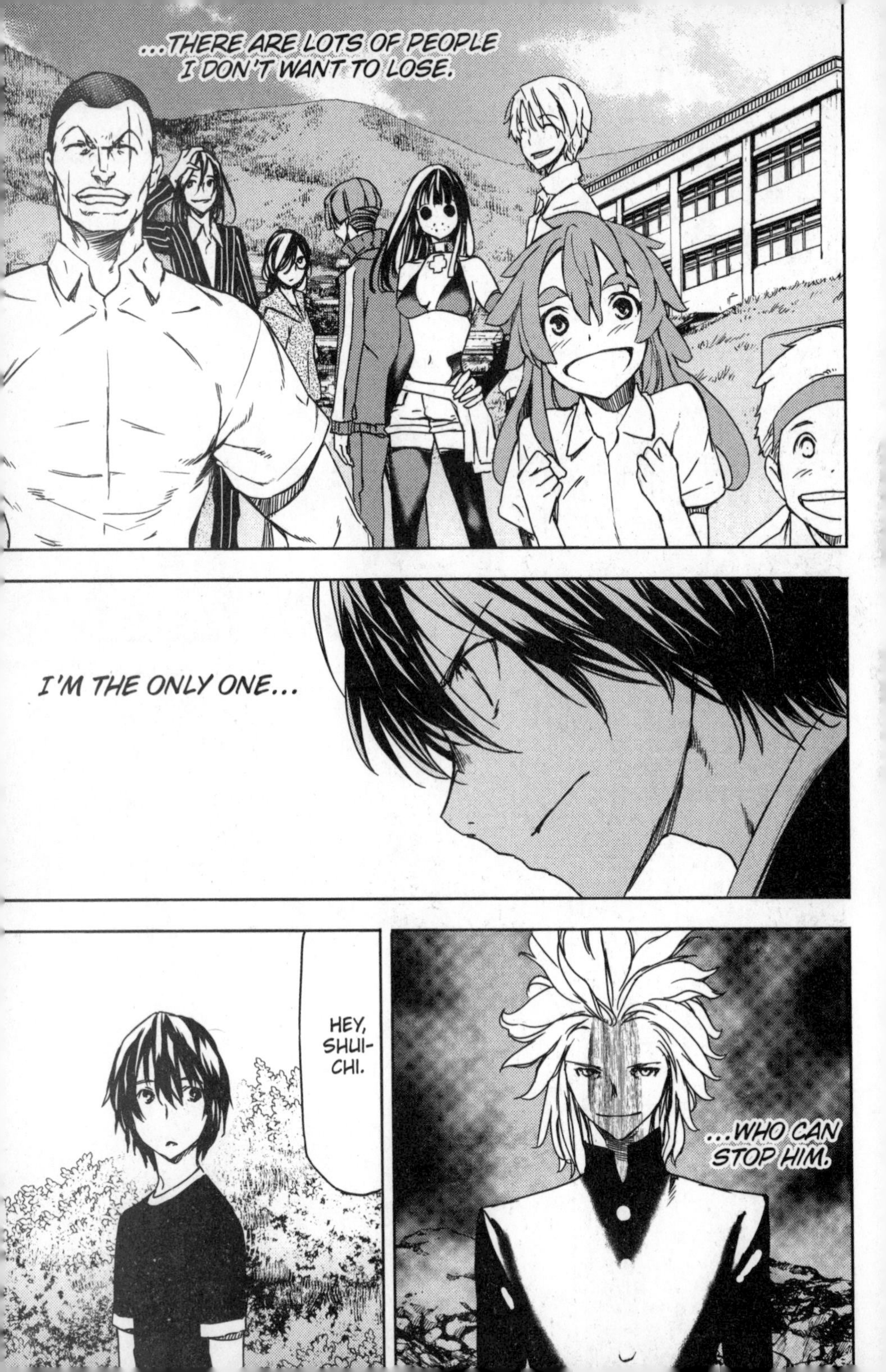
...THERE ARE LOTS OF PEOPLE I DON'T WANT TO LOSE.
I'M THE ONLY ONE...
...WHO CAN STOP HIM.
HEY, SHUI-CHI.

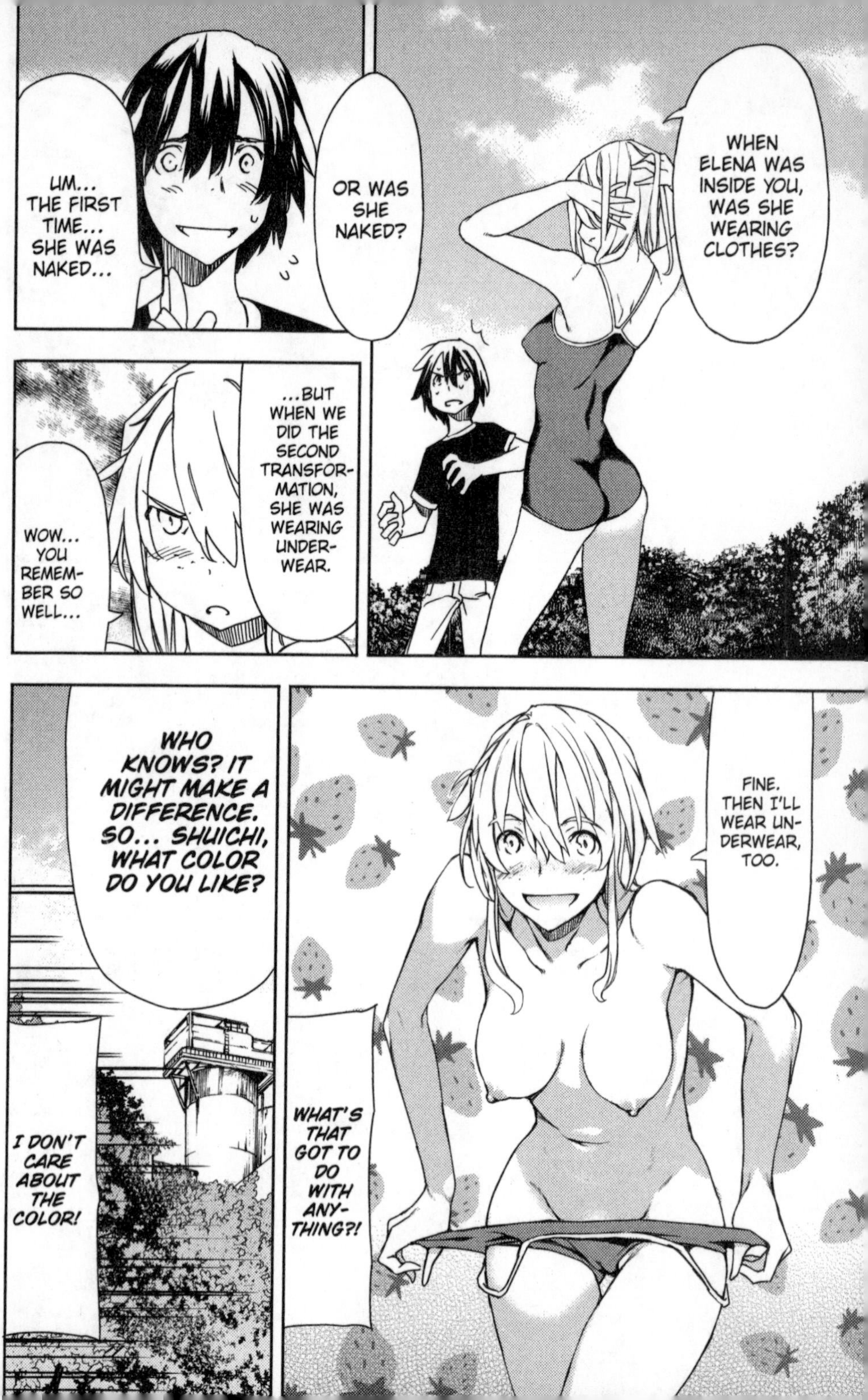
WHEN ELENA WAS INSIDE YOU, WAS SHE WEARING CLOTHES?
OR WAS SHE NAKED?
UM... THE FIRST TIME... SHE WAS NAKED...
...BUT WHEN WE DID THE SECOND TRANSFORMATION, SHE WAS WEARING UNDERWEAR.
WOW... YOU REMEMBER SO WELL...
FINE. THEN I'LL WEAR UNDERWEAR, TOO.
WHAT'S THAT GOT TO DO WITH ANYTHING?!
WHO KNOWS? IT MIGHT MAKE A DIFFERENCE. SO... SHUICHI, WHAT COLOR DO YOU LIKE?
I DON'T CARE ABOUT THE COLOR!

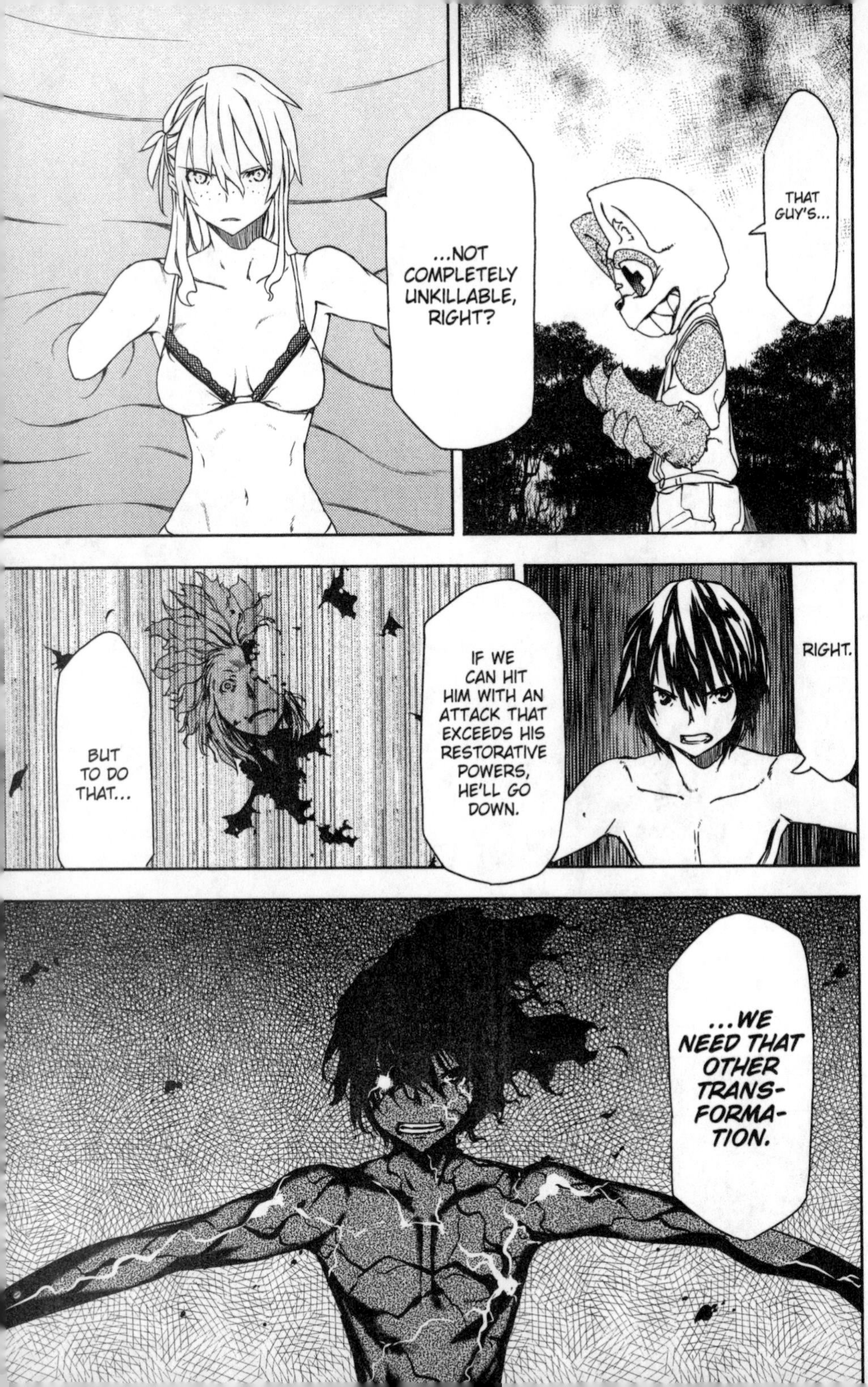
THAT GUY'S...
...NOT COMPLETELY UNKILLABLE, RIGHT?
RIGHT.
IF WE CAN HIT HIM WITH AN ATTACK THAT EXCEEDS HIS RESTORATIVE POWERS, HE'LL GO DOWN.
BUT TO DO THAT...
...WE NEED THAT OTHER TRANS-FORMA-TION.

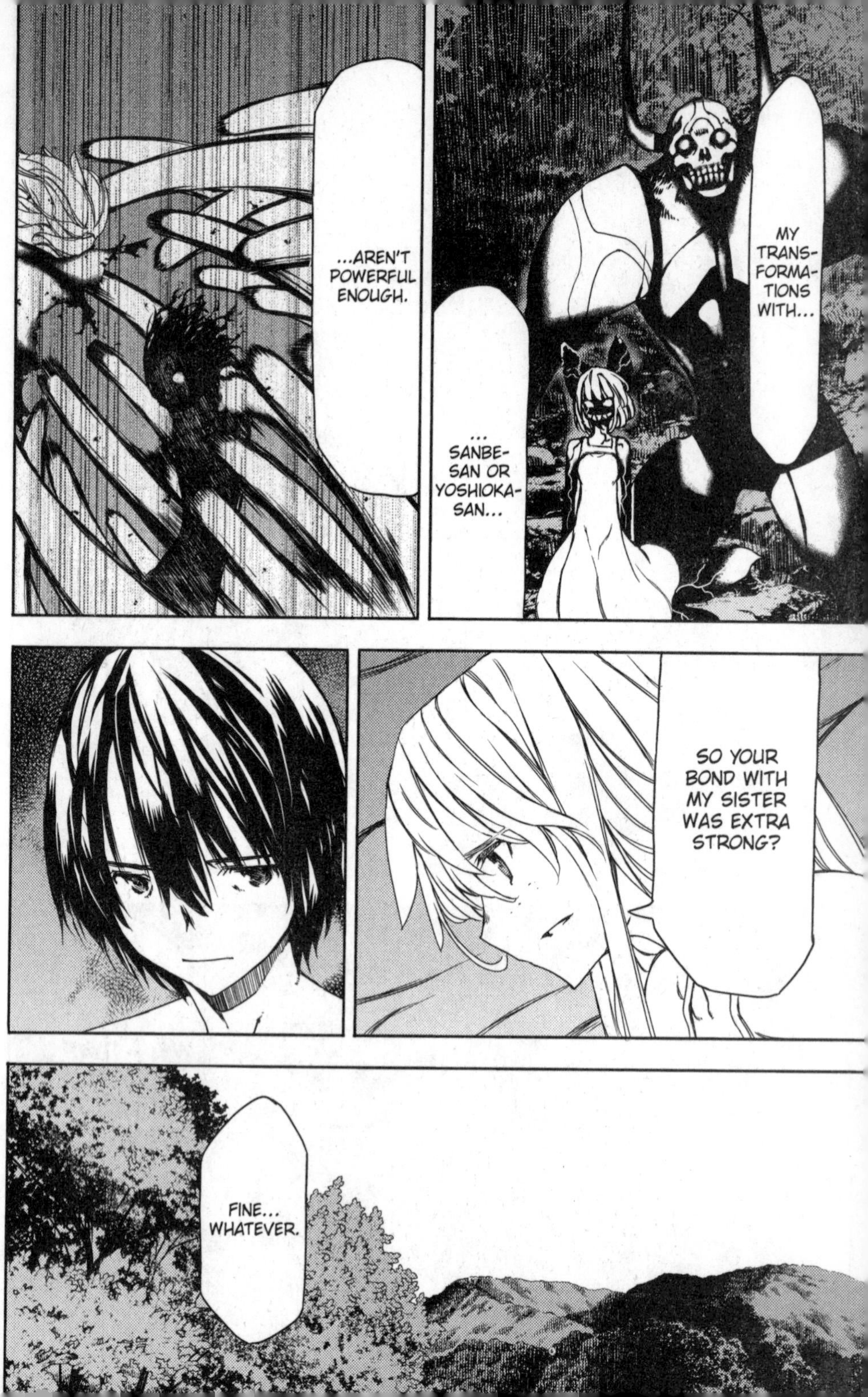
MY TRANS-FORMA-TIONS WITH...
... SANBE-SAN OR YOSHIOKA-SAN...
...AREN'T POWERFUL ENOUGH.
SO YOUR BOND WITH MY SISTER WAS EXTRA STRONG?
FINE... WHATEVER.

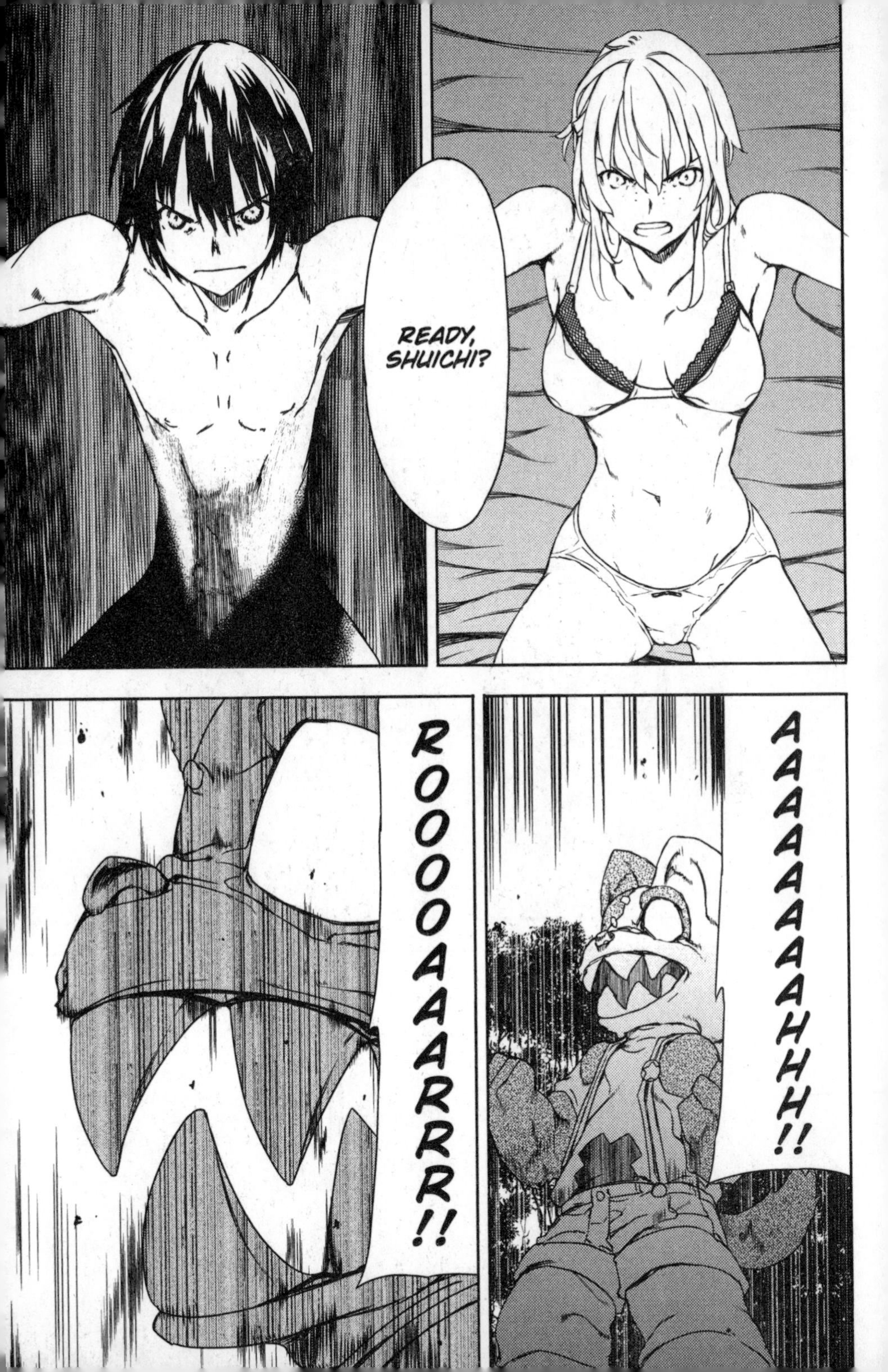
READY, SHUICHI?
AAAAAAAAAHHH!!
ROOOOAAARRR!!

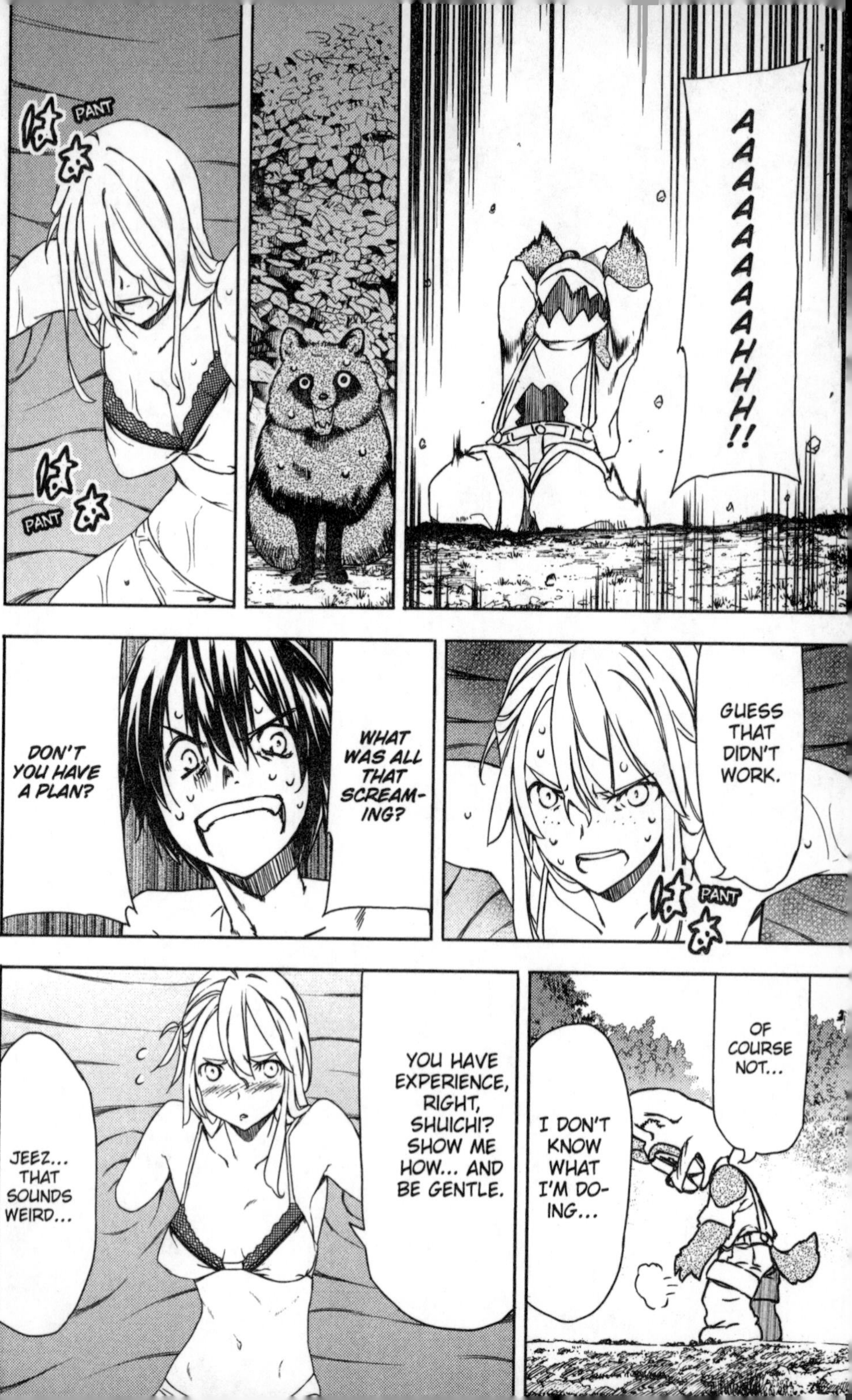
AAAAAAAAHHH!!
はぁ PANT
はぁ PANT
GUESS THAT DIDN'T WORK.
はぁ PANT
WHAT WAS ALL THAT SCREAM-ING?
DON'T YOU HAVE A PLAN?
OF COURSE NOT...
I DON'T KNOW WHAT I'M DO-ING...
YOU HAVE EXPERIENCE, RIGHT, SHUICHI? SHOW ME HOW... AND BE GENTLE.
JEEZ... THAT SOUNDS WEIRD...

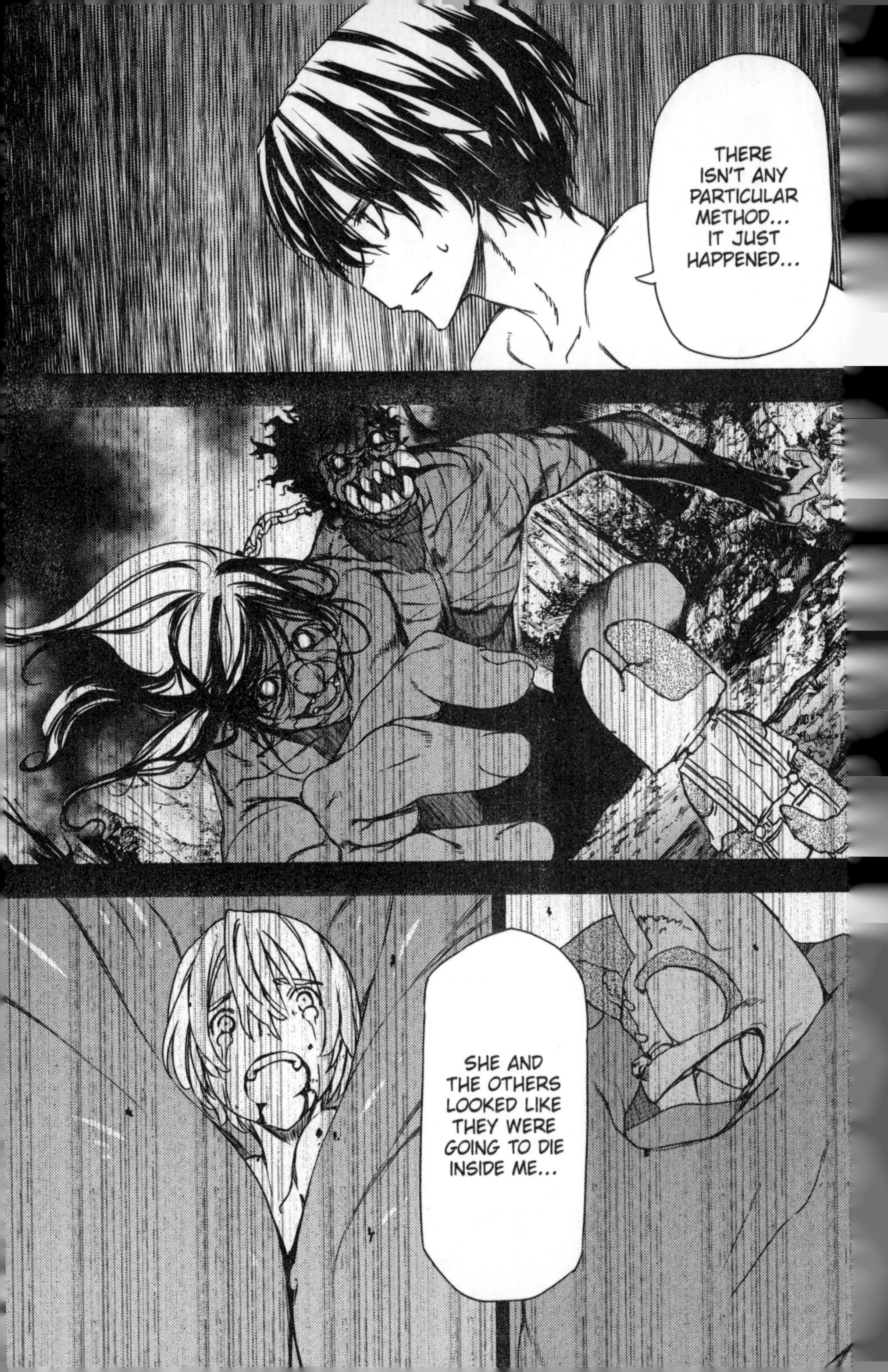
THERE ISN'T ANY PARTICULAR METHOD... IT JUST HAPPENED...
SHE AND THE OTHERS LOOKED LIKE THEY WERE GOING TO DIE INSIDE ME...

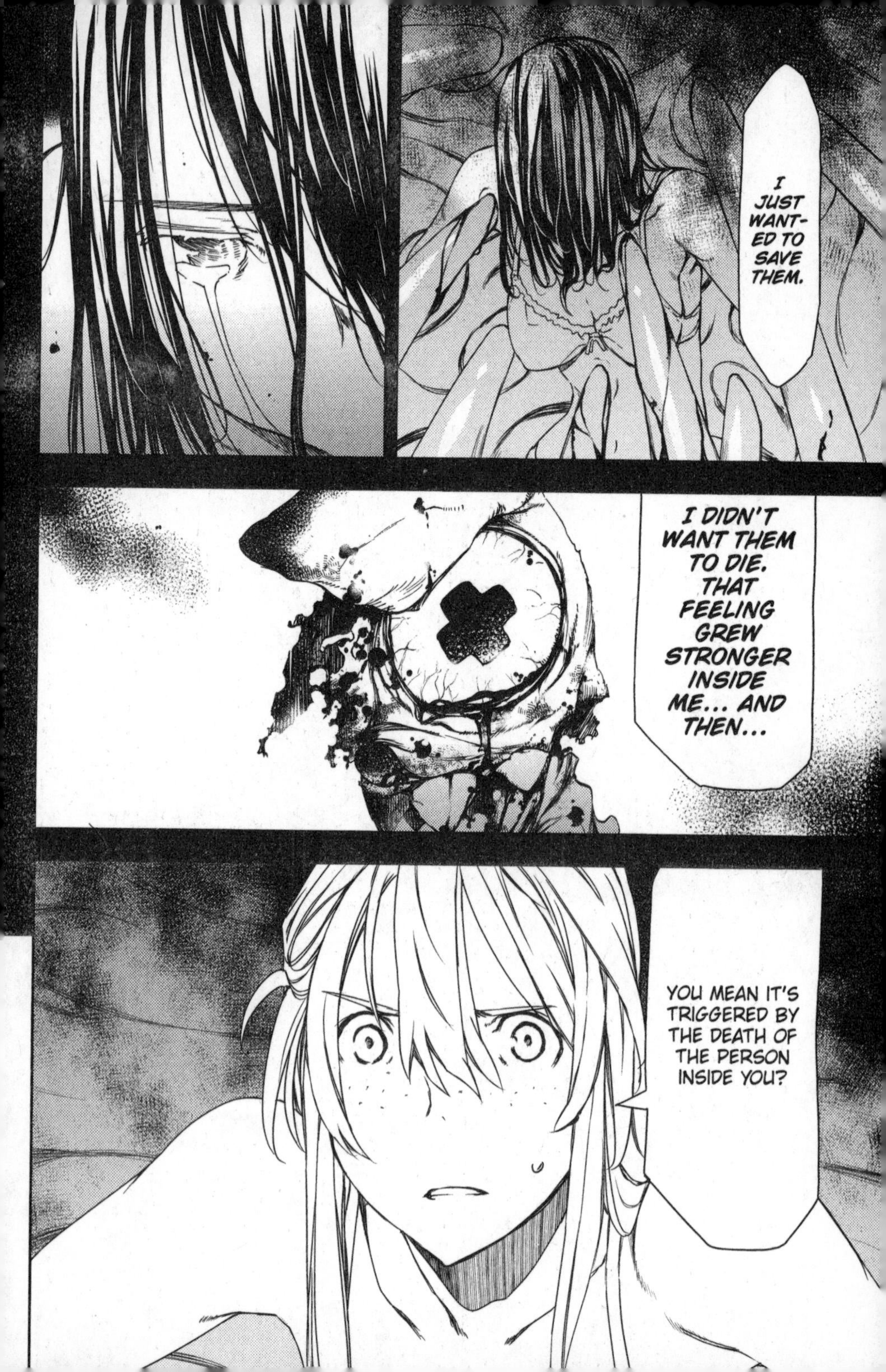
I JUST WANT-ED TO SAVE THEM.
I DIDN'T WANT THEM TO DIE. THAT FEELING GREW STRONGER INSIDE ME... AND THEN...
YOU MEAN IT'S TRIGGERED BY THE DEATH OF THE PERSON INSIDE YOU?

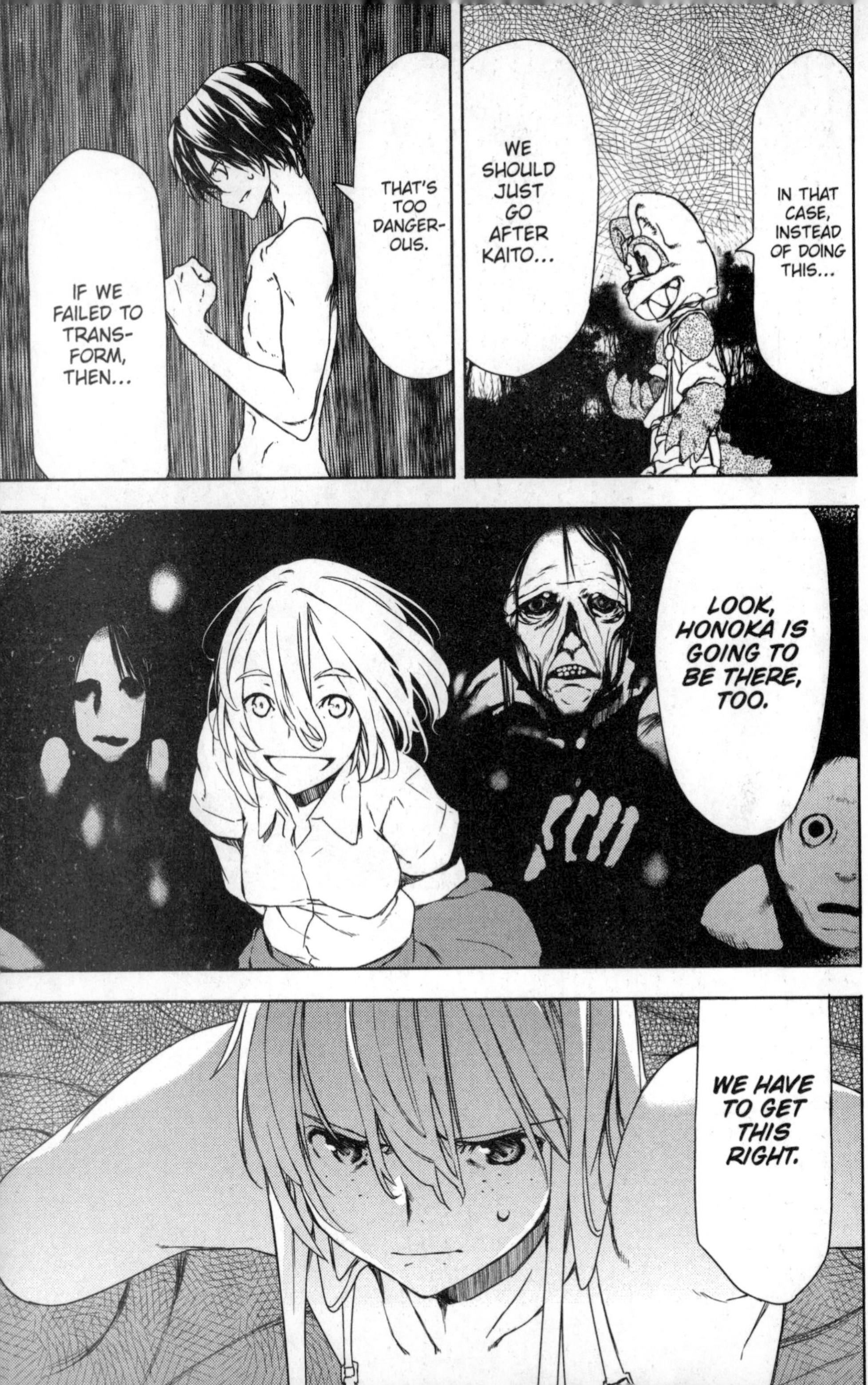
IN THAT CASE, INSTEAD OF DOING THIS...
WE SHOULD JUST GO AFTER KAITO...
THAT'S TOO DANGER-OUS.
IF WE FAILED TO TRANS-FORM, THEN...
LOOK, HONOKA IS GOING TO BE THERE, TOO.
WE HAVE TO GET THIS RIGHT.

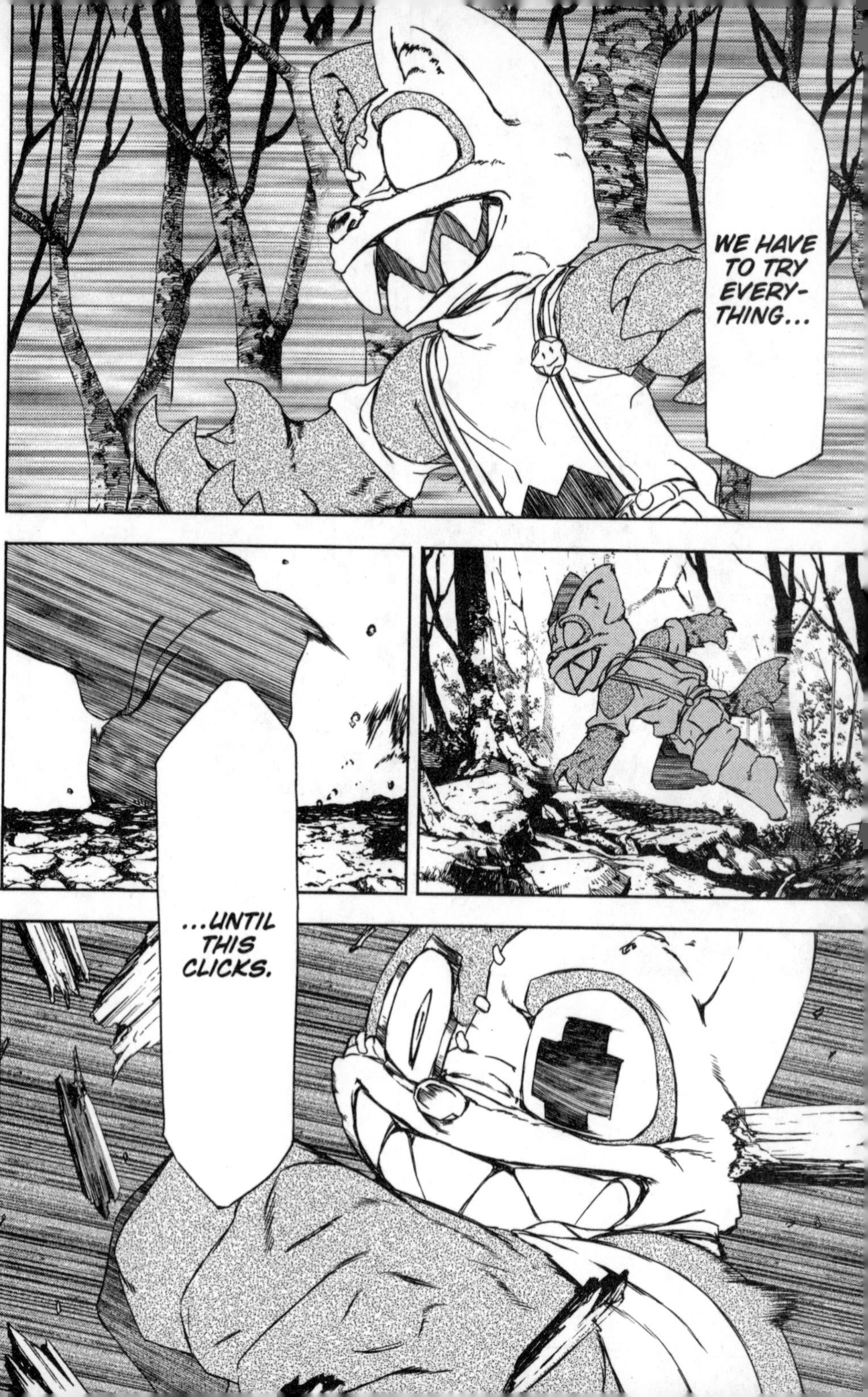
WE HAVE TO TRY EVERY-THING...
...UNTIL THIS CLICKS.

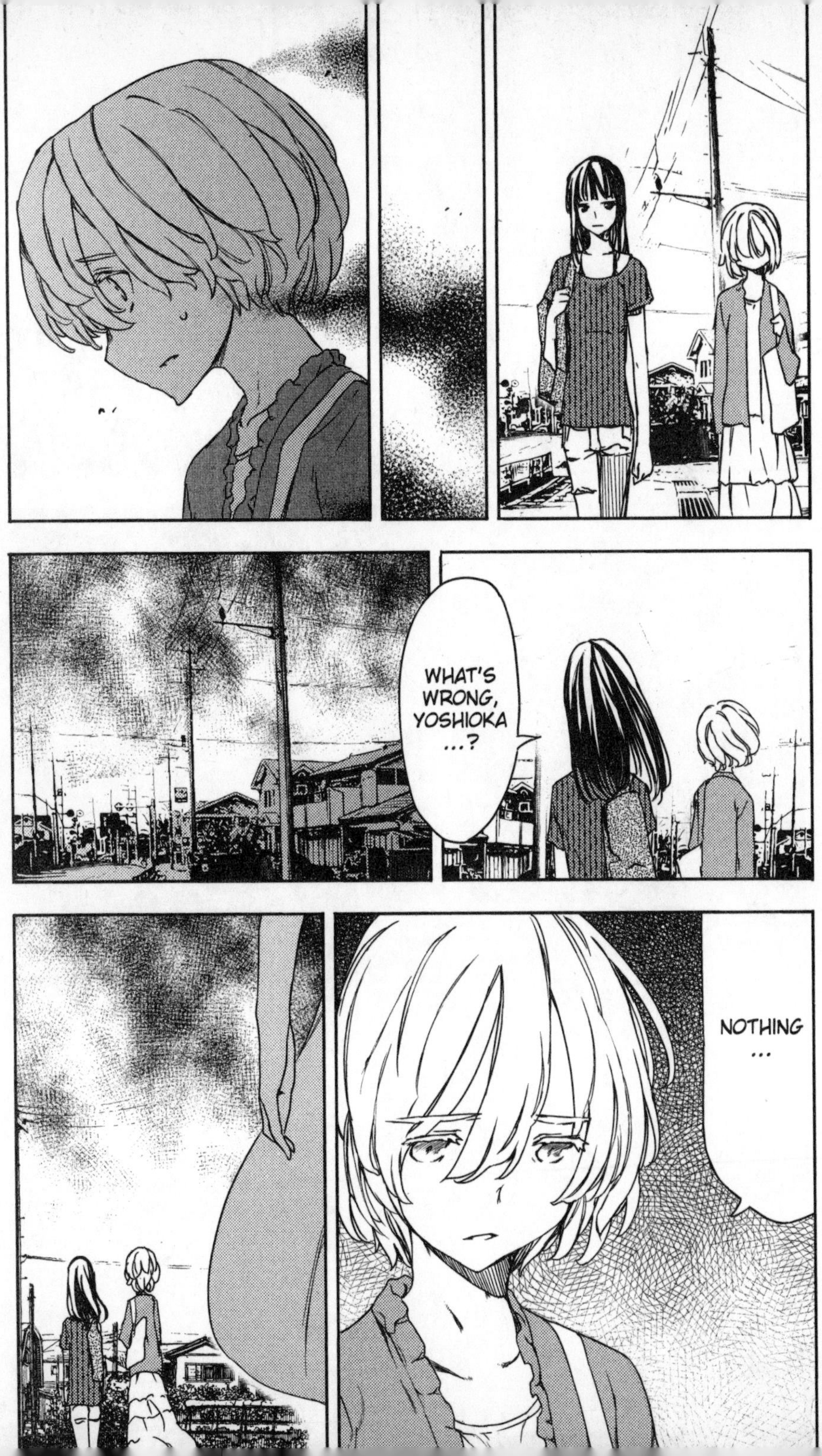
WHAT'S WRONG, YOSHIOKA ...?
NOTHING ...

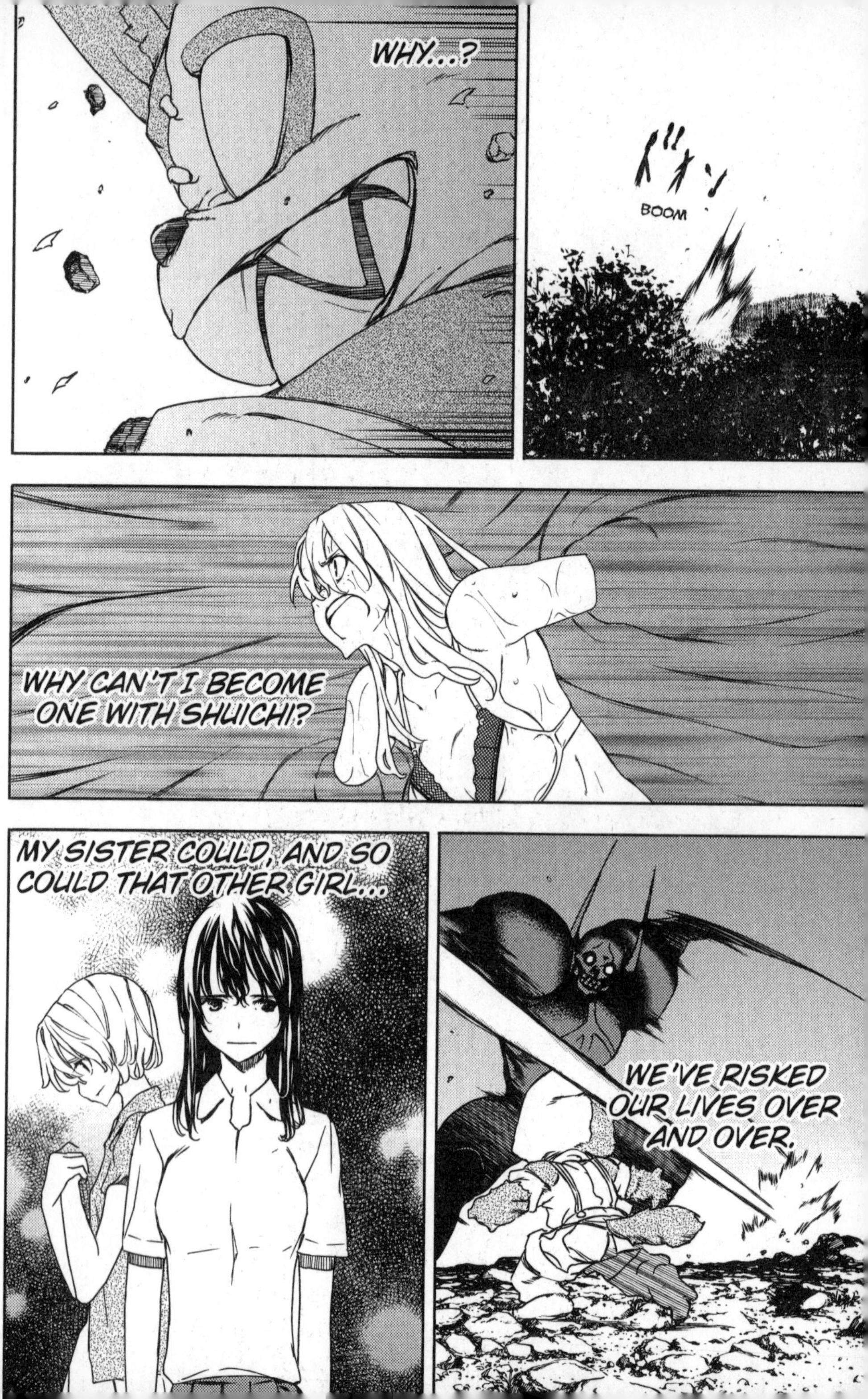
ドオン
BOOM
WHY...?
WHY CAN'T I BECOME ONE WITH SHUICHI?
WE'VE RISKED OUR LIVES OVER AND OVER.
MY SISTER COULD, AND SO COULD THAT OTHER GIRL...

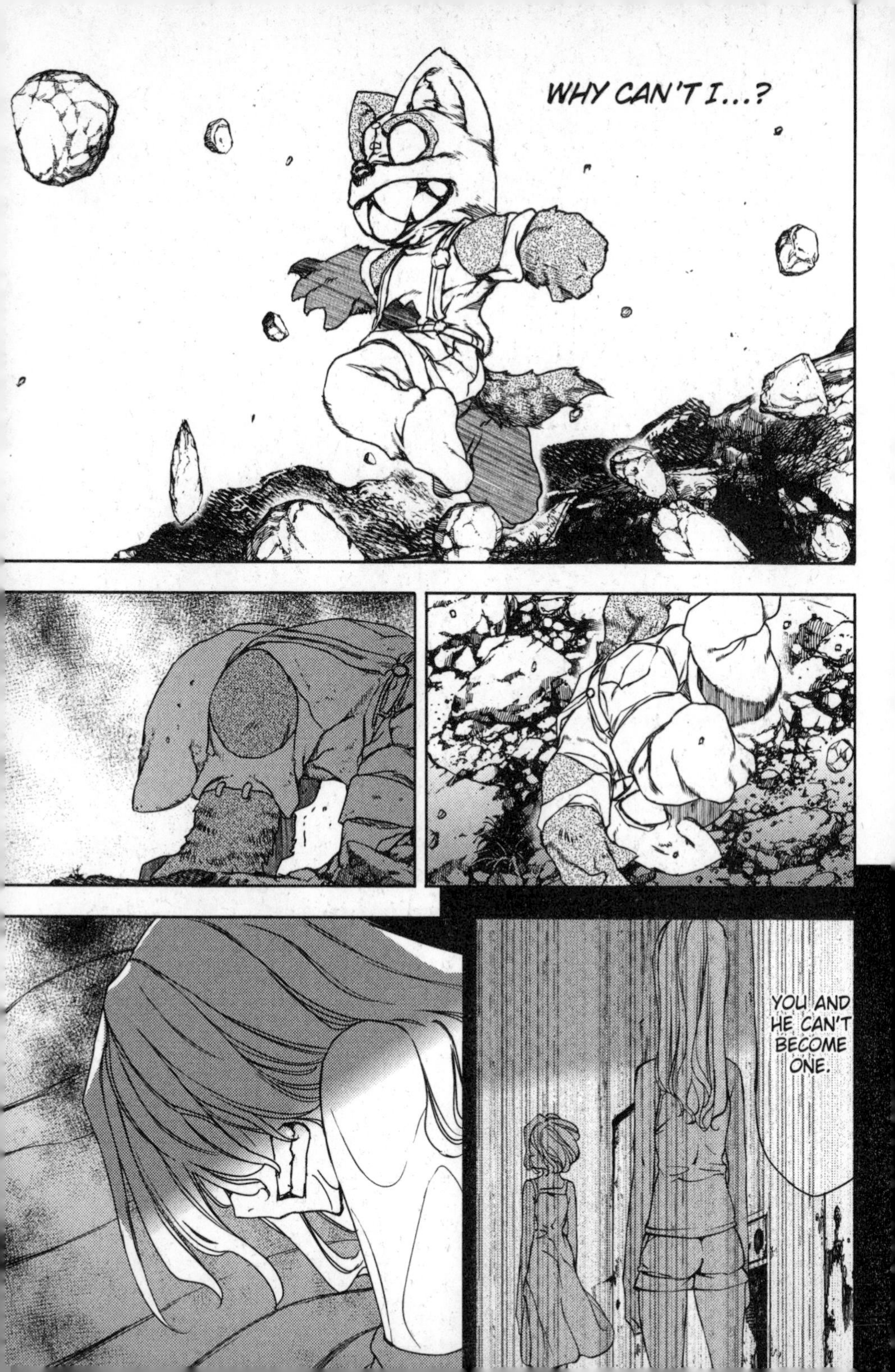
WHY CAN'T I...?
YOU AND HE CAN'T BECOME ONE.

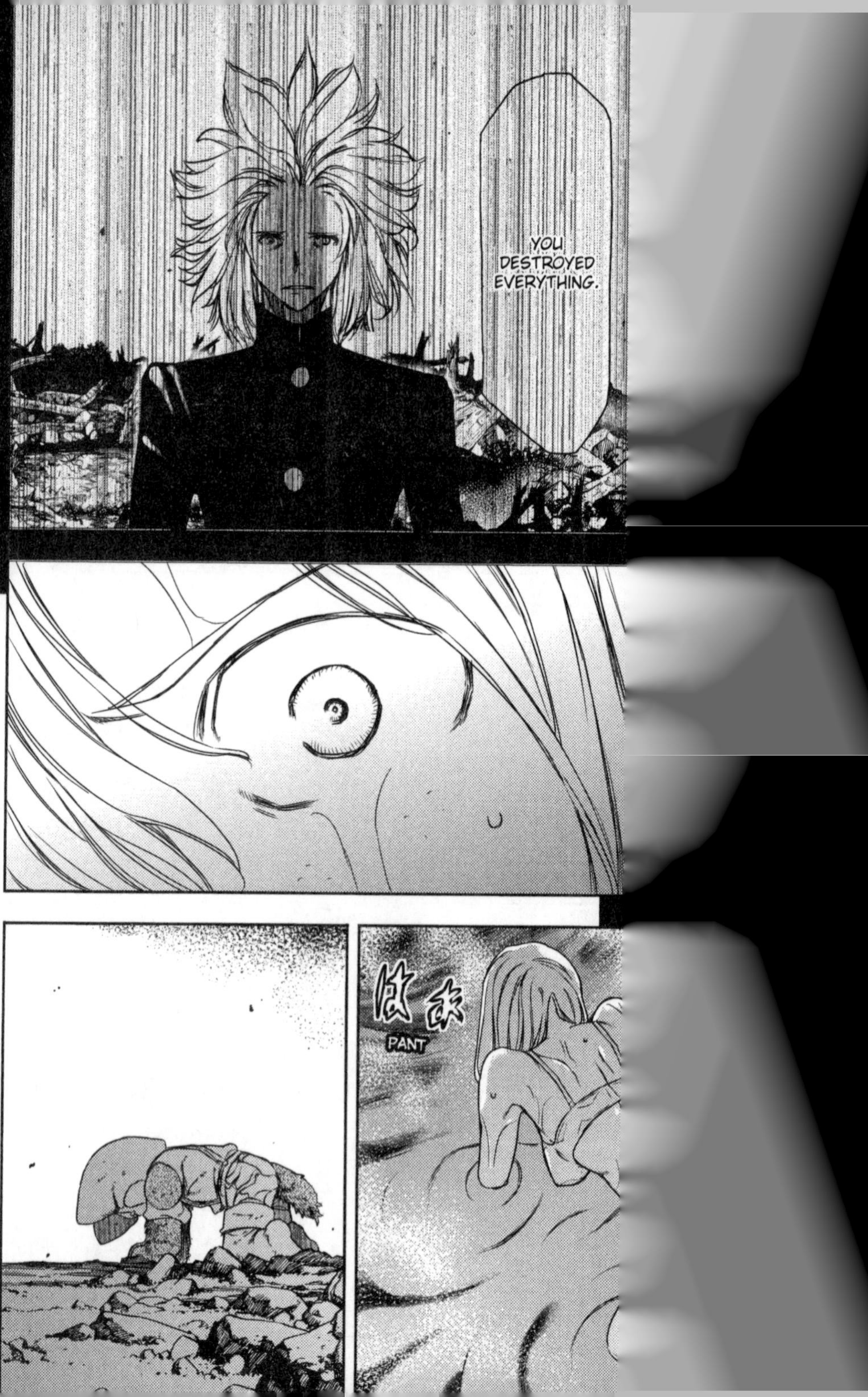
YOU DESTROYED EVERYTHING.
PANT

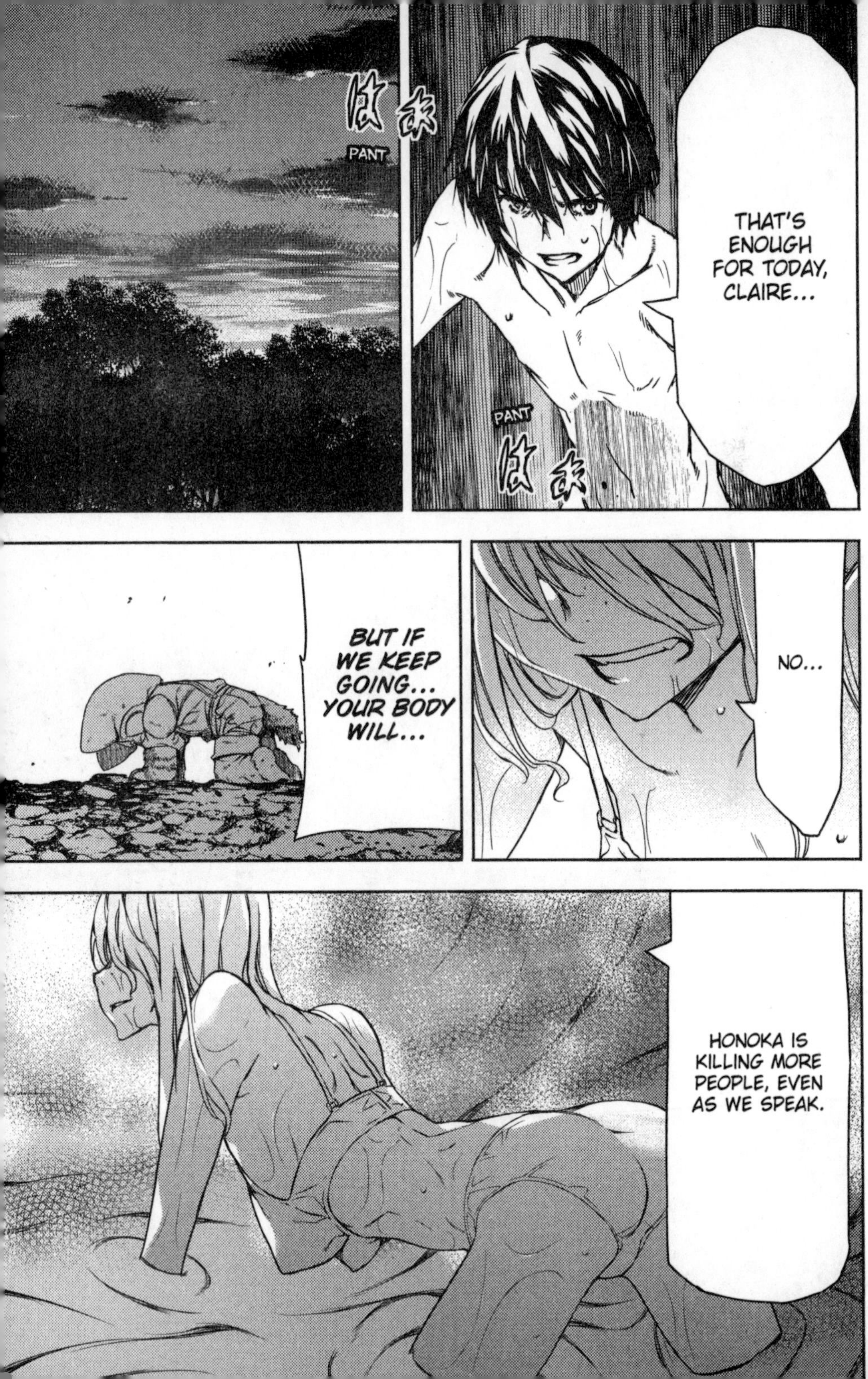
THAT'S ENOUGH FOR TODAY, CLAIRE...
PANT
PANT
NO...
BUT IF WE KEEP GOING... YOUR BODY WILL...
HONOKA IS KILLING MORE PEOPLE, EVEN AS WE SPEAK.

YOU'RE THE ONLY ONE WHO CAN STOP HER, RIGHT, SHUICHI?

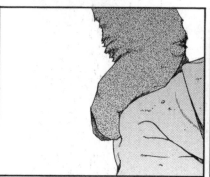

YOU KNOW... THERE'S SOMETHING I WANTED TO APOLOGIZE TO YOU ABOUT.

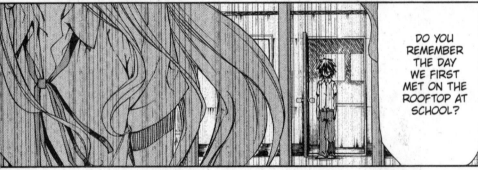

DO YOU REMEMBER THE DAY WE FIRST MET ON THE ROOFTOP AT SCHOOL?

I PUSHED YOU OFF...

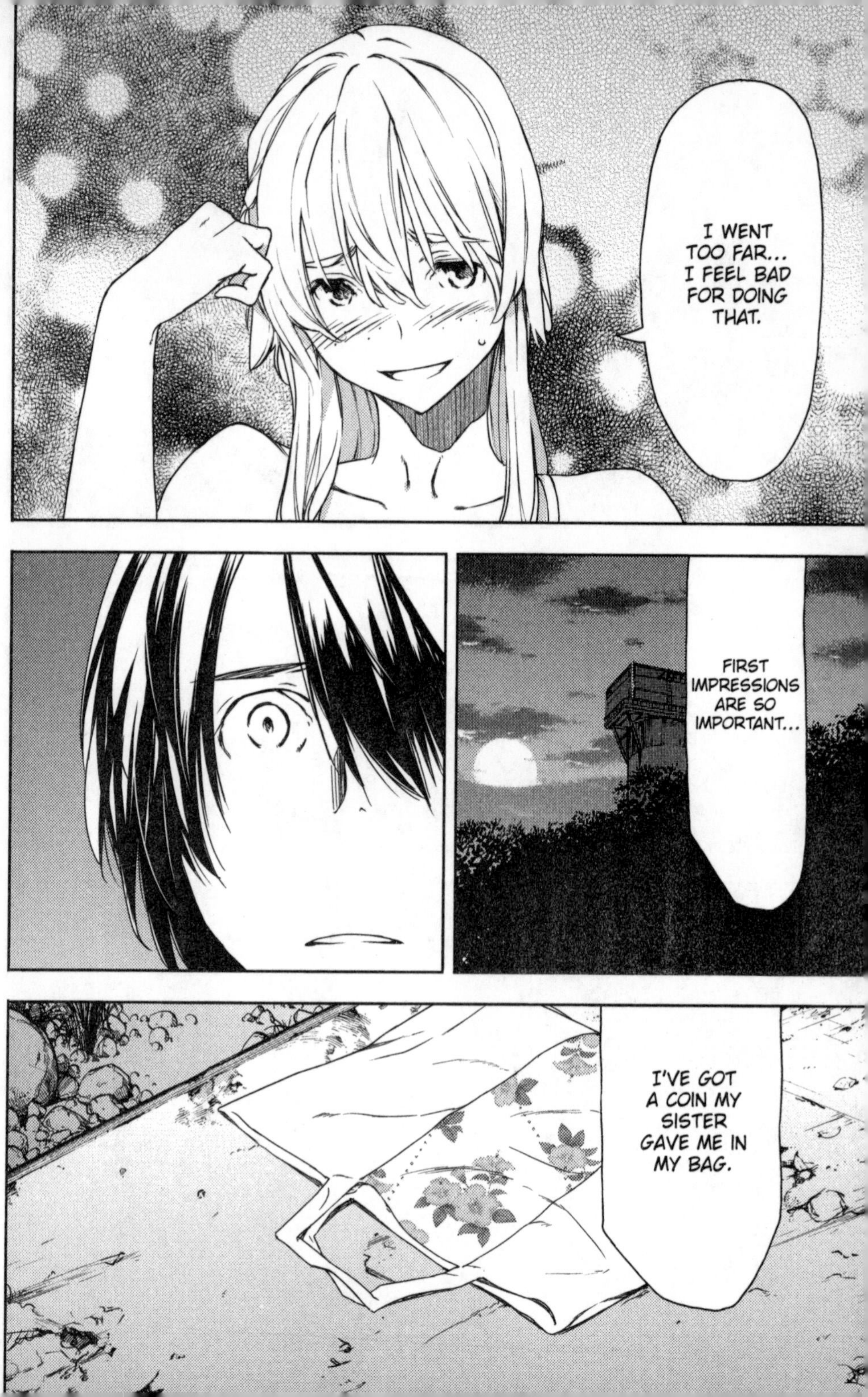
I WENT TOO FAR... I FEEL BAD FOR DOING THAT.
FIRST IMPRESSIONS ARE SO IMPORTANT...
I'VE GOT A COIN MY SISTER GAVE ME IN MY BAG.

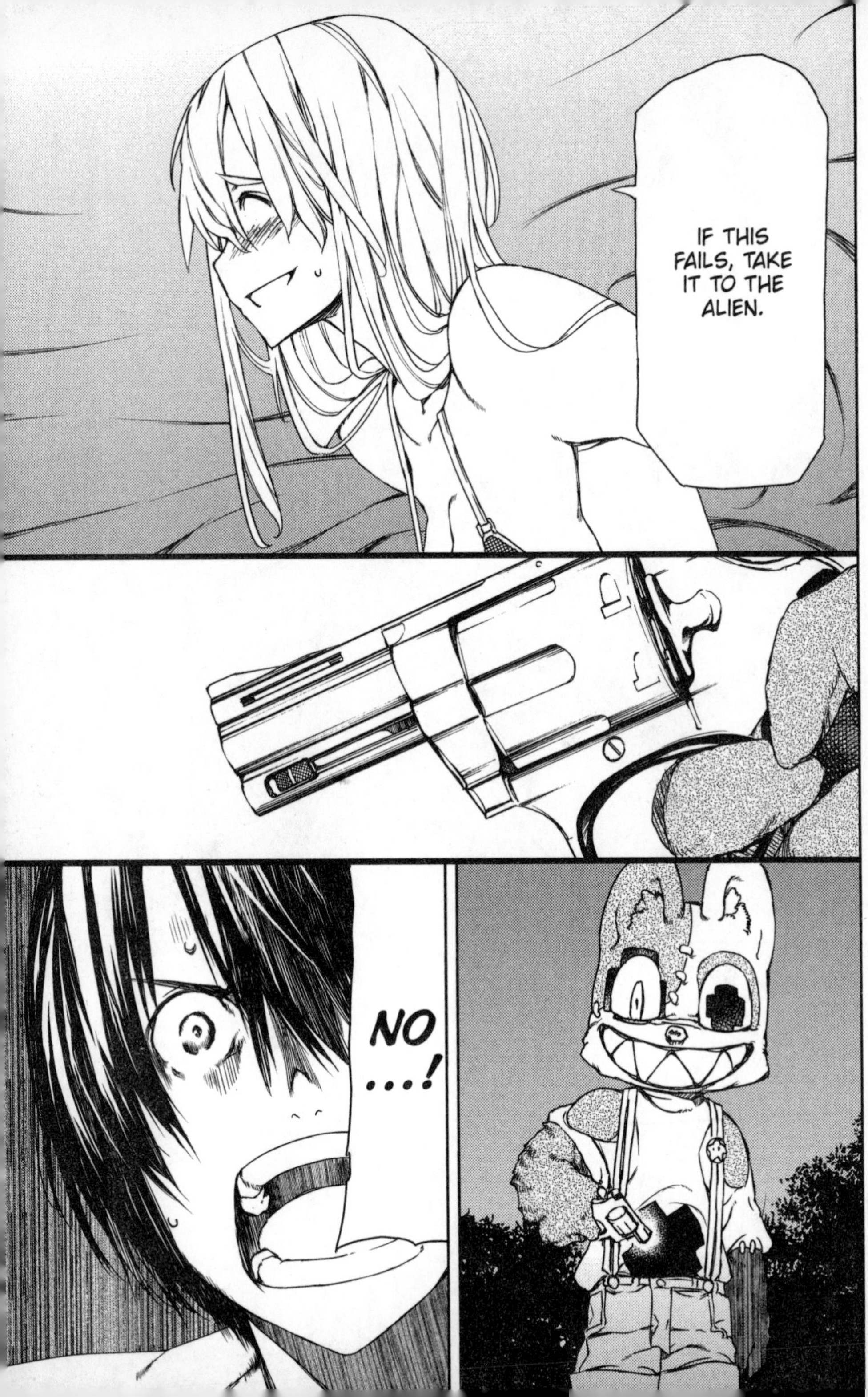
IF THIS FAILS, TAKE IT TO THE ALIEN.
NO ...!

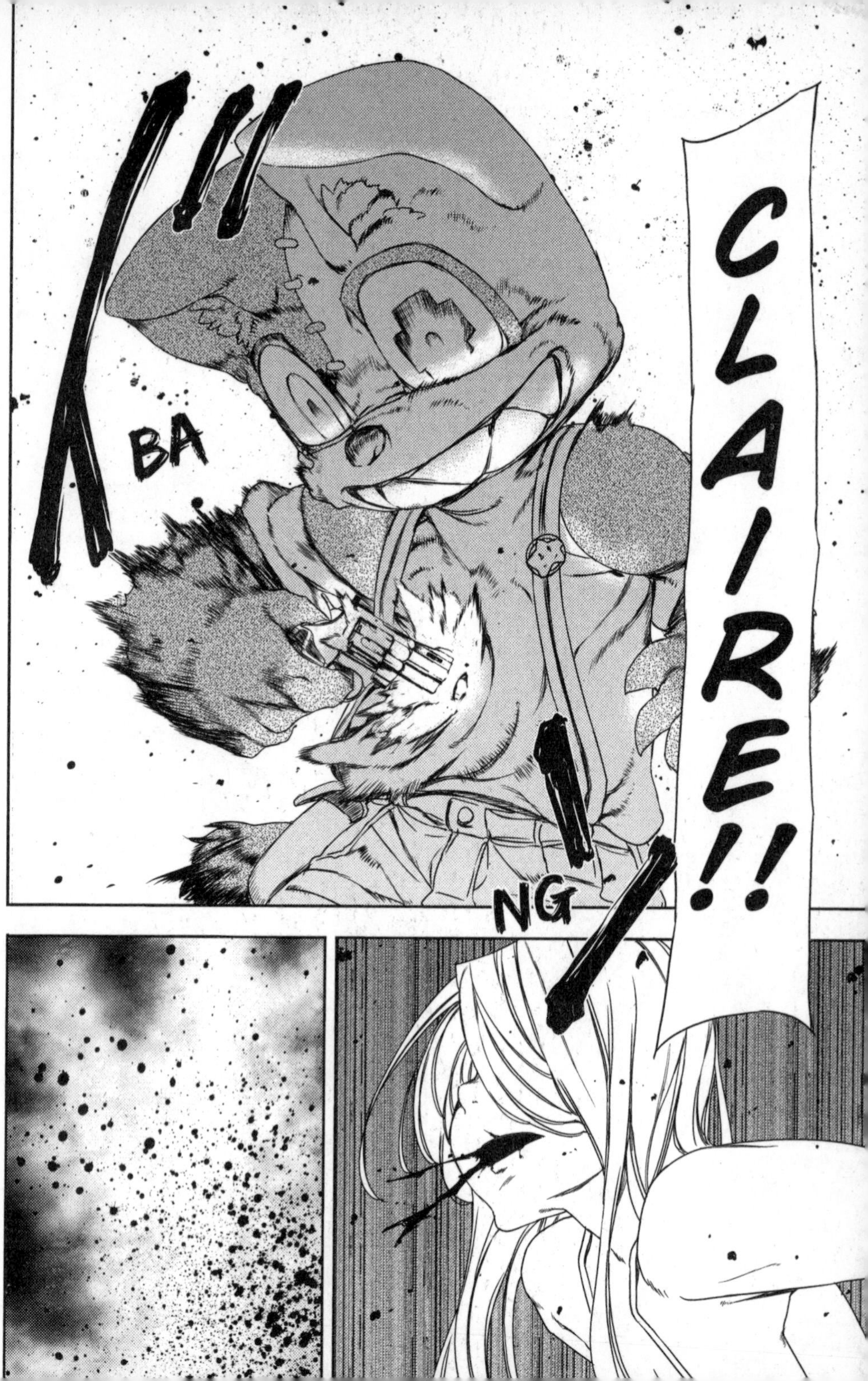
CLAIRE!!
BA
NG

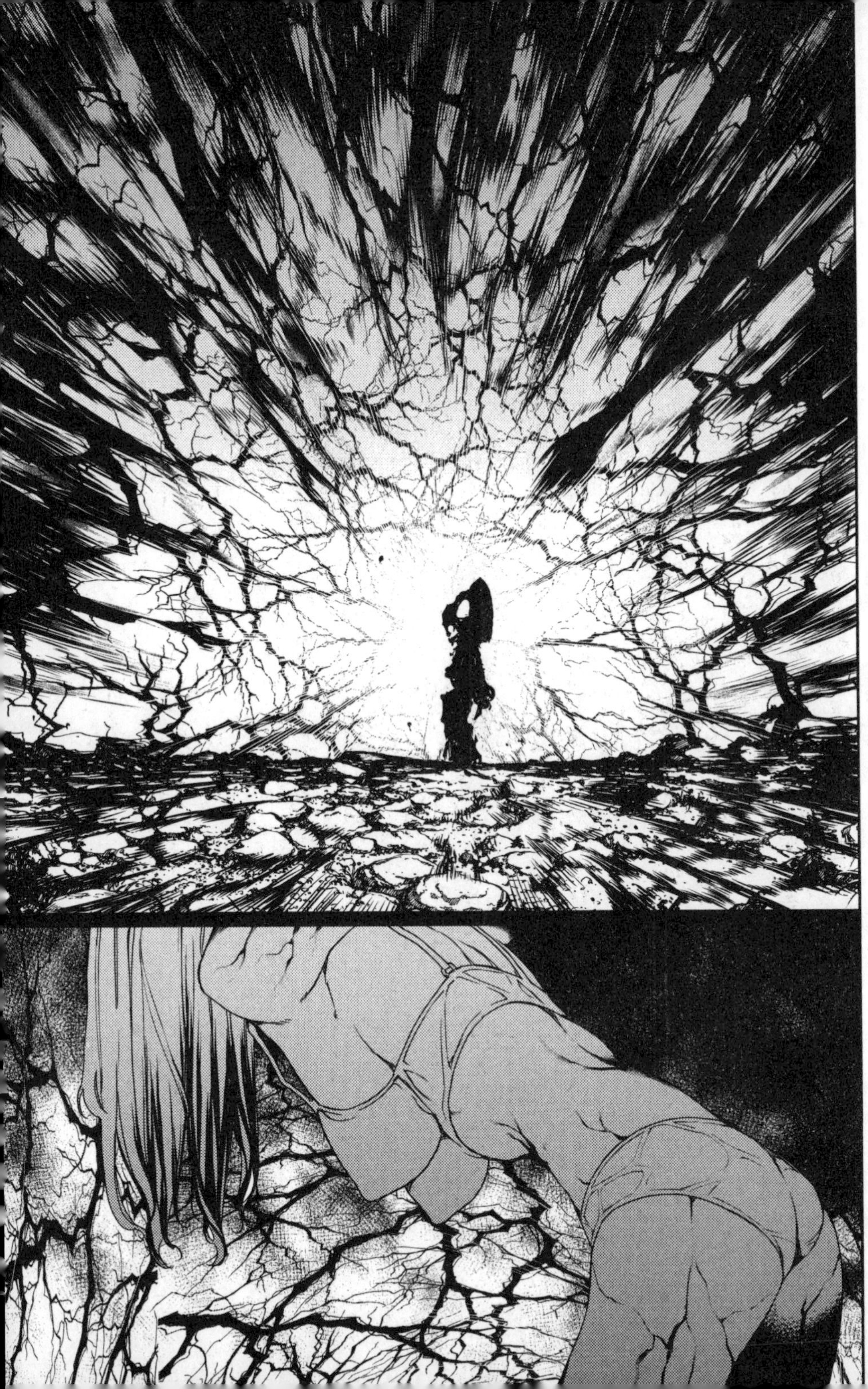

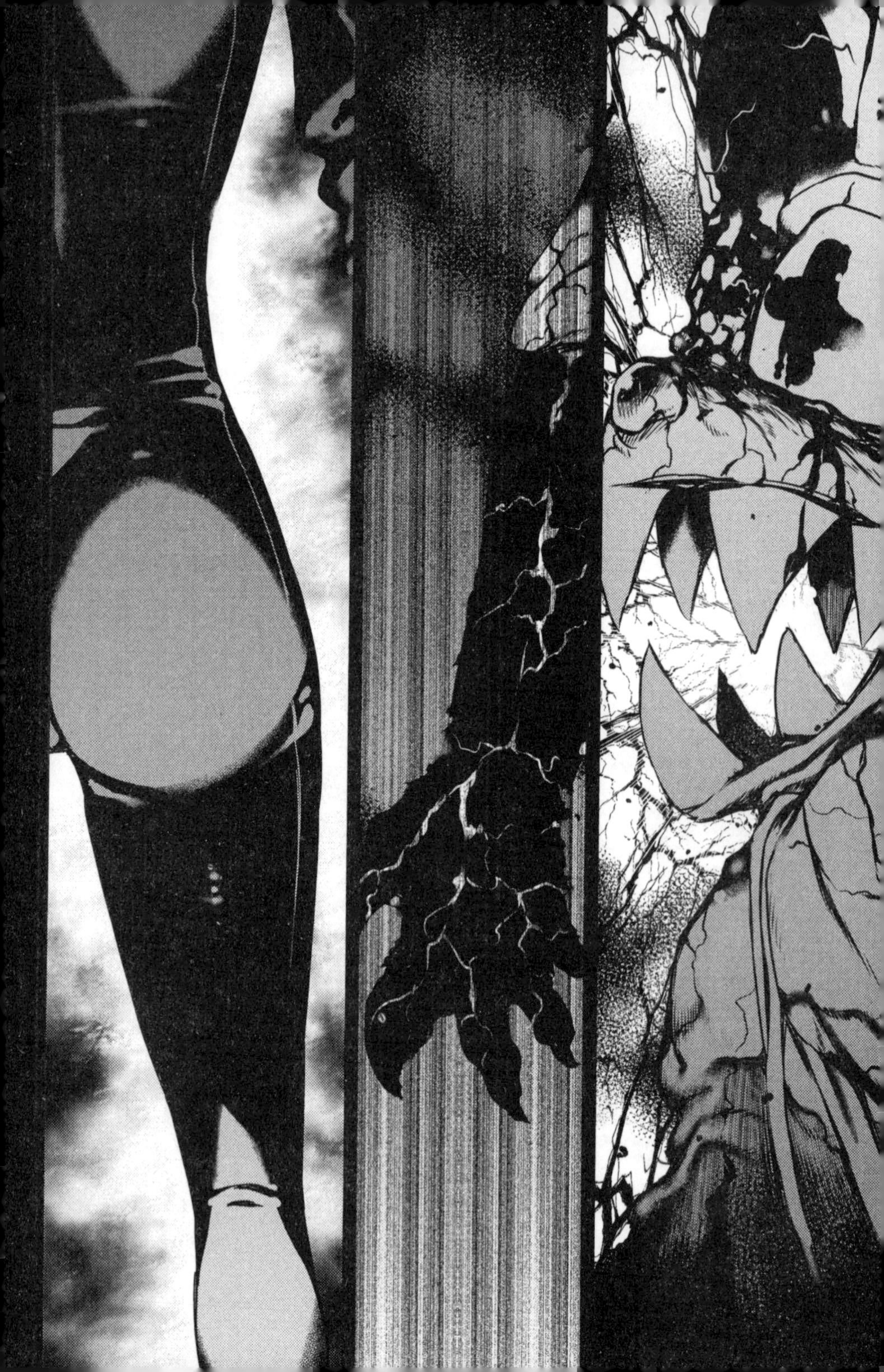

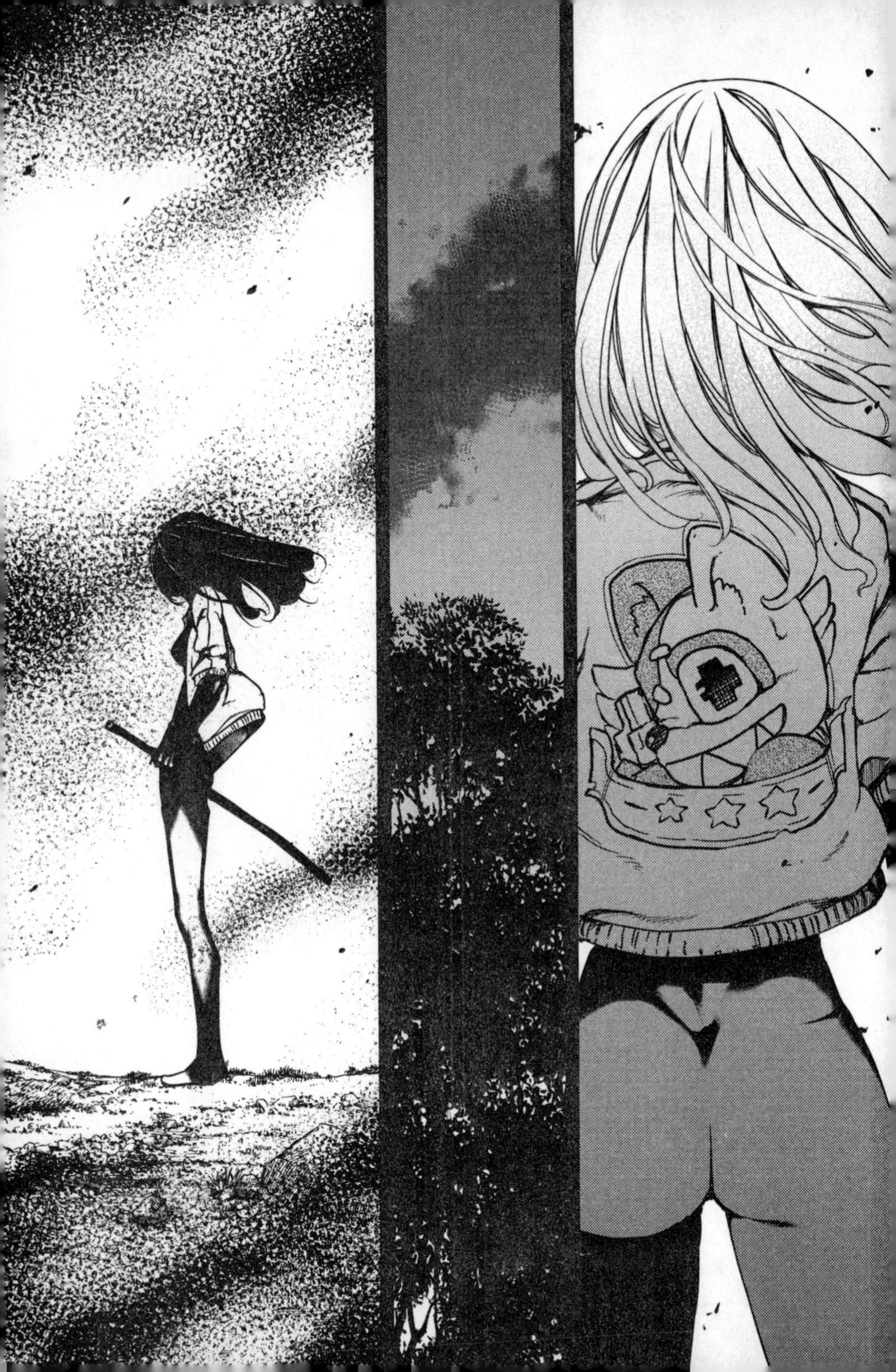

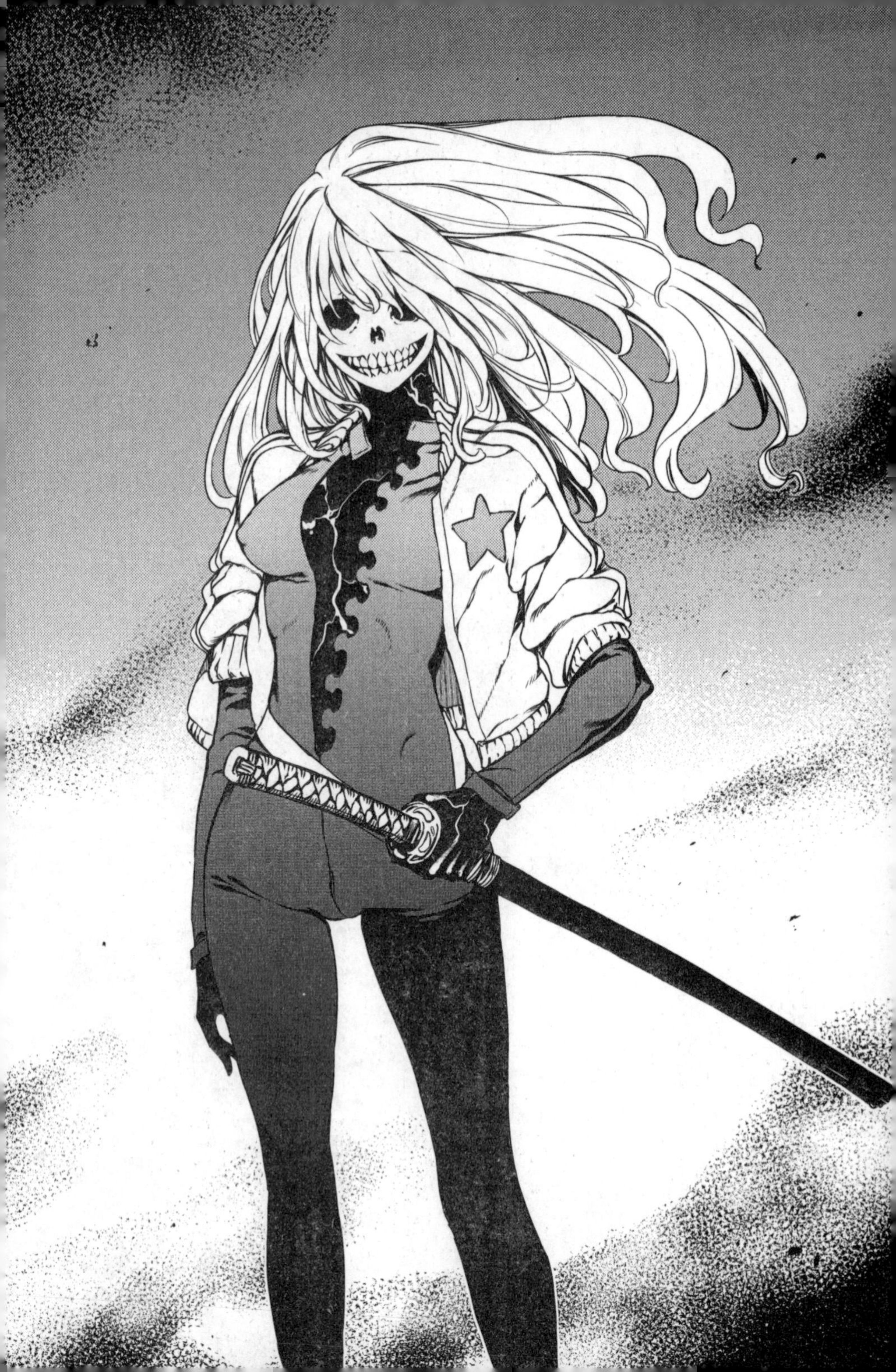

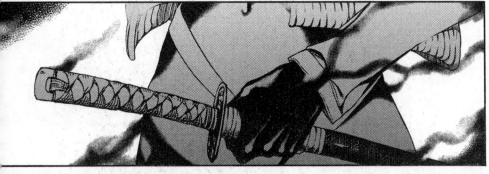

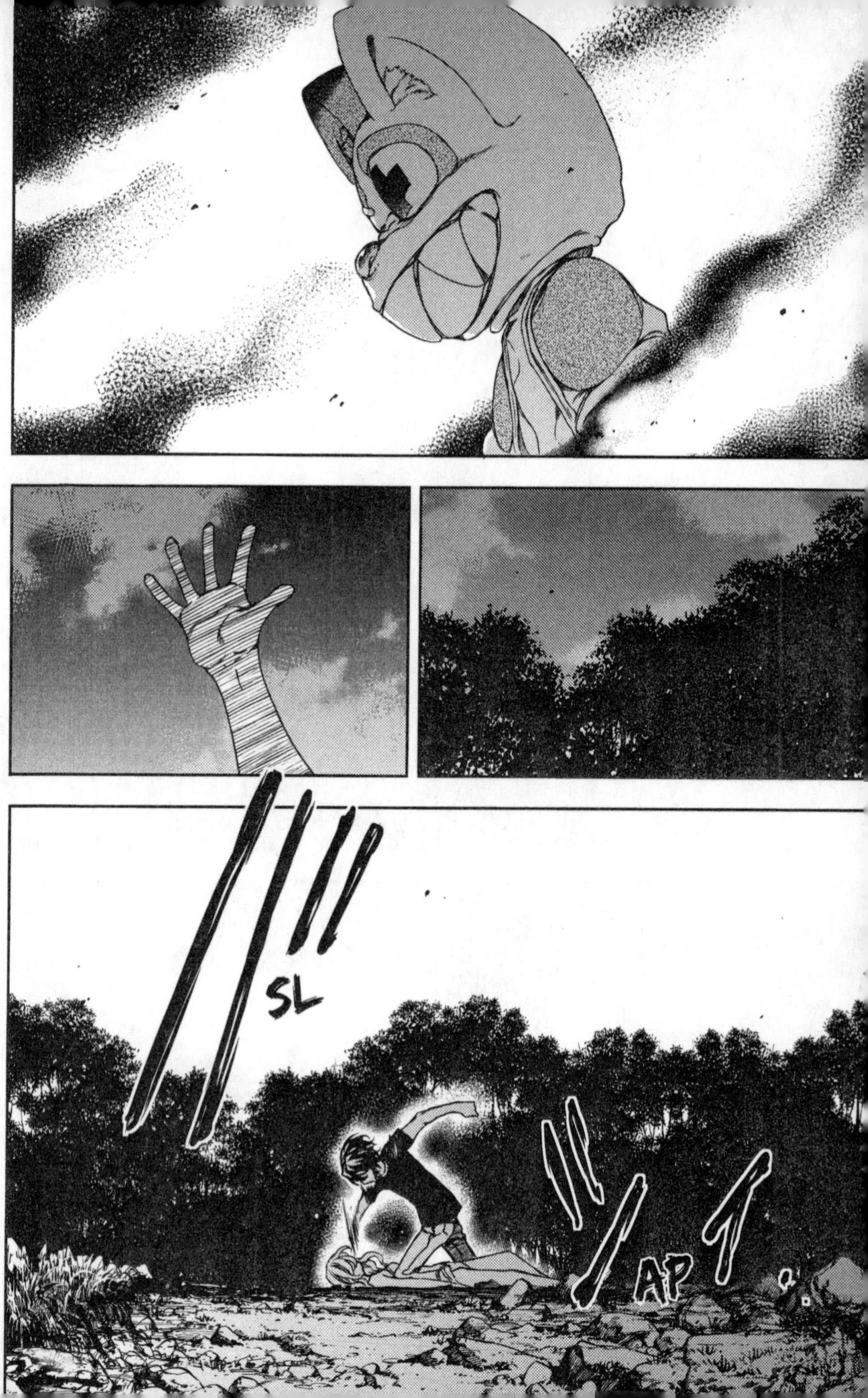
SL
AP

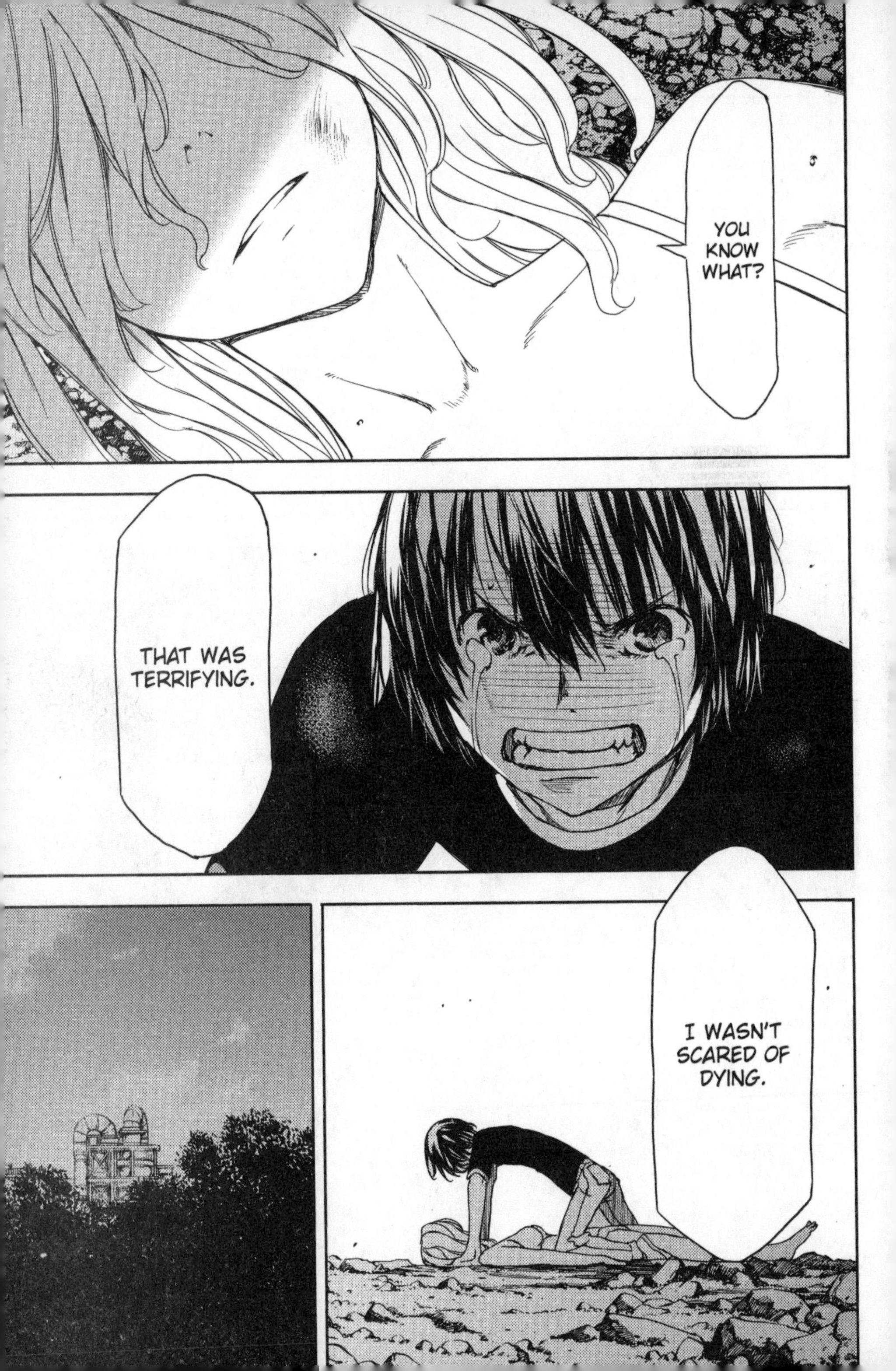
YOU KNOW WHAT?
THAT WAS TERRIFYING.
I WASN'T SCARED OF DYING.

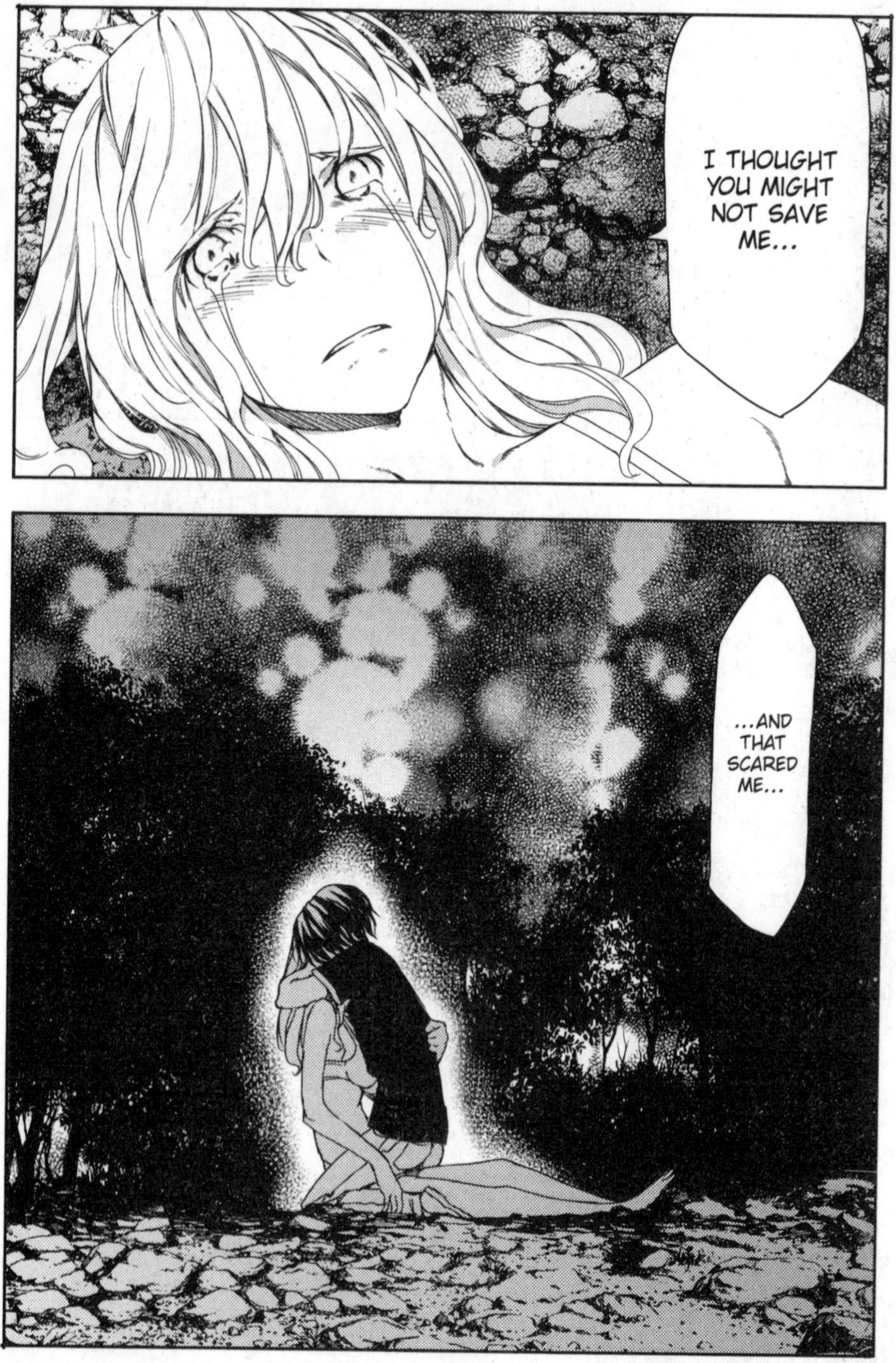
I THOUGHT YOU MIGHT NOT SAVE ME...
...AND THAT SCARED ME...

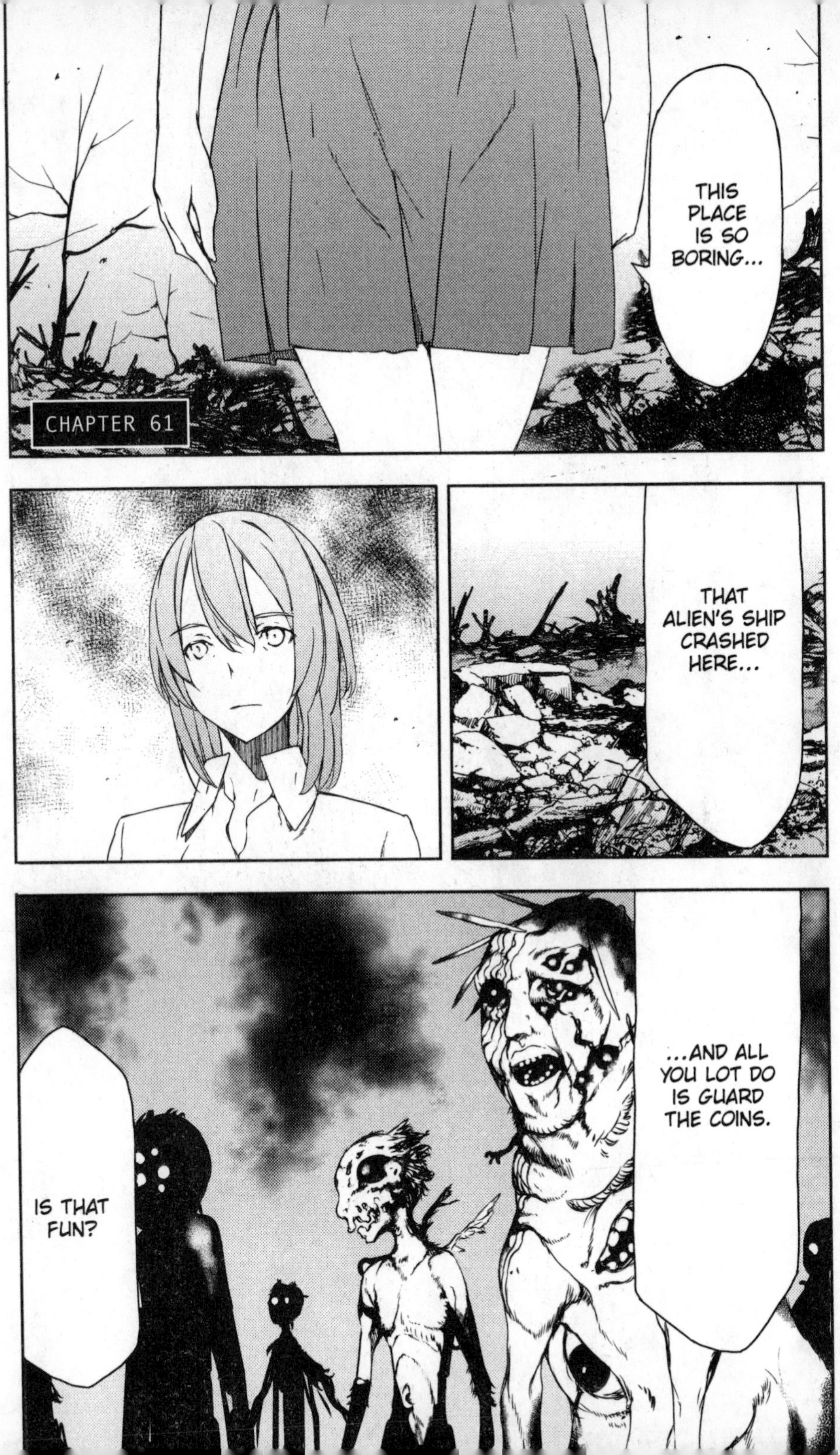
THIS PLACE IS SO BORING...
CHAPTER 61
THAT ALIEN'S SHIP CRASHED HERE...
...AND ALL YOU LOT DO IS GUARD THE COINS.
IS THAT FUN?

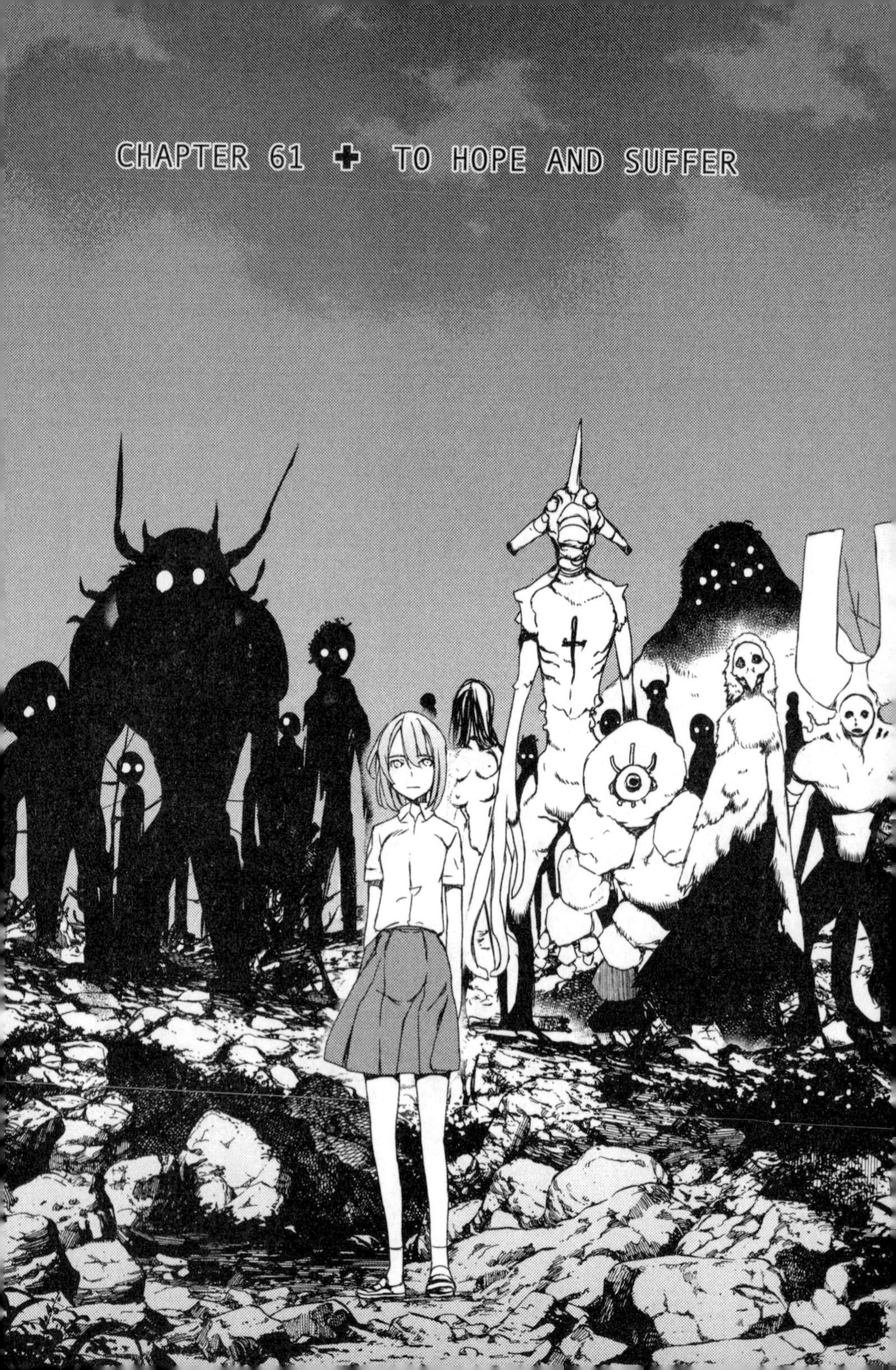
CHAPTER 61 + TO HOPE AND SUFFER

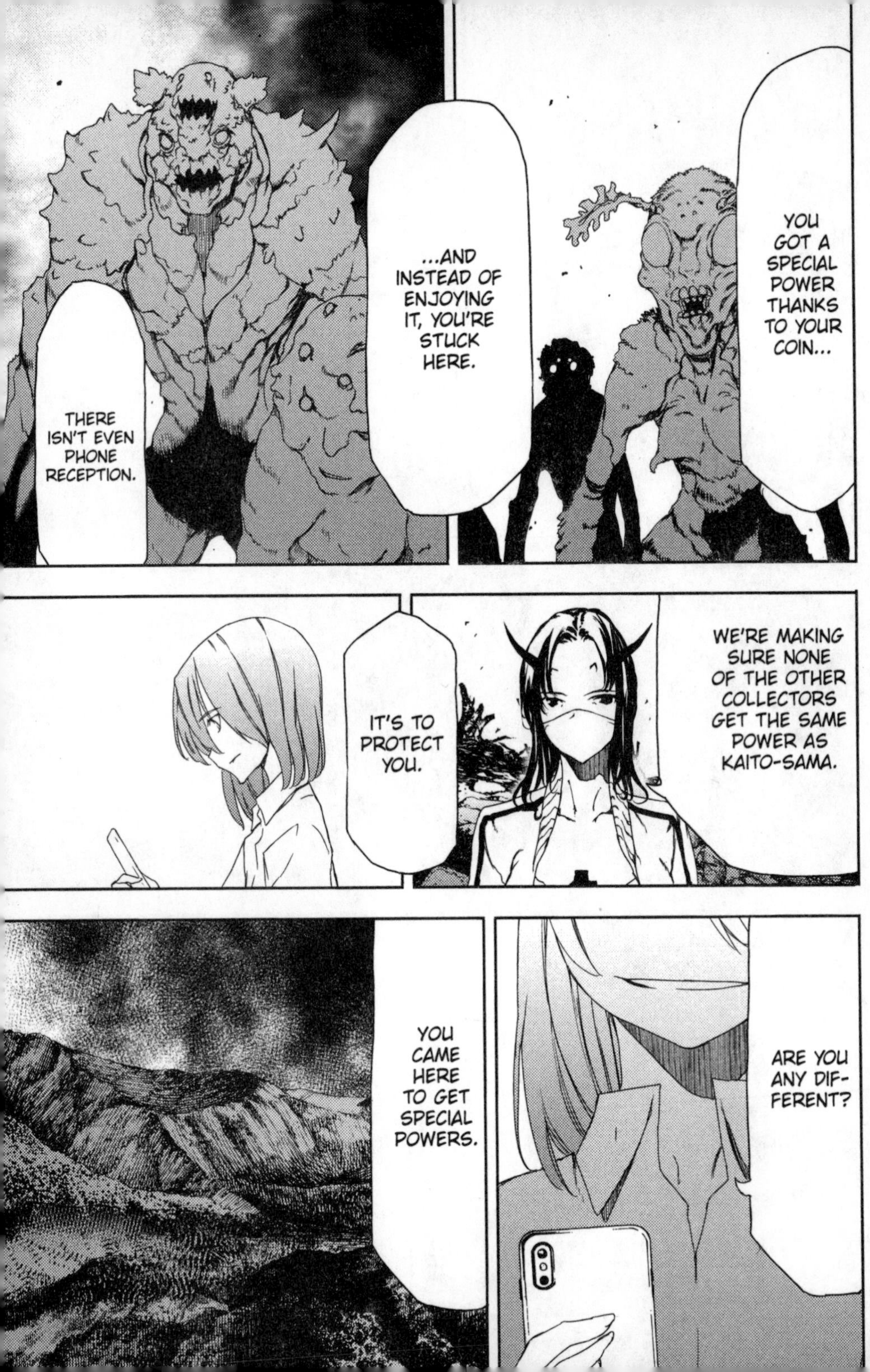
YOU GOT A SPECIAL POWER THANKS TO YOUR COIN...
...AND INSTEAD OF ENJOYING IT, YOU'RE STUCK HERE.
THERE ISN'T EVEN PHONE RECEPTION.
WE'RE MAKING SURE NONE OF THE OTHER COLLECTORS GET THE SAME POWER AS KAITO-SAMA.
IT'S TO PROTECT YOU.
ARE YOU ANY DIF-FERENT?
YOU CAME HERE TO GET SPECIAL POWERS.

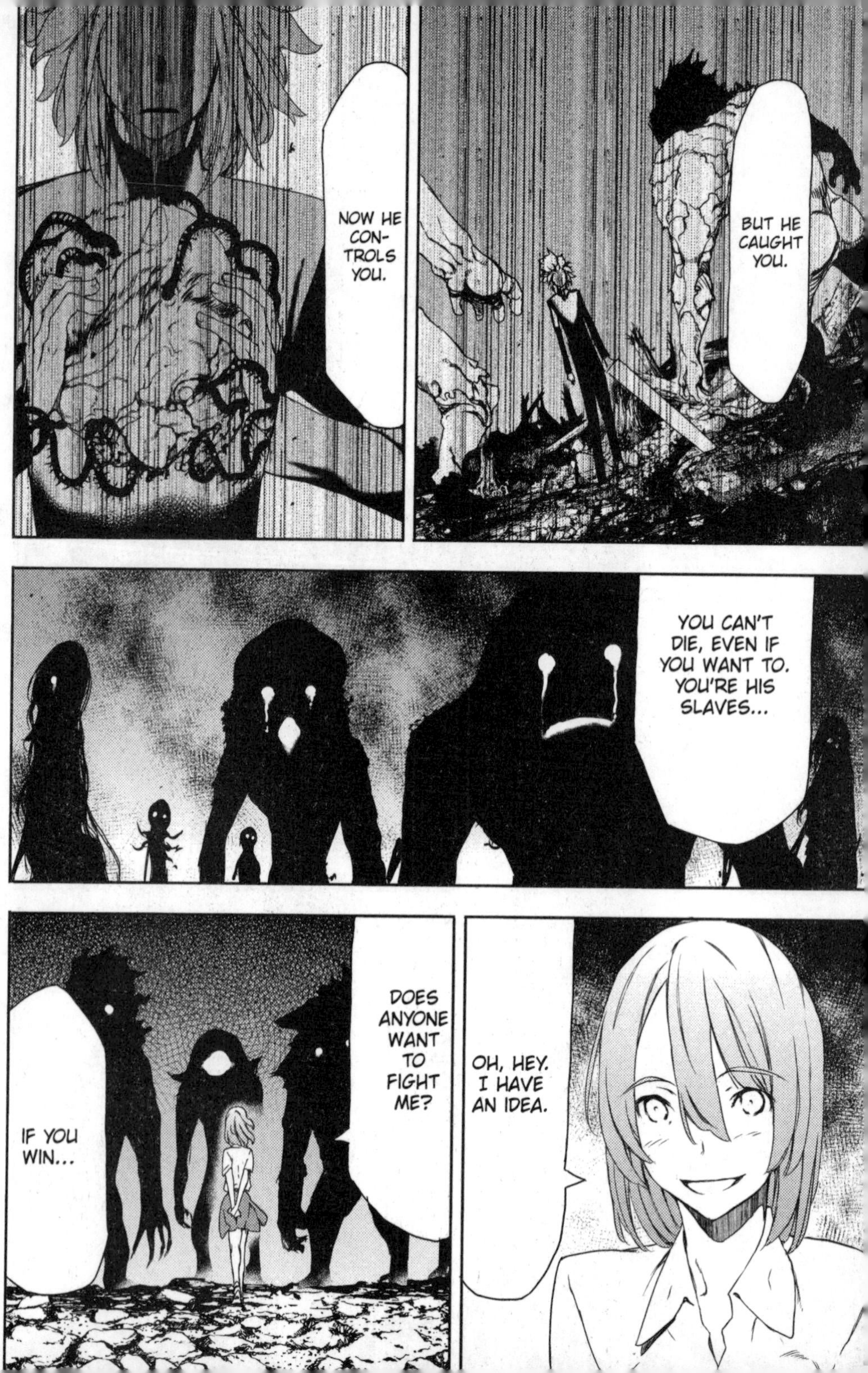
BUT HE CAUGHT YOU.
NOW HE CON-TROLS YOU.
YOU CAN'T DIE, EVEN IF YOU WANT TO. YOU'RE HIS SLAVES...
OH, HEY. I HAVE AN IDEA.
DOES ANYONE WANT TO FIGHT ME?
IF YOU WIN...

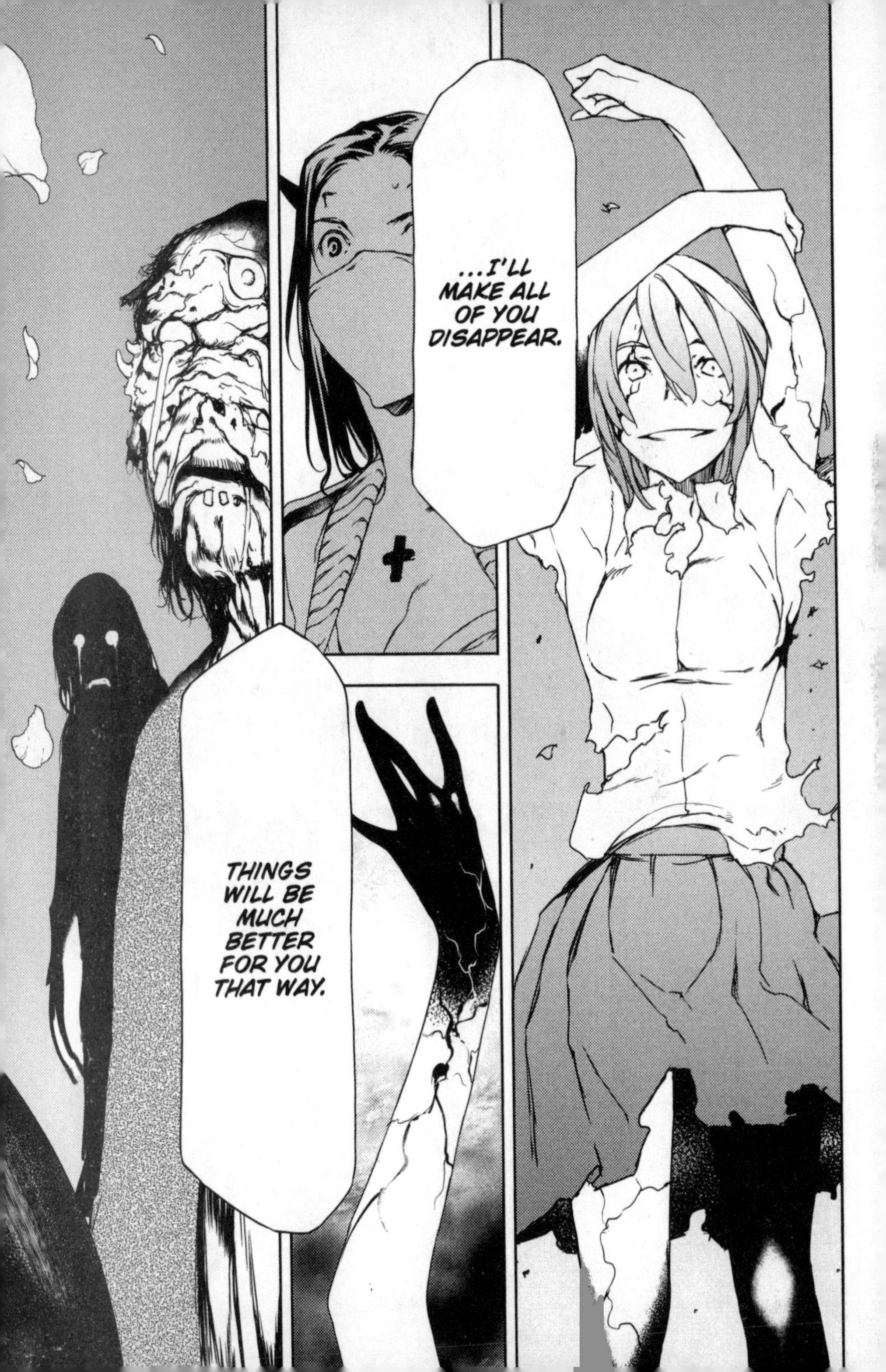
...I'LL MAKE ALL OF YOU DISAPPEAR.
THINGS WILL BE MUCH BETTER FOR YOU THAT WAY.

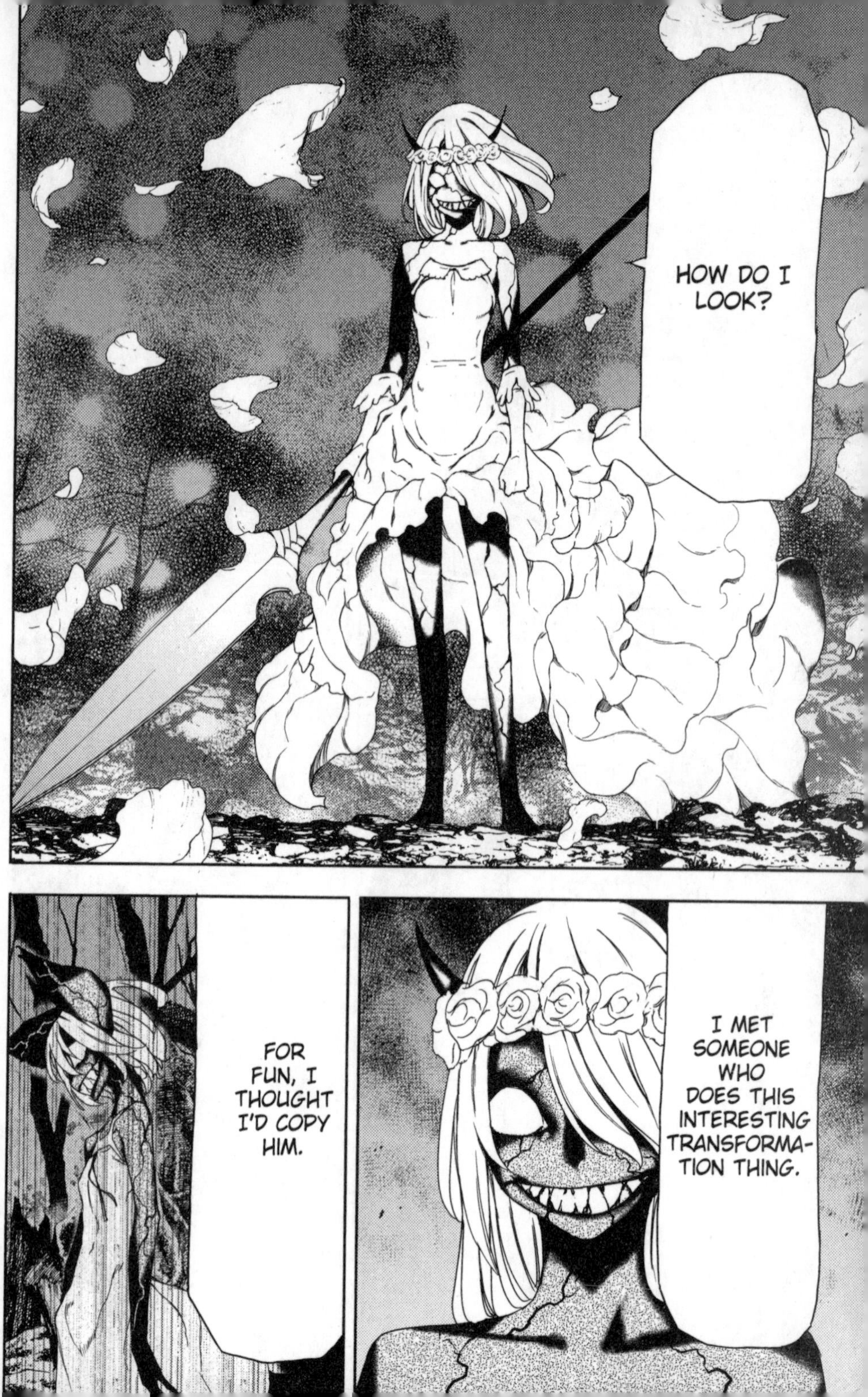
HOW DO I LOOK?
I MET SOMEONE WHO DOES THIS INTERESTING TRANSFORMATION THING.
FOR FUN, I THOUGHT I'D COPY HIM.

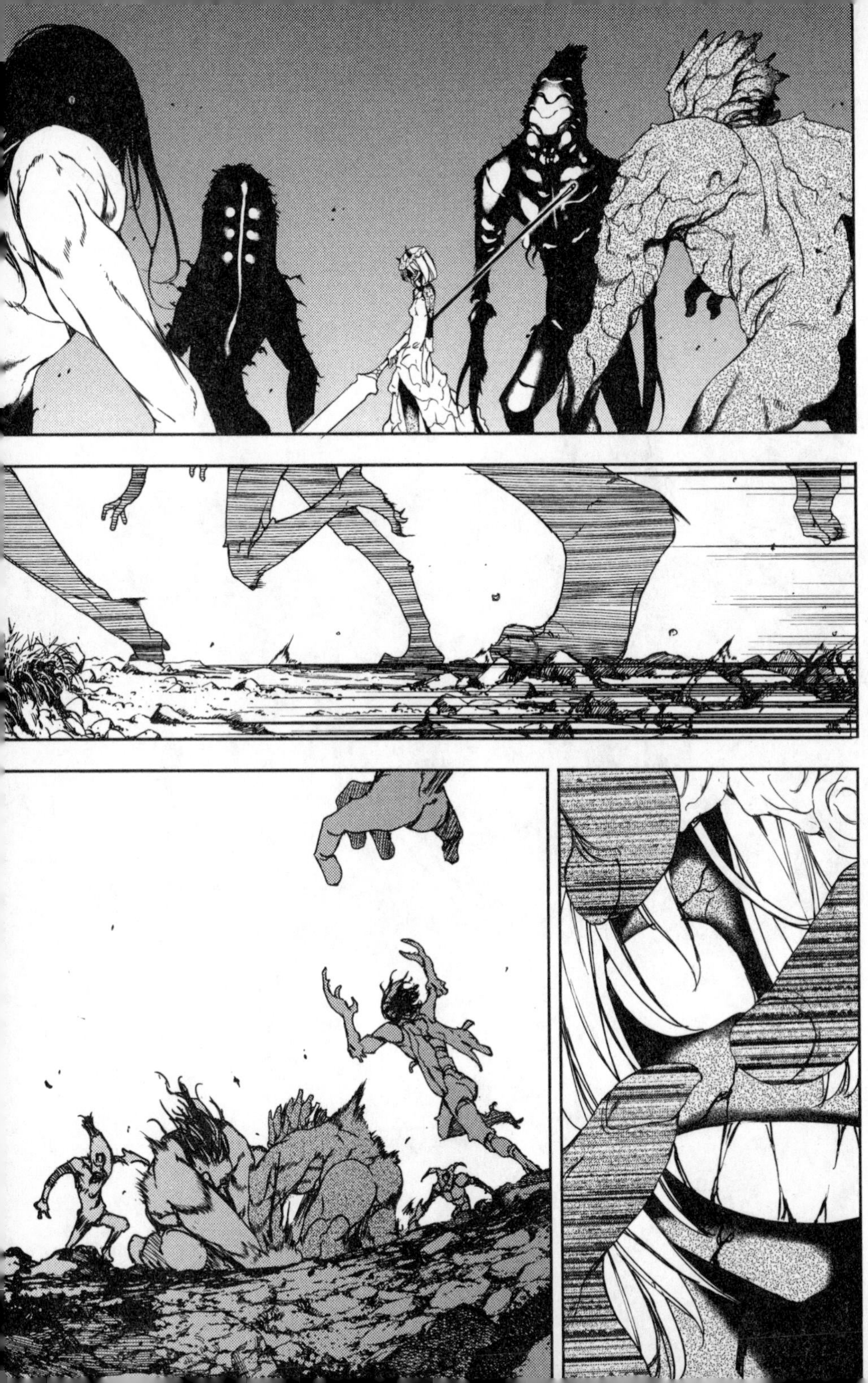

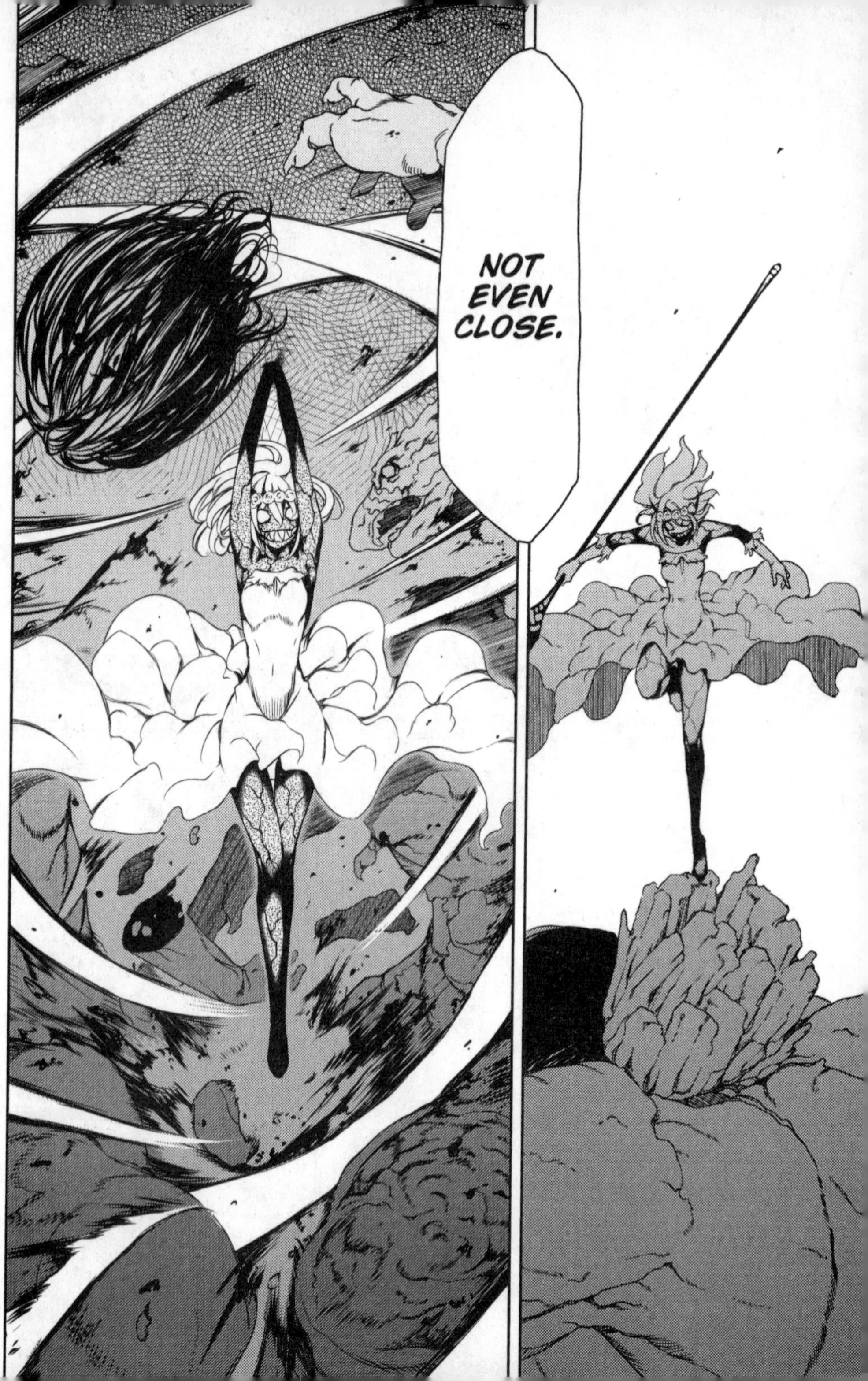
NOT EVEN CLOSE.

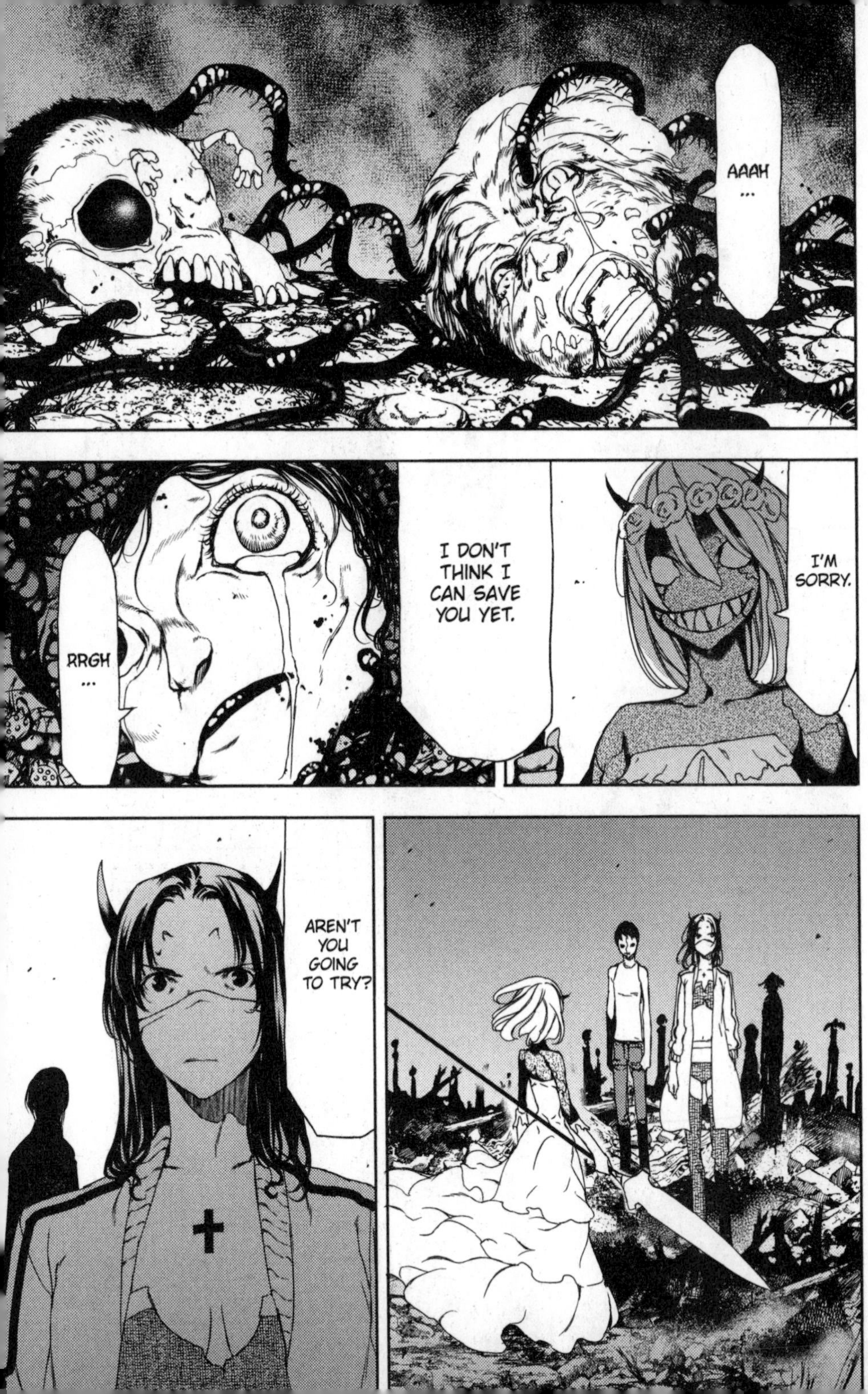
AAAH ...
I'M SORRY.
I DON'T THINK I CAN SAVE YOU YET.
RRGH ...
AREN'T YOU GOING TO TRY?

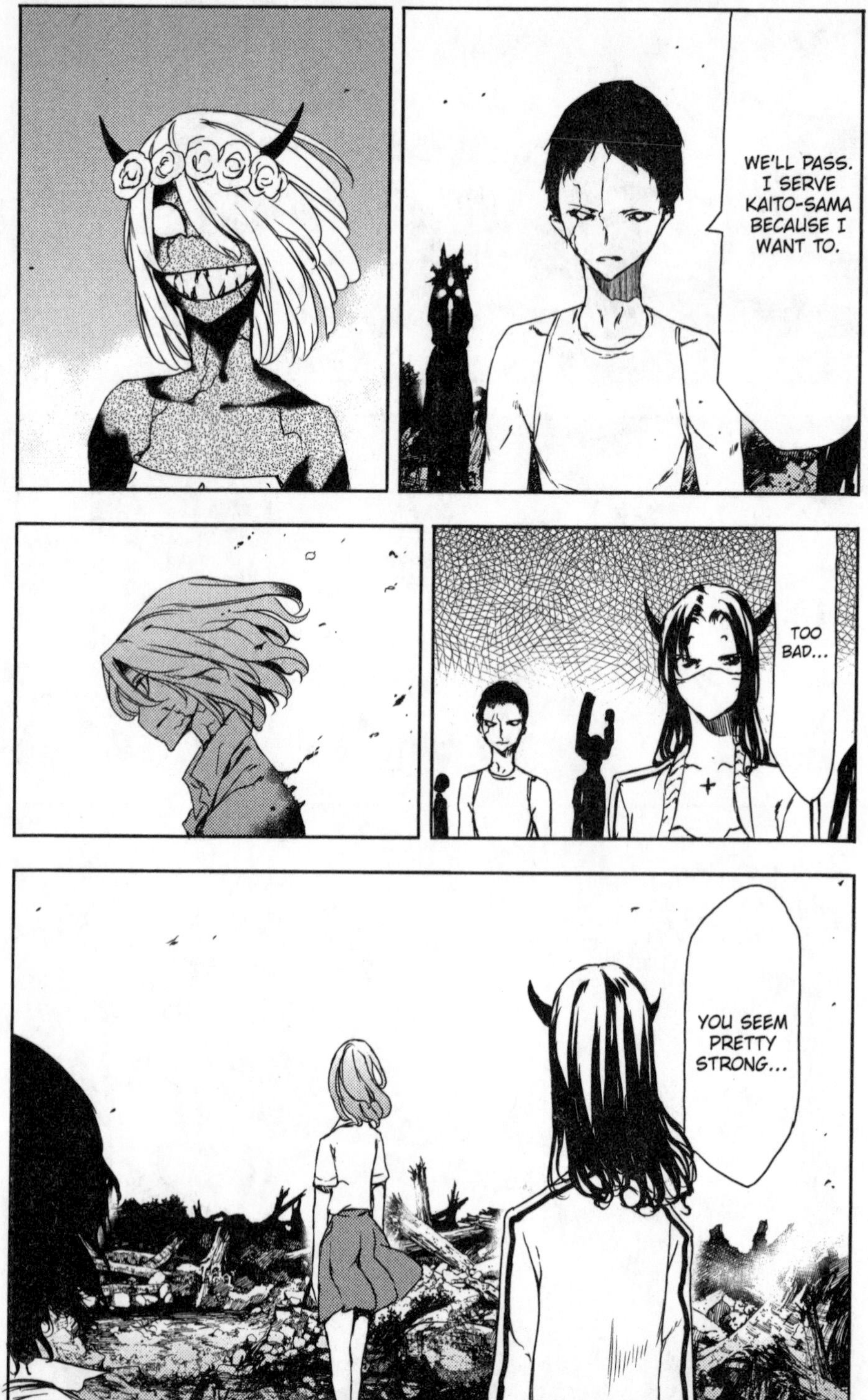
WE'LL PASS. I SERVE KAITO-SAMA BECAUSE I WANT TO.
TOO BAD...
YOU SEEM PRETTY STRONG...

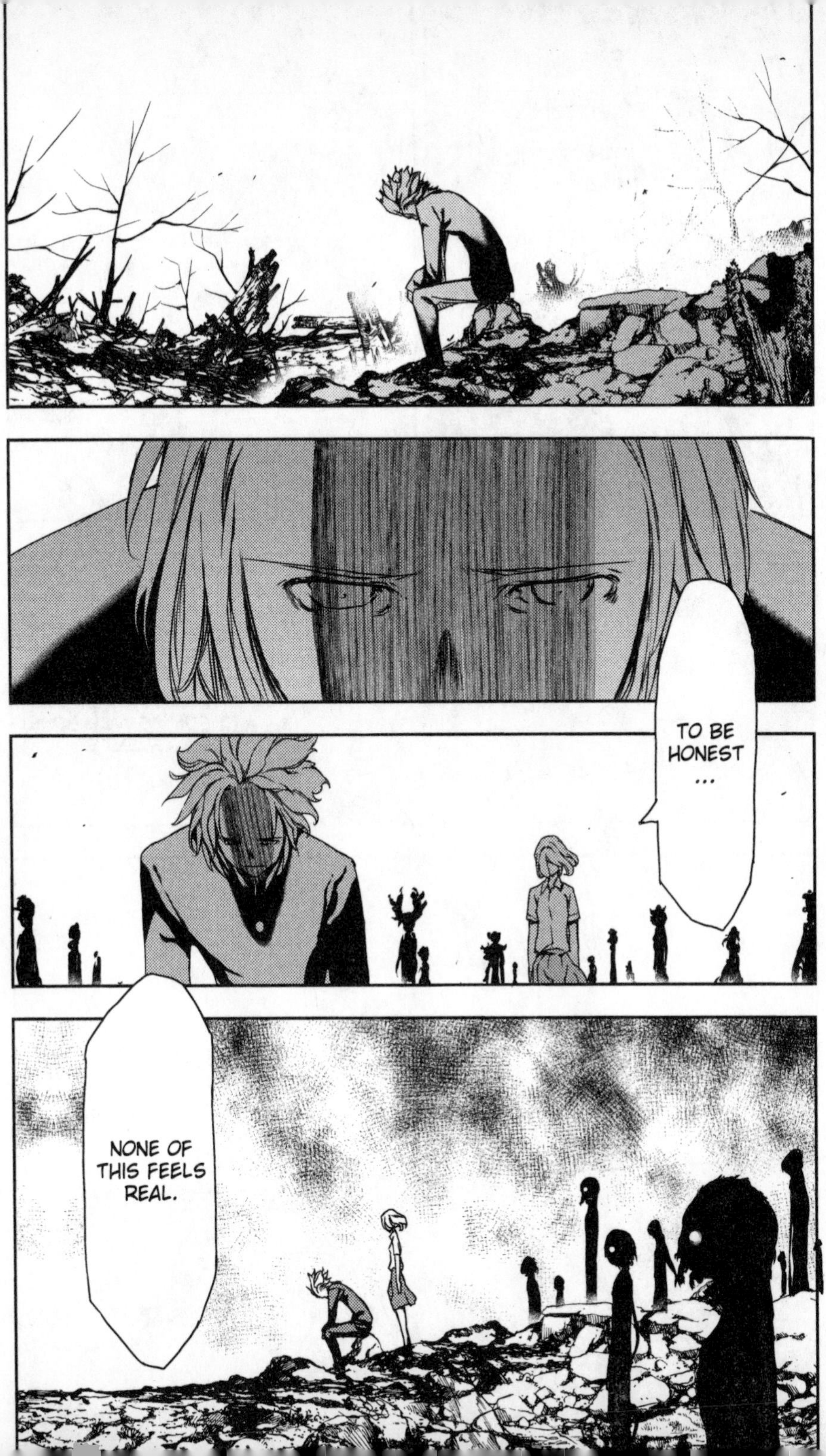
TO BE HONEST ...
NONE OF THIS FEELS REAL.

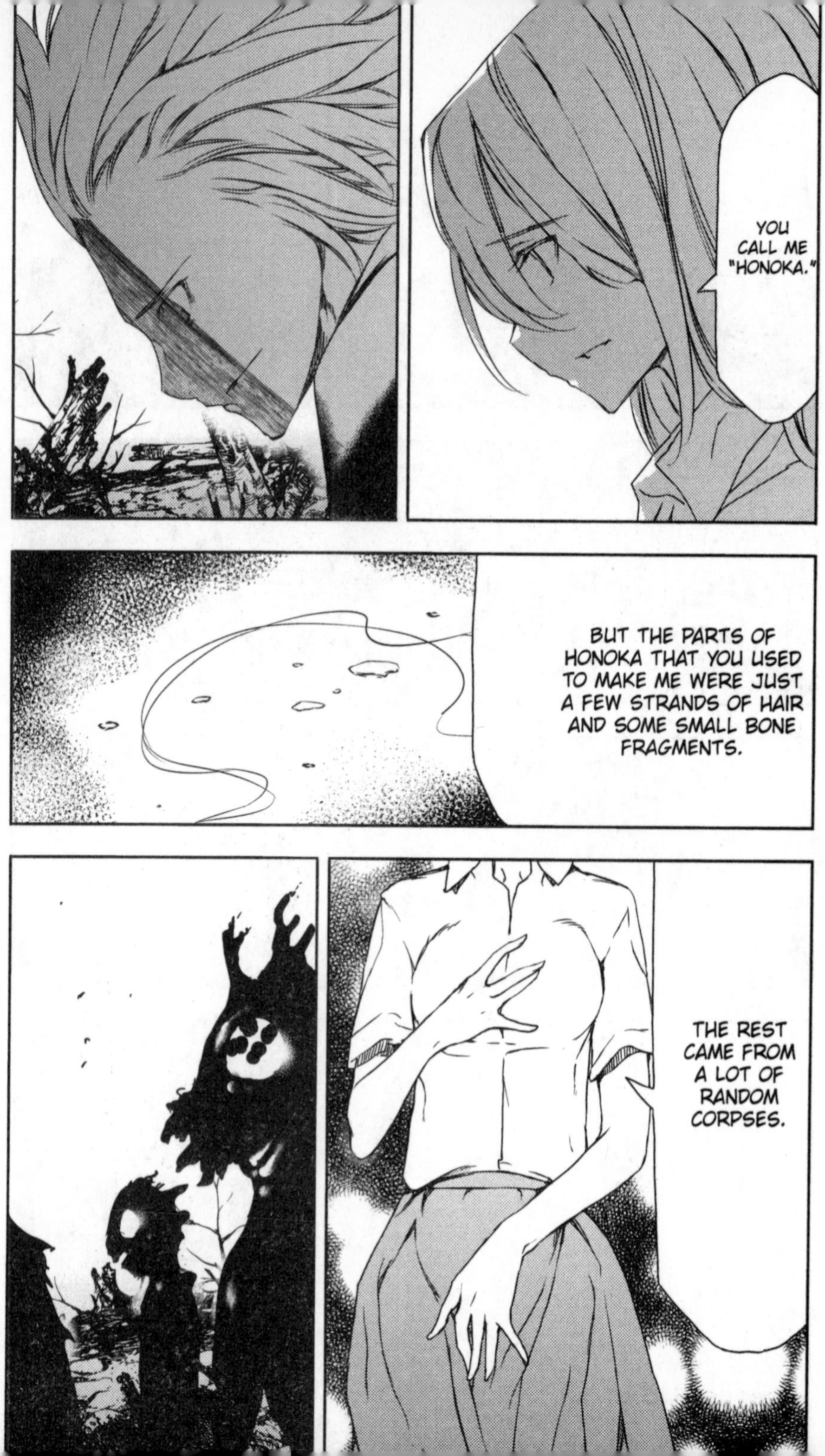
YOU CALL ME "HONOKA."
BUT THE PARTS OF HONOKA THAT YOU USED TO MAKE ME WERE JUST A FEW STRANDS OF HAIR AND SOME SMALL BONE FRAGMENTS.
THE REST CAME FROM A LOT OF RANDOM CORPSES.

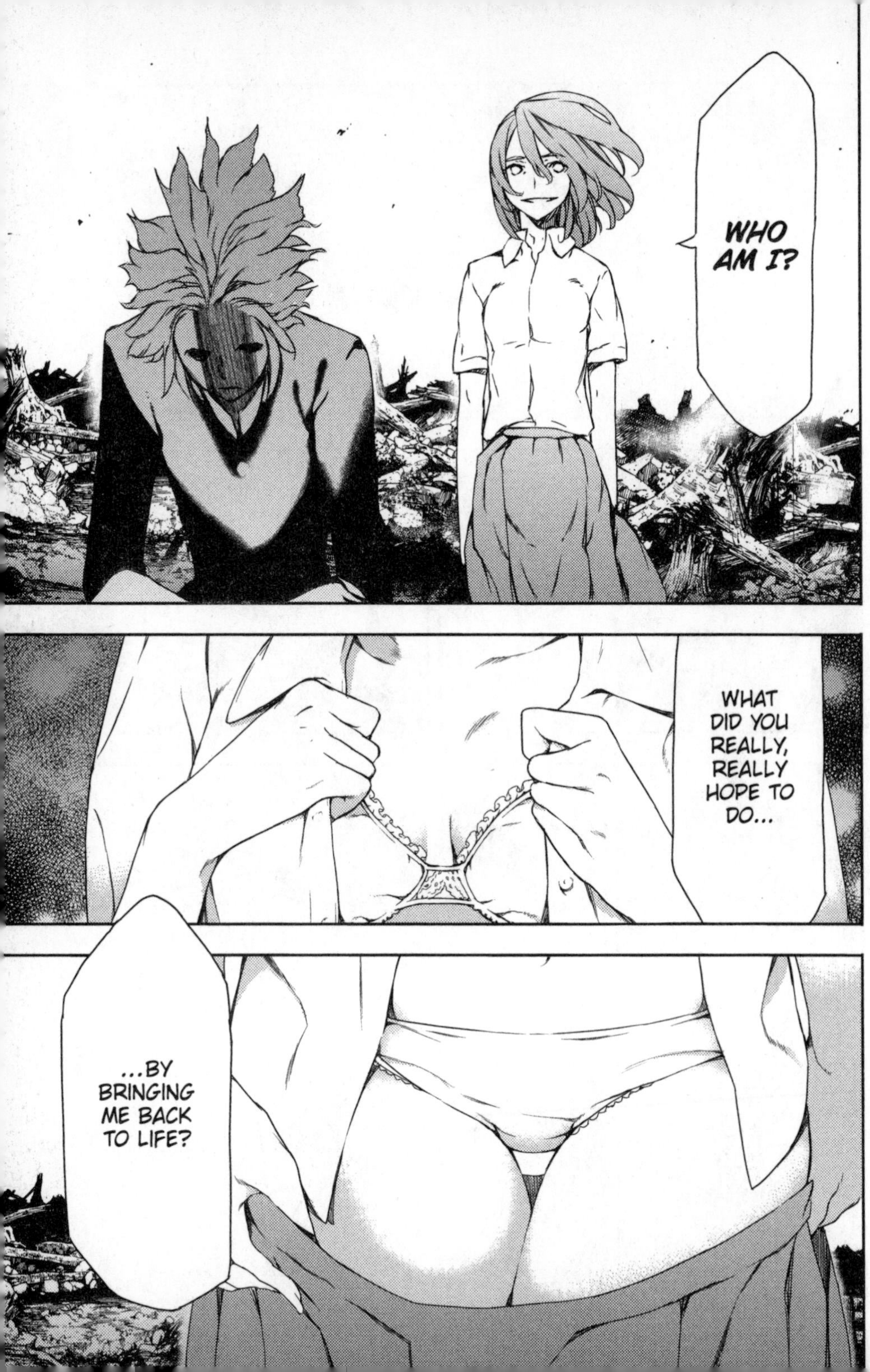
WHO AM I?
WHAT DID YOU REALLY, REALLY HOPE TO DO...
...BY BRINGING ME BACK TO LIFE?

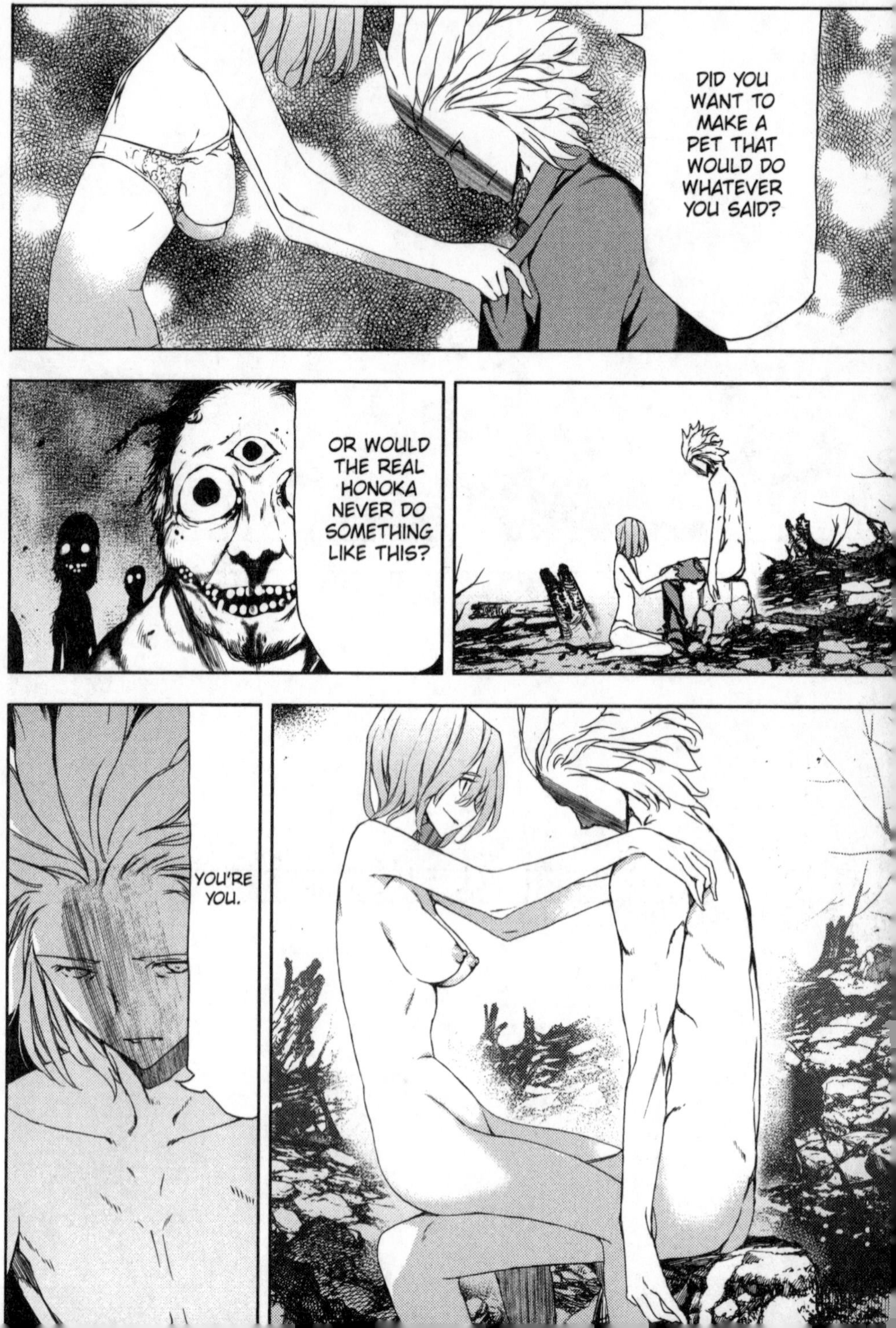
DID YOU WANT TO MAKE A PET THAT WOULD DO WHATEVER YOU SAID?
OR WOULD THE REAL HONOKA NEVER DO SOMETHING LIKE THIS?
YOU'RE YOU.

YOU SHOULD DO WHATEVER YOU WANT.

FOOF

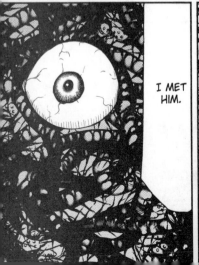

I MET HIM.

OH, HEY!

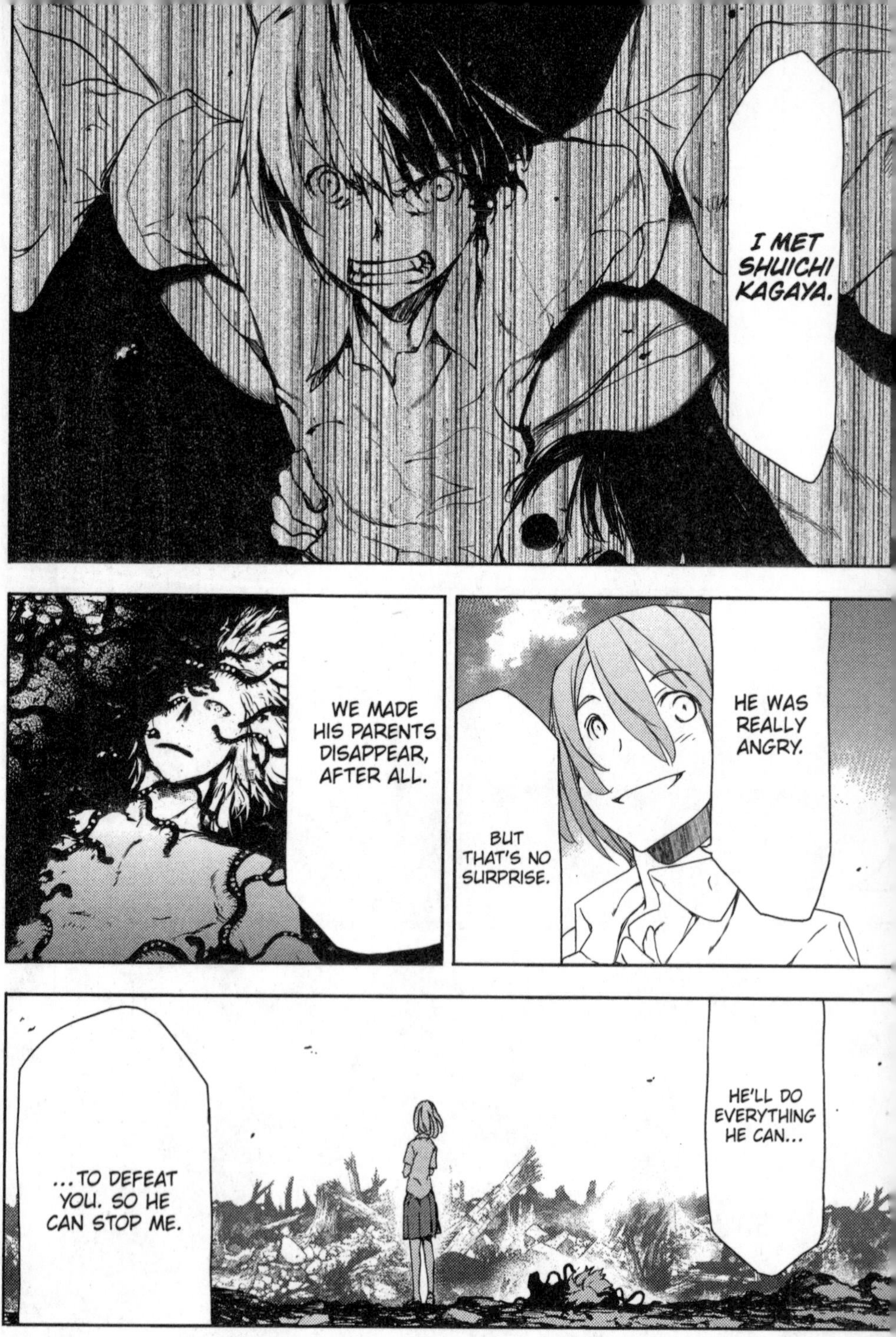
I MET SHUICHI KAGAYA.
HE WAS REALLY ANGRY.
BUT THAT'S NO SURPRISE.
WE MADE HIS PARENTS DISAPPEAR, AFTER ALL.
HE'LL DO EVERYTHING HE CAN...
...TO DEFEAT YOU. SO HE CAN STOP ME.

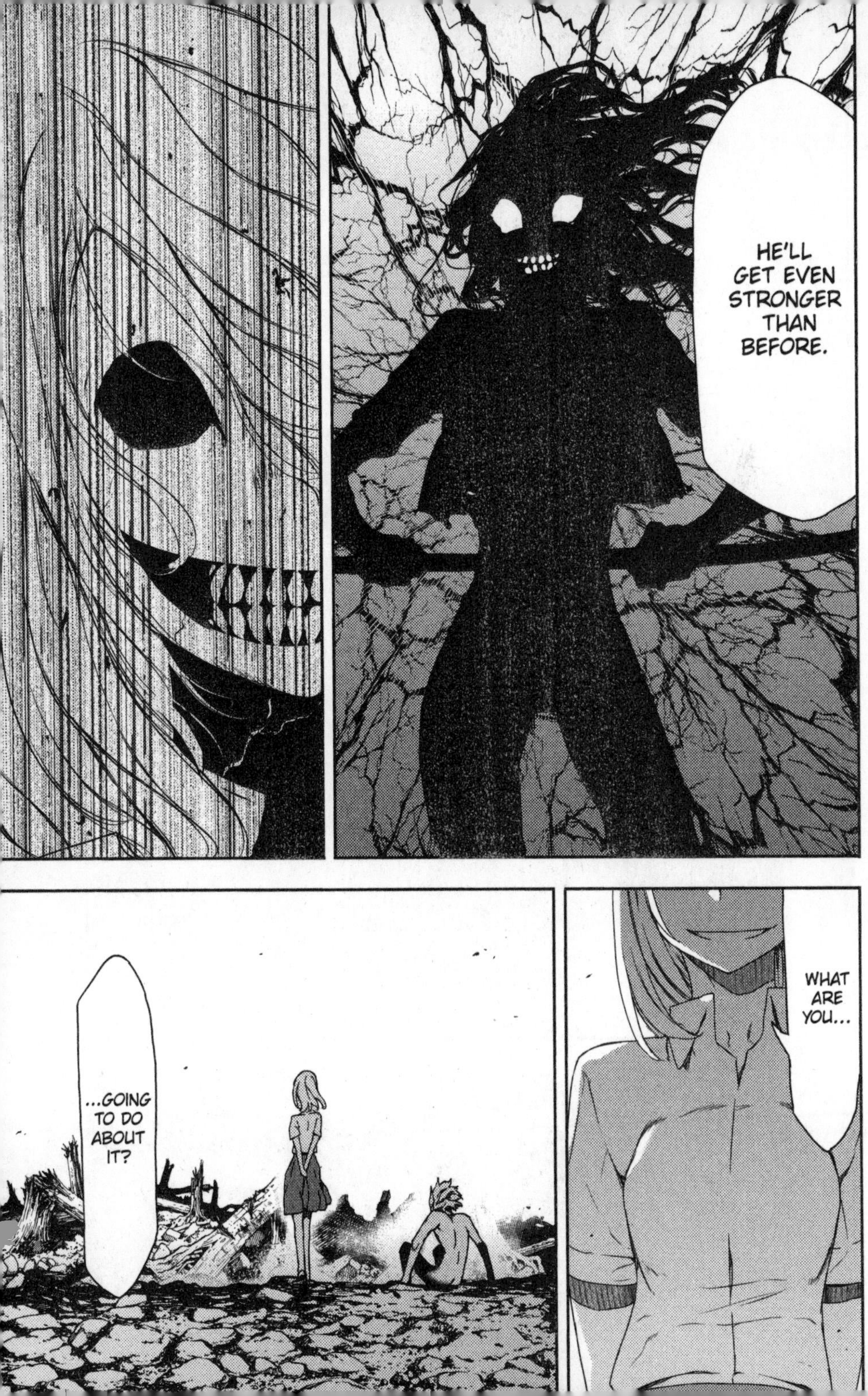
HE'LL GET EVEN STRONGER THAN BEFORE.
WHAT ARE YOU...
...GOING TO DO ABOUT IT?

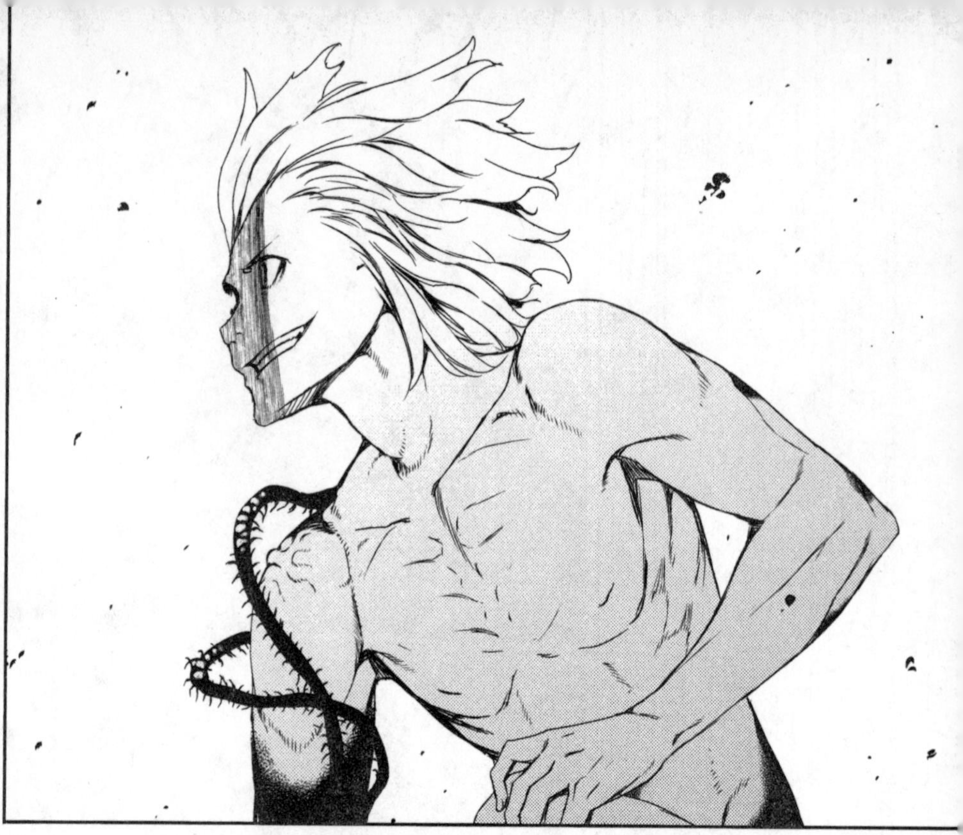

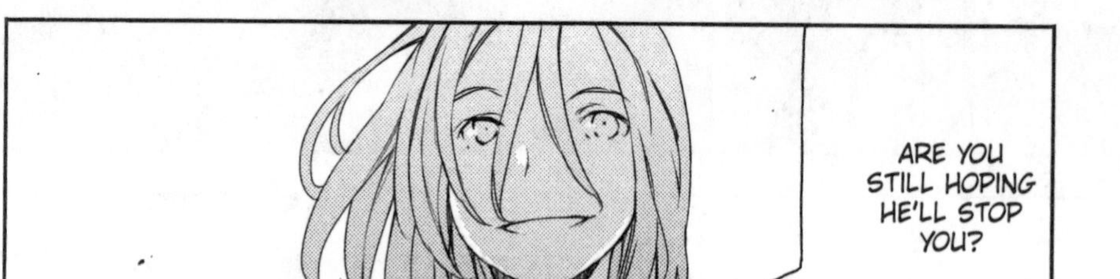
ARE YOU STILL HOPING HE'LL STOP YOU?

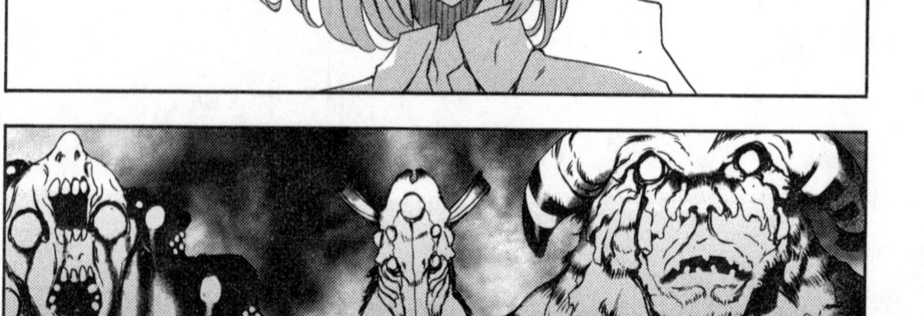

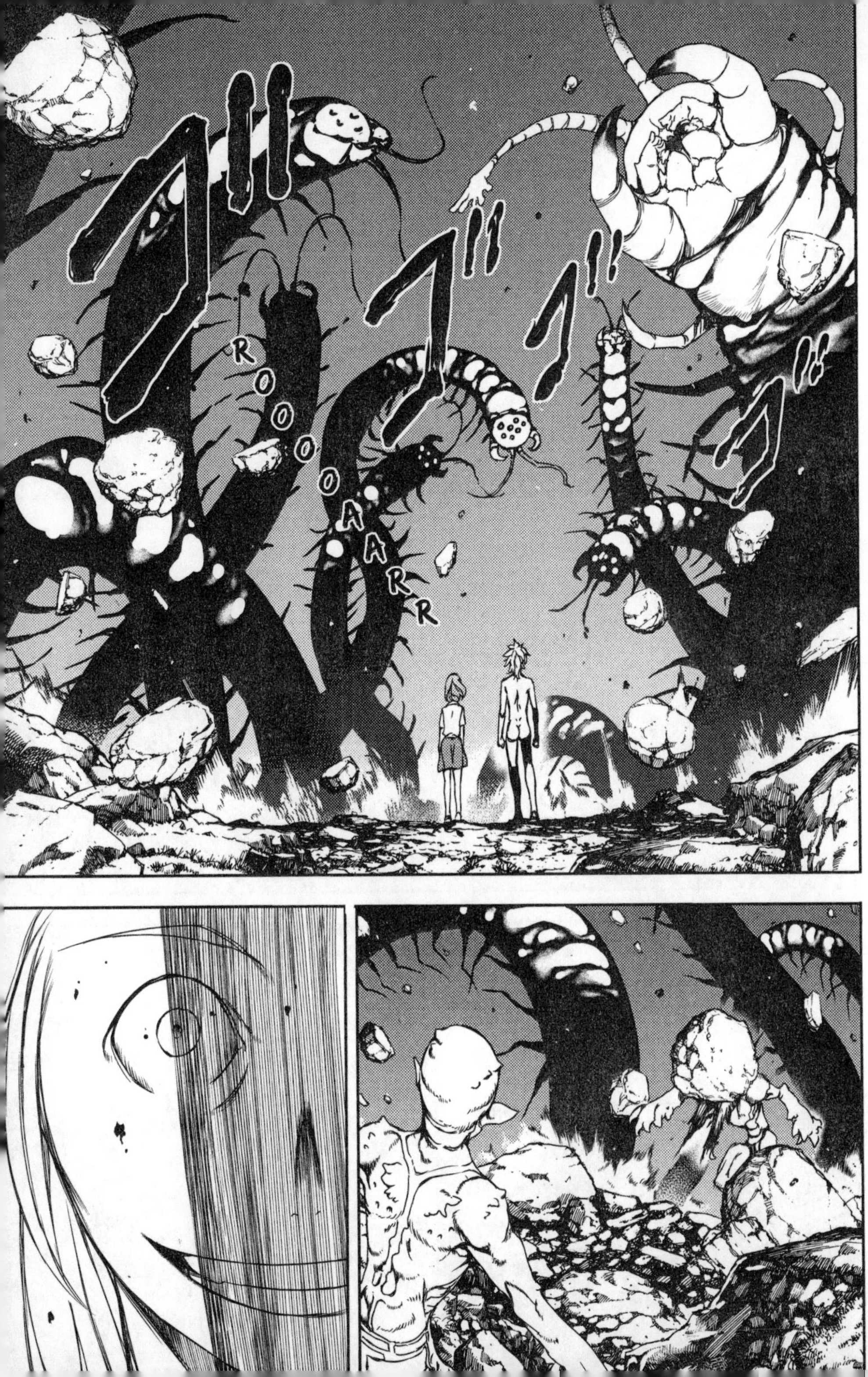
ROOOOAARR

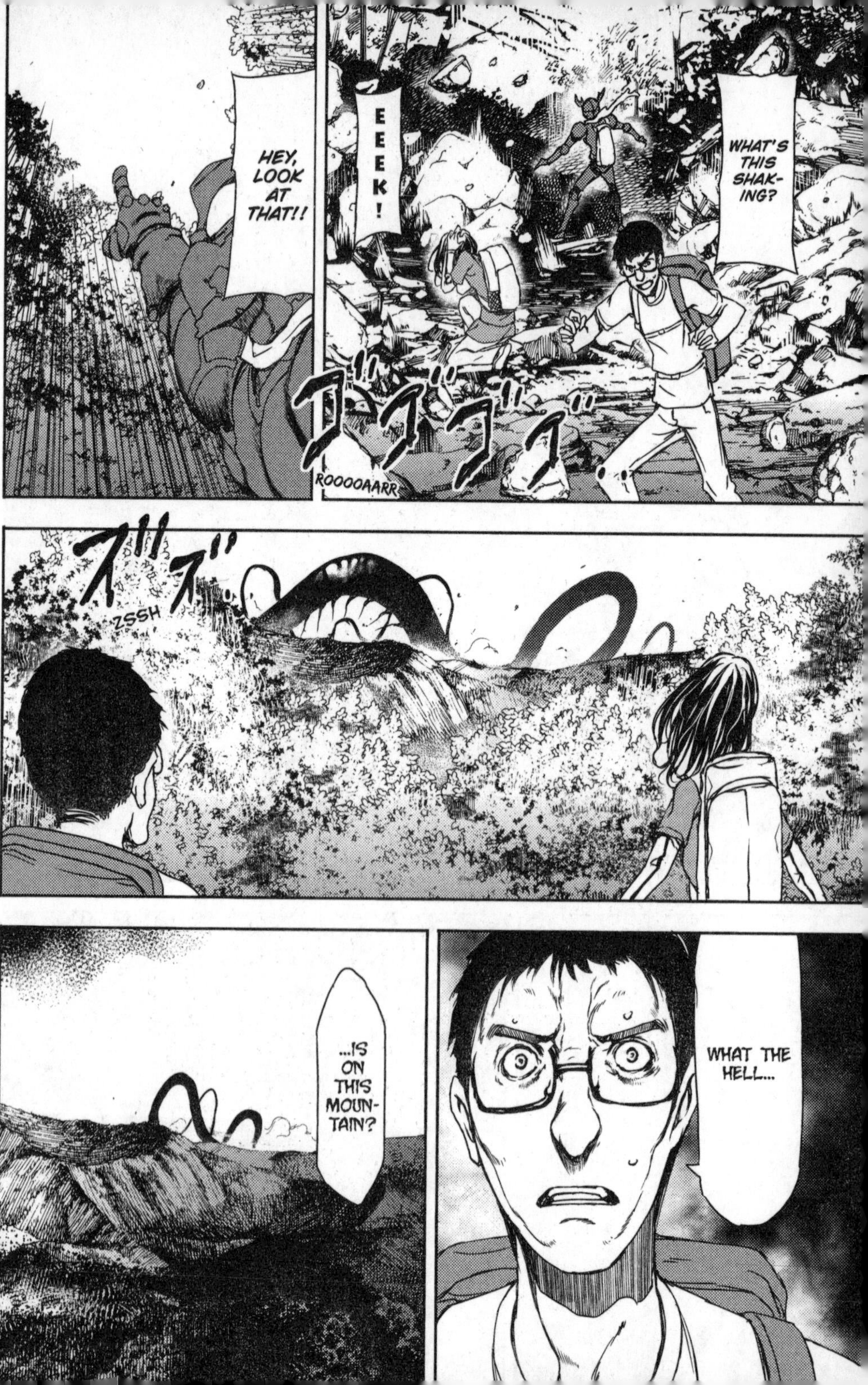
WHAT'S THIS SHAKING?
EEEK!
ROOOOAARR
HEY, LOOK AT THAT!!
ZSSH
WHAT THE HELL...
...IS ON THIS MOUNTAIN?

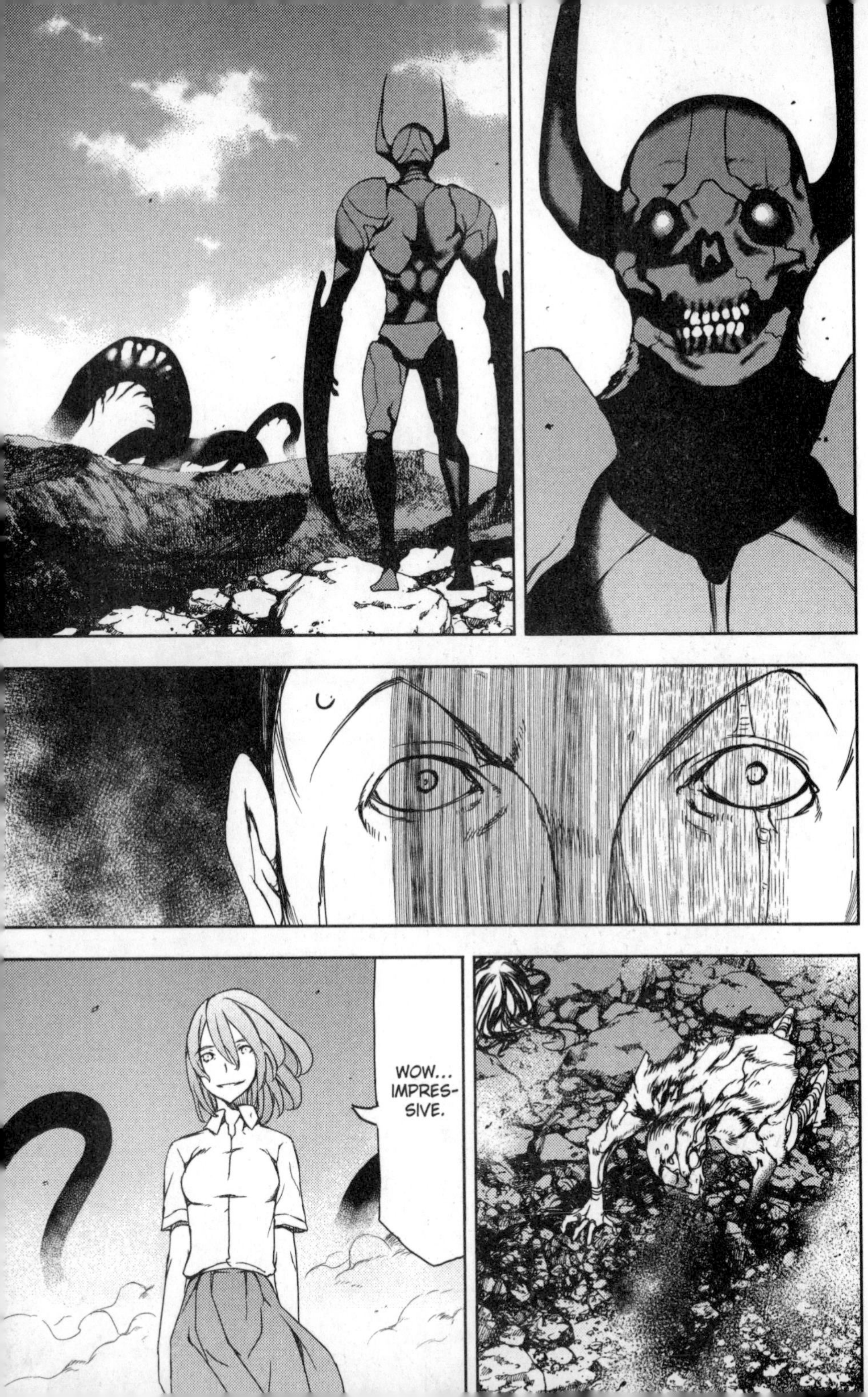
WOW... IMPRES-SIVE.

THIS MUST BE YOUR TRUE STRENGTH.

WHY DIDN'T YOU USE IT BEFORE?

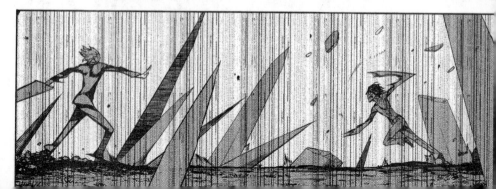

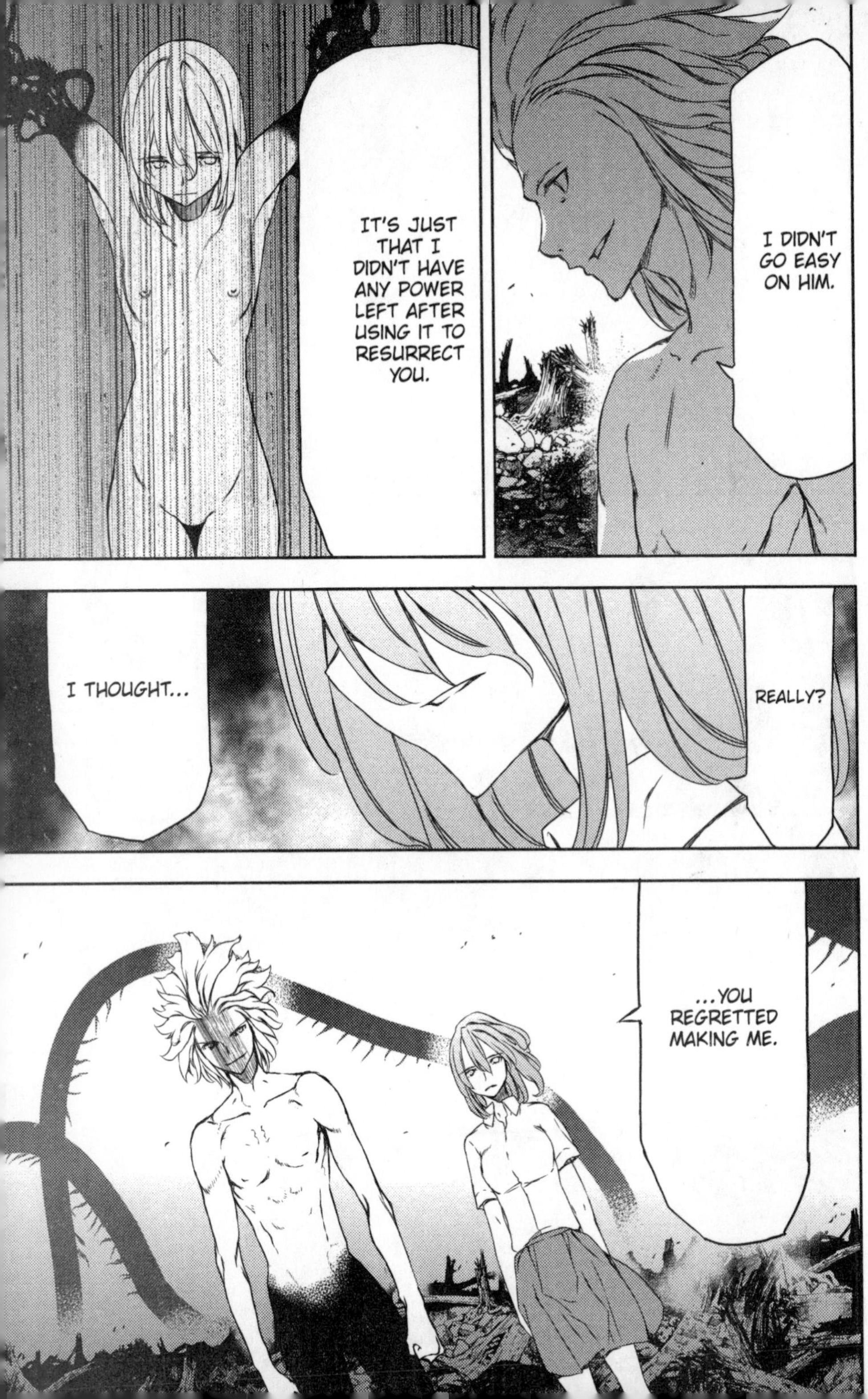
I DIDN'T GO EASY ON HIM.
IT'S JUST THAT I DIDN'T HAVE ANY POWER LEFT AFTER USING IT TO RESURRECT YOU.
REALLY?
I THOUGHT...
...YOU REGRETTED MAKING ME.

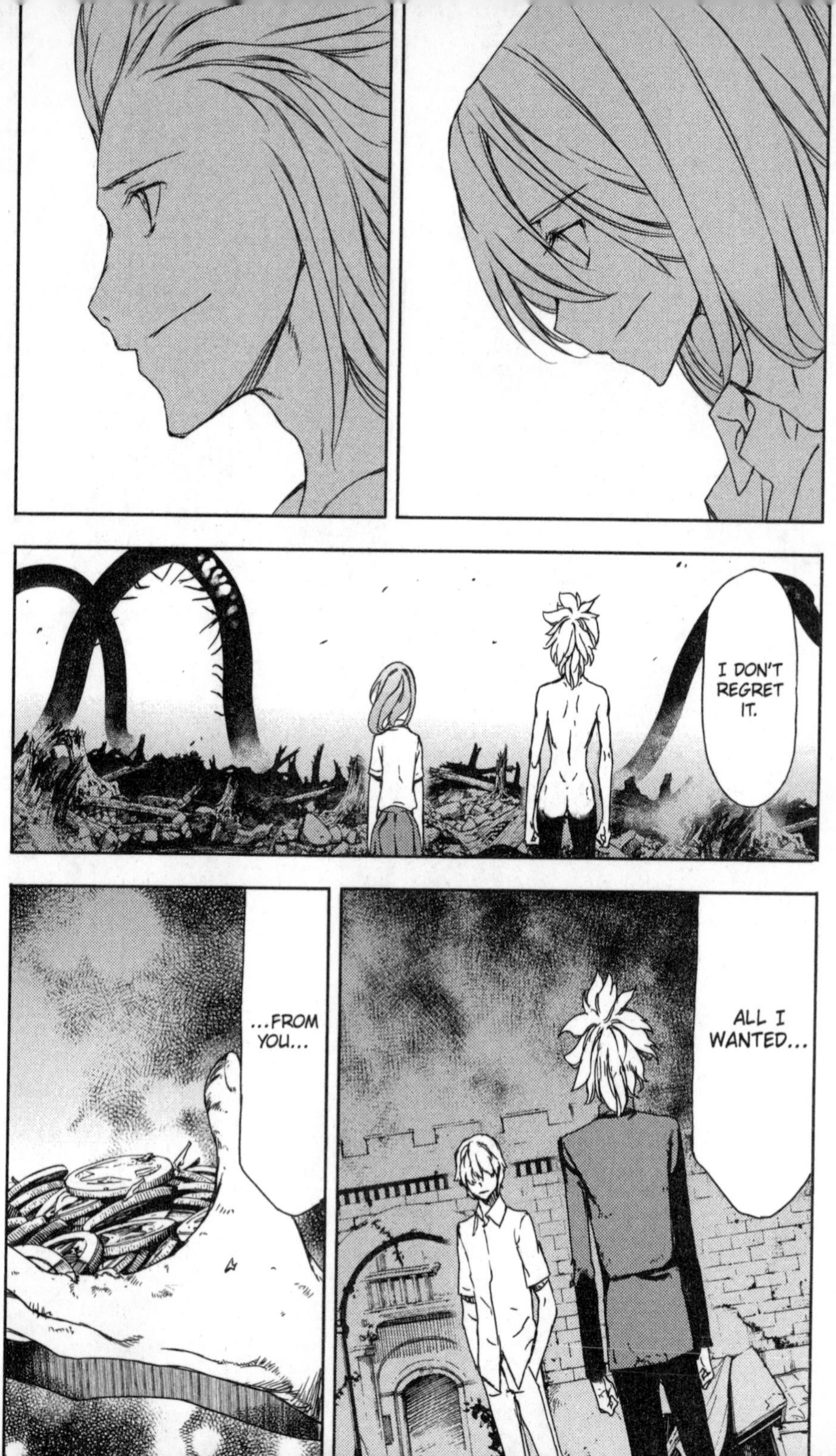
I DON'T REGRET IT.
ALL I WANTED...
...FROM YOU...

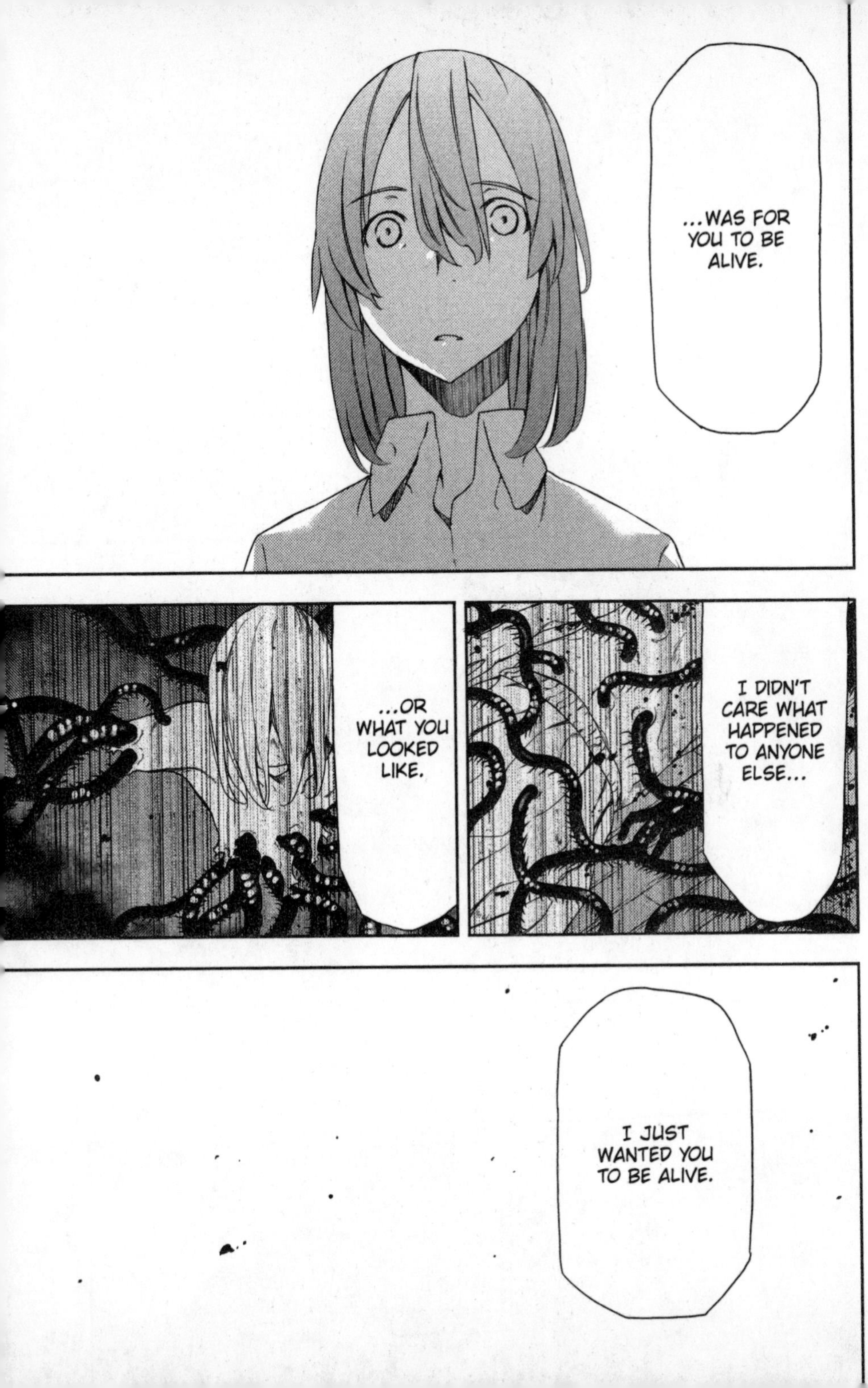
...WAS FOR YOU TO BE ALIVE.
I DIDN'T CARE WHAT HAPPENED TO ANYONE ELSE...
...OR WHAT YOU LOOKED LIKE.
I JUST WANTED YOU TO BE ALIVE.

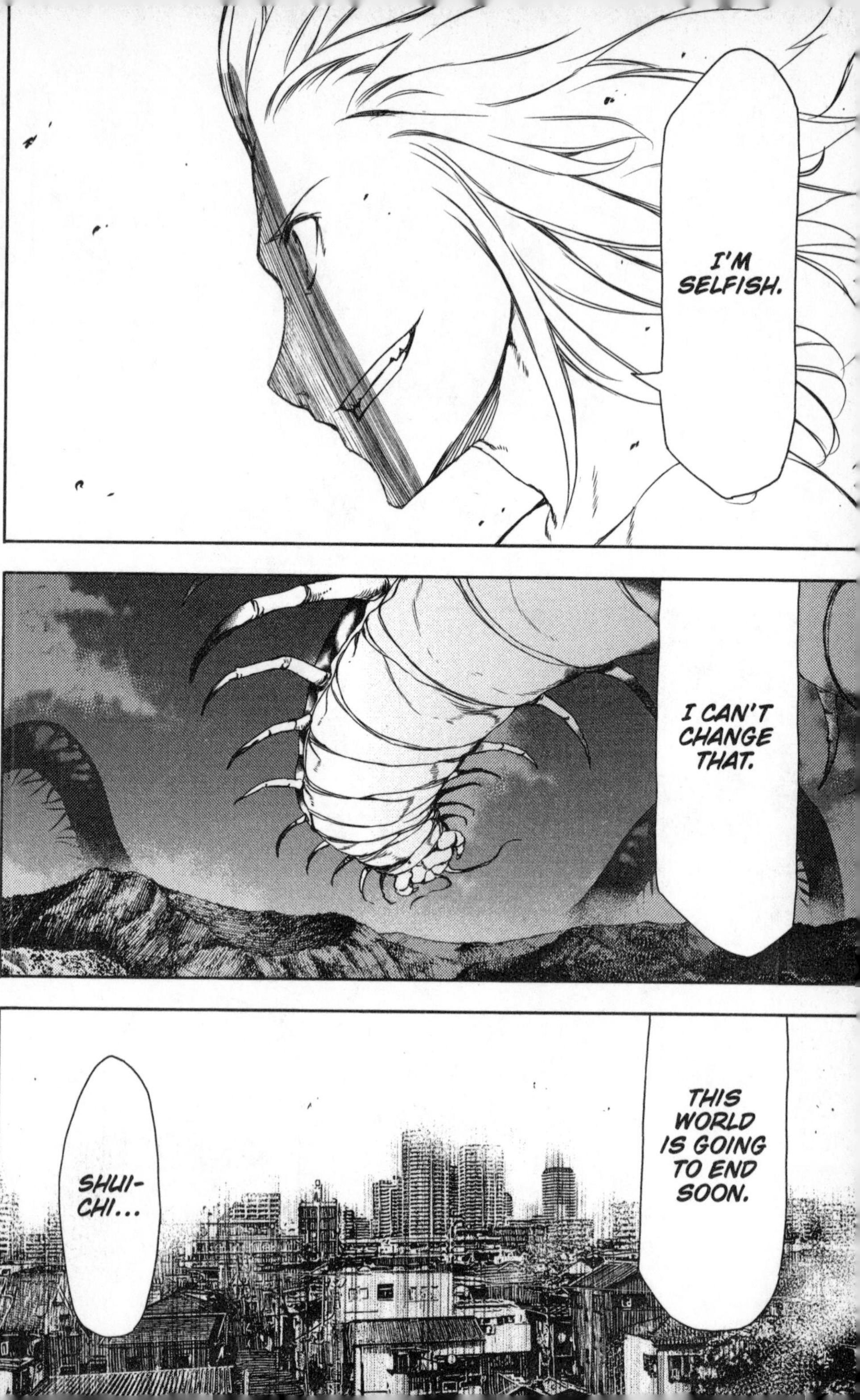
I'M SELFISH.
I CAN'T CHANGE THAT.
THIS WORLD IS GOING TO END SOON.
SHUI-CHI...

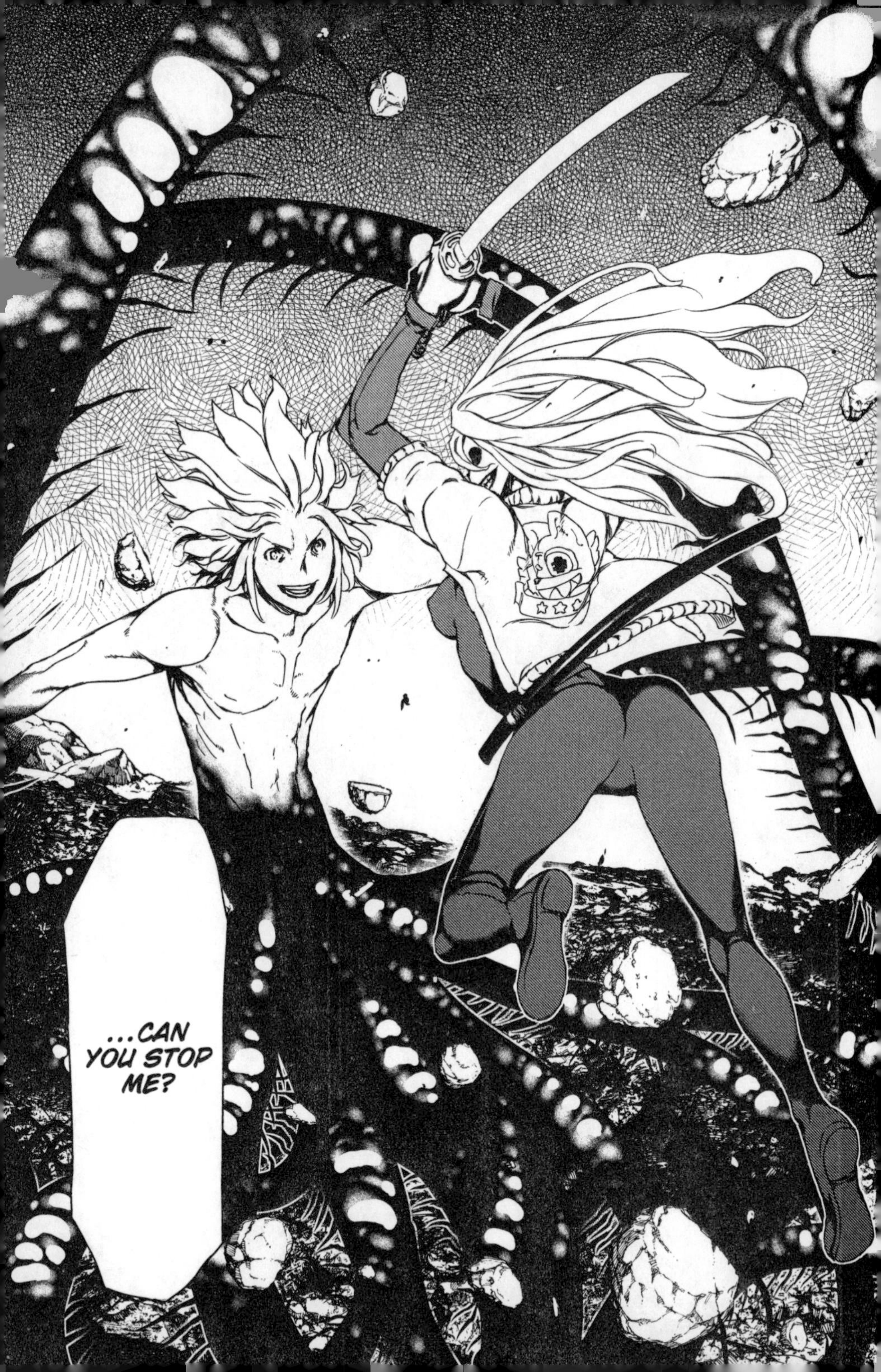
...CAN YOU STOP ME?

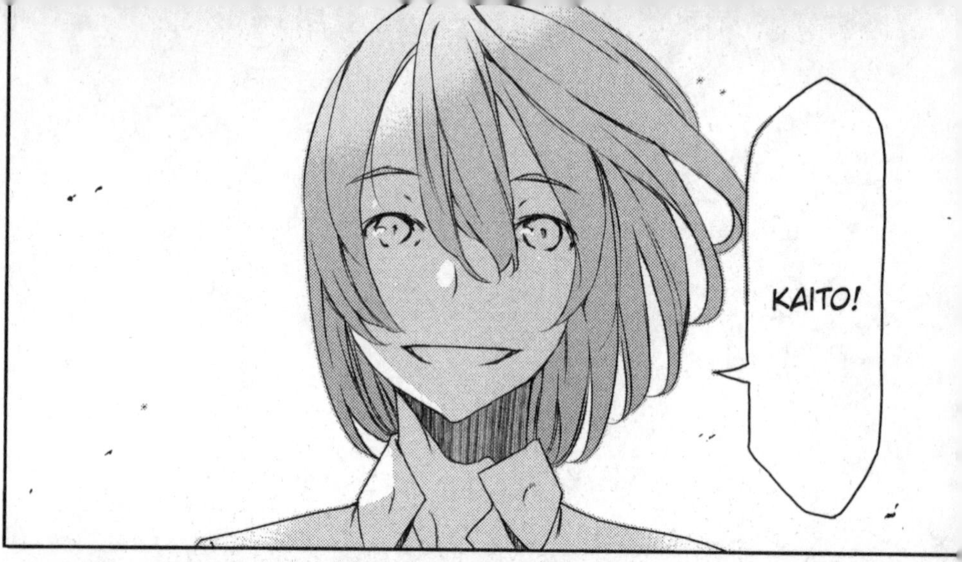
KAITO!

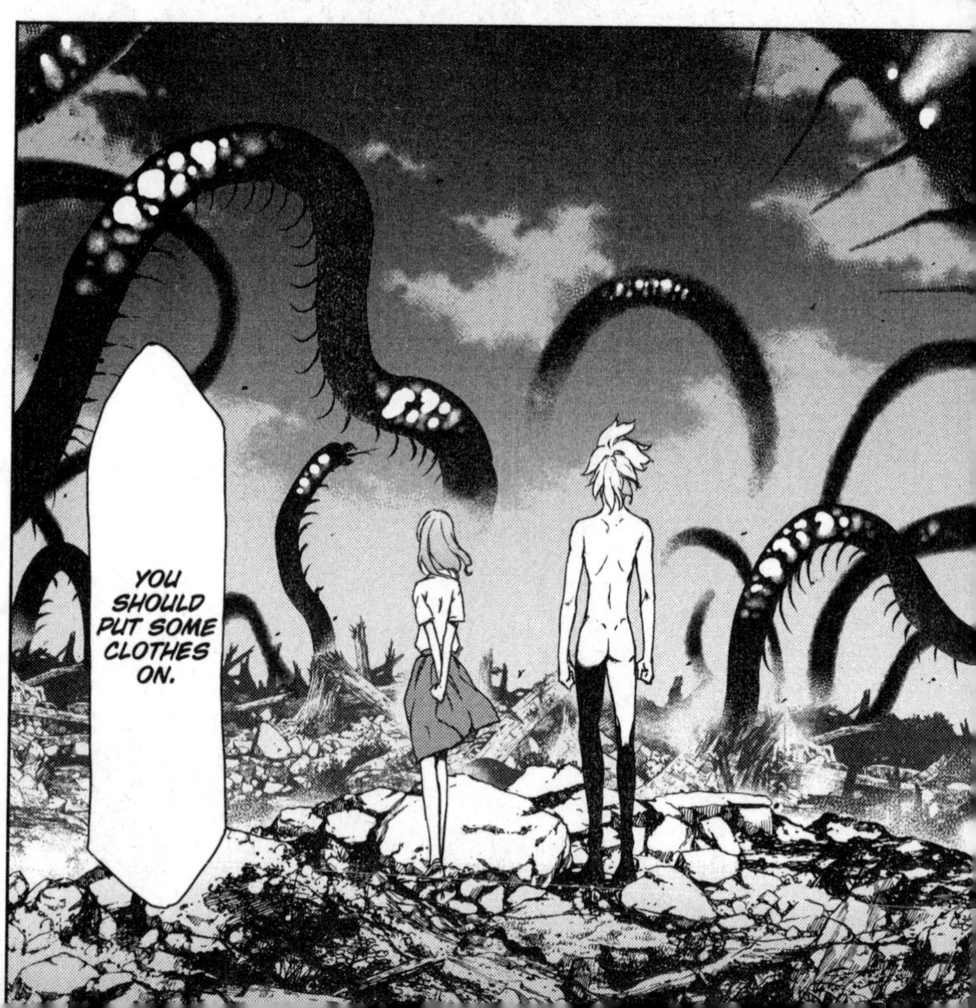
YOU SHOULD PUT SOME CLOTHES ON.

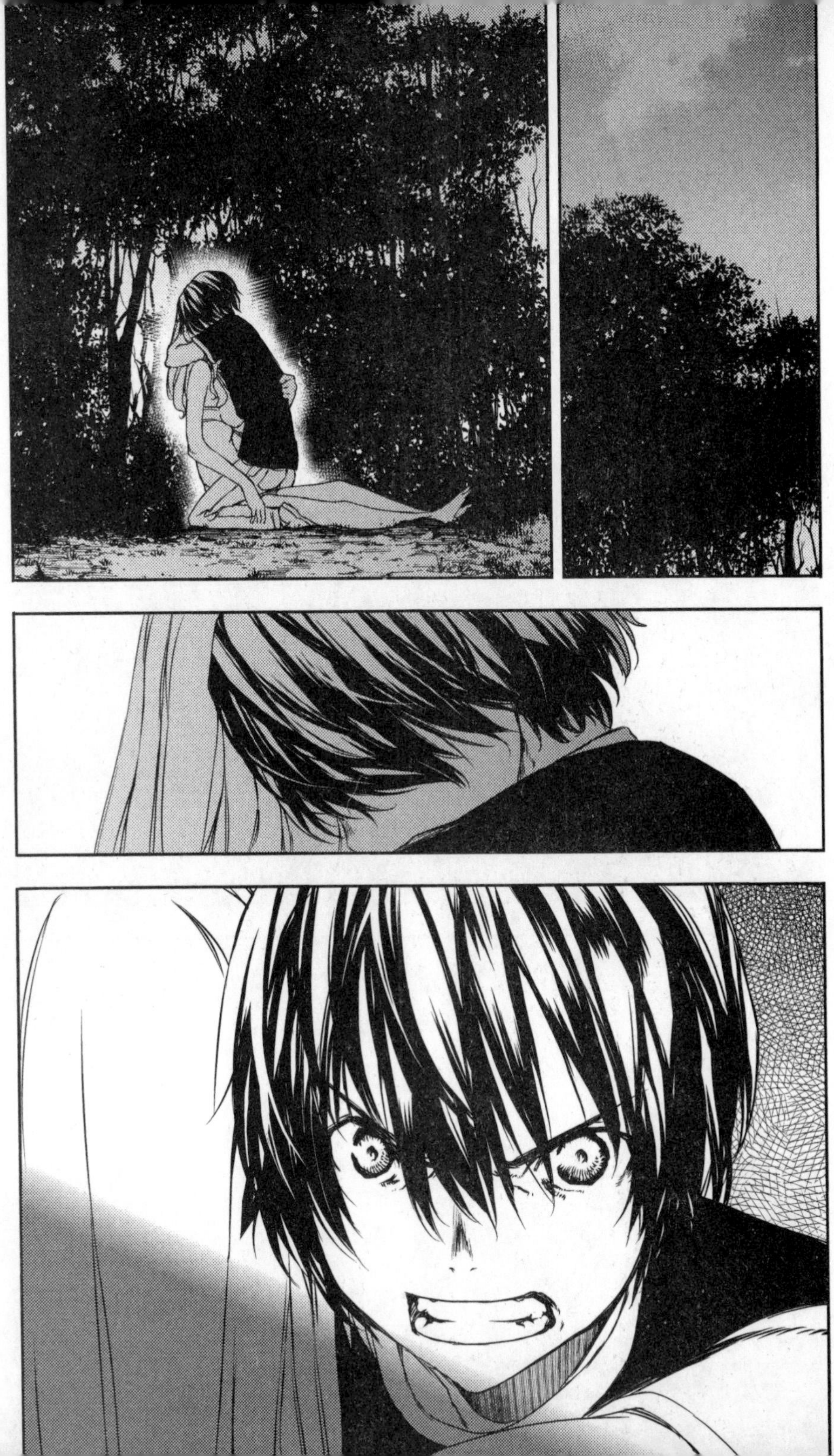

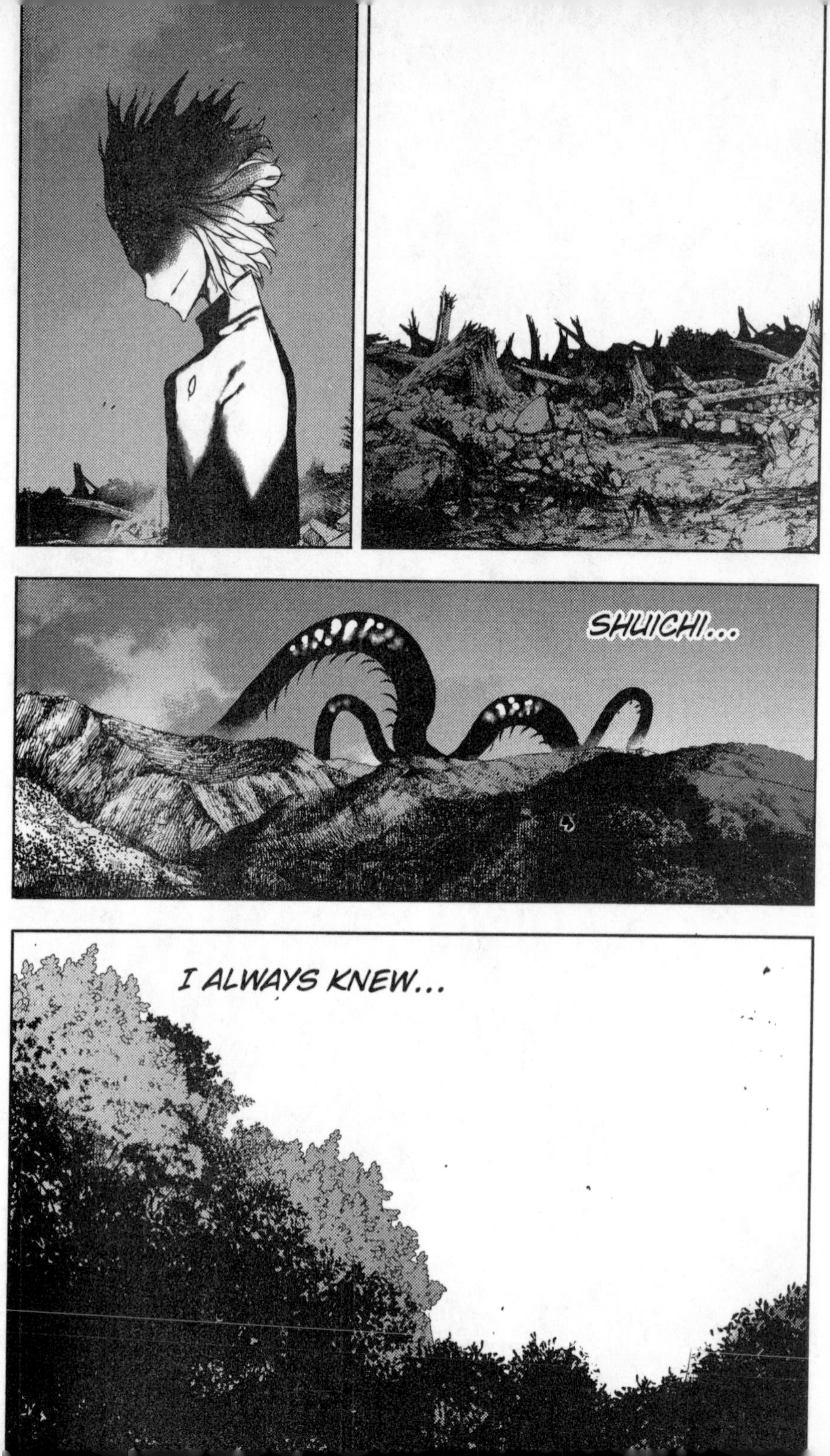
SHUICHI...
I ALWAYS KNEW...

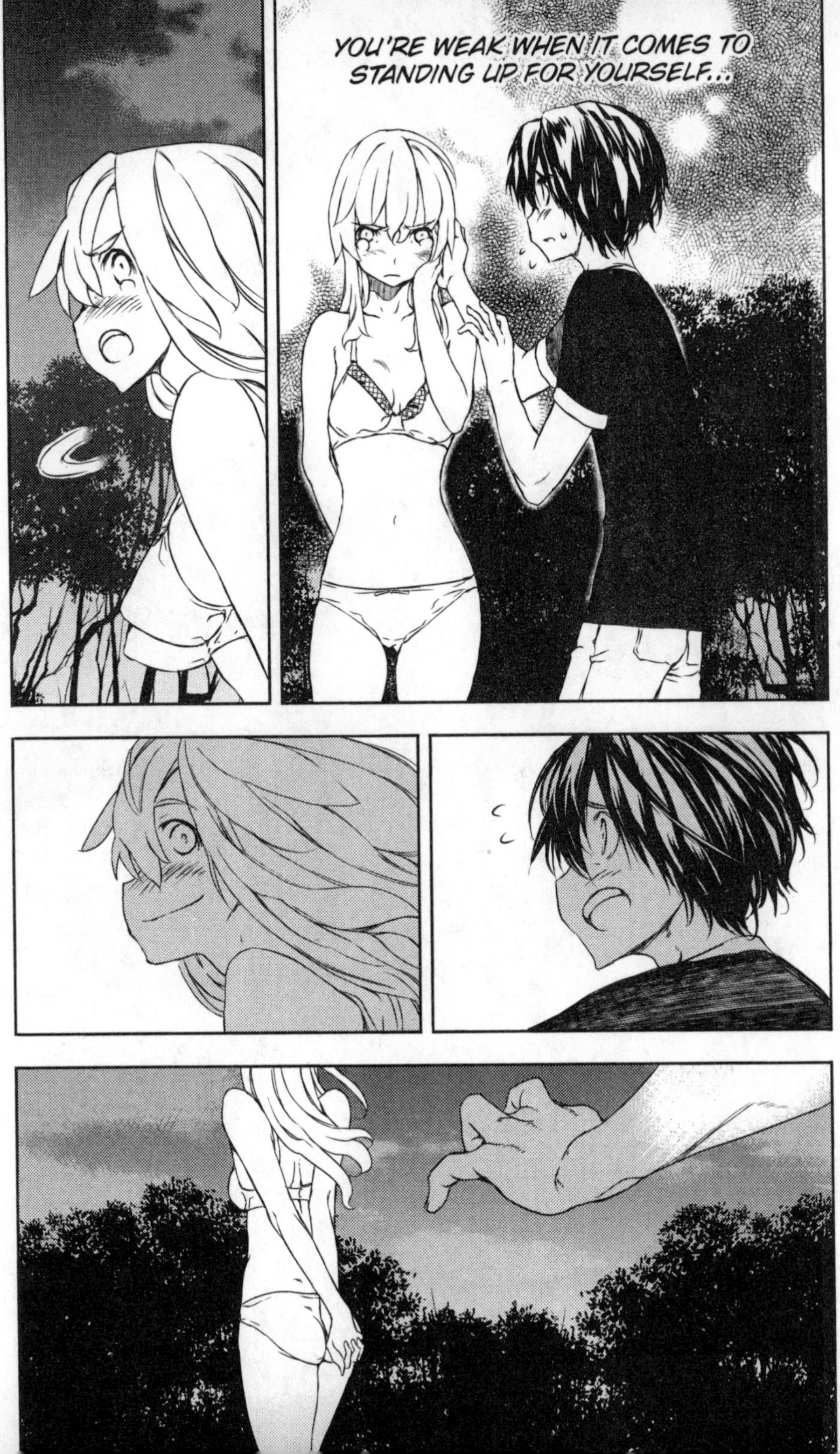
YOU'RE WEAK WHEN IT COMES TO STANDING UP FOR YOURSELF...

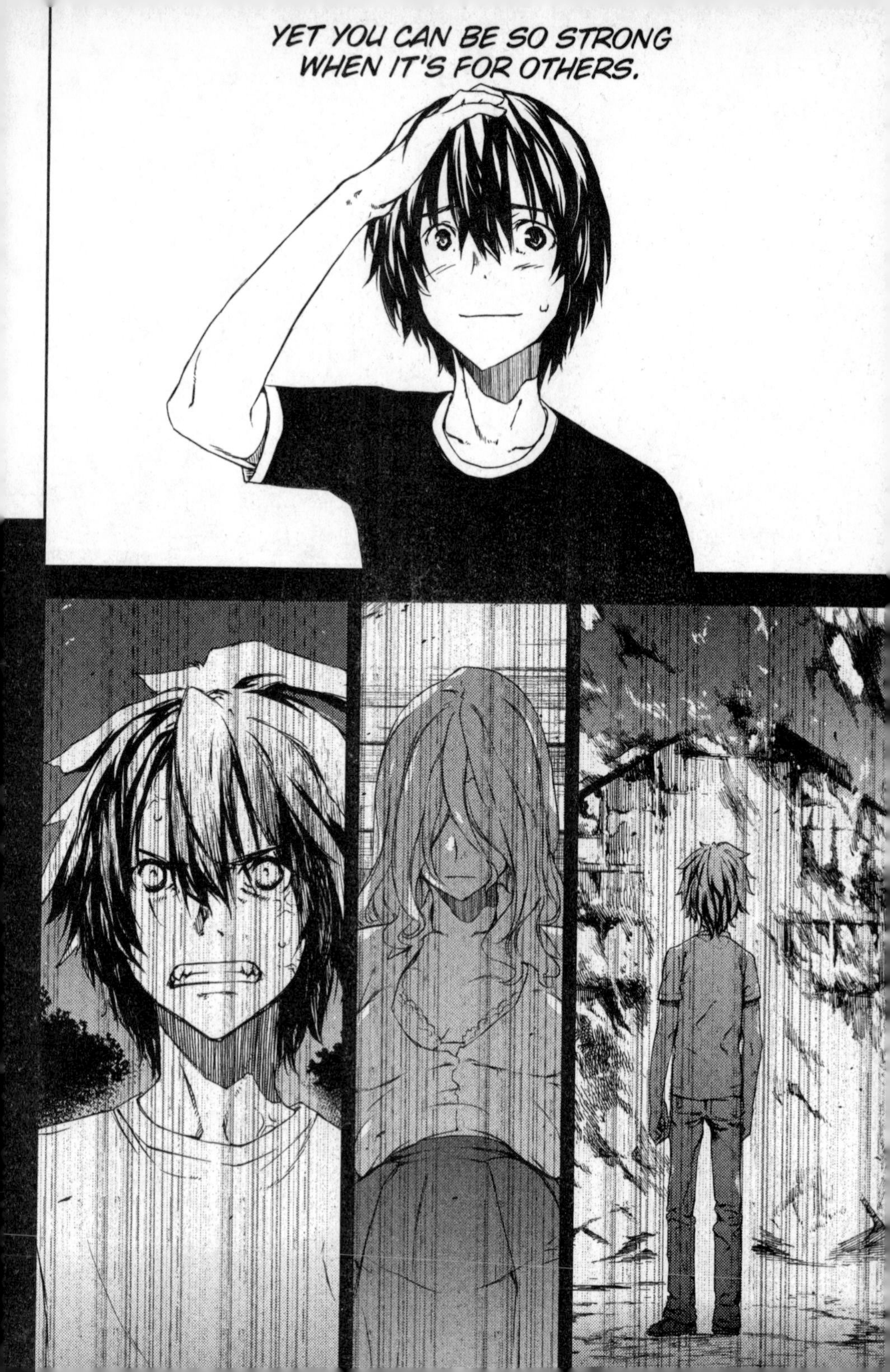
YET YOU CAN BE SO STRONG WHEN IT'S FOR OTHERS.

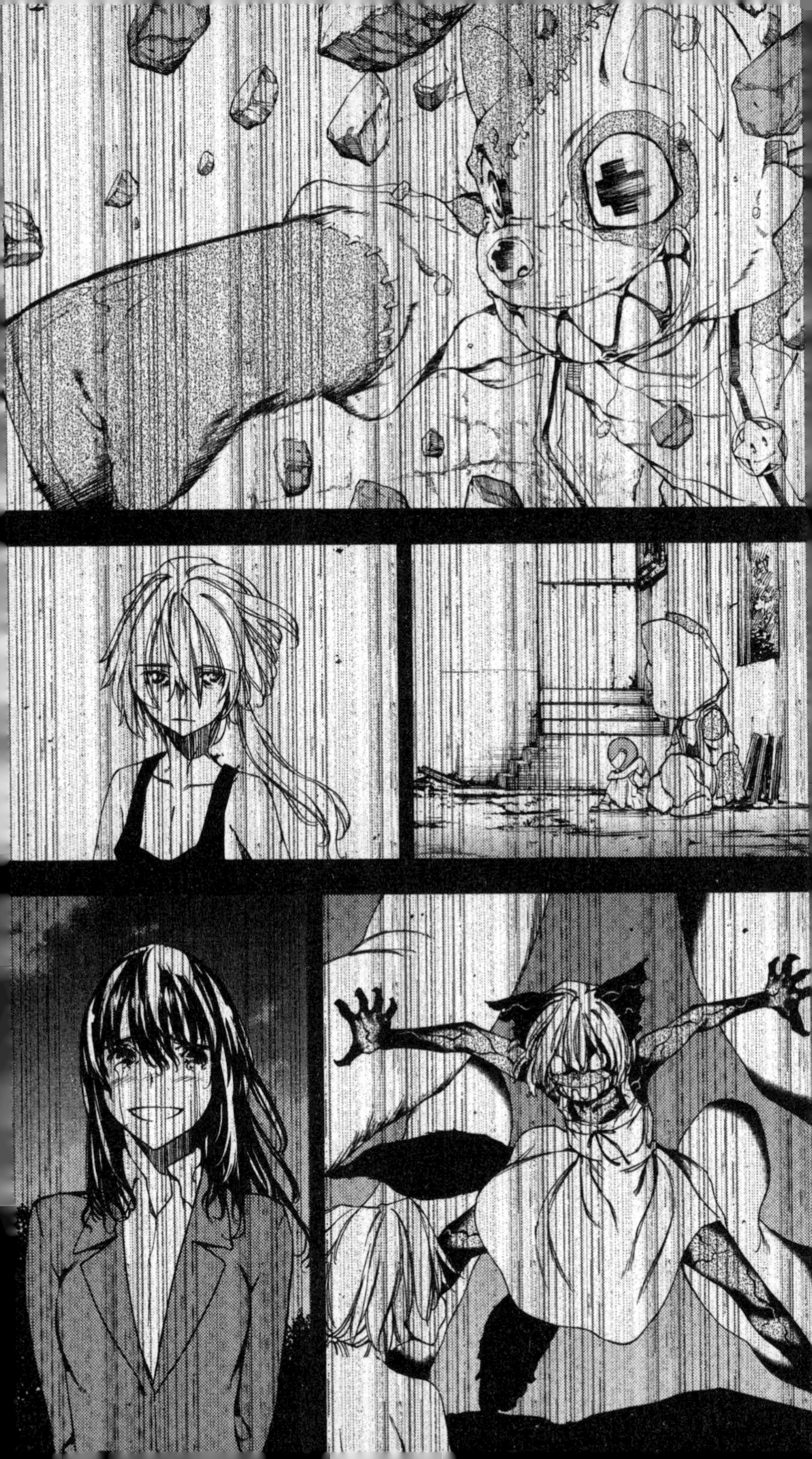

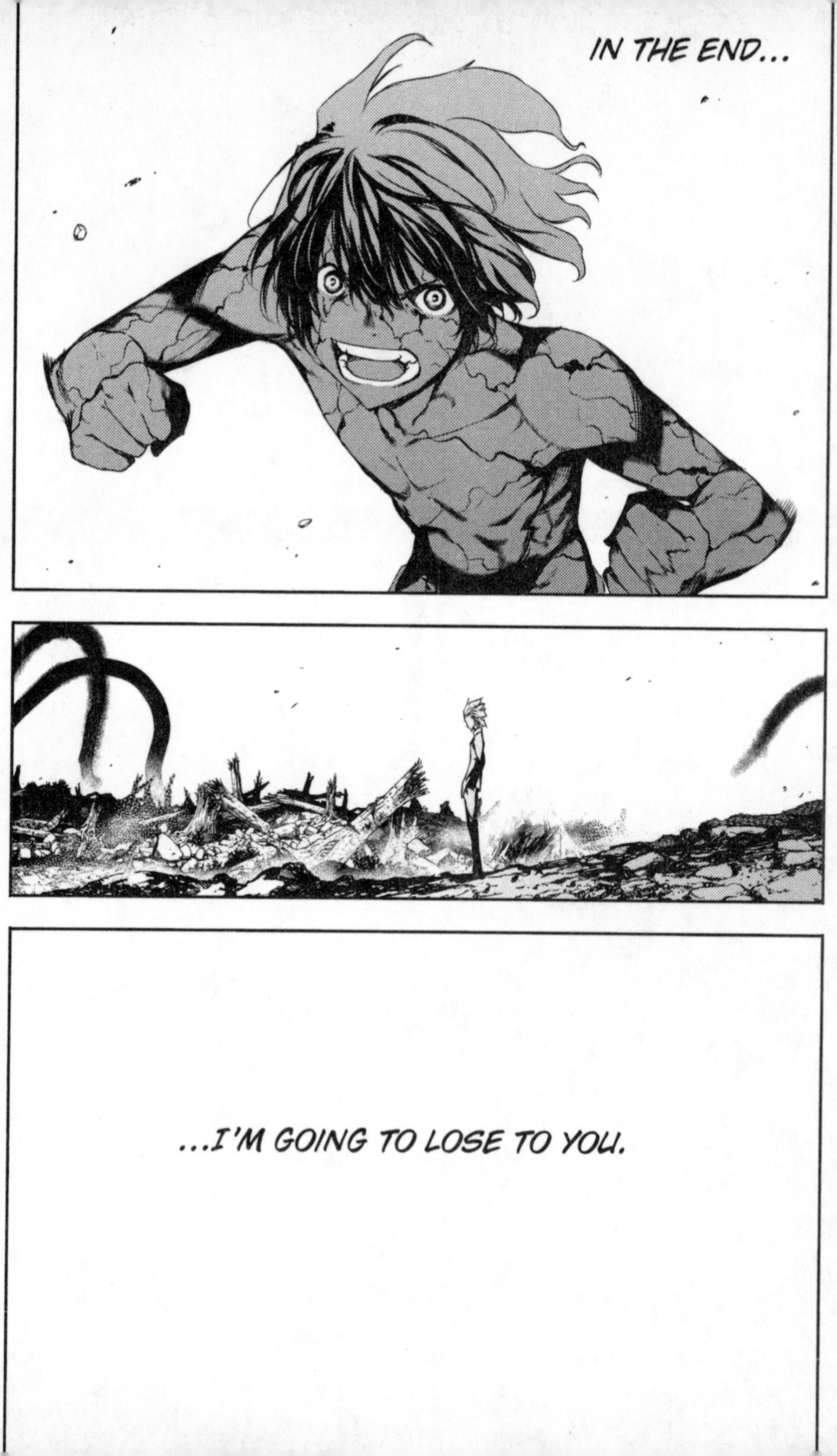
IN THE END...
...I'M GOING TO LOSE TO YOU.

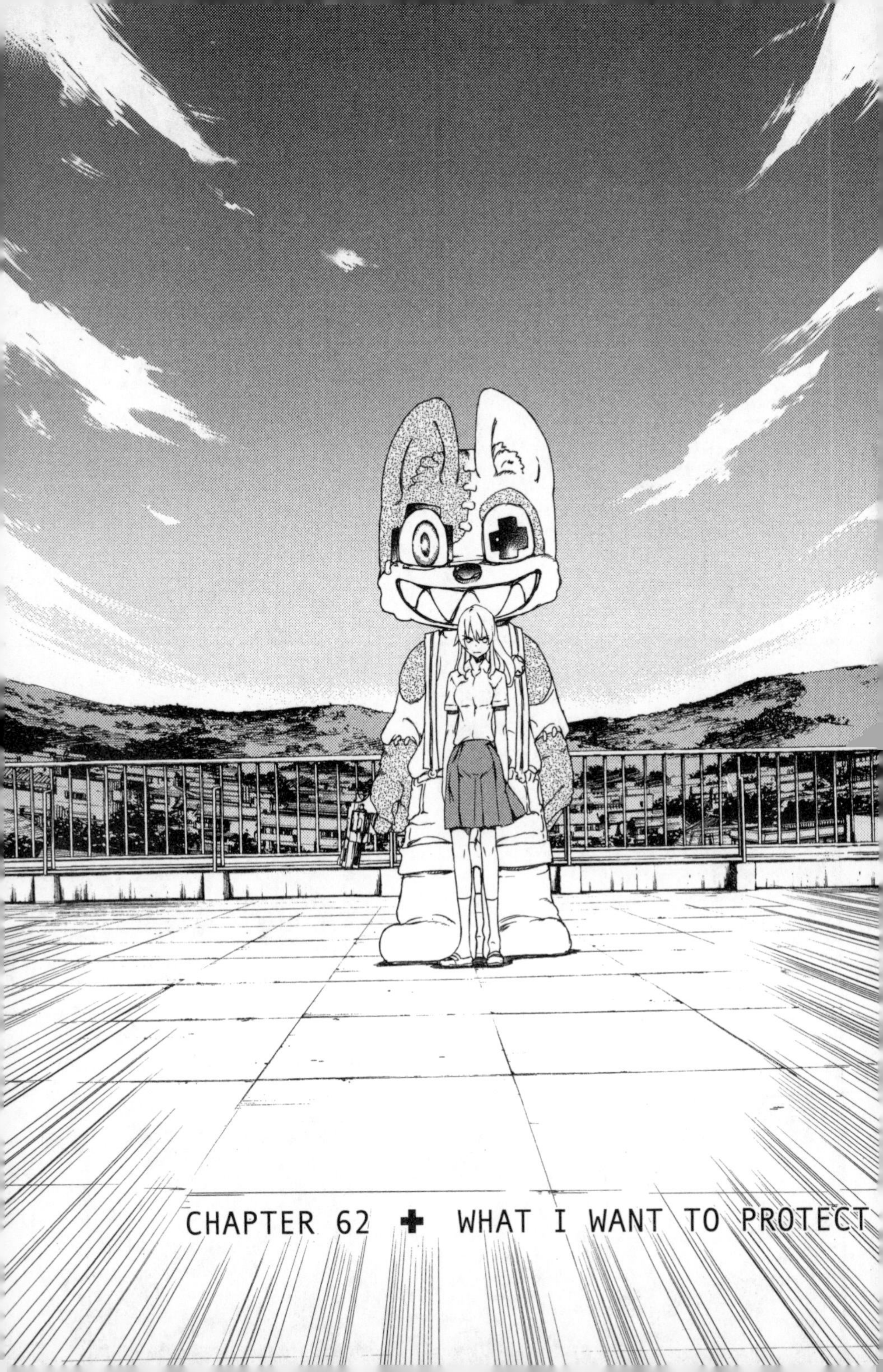

CHAPTER 62 ✚ WHAT I WANT TO PROTECT

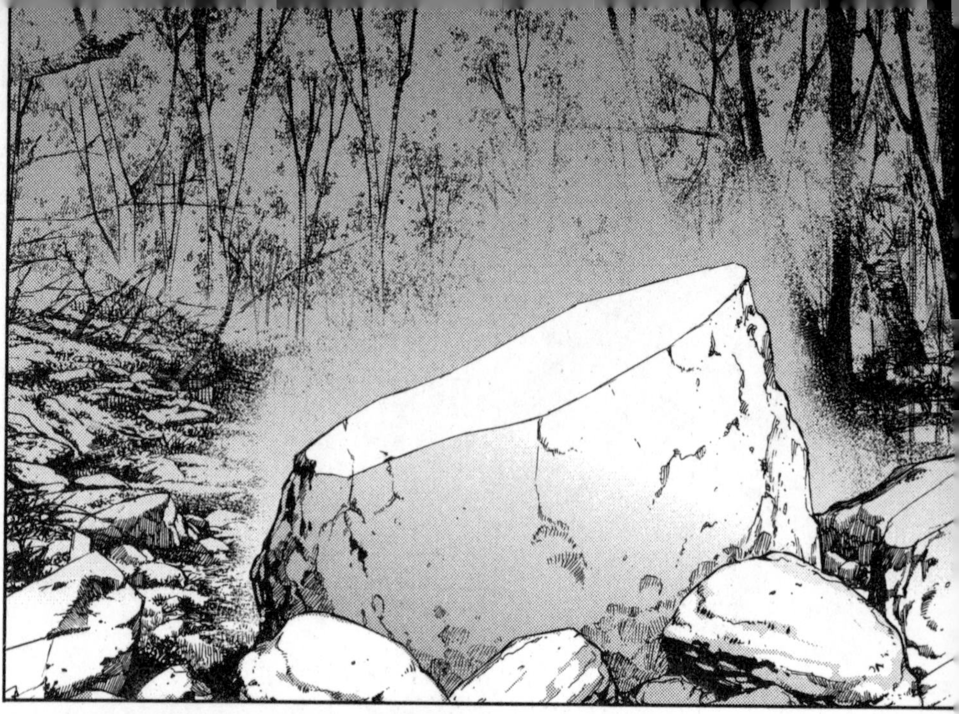
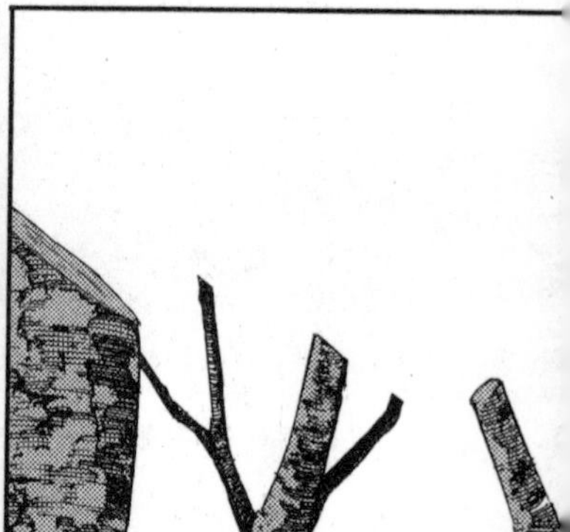
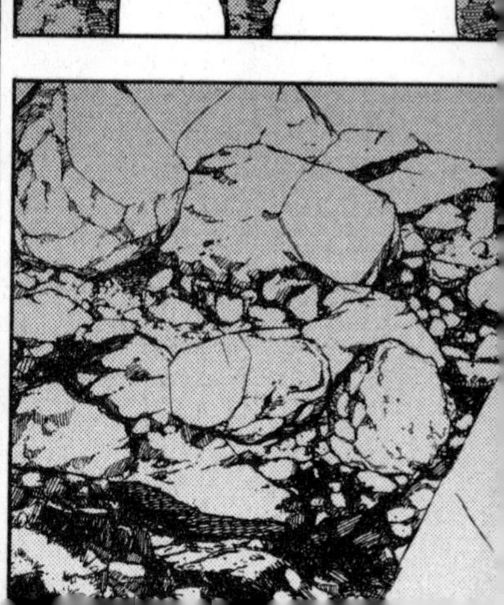
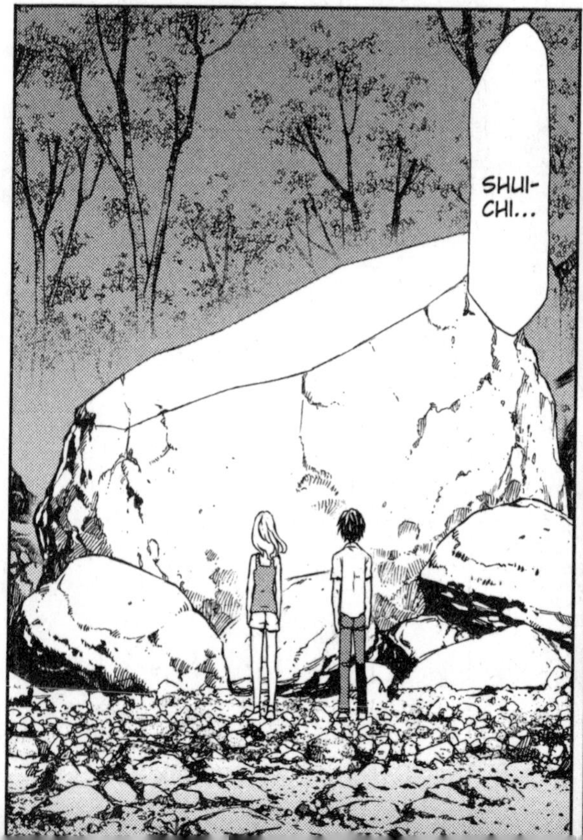
SHUI-CHI...

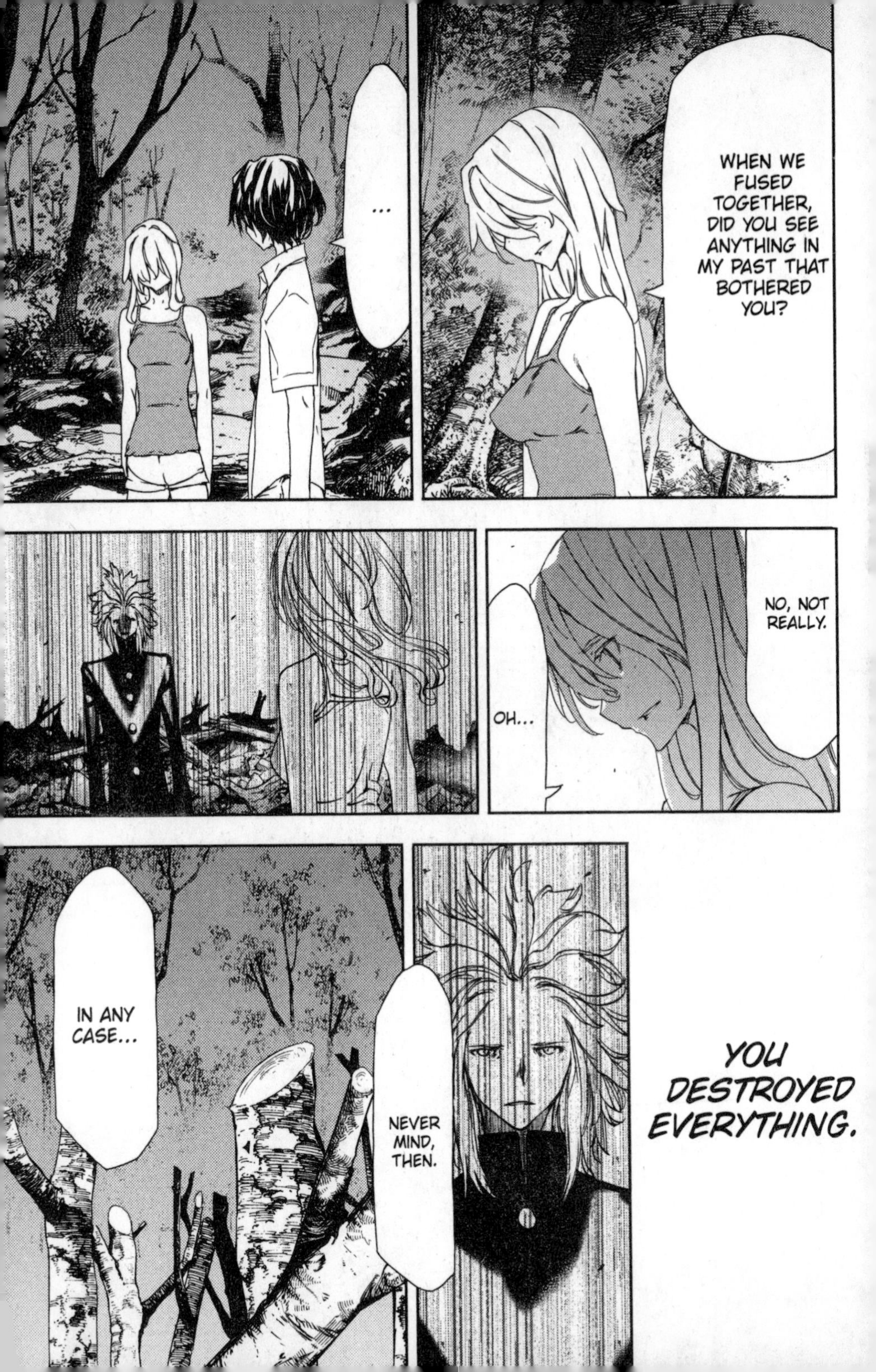
WHEN WE FUSED TOGETHER, DID YOU SEE ANYTHING IN MY PAST THAT BOTHERED YOU?
...
NO, NOT REALLY.
OH...
IN ANY CASE...
NEVER MIND, THEN.
YOU DESTROYED EVERYTHING.

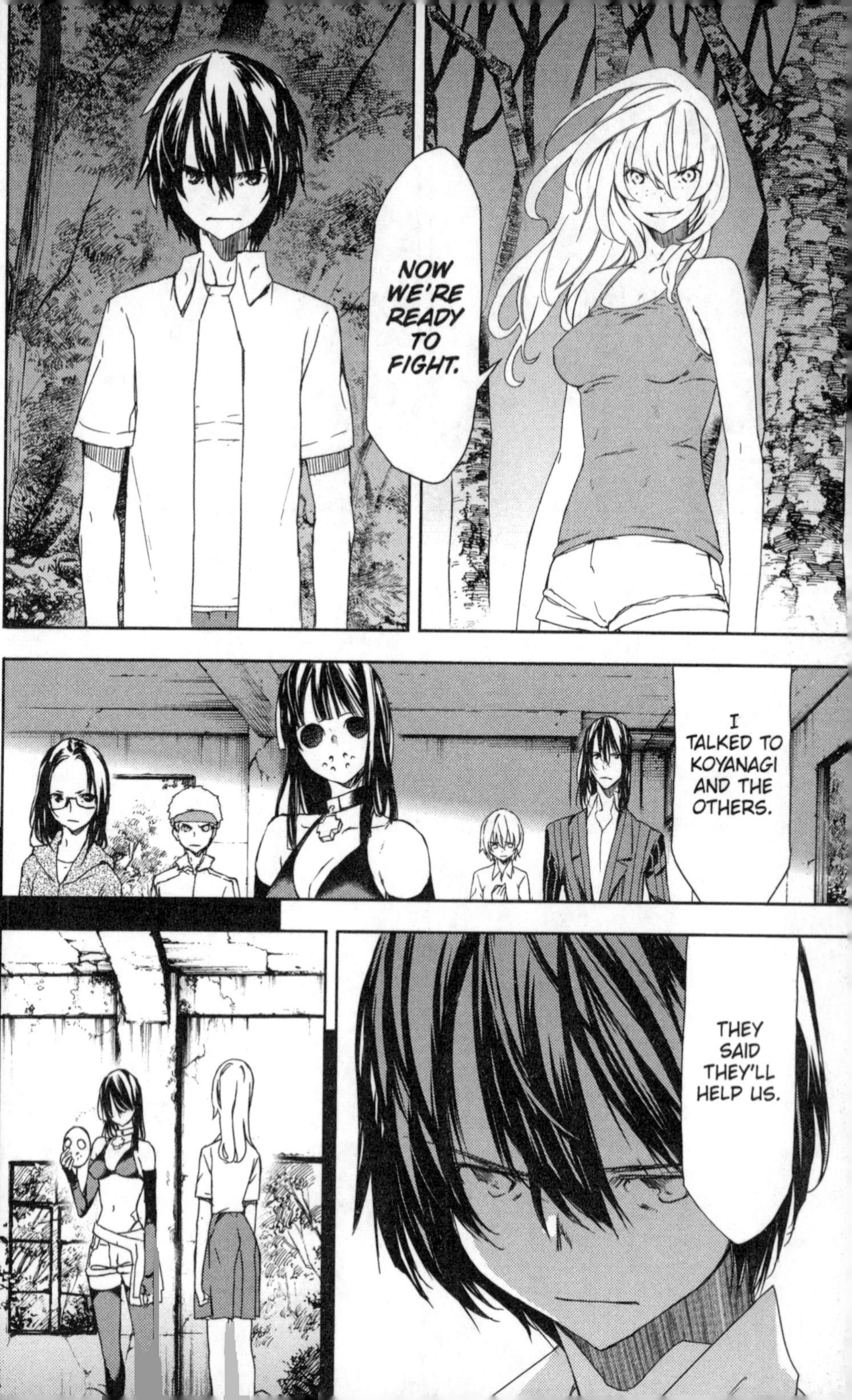
NOW WE'RE READY TO FIGHT.
I TALKED TO KOYANAGI AND THE OTHERS.
THEY SAID THEY'LL HELP US.

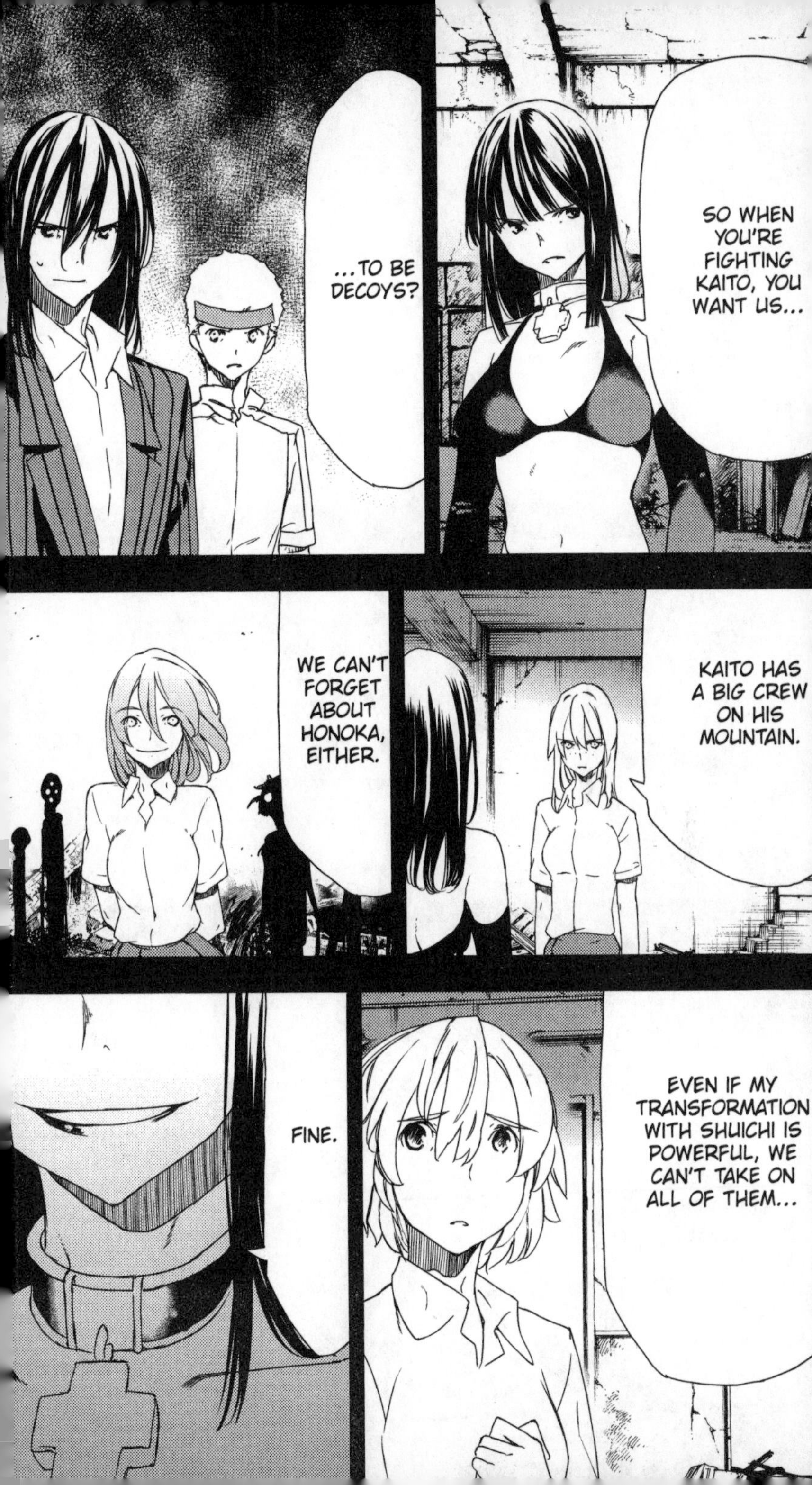
SO WHEN YOU'RE FIGHTING KAITO, YOU WANT US...
...TO BE DECOYS?
KAITO HAS A BIG CREW ON HIS MOUNTAIN.
WE CAN'T FORGET ABOUT HONOKA, EITHER.
EVEN IF MY TRANSFORMATION WITH SHUICHI IS POWERFUL, WE CAN'T TAKE ON ALL OF THEM...
FINE.

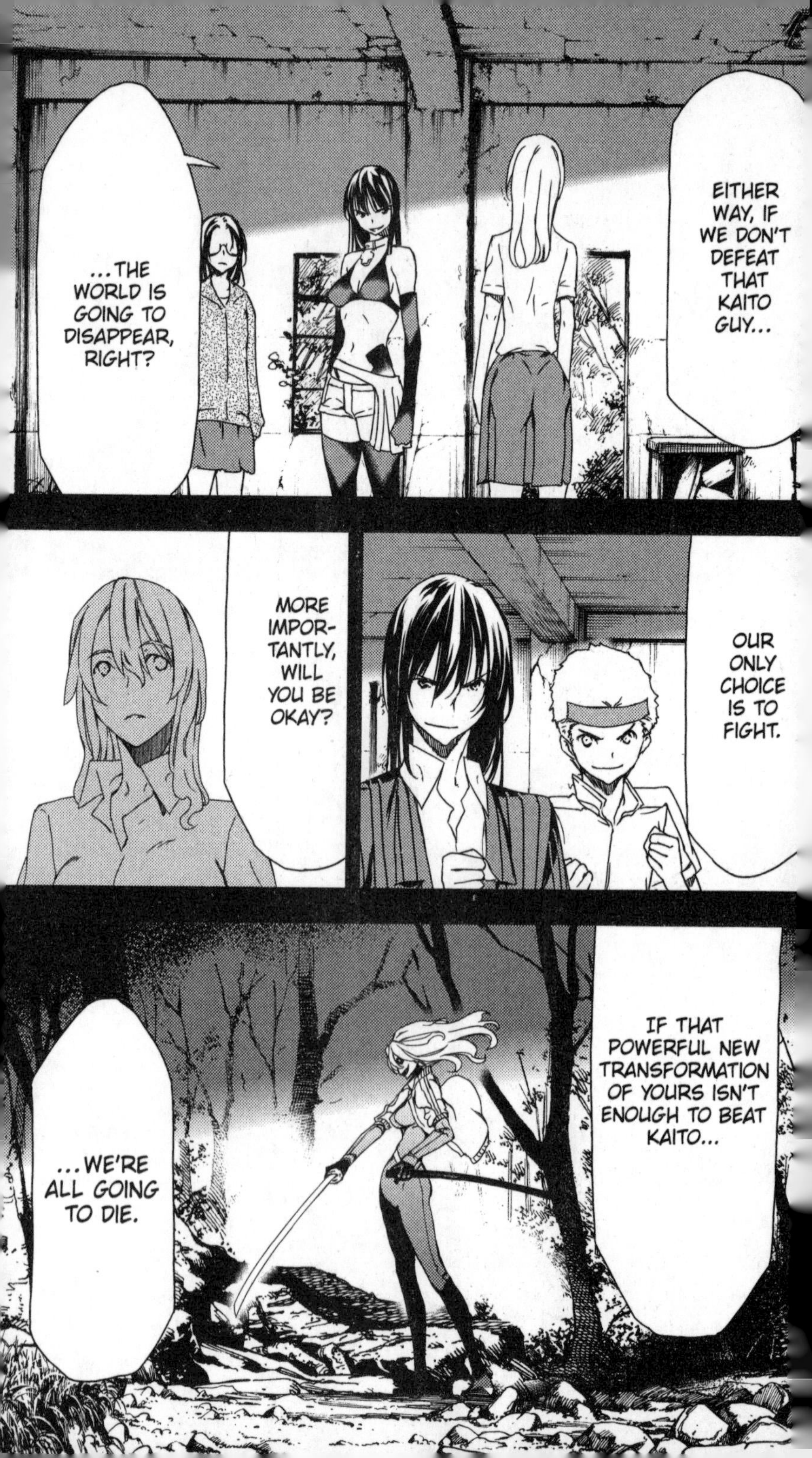
EITHER WAY, IF WE DON'T DEFEAT THAT KAITO GUY...
...THE WORLD IS GOING TO DISAPPEAR, RIGHT?
OUR ONLY CHOICE IS TO FIGHT.
MORE IMPORTANTLY, WILL YOU BE OKAY?
IF THAT POWERFUL NEW TRANSFORMATION OF YOURS ISN'T ENOUGH TO BEAT KAITO...
...WE'RE ALL GOING TO DIE.

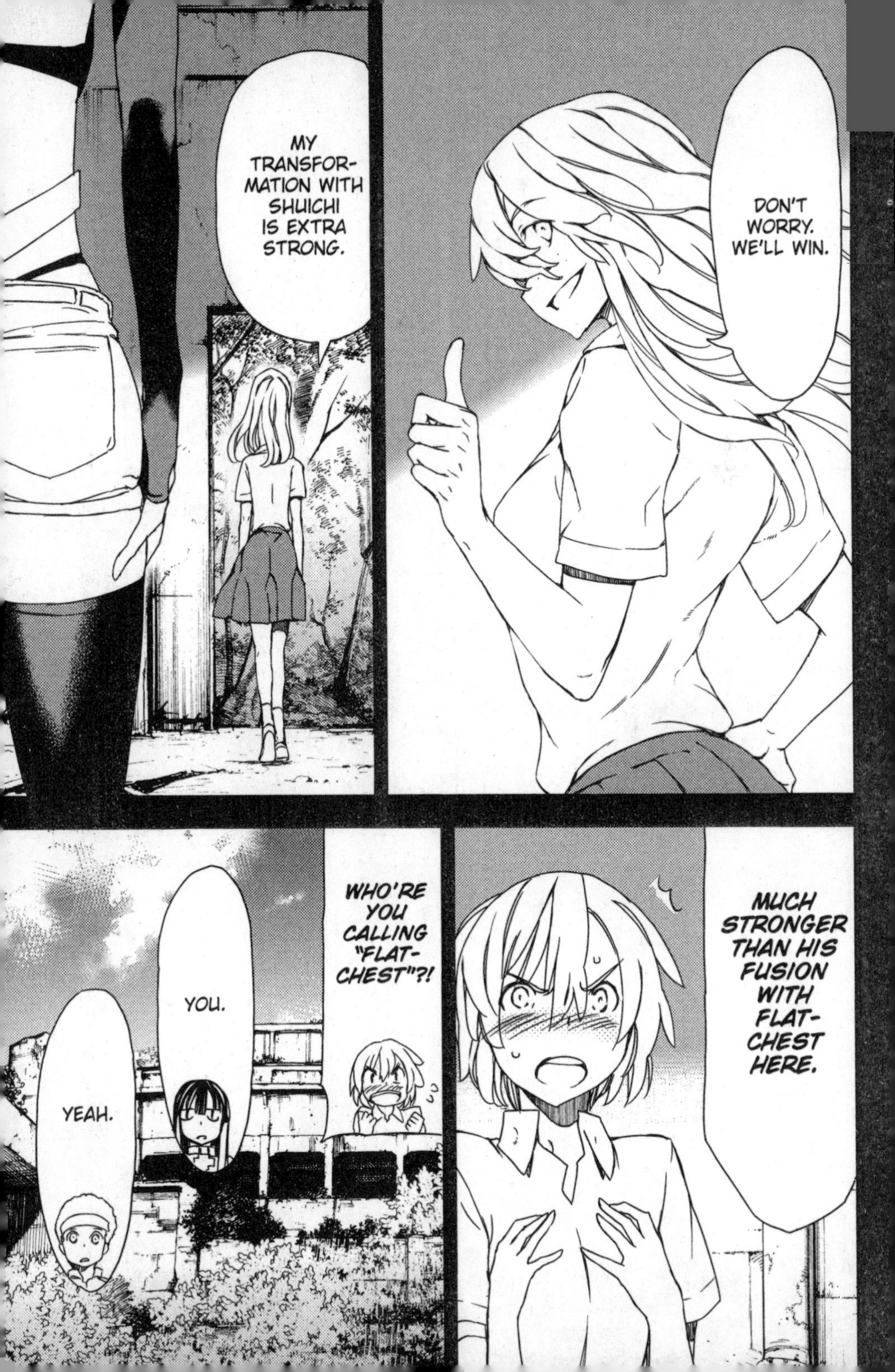
DON'T WORRY. WE'LL WIN.
MY TRANSFOR-MATION WITH SHUICHI IS EXTRA STRONG.
MUCH STRONGER THAN HIS FUSION WITH FLAT-CHEST HERE.
WHO'RE YOU CALLING "FLAT-CHEST"?!
YOU.
YEAH.

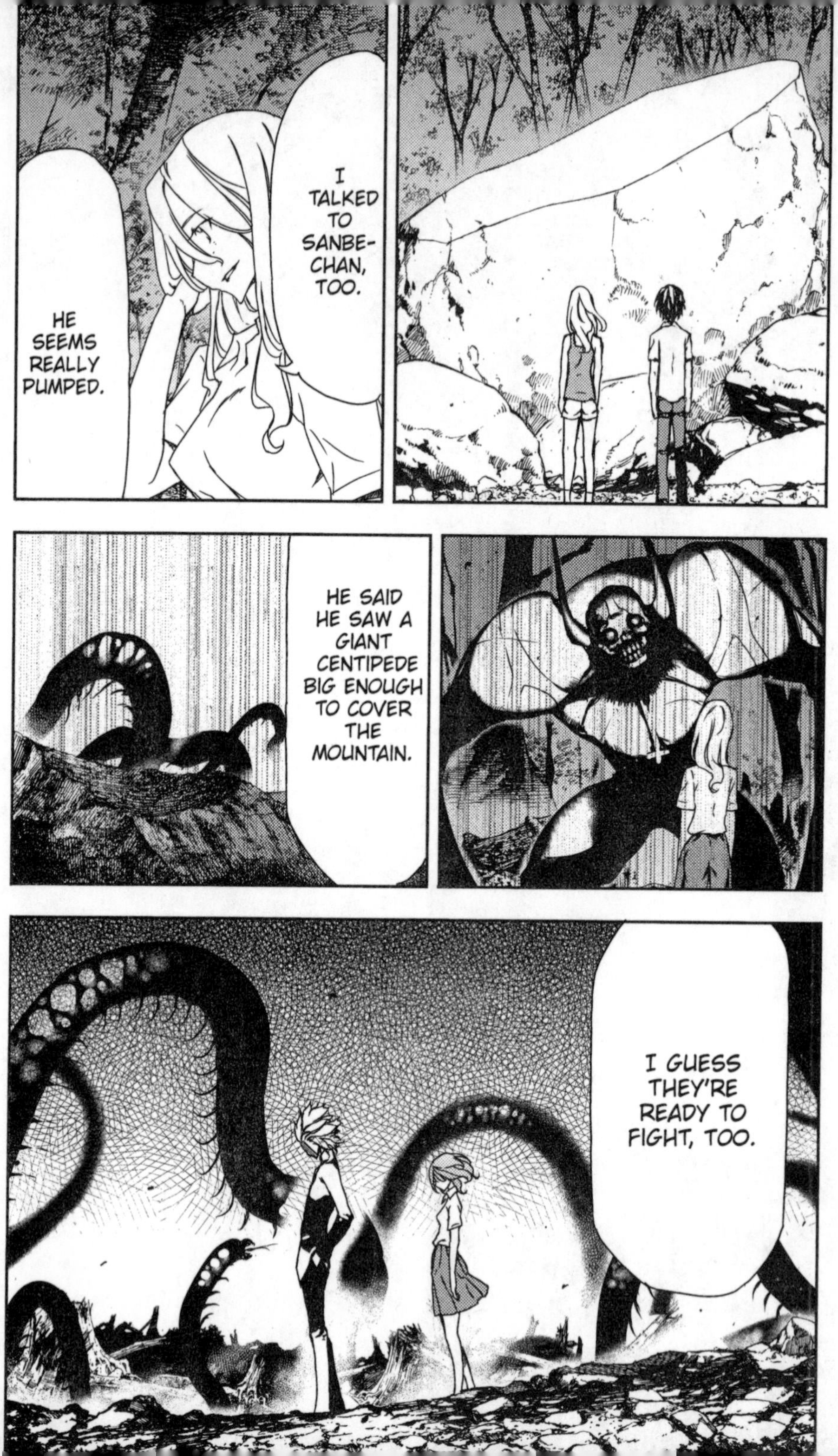
I TALKED TO SANBE-CHAN, TOO.
HE SEEMS REALLY PUMPED.
HE SAID HE SAW A GIANT CENTIPEDE BIG ENOUGH TO COVER THE MOUNTAIN.
I GUESS THEY'RE READY TO FIGHT, TOO.

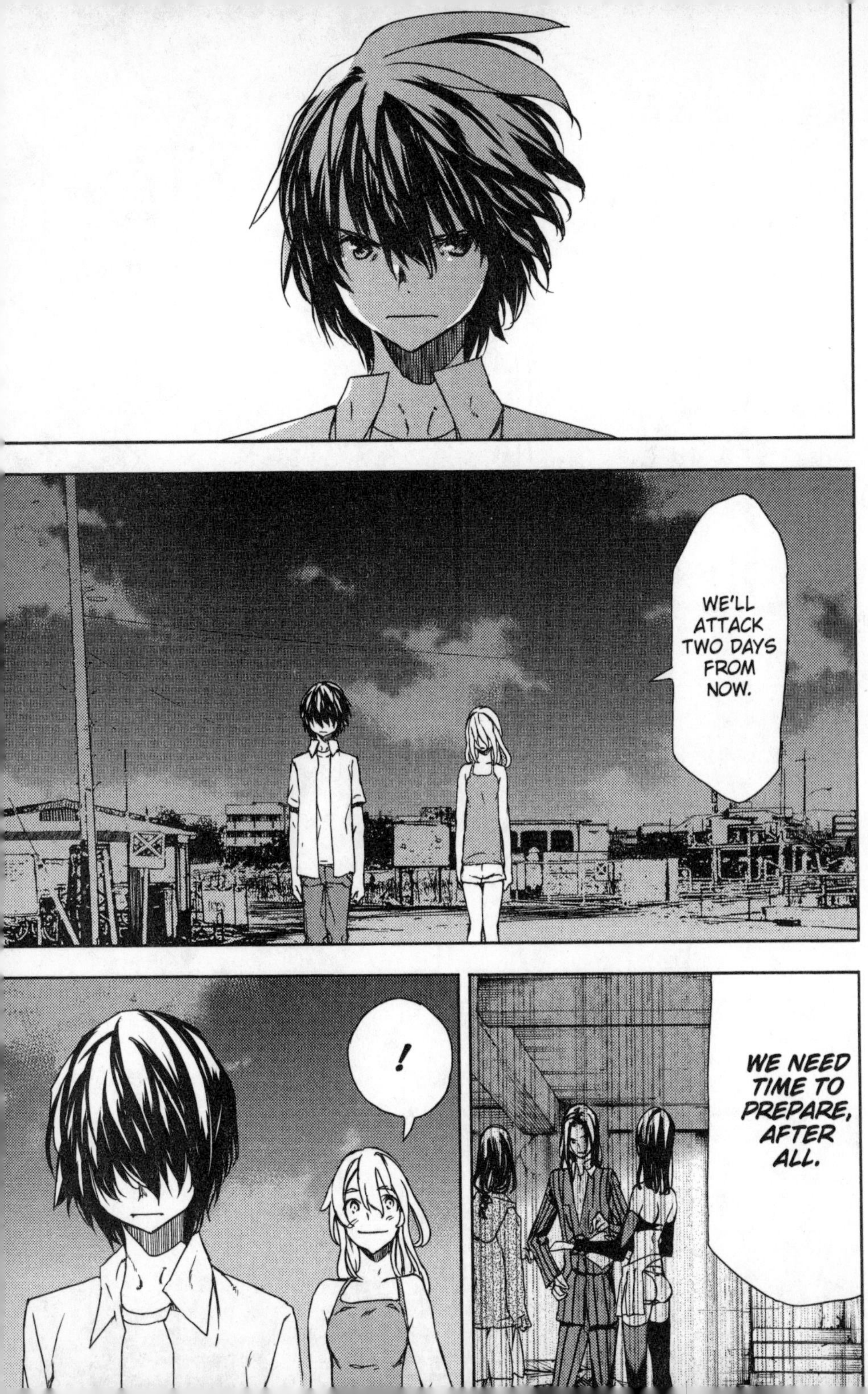
WE'LL ATTACK TWO DAYS FROM NOW.
WE NEED TIME TO PREPARE, AFTER ALL.
!

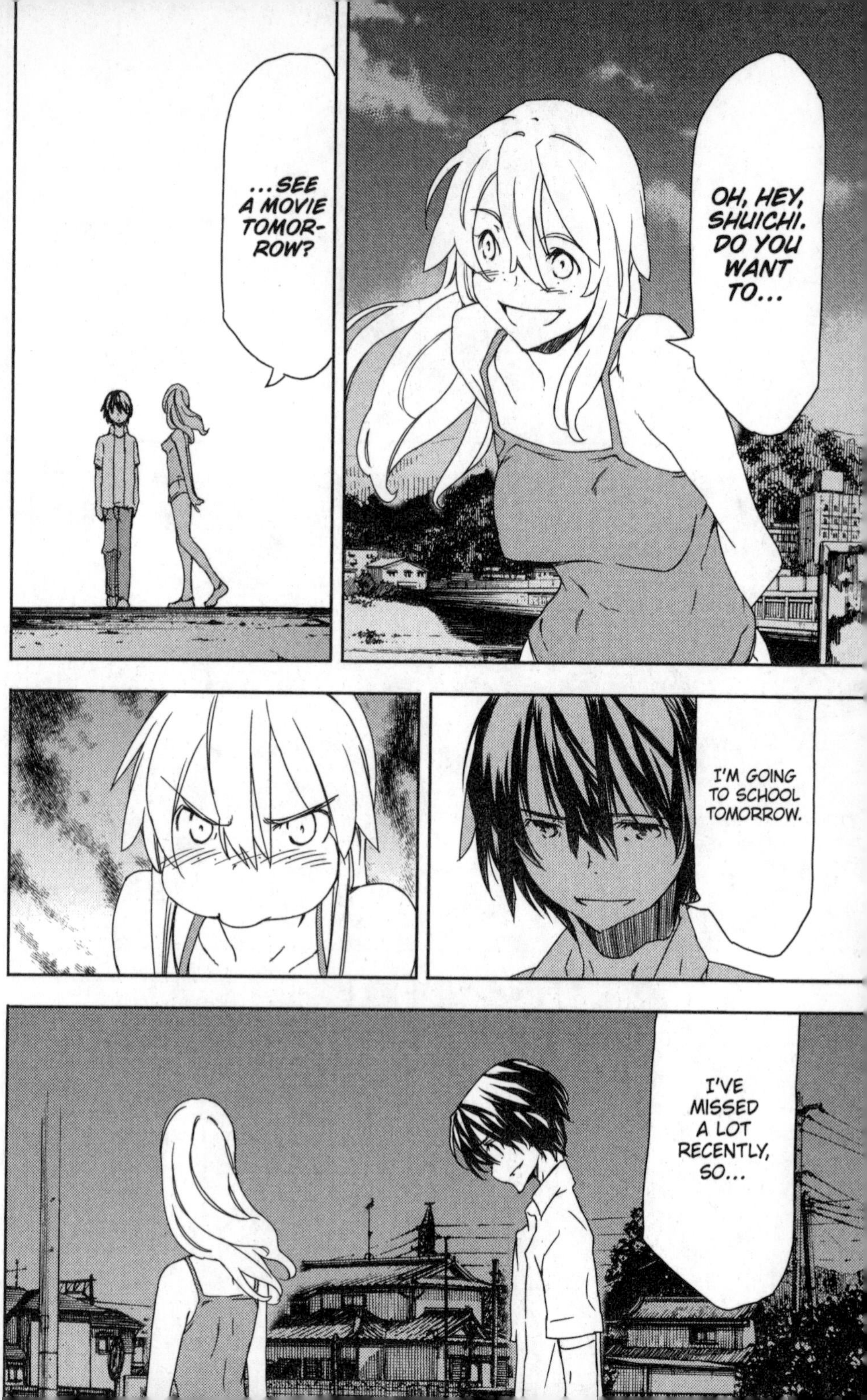
OH, HEY, SHUICHI. DO YOU WANT TO...
...SEE A MOVIE TOMOR-ROW?
I'M GOING TO SCHOOL TOMORROW.
I'VE MISSED A LOT RECENTLY, SO...

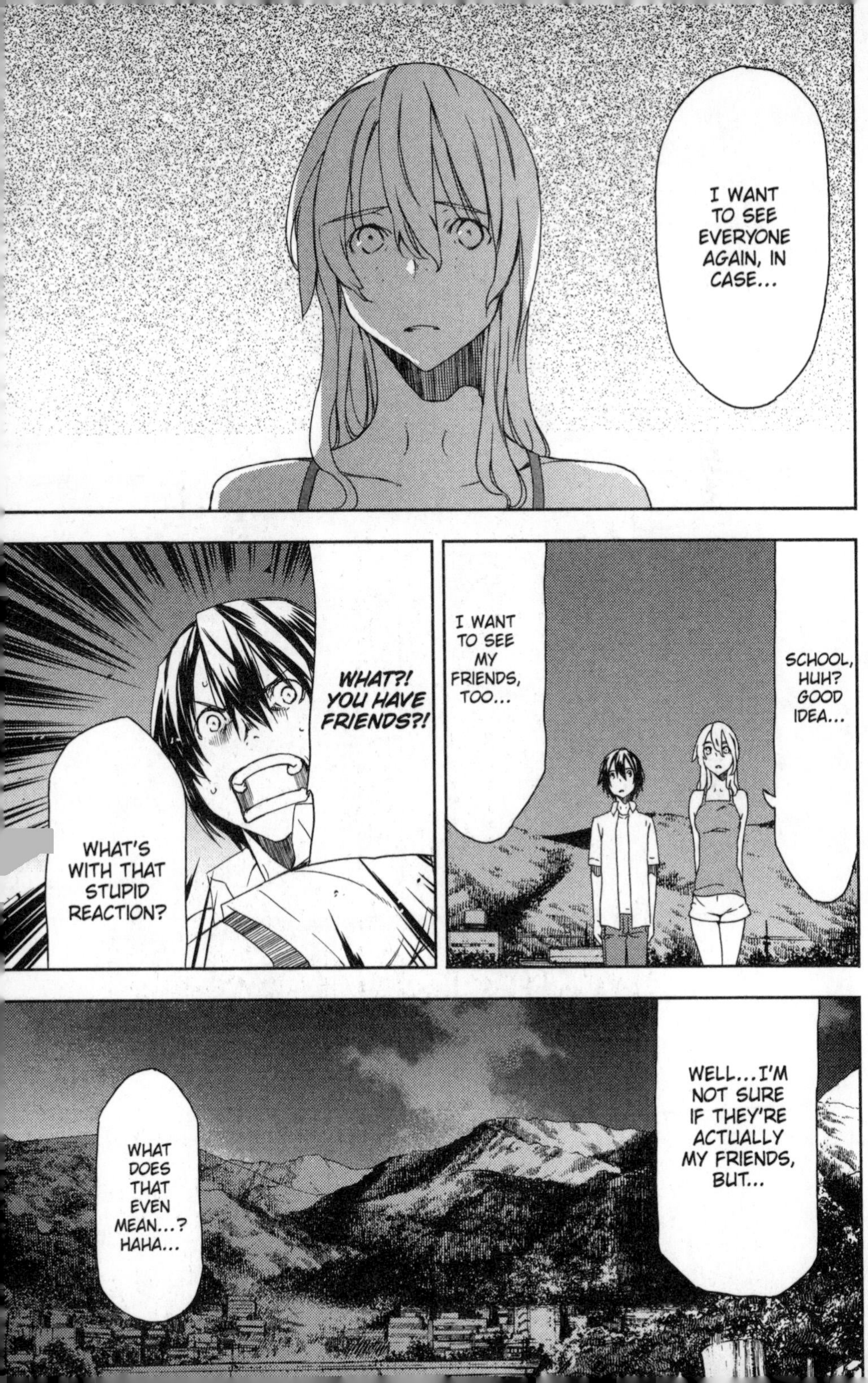
I WANT TO SEE EVERYONE AGAIN, IN CASE...
SCHOOL, HUH? GOOD IDEA...
I WANT TO SEE MY FRIENDS, TOO...
WHAT?! YOU HAVE FRIENDS?!
WHAT'S WITH THAT STUPID REACTION?
WELL...I'M NOT SURE IF THEY'RE ACTUALLY MY FRIENDS, BUT...
WHAT DOES THAT EVEN MEAN...? HAHA...

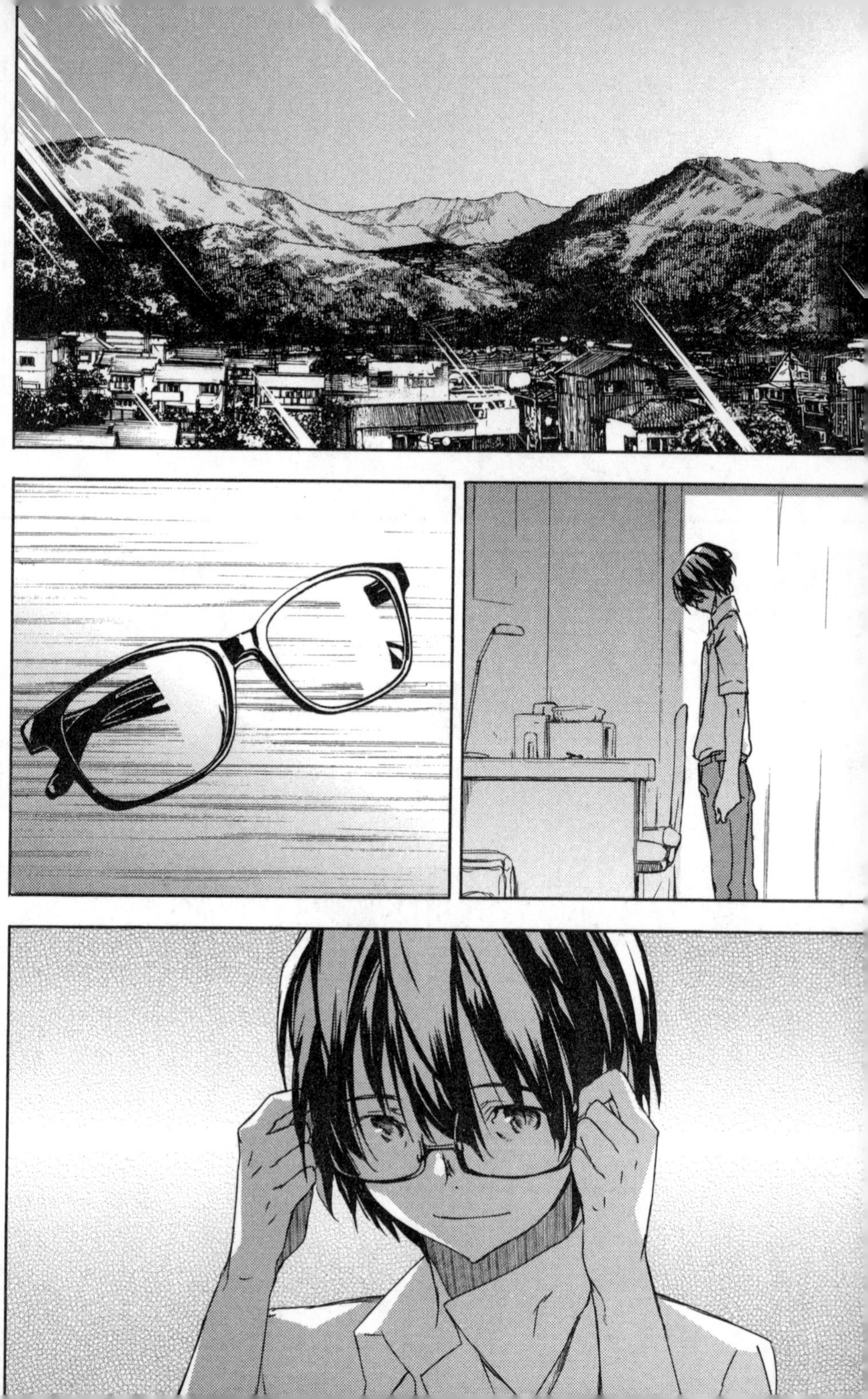

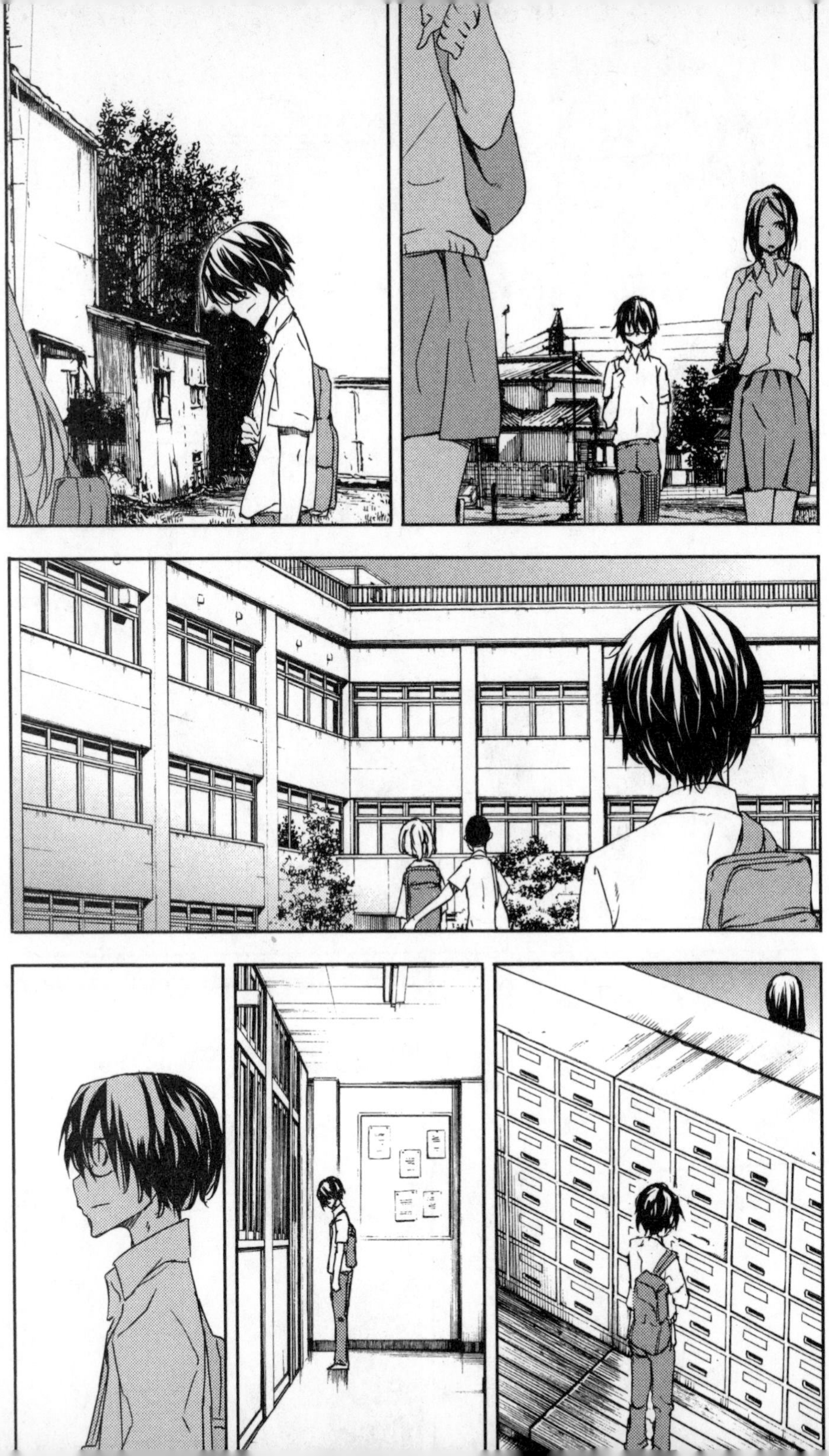

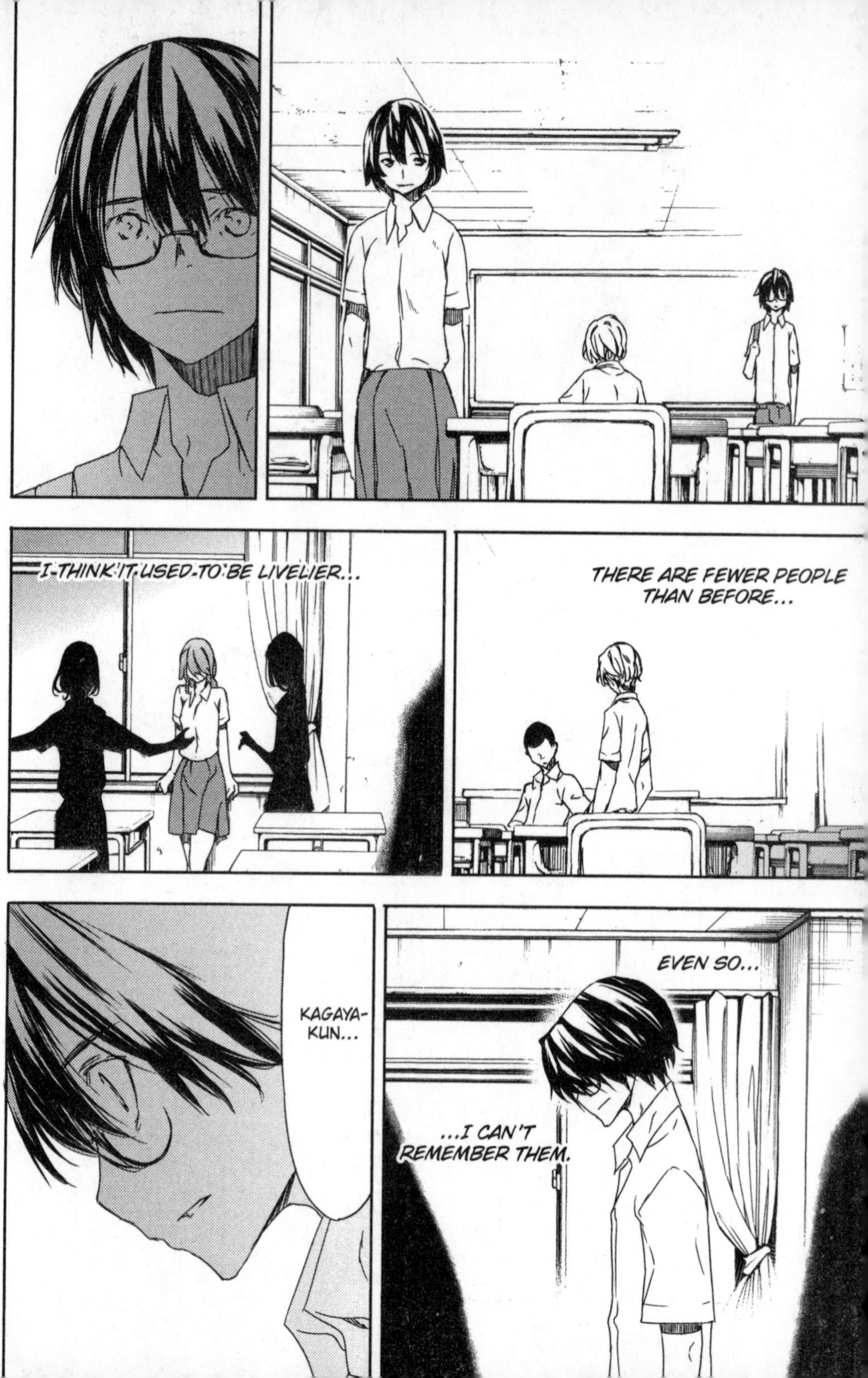
THERE ARE FEWER PEOPLE THAN BEFORE...
I THINK IT USED TO BE LIVELIER...
EVEN SO...
...I CAN'T REMEMBER THEM.
KAGAYA-KUN...

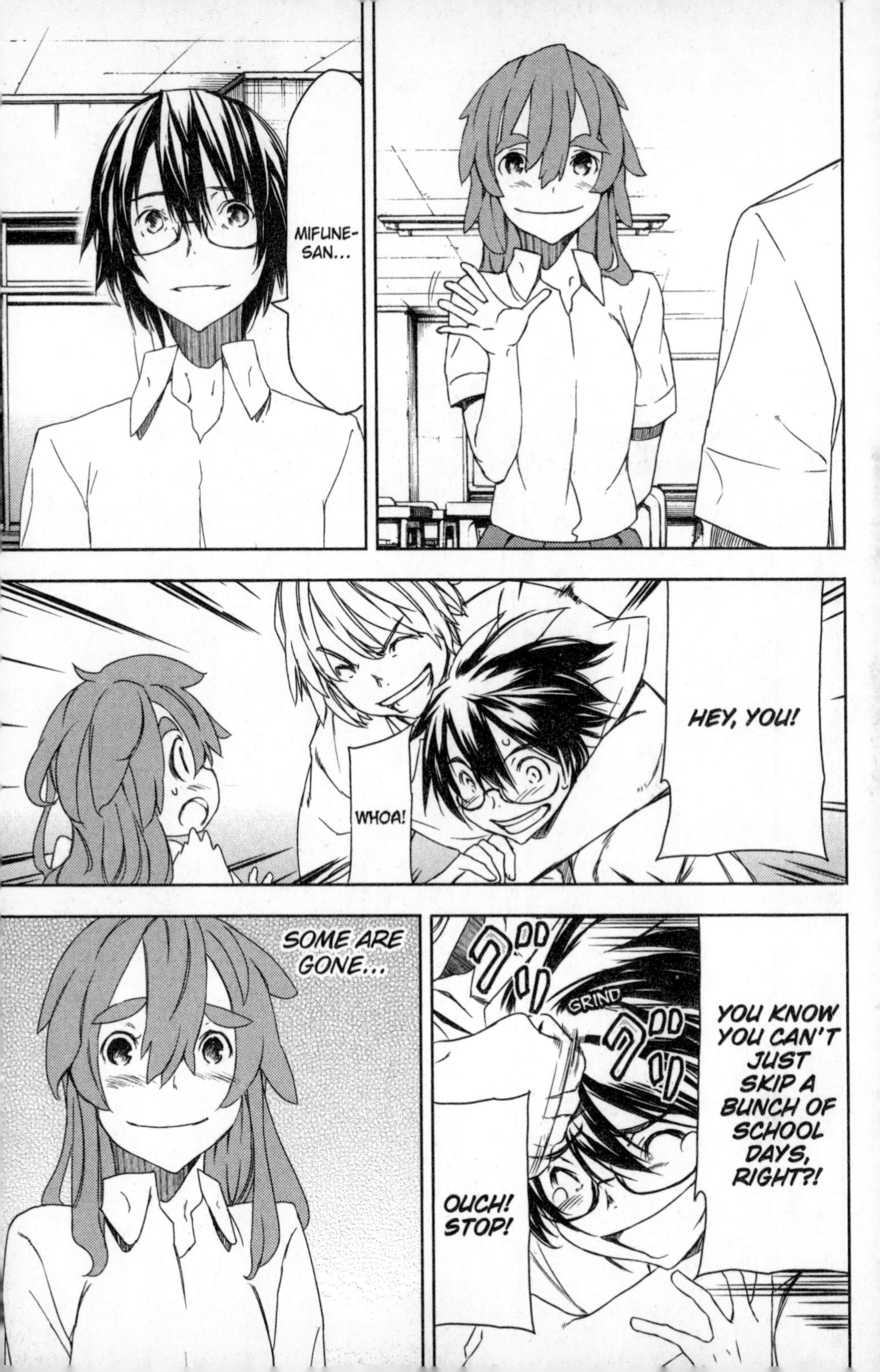
MIFUNE-SAN...
HEY, YOU!
WHOA!
YOU KNOW YOU CAN'T JUST SKIP A BUNCH OF SCHOOL DAYS, RIGHT?!
GRIND
OUCH! STOP!
SOME ARE GONE...

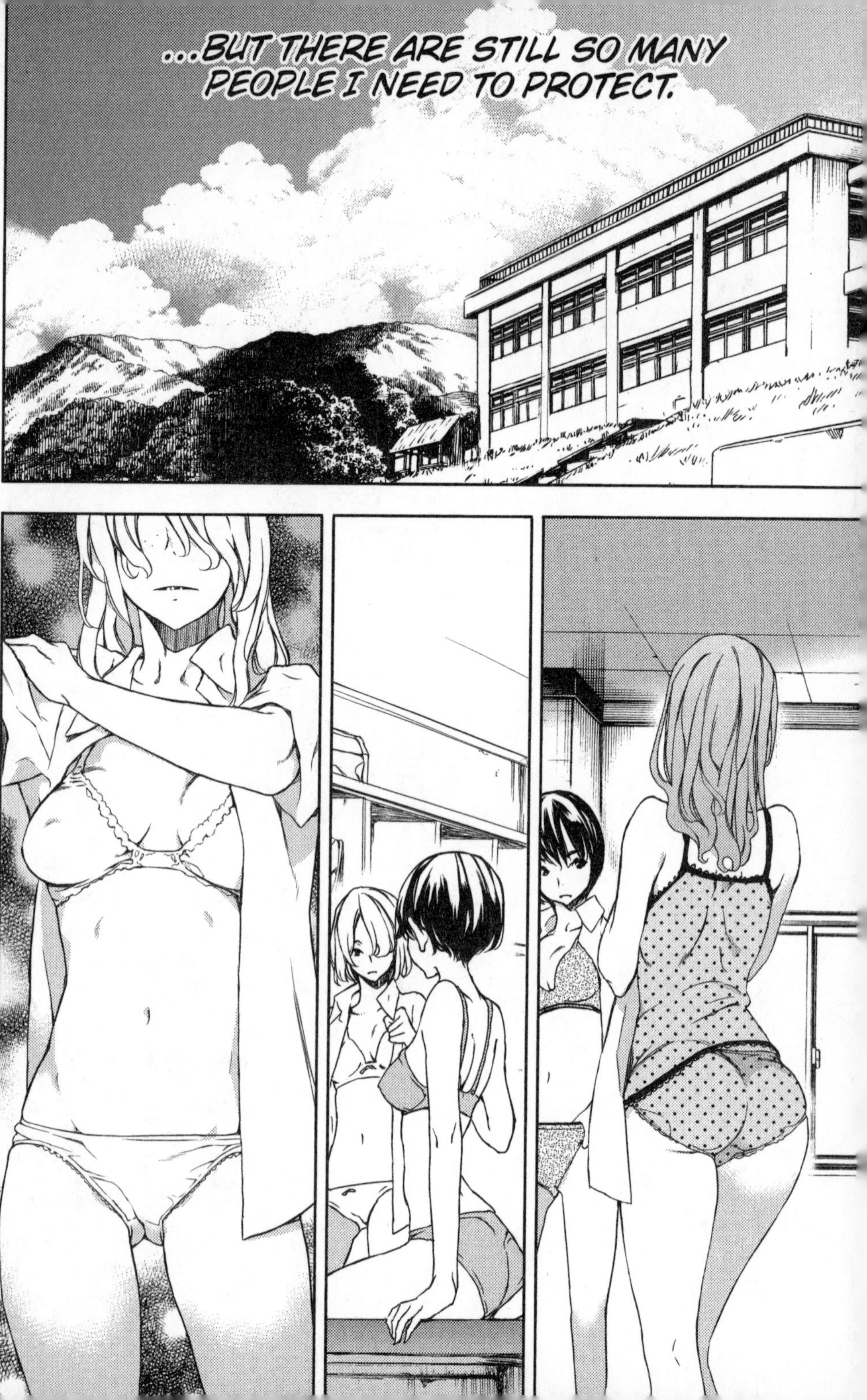
...BUT THERE ARE STILL SO MANY PEOPLE I NEED TO PROTECT.

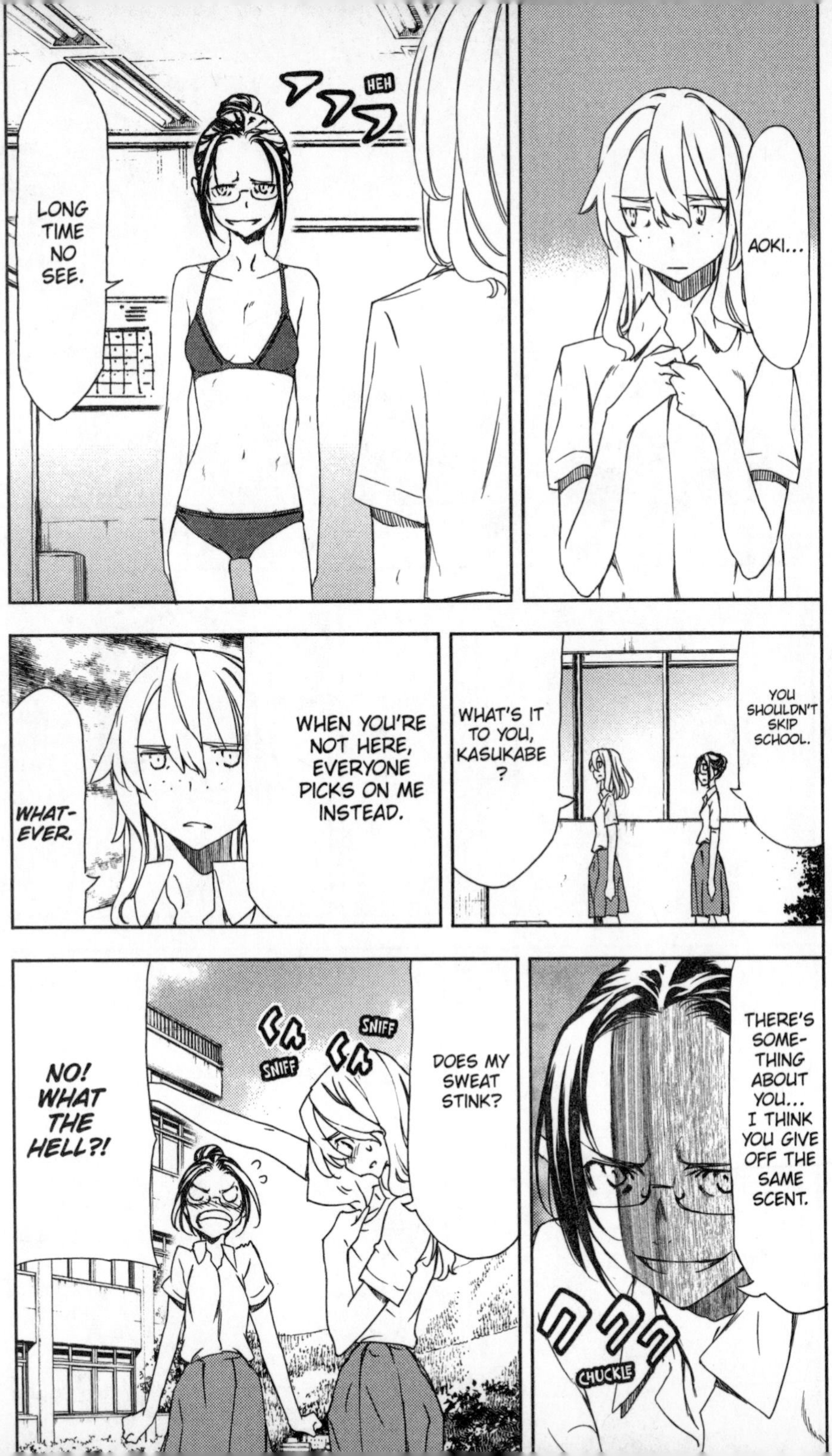
AOKI...
HEH
LONG TIME NO SEE.
YOU SHOULDN'T SKIP SCHOOL.
WHAT'S IT TO YOU, KASUKABE?
WHEN YOU'RE NOT HERE, EVERYONE PICKS ON ME INSTEAD.
WHAT-EVER.
THERE'S SOME-THING ABOUT YOU... I THINK YOU GIVE OFF THE SAME SCENT.
CHUCKLE
DOES MY SWEAT STINK?
SNIFF
SNIFF
NO! WHAT THE HELL?!

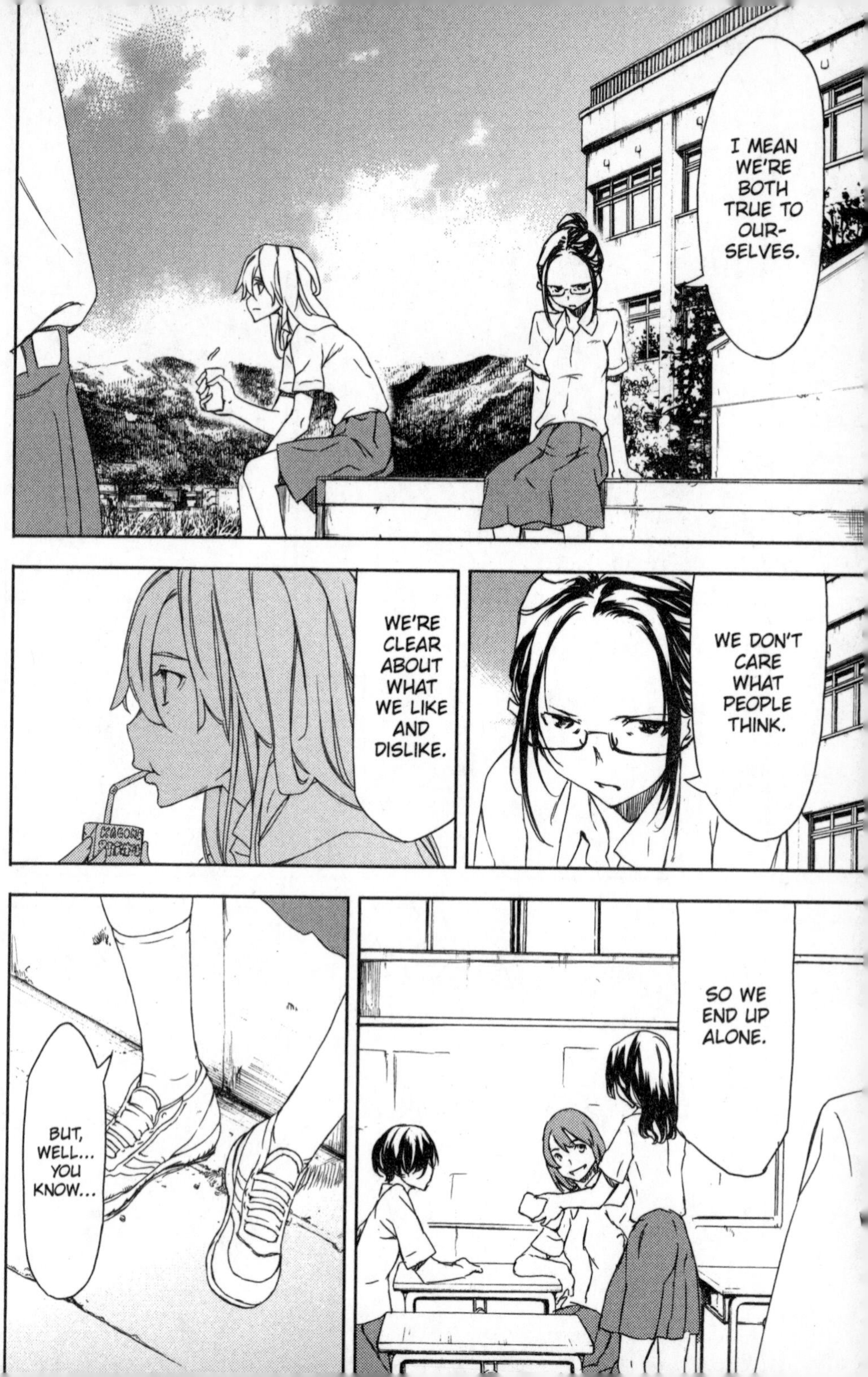
I MEAN WE'RE BOTH TRUE TO OUR-SELVES.
WE DON'T CARE WHAT PEOPLE THINK.
WE'RE CLEAR ABOUT WHAT WE LIKE AND DISLIKE.
SO WE END UP ALONE.
BUT, WELL... YOU KNOW...

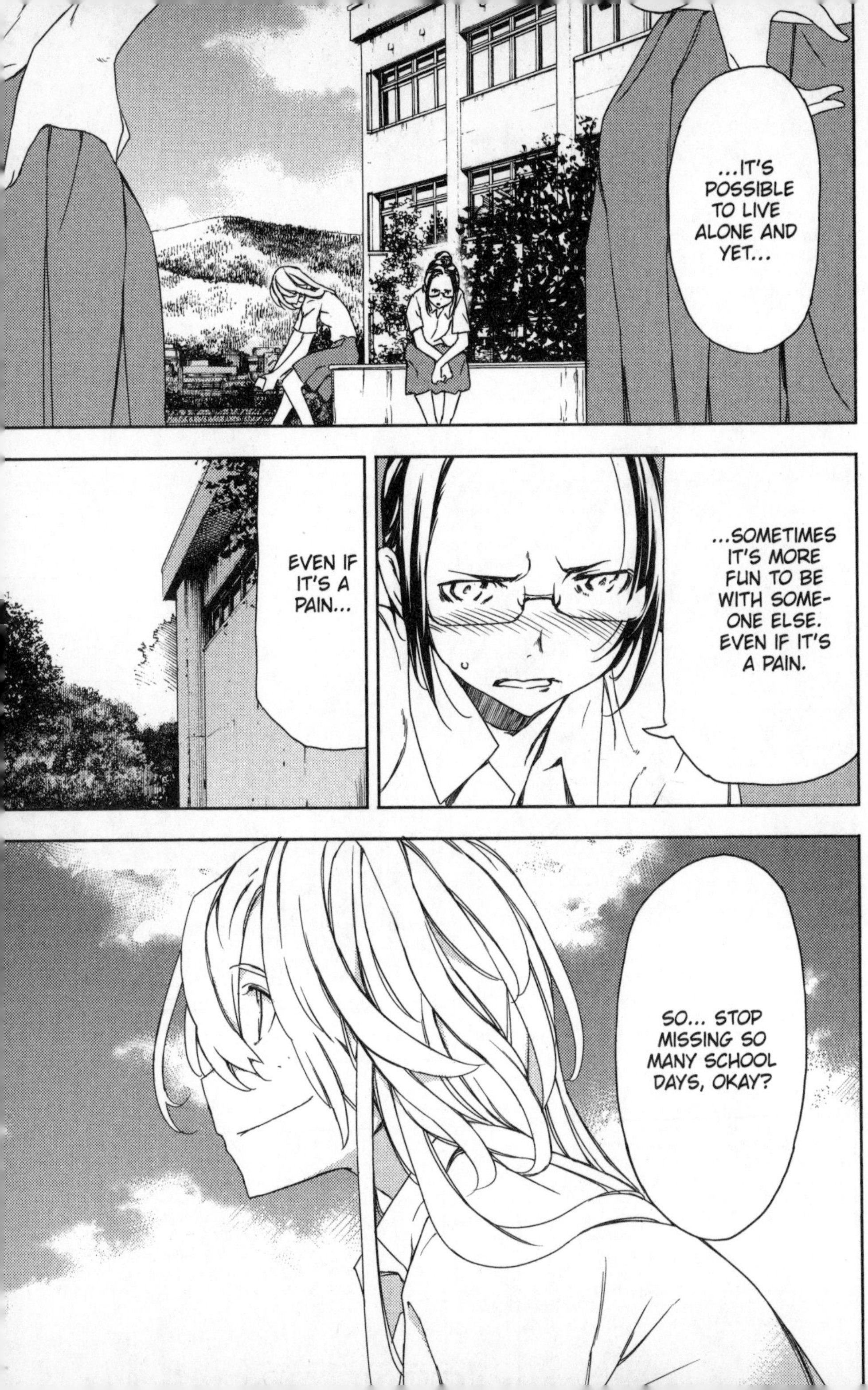
...IT'S POSSIBLE TO LIVE ALONE AND YET...
...SOMETIMES IT'S MORE FUN TO BE WITH SOME-ONE ELSE. EVEN IF IT'S A PAIN.
EVEN IF IT'S A PAIN...
SO... STOP MISSING SO MANY SCHOOL DAYS, OKAY?

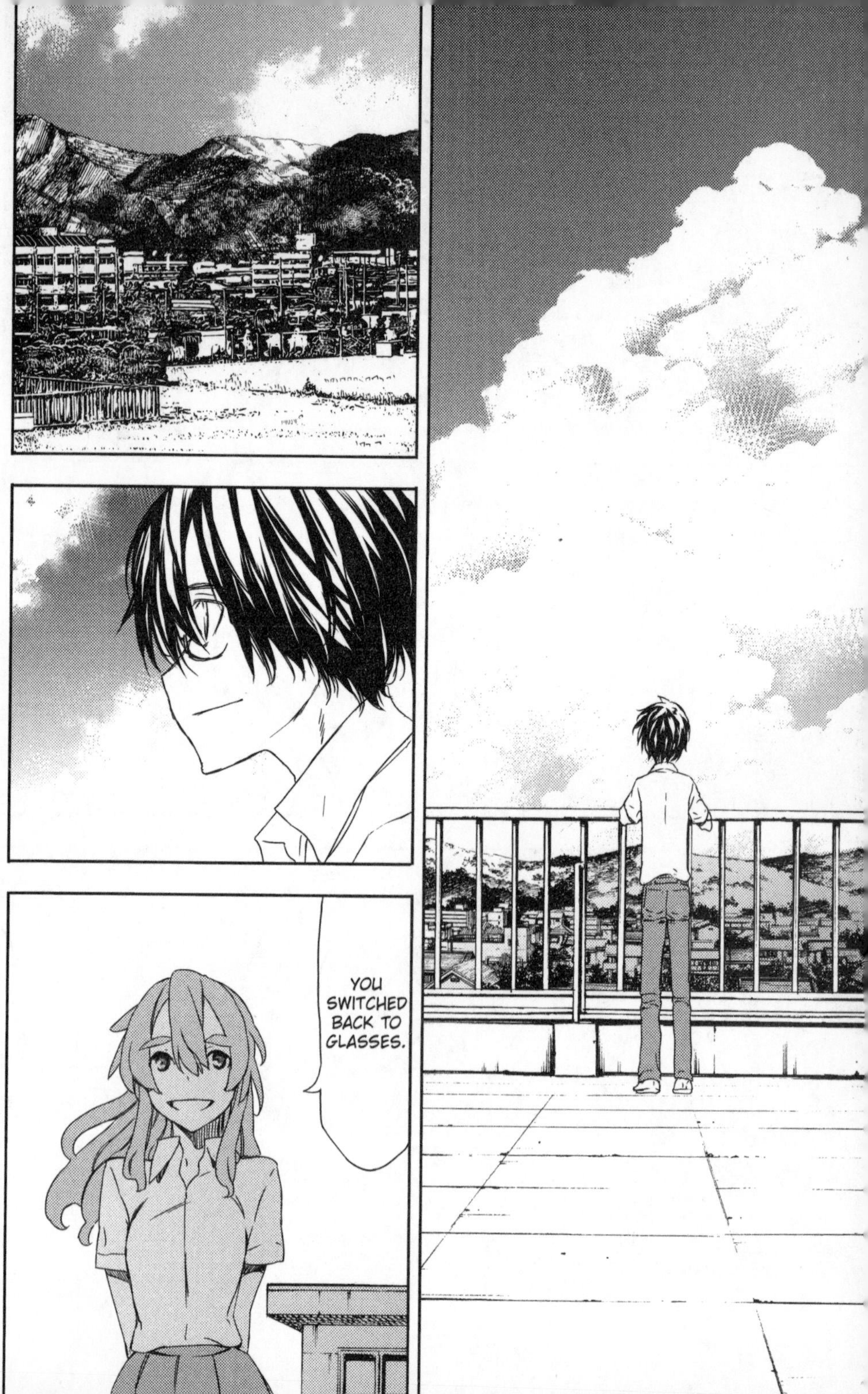
YOU SWITCHED BACK TO GLASSES.

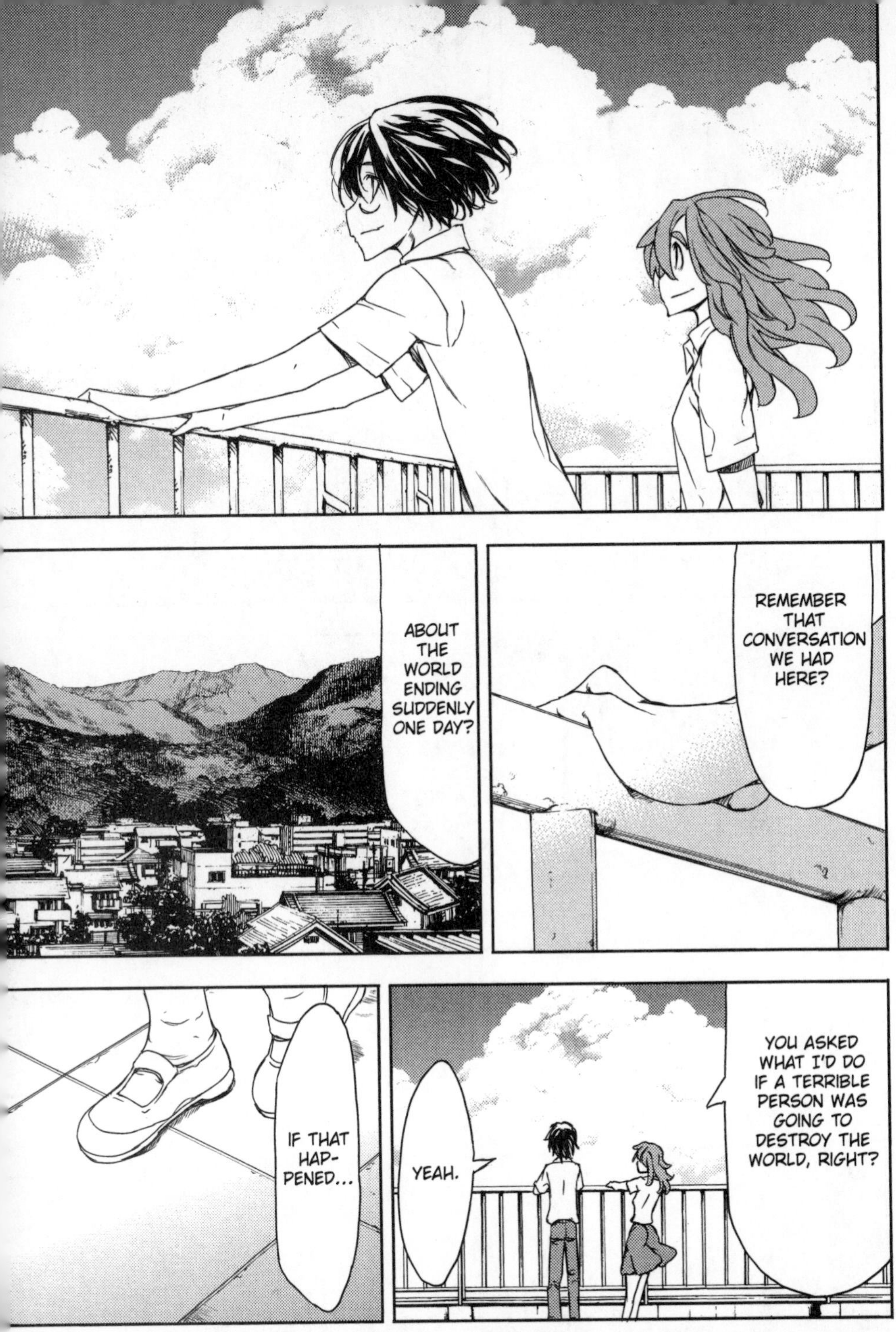
REMEMBER THAT CONVERSATION WE HAD HERE?
ABOUT THE WORLD ENDING SUDDENLY ONE DAY?
YOU ASKED WHAT I'D DO IF A TERRIBLE PERSON WAS GOING TO DESTROY THE WORLD, RIGHT?
YEAH.
IF THAT HAP-PENED...

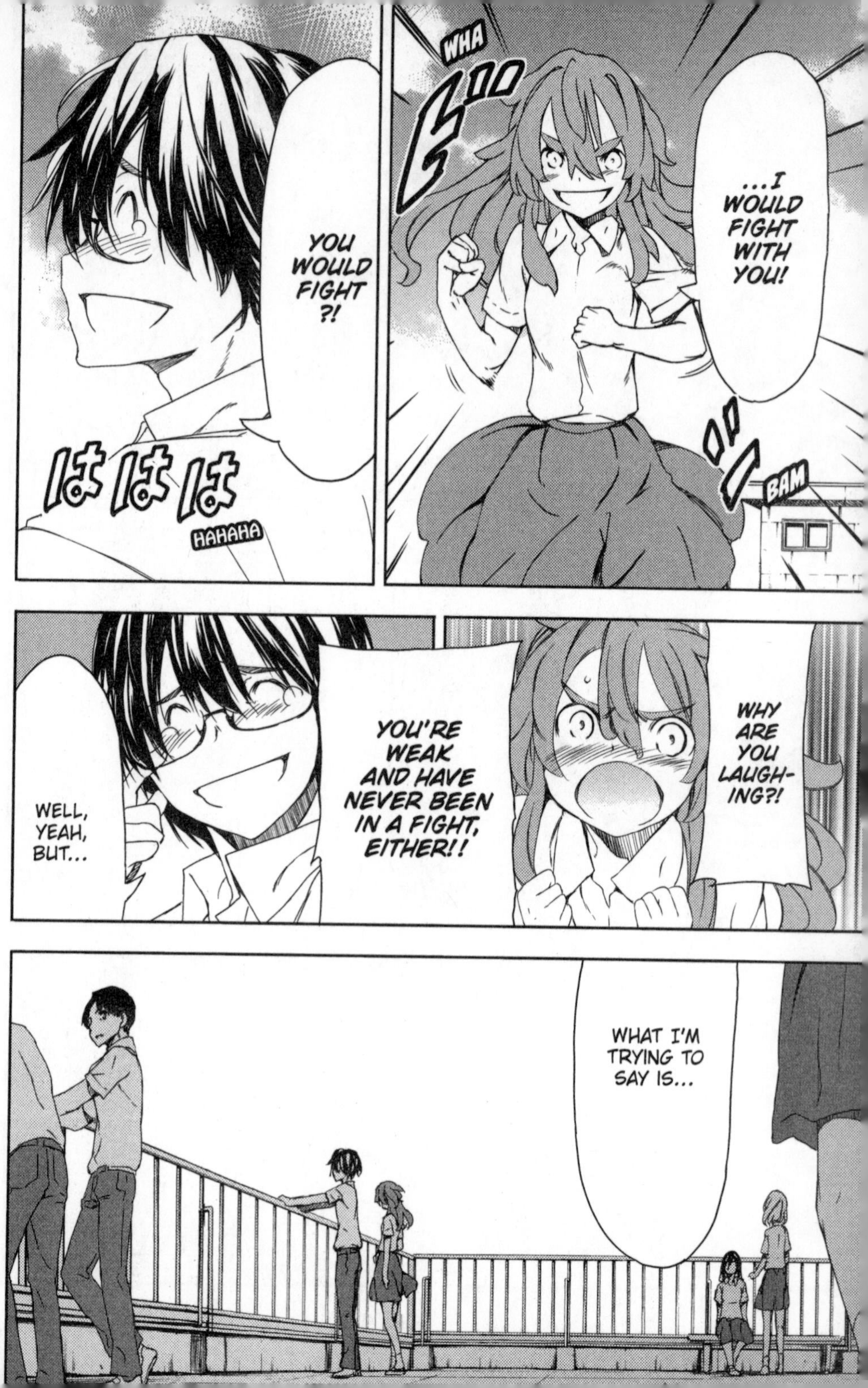
WHA
...I WOULD FIGHT WITH YOU!
BAM
YOU WOULD FIGHT?!
ははは
HAHAHA
WHY ARE YOU LAUGH-ING?!
YOU'RE WEAK AND HAVE NEVER BEEN IN A FIGHT, EITHER!!
WELL, YEAH, BUT...
WHAT I'M TRYING TO SAY IS...

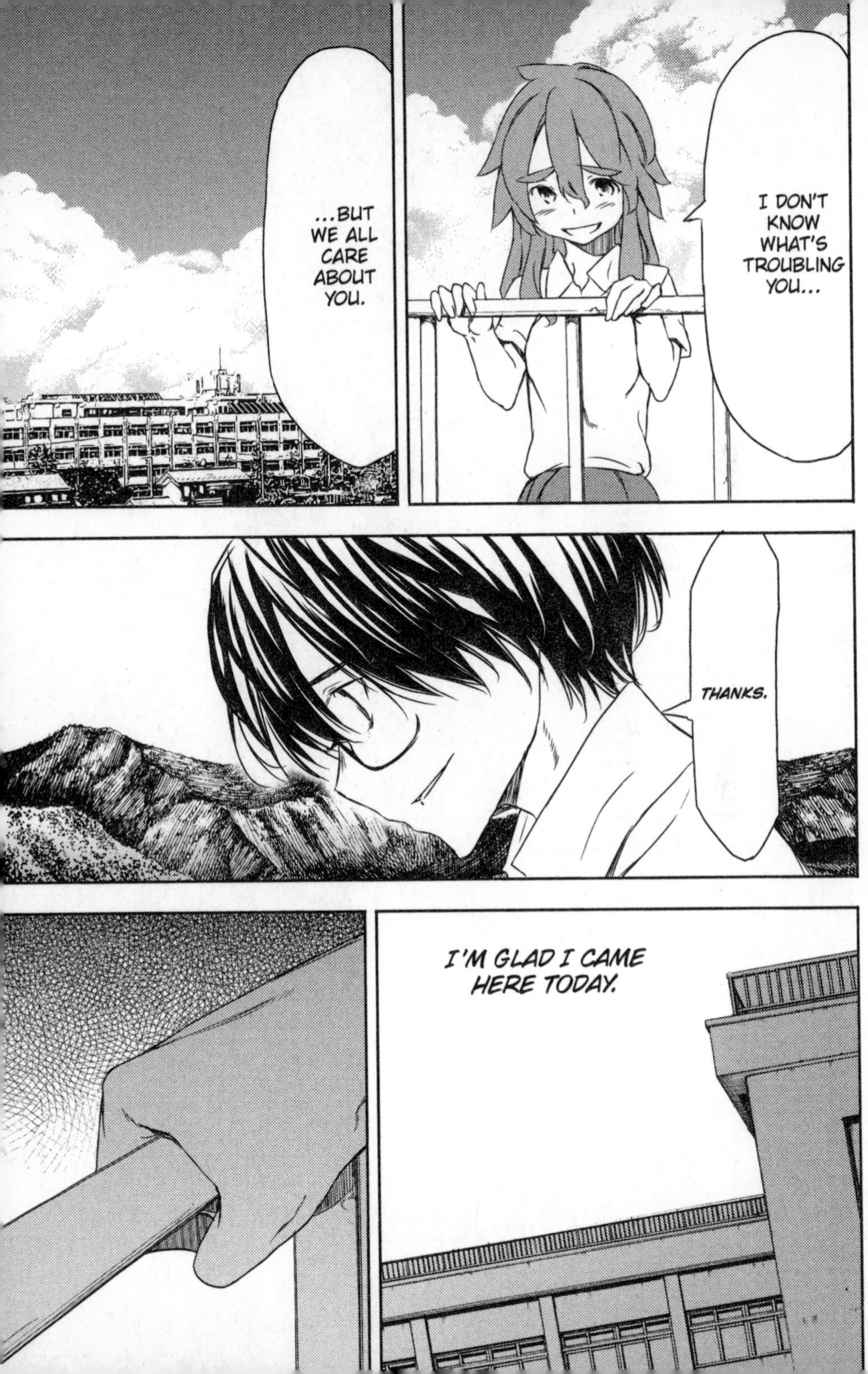
I DON'T KNOW WHAT'S TROUBLING YOU...
...BUT WE ALL CARE ABOUT YOU.
THANKS.
I'M GLAD I CAME HERE TODAY.

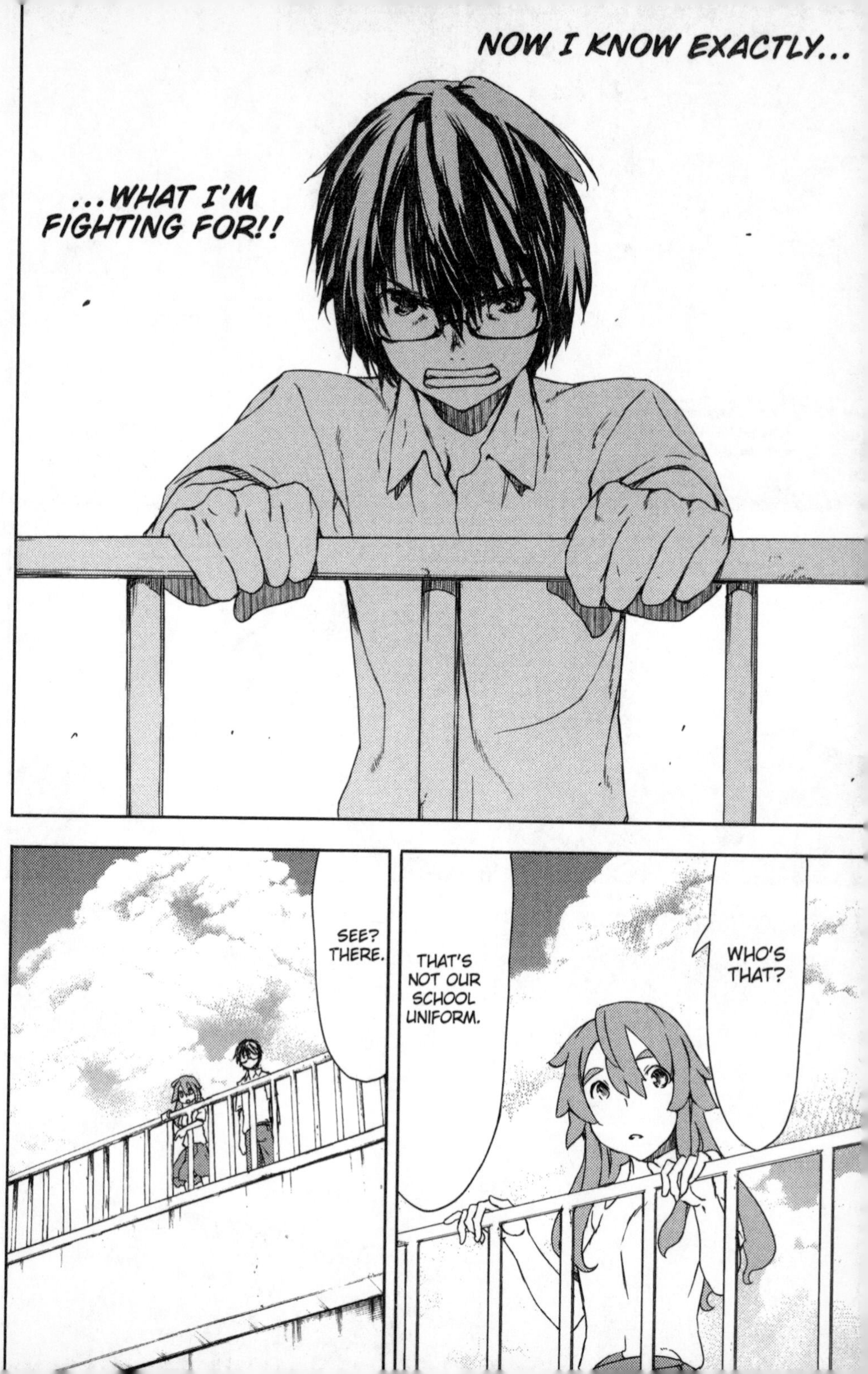
NOW I KNOW EXACTLY...
...WHAT I'M FIGHTING FOR!!
WHO'S THAT?
THAT'S NOT OUR SCHOOL UNIFORM.
SEE? THERE.

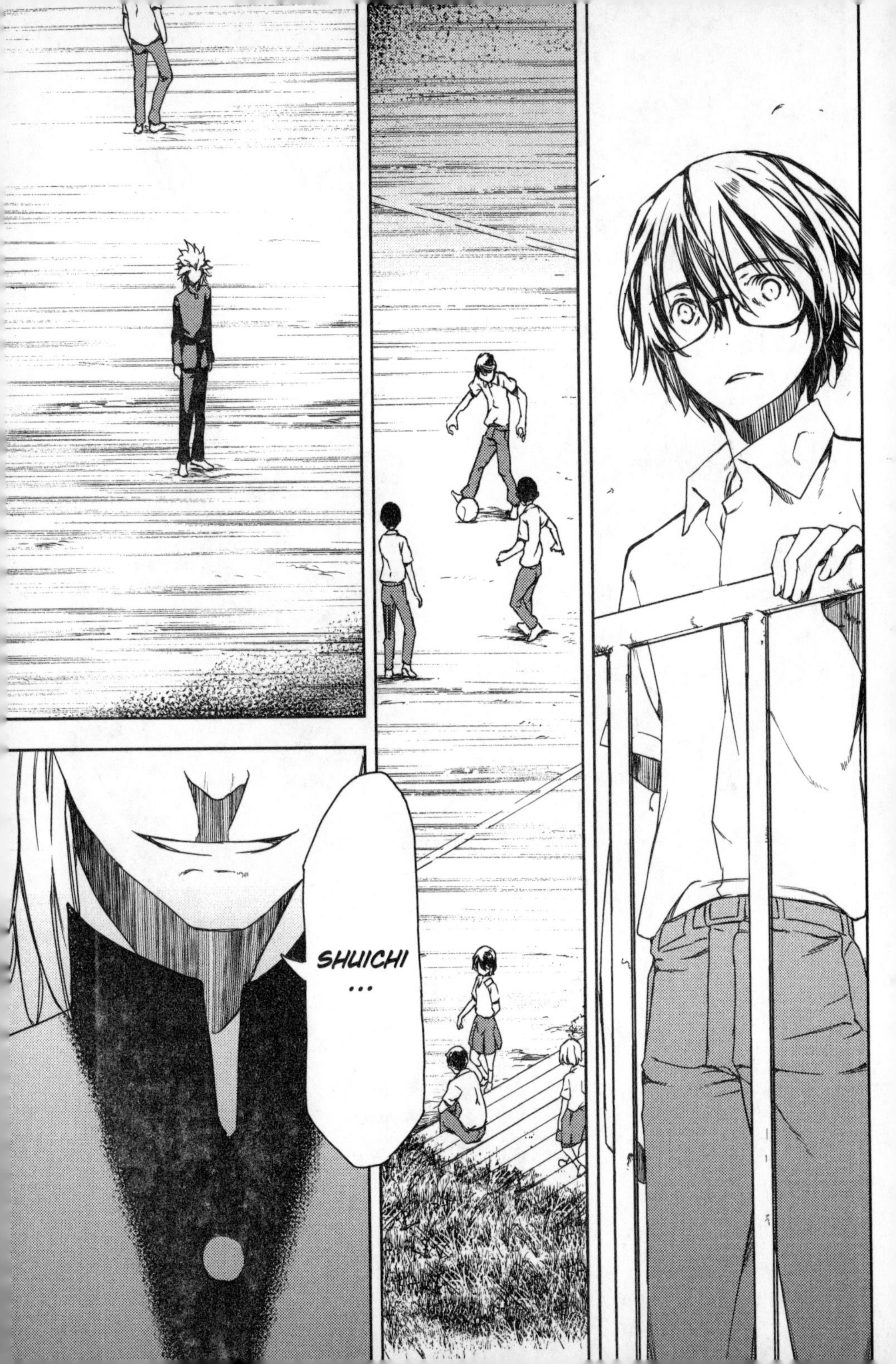
SHUICHI
...

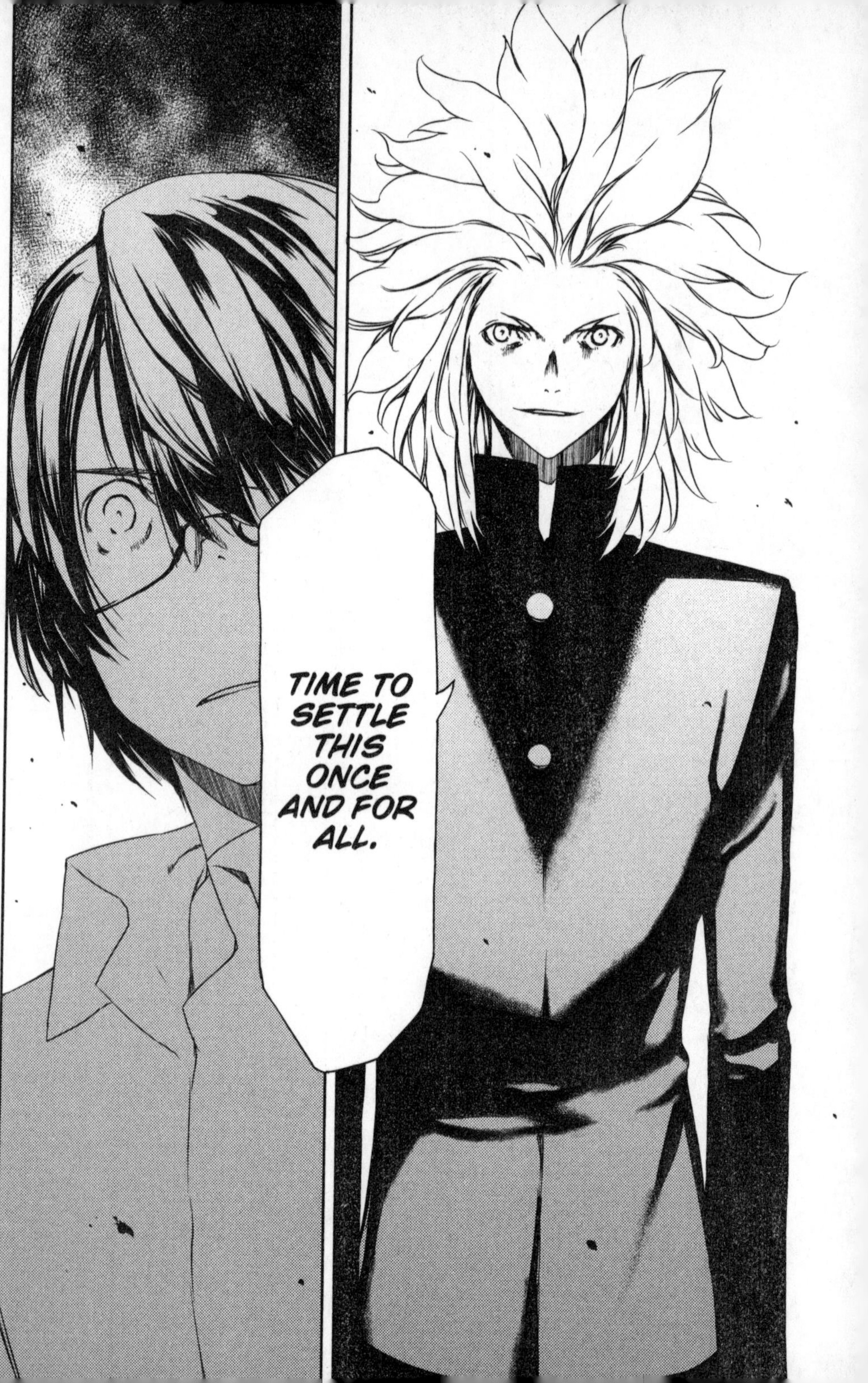
TIME TO SETTLE THIS ONCE AND FOR ALL.

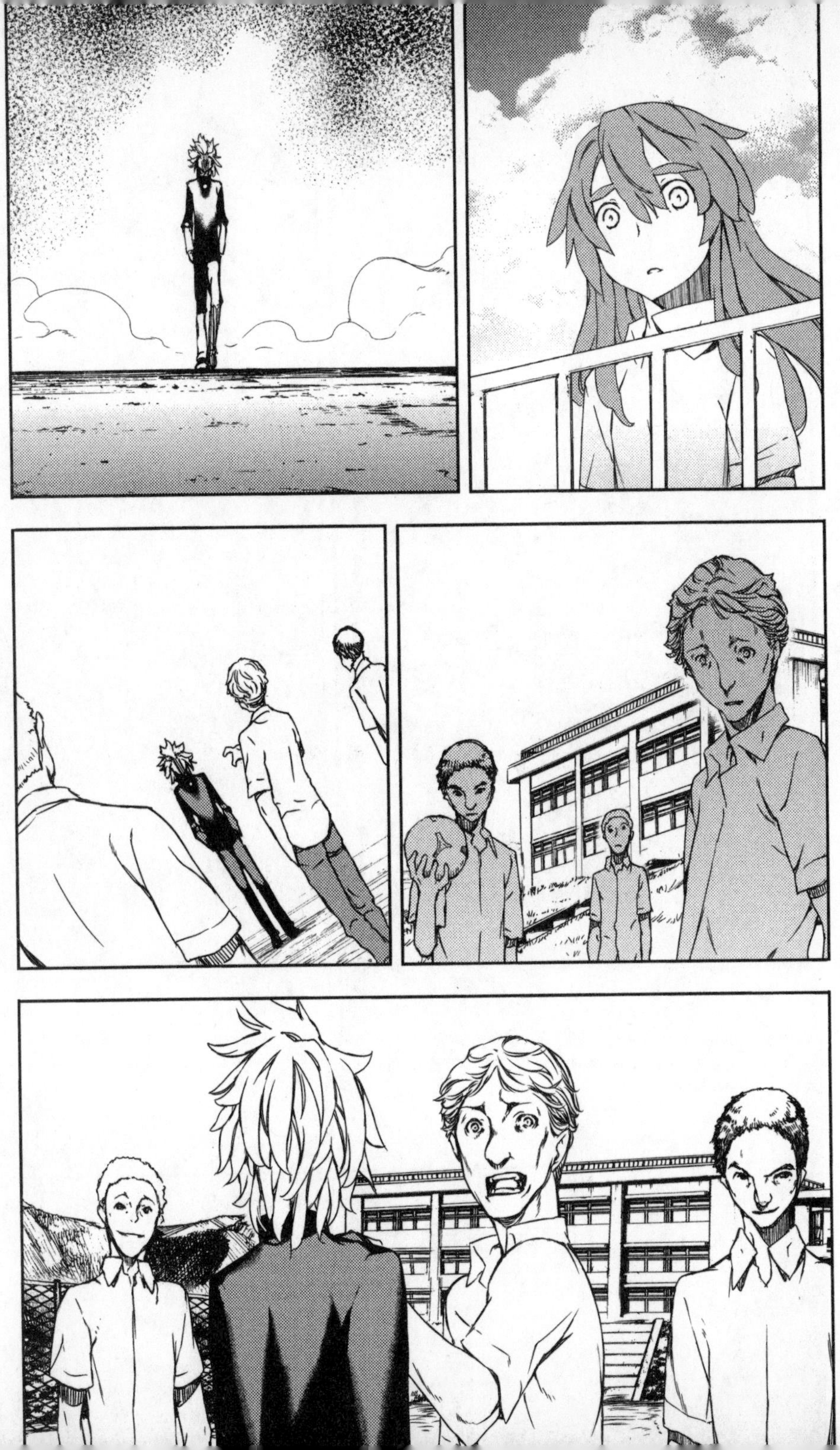

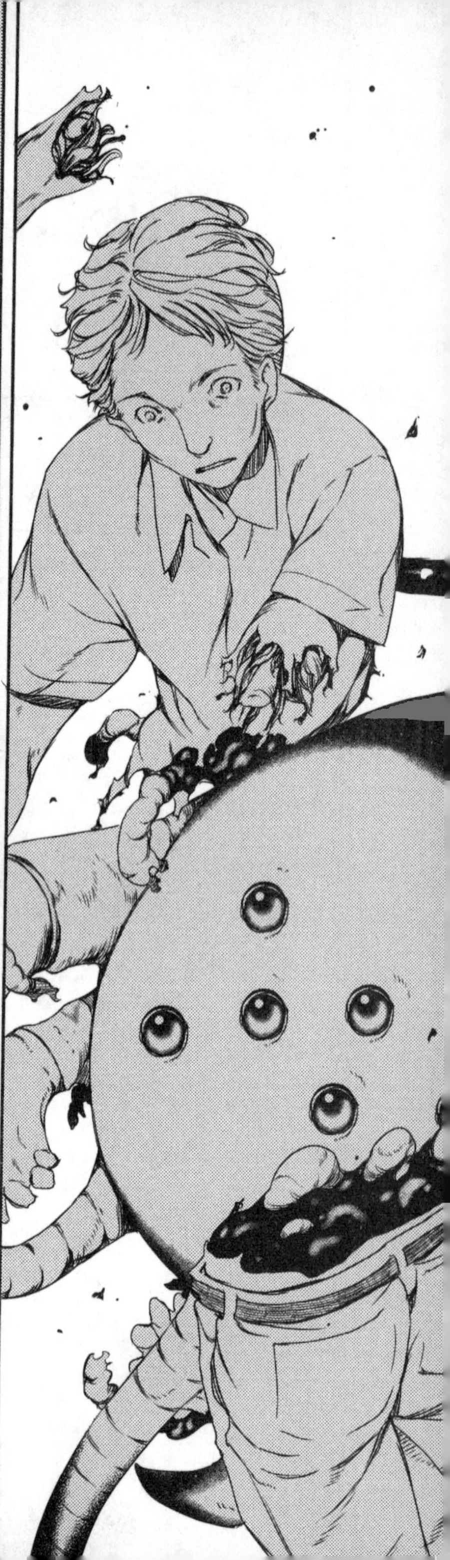
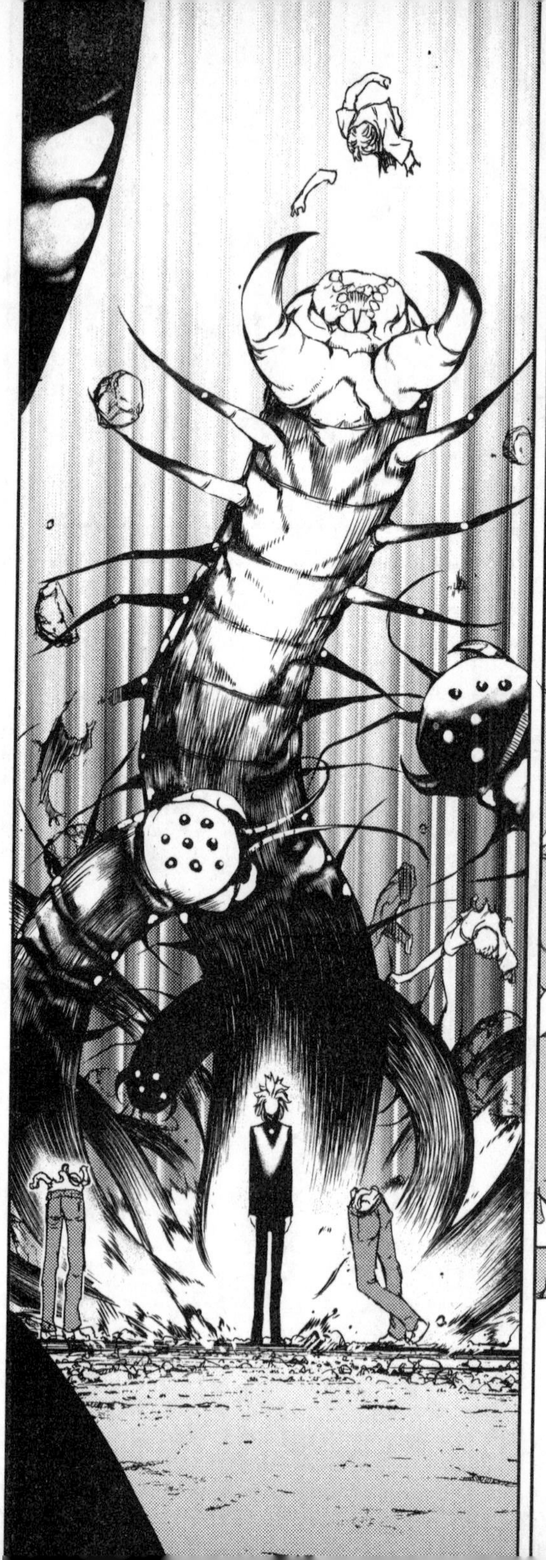

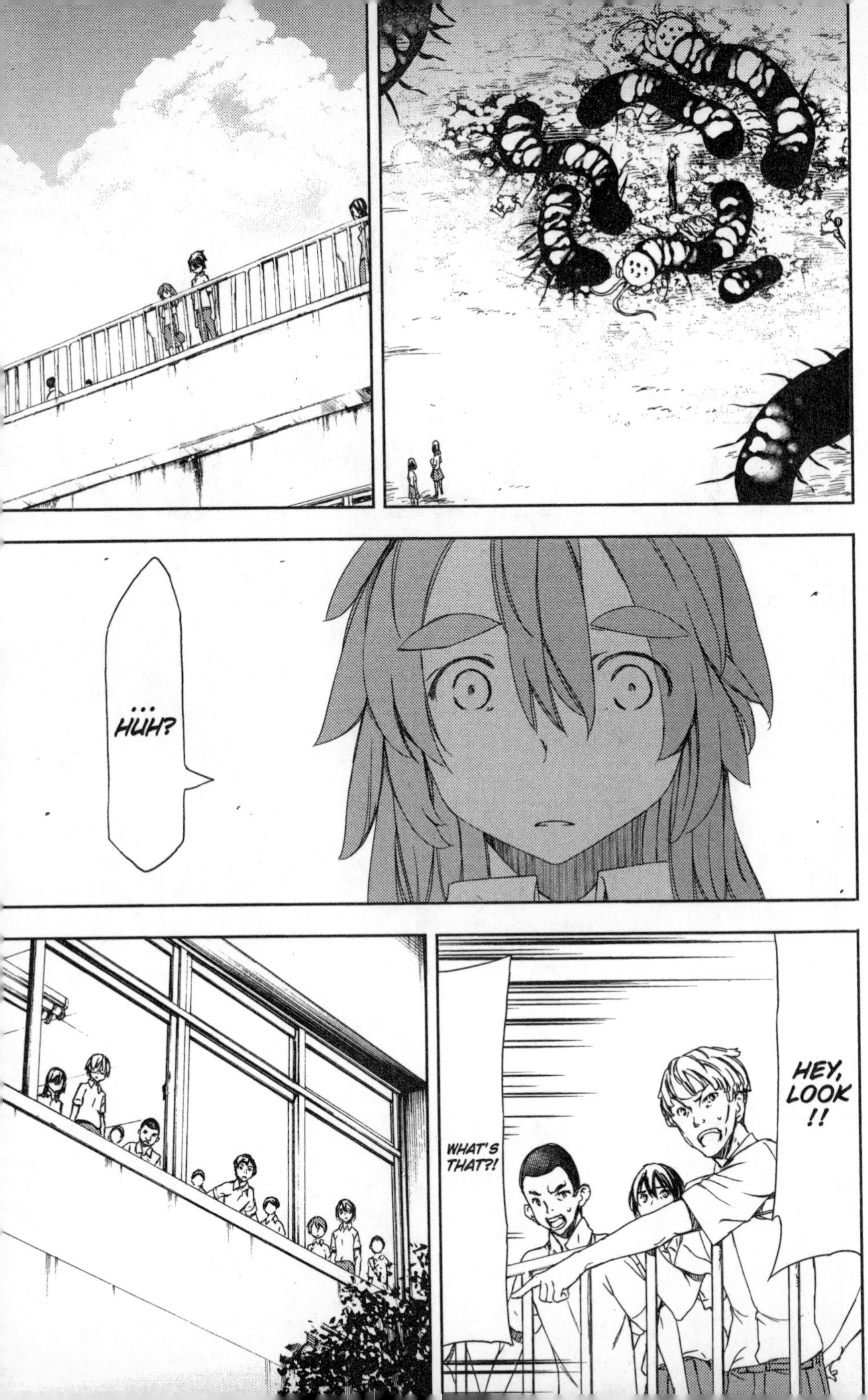
...HUH?
HEY, LOOK!!
WHAT'S THAT?!

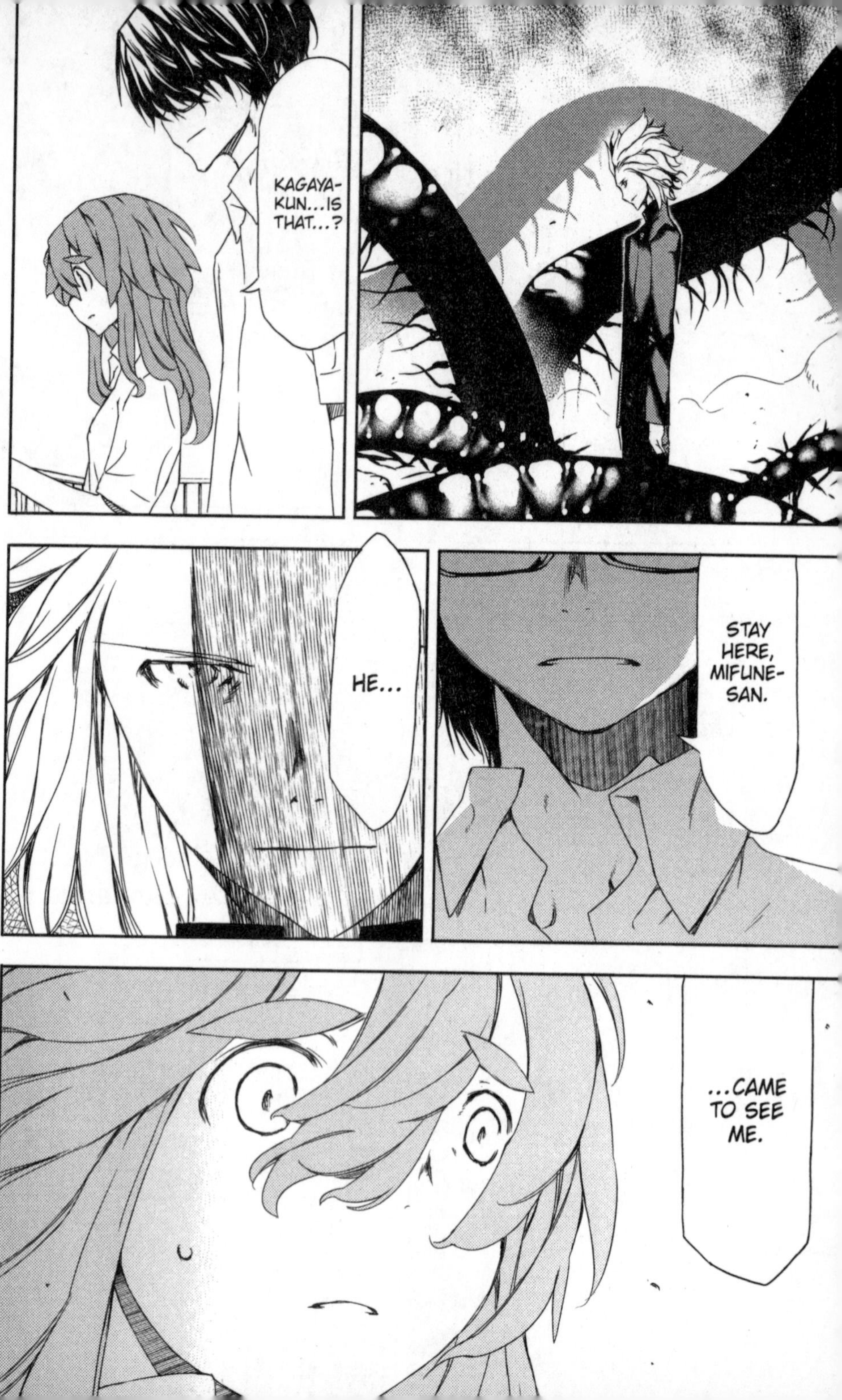
KAGAYA-KUN...IS THAT...?
STAY HERE, MIFUNE-SAN.
HE...
...CAME TO SEE ME.

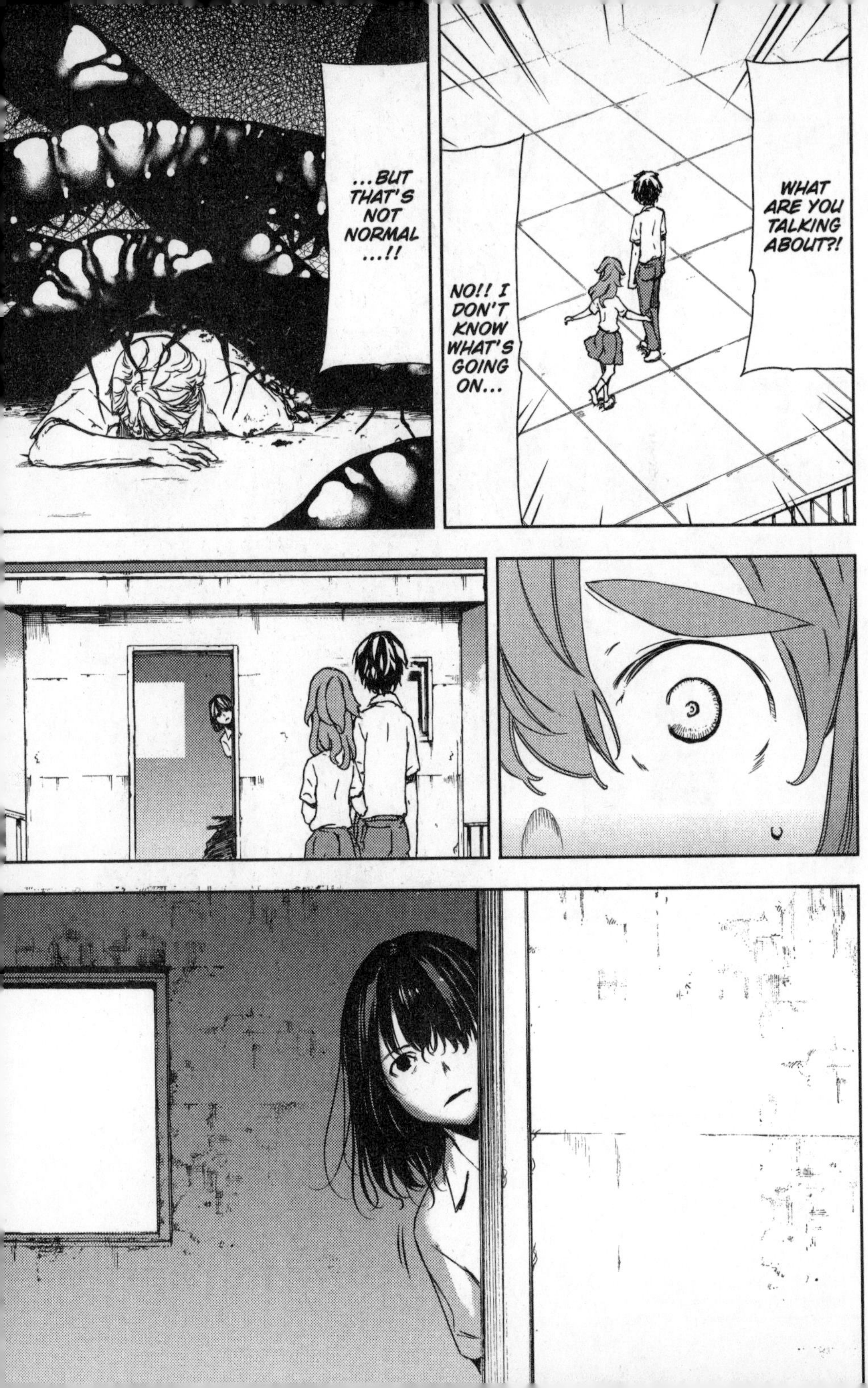
WHAT ARE YOU TALKING ABOUT?!
NO!! I DON'T KNOW WHAT'S GOING ON...
...BUT THAT'S NOT NORMAL...!!

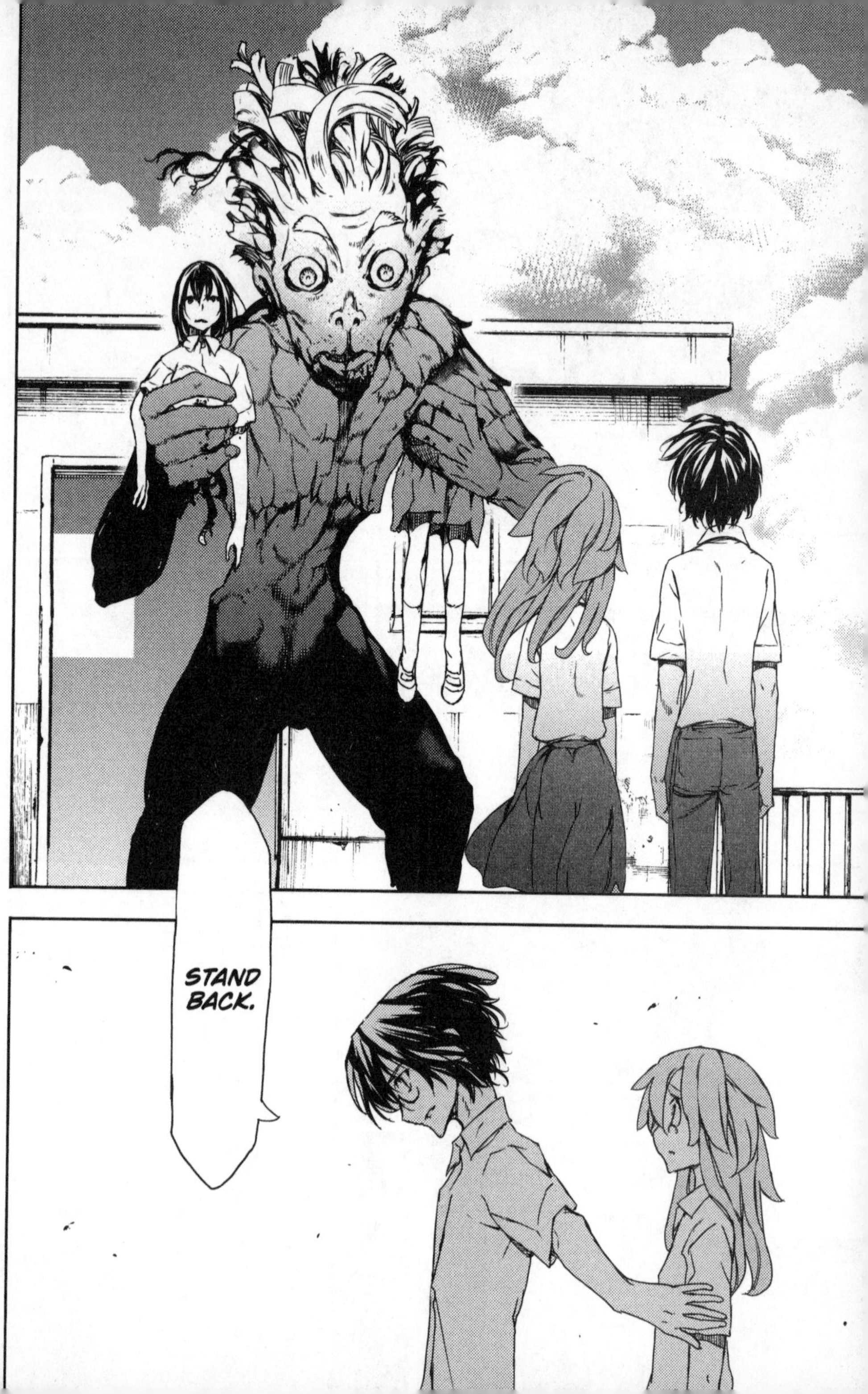
STAND BACK.

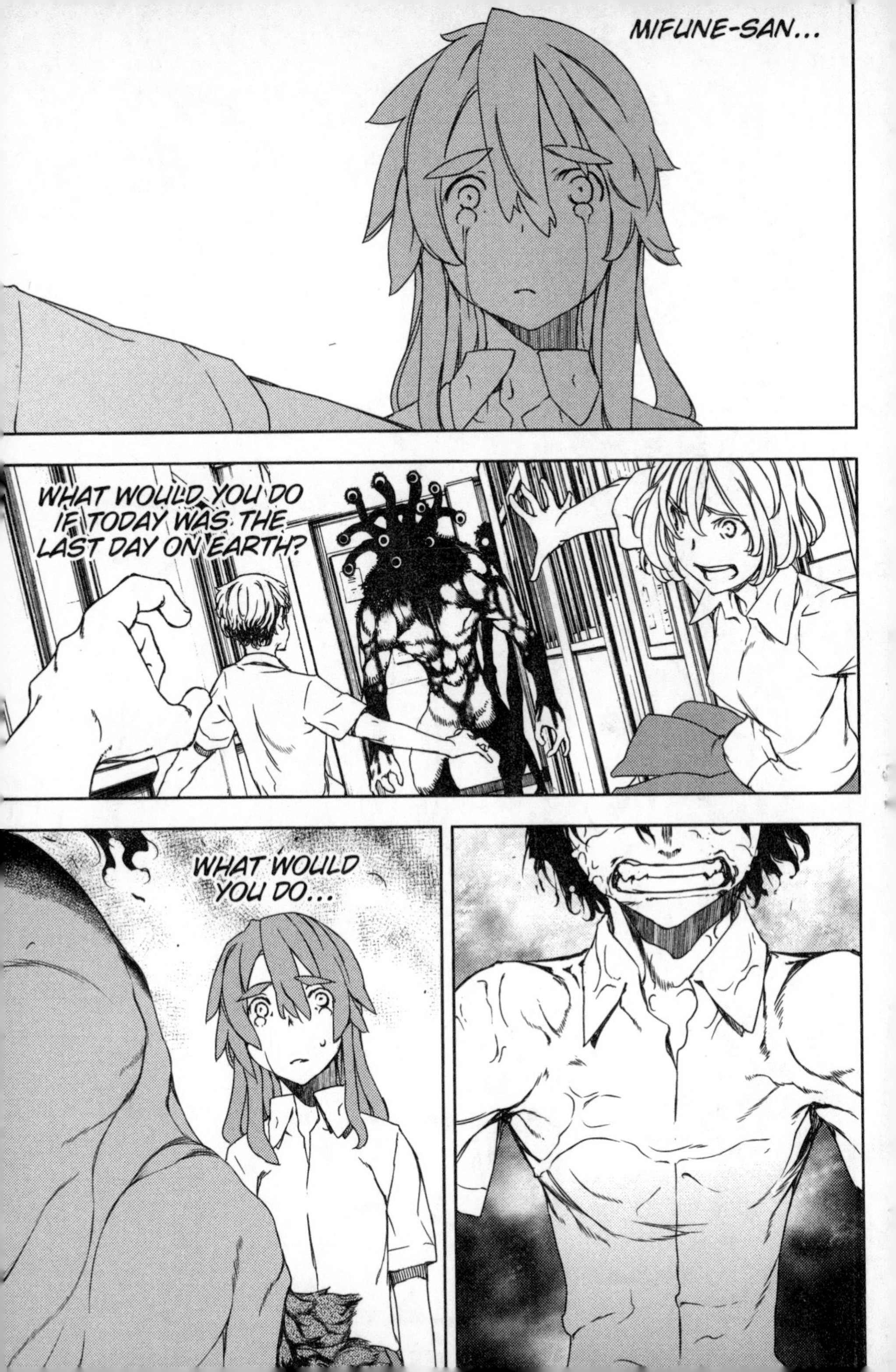
MIFUNE-SAN...
WHAT WOULD YOU DO IF TODAY WAS THE LAST DAY ON EARTH?
WHAT WOULD YOU DO...

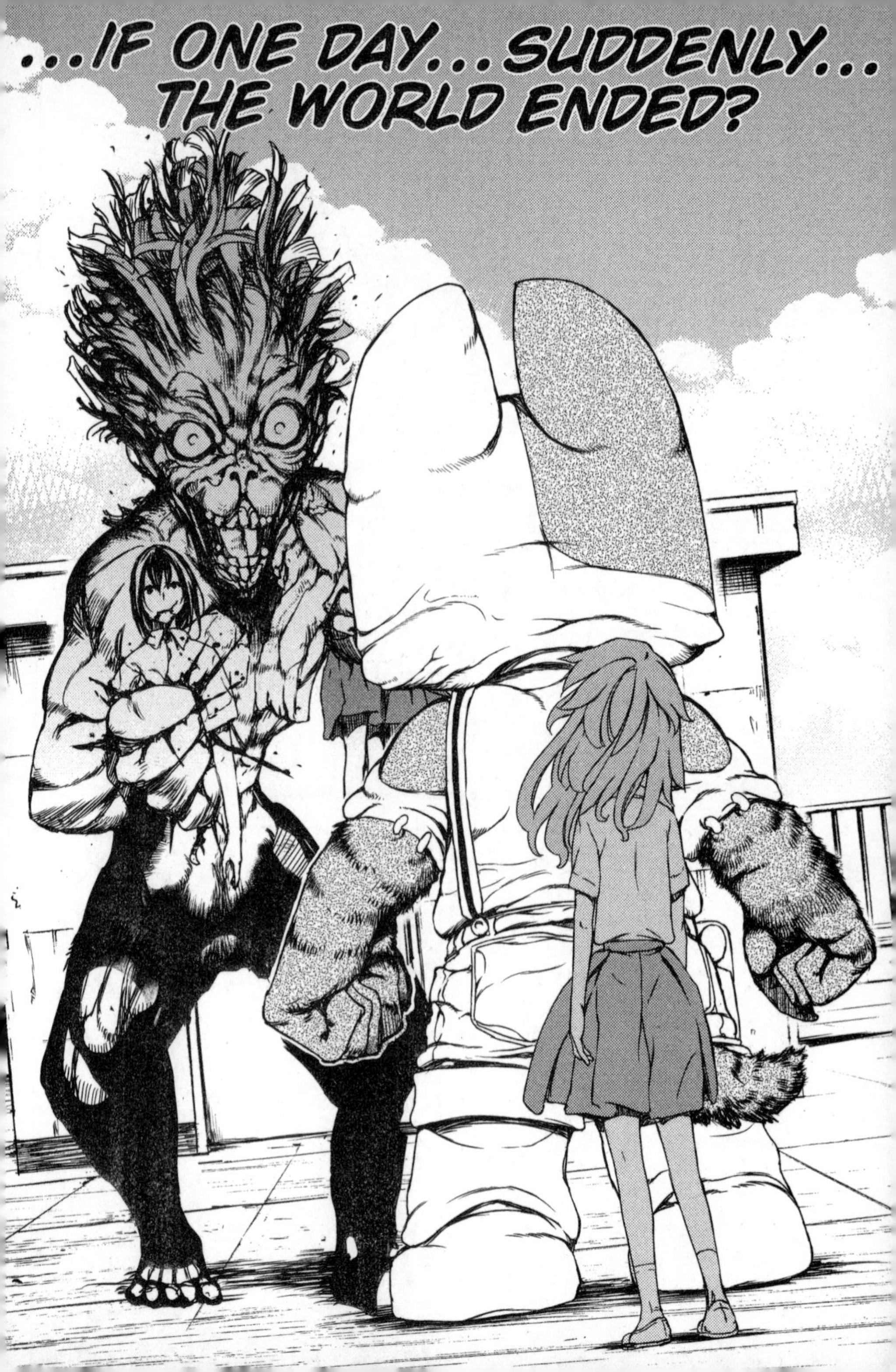
...IF ONE DAY...SUDDENLY...
THE WORLD ENDED?

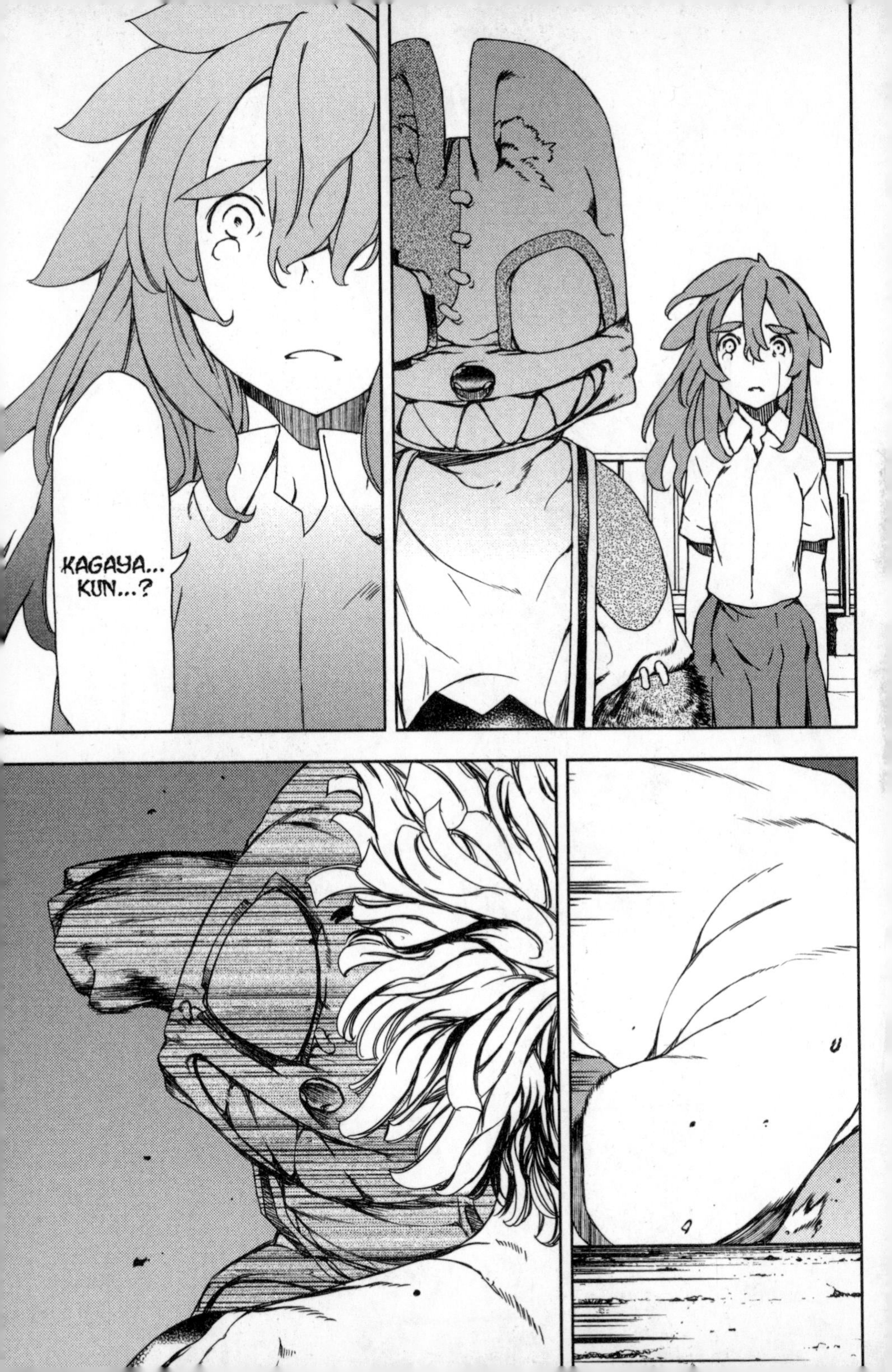
KAGAYA...
KUN...?

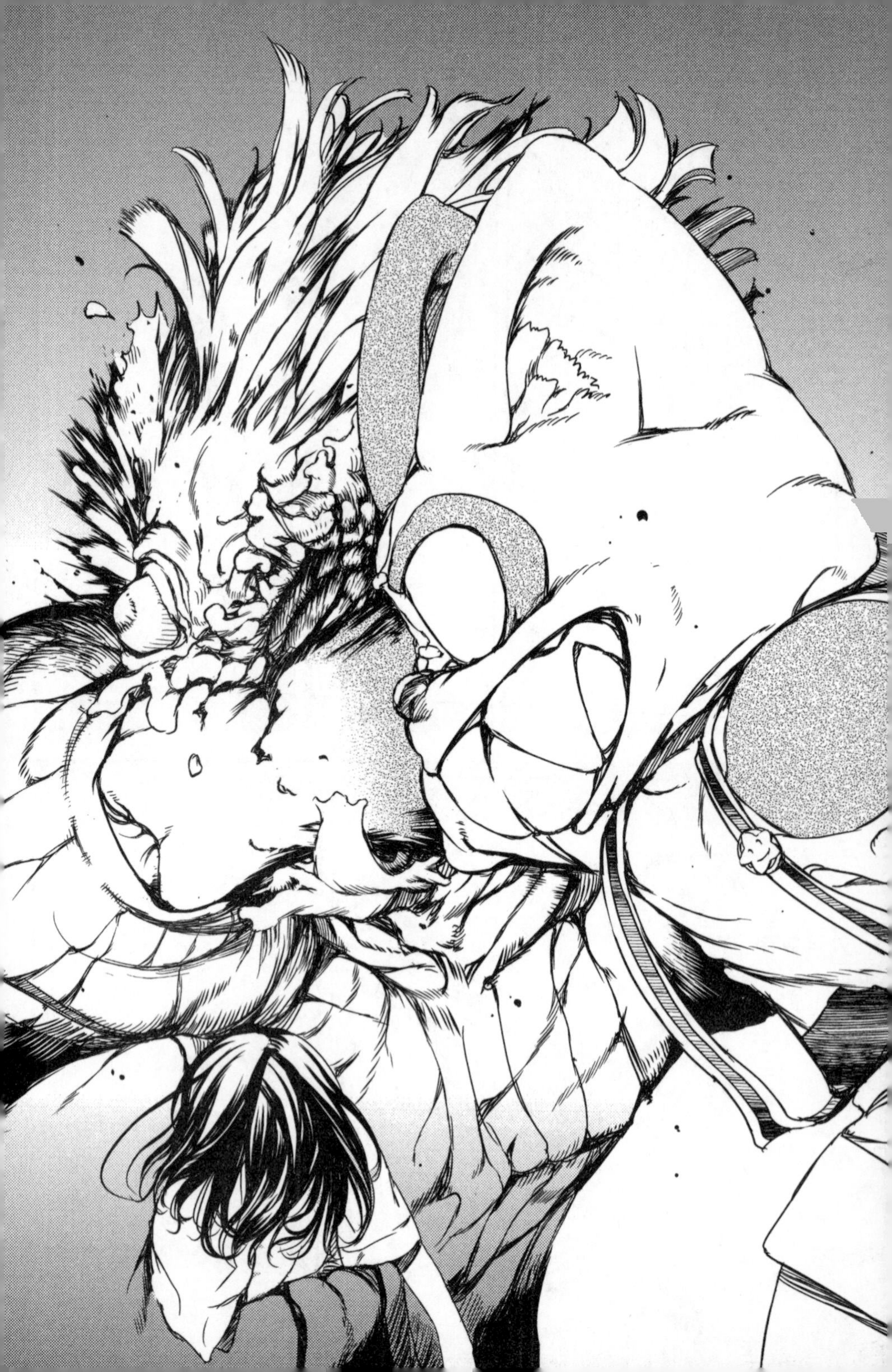

NOW THAT PEOPLE HAVE SEEN ME LIKE THIS...

...I...

CHAPTER 63

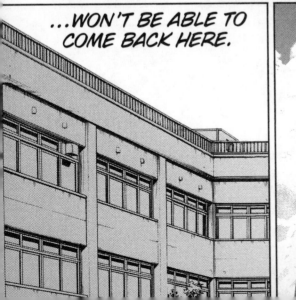

...WON'T BE ABLE TO COME BACK HERE.

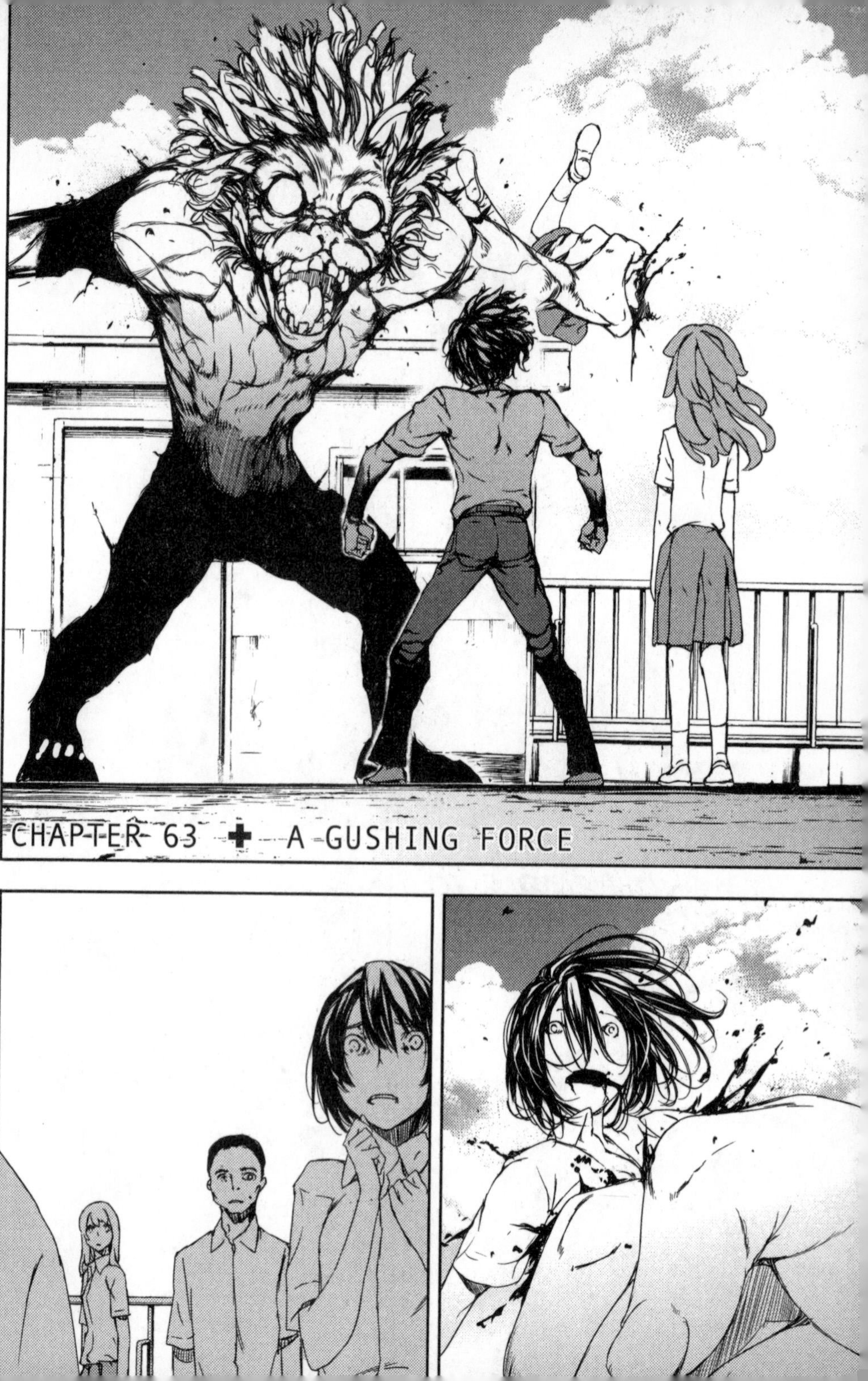
CHAPTER 63 ✚ A GUSHING FORCE

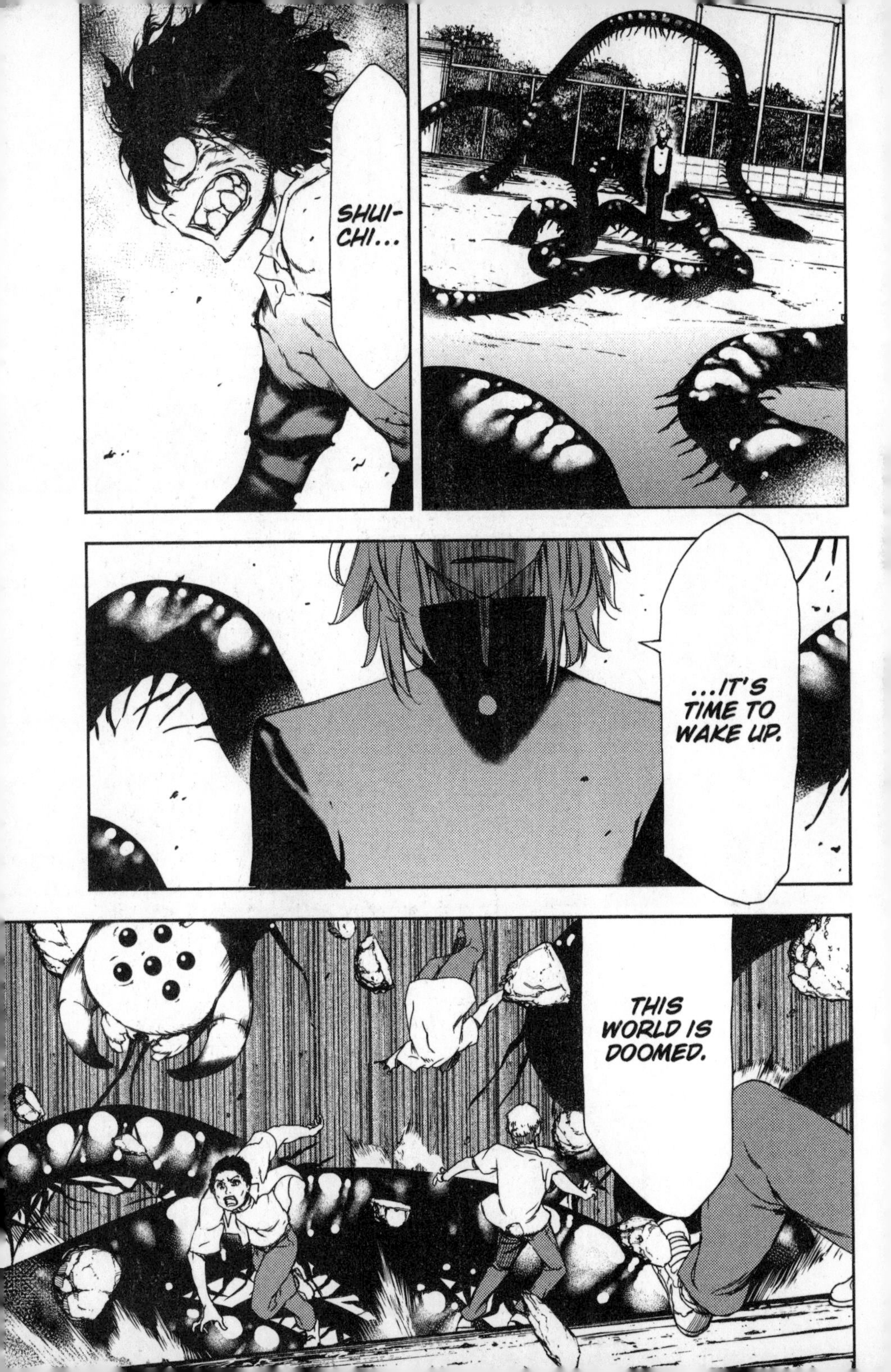
SHUI-CHI...
...IT'S TIME TO WAKE UP.
THIS WORLD IS DOOMED.

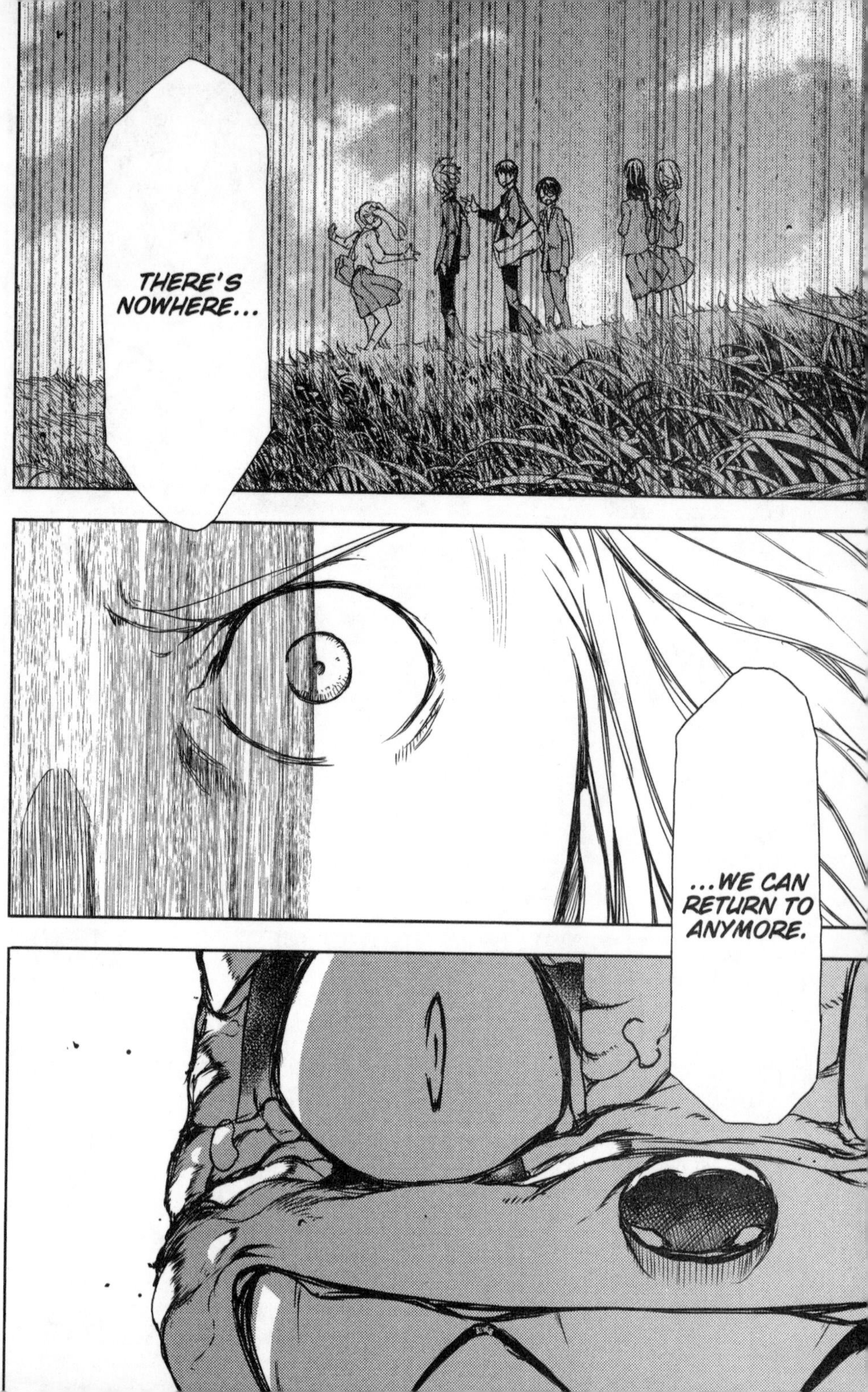
THERE'S NOWHERE...
...WE CAN RETURN TO ANYMORE.

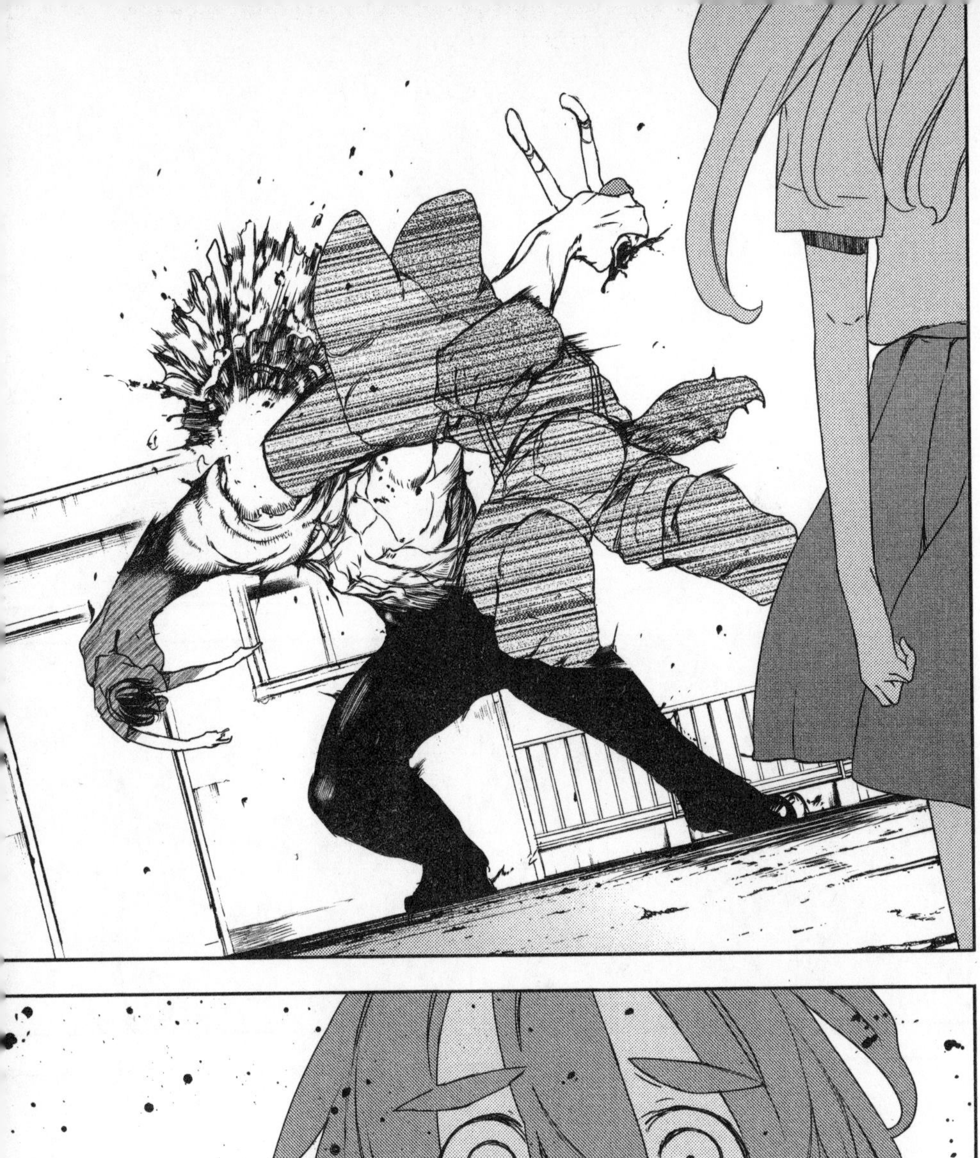
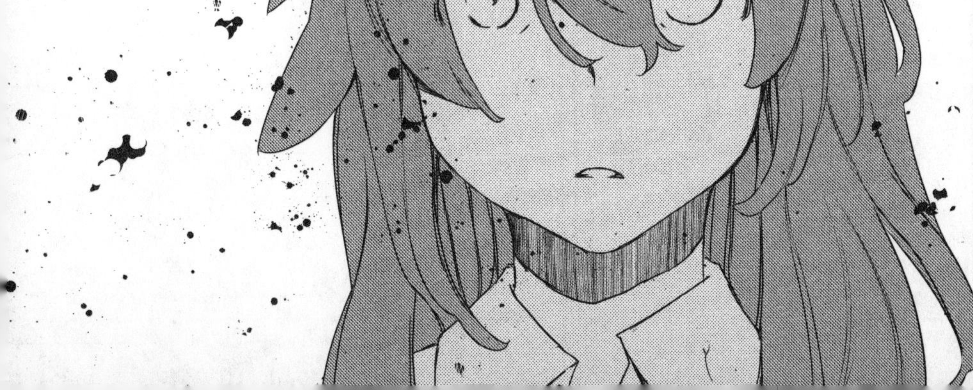

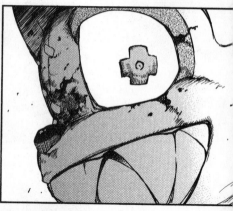

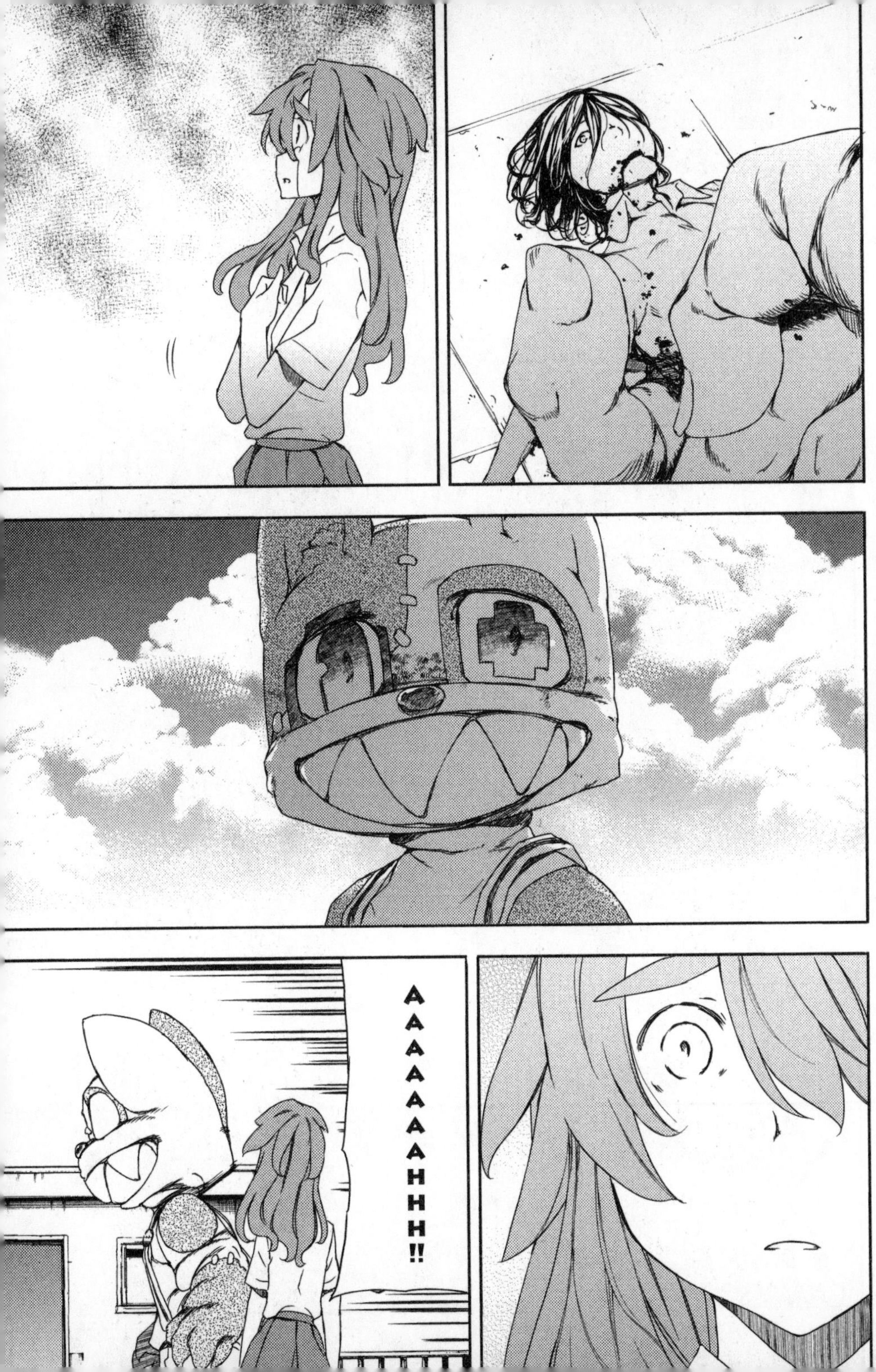
AAAAAAAAHHH!!

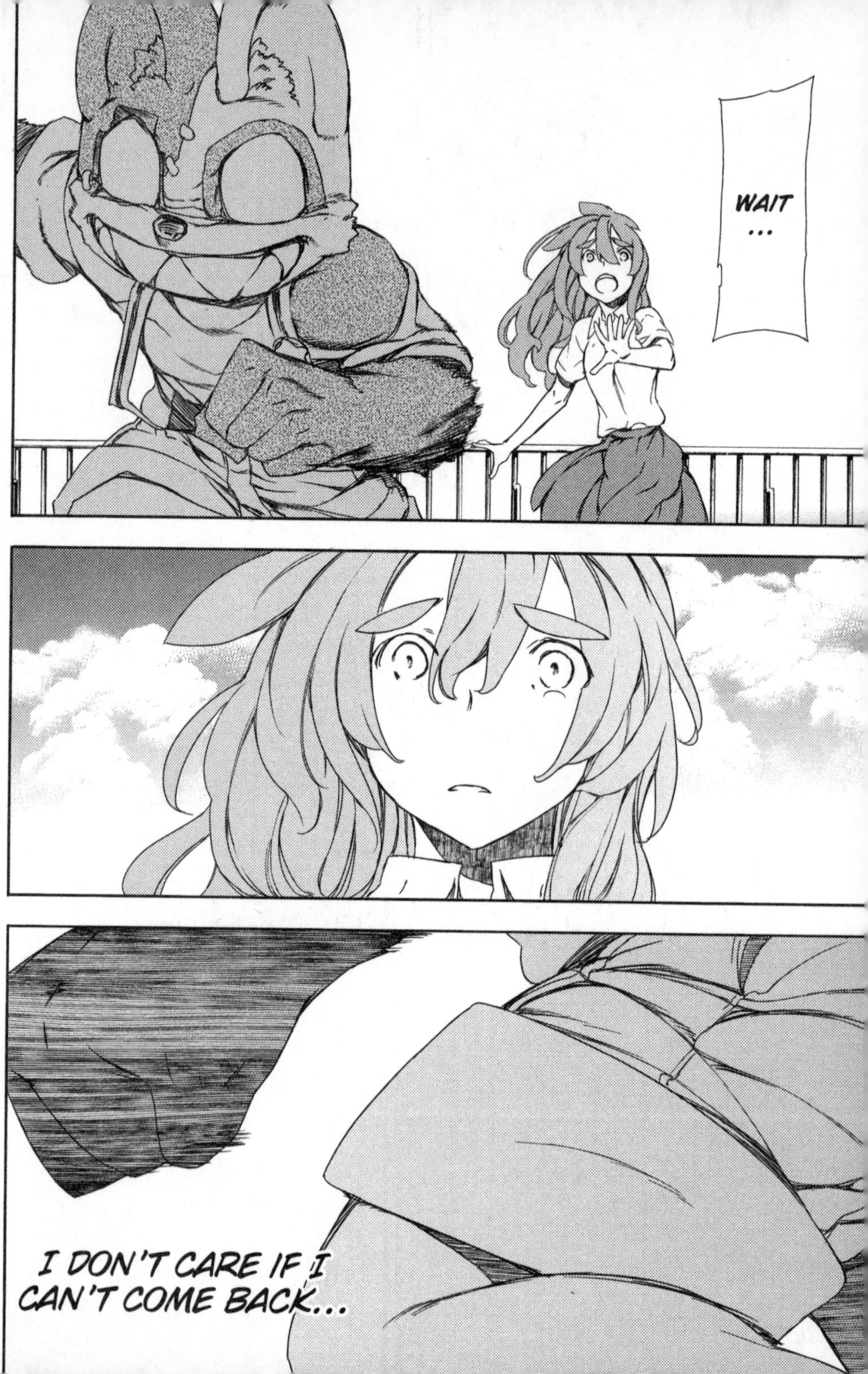
WAIT
...
I DON'T CARE IF I CAN'T COME BACK...

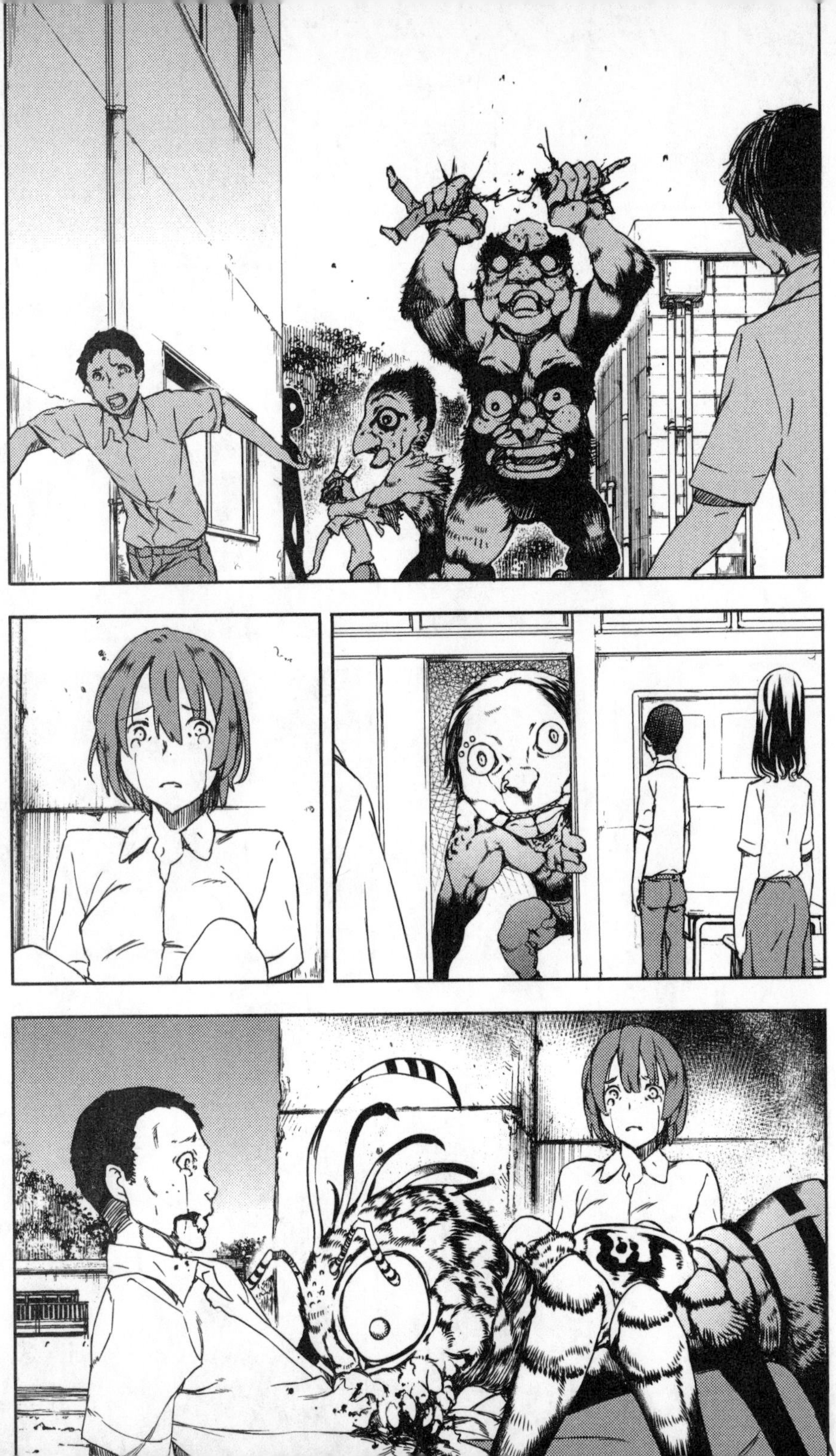

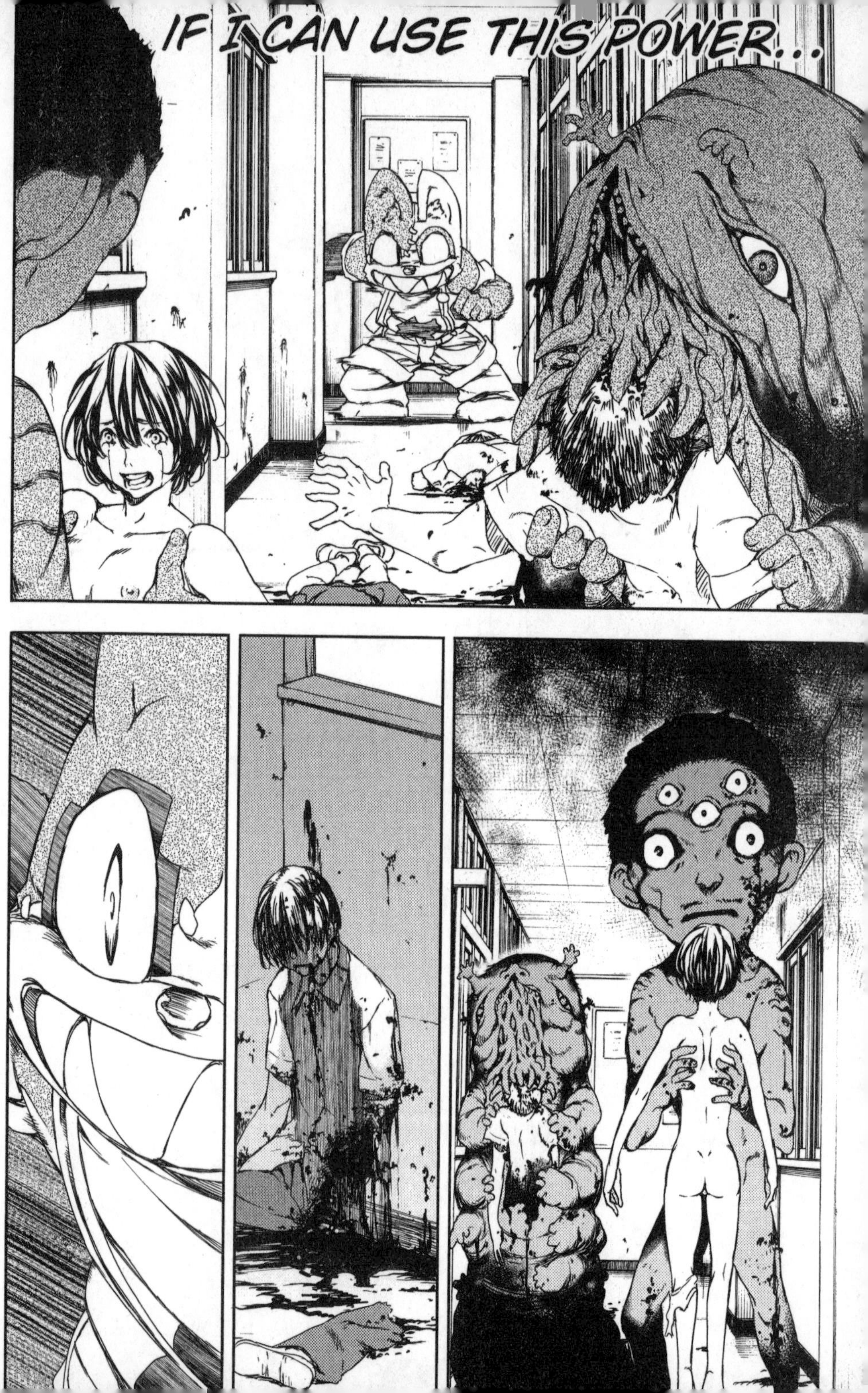
IF I CAN USE THIS POWER...

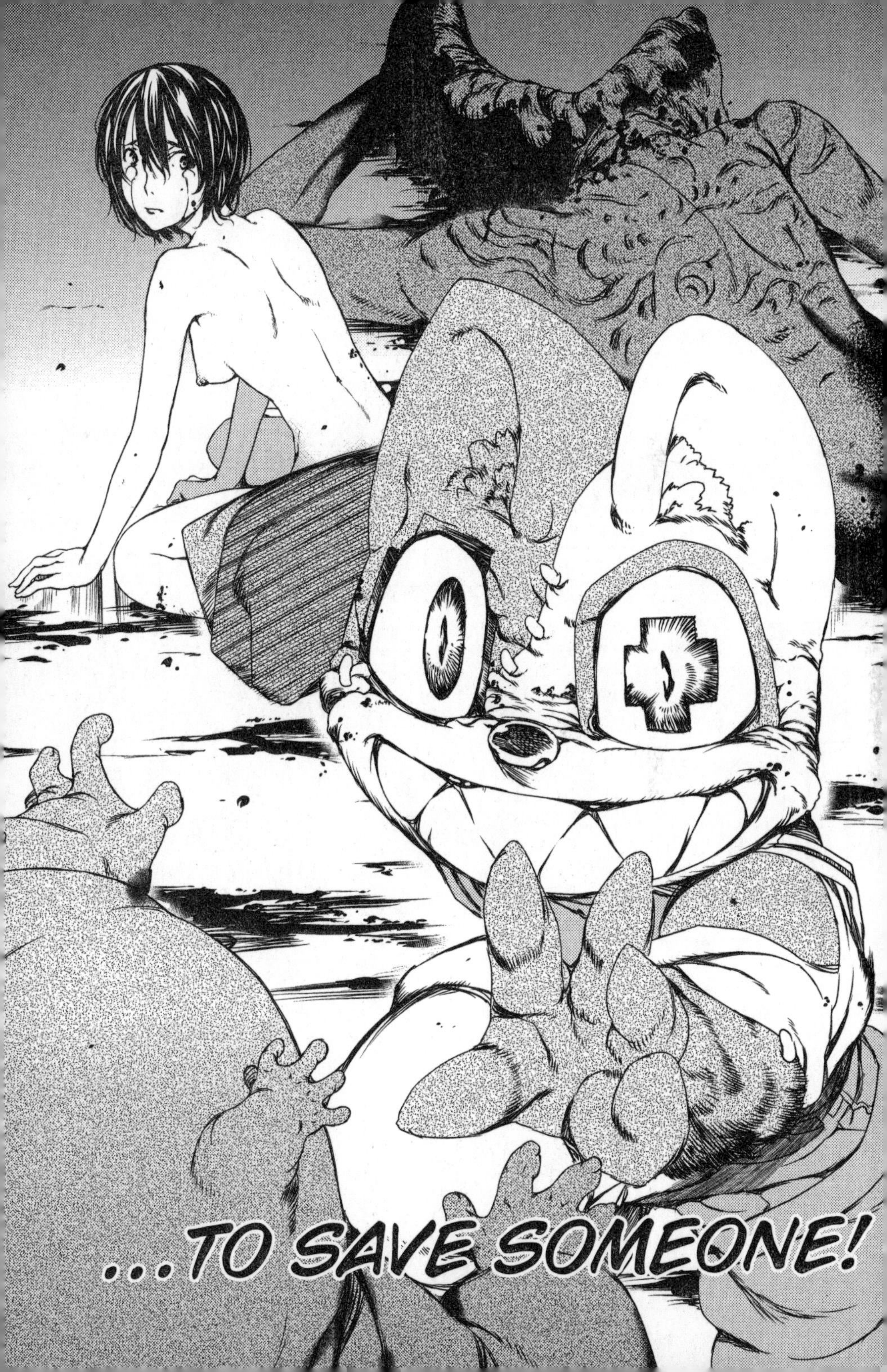
...TO SAVE SOMEONE!

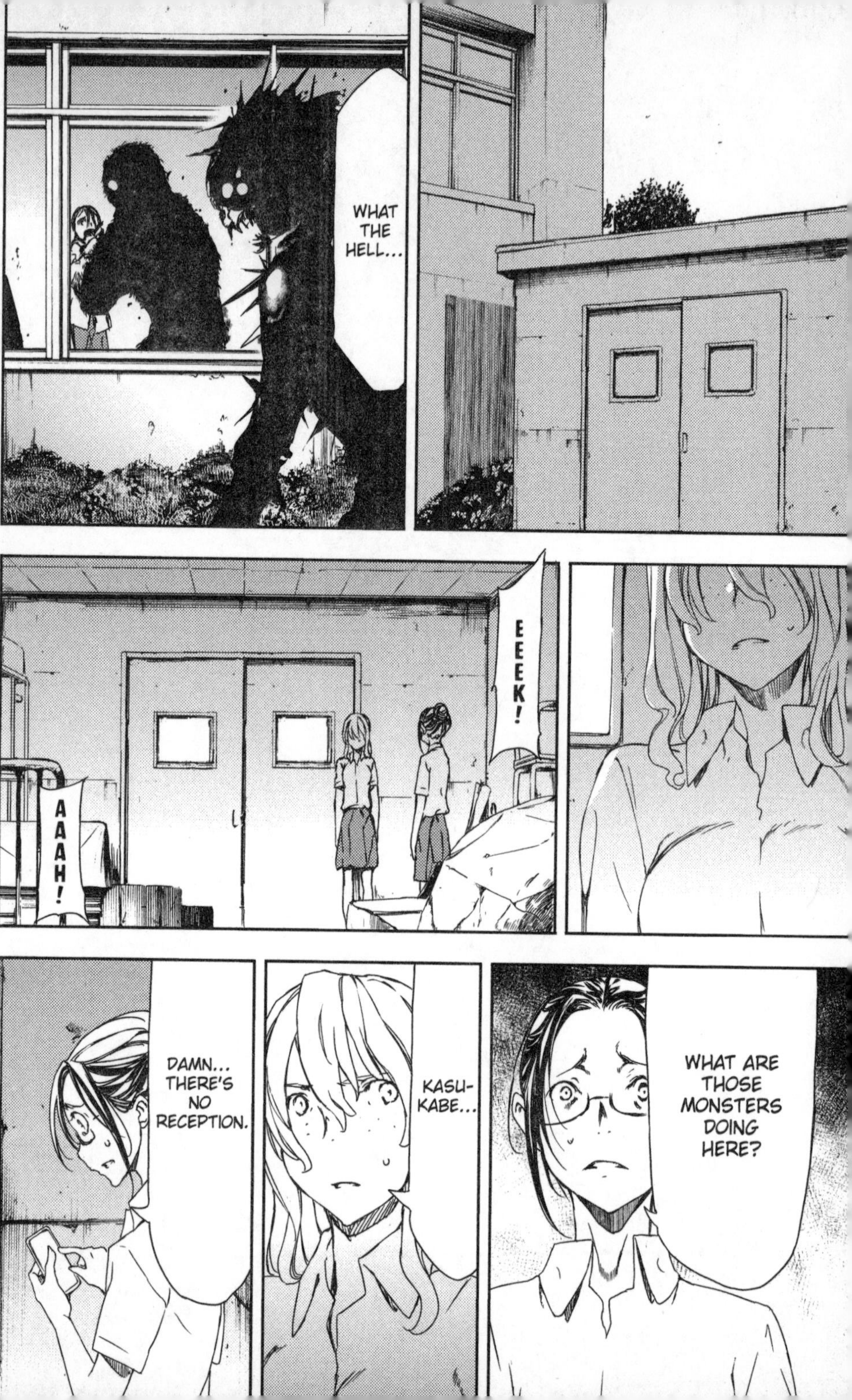
WHAT THE HELL...
EEEK!
AAAH!
WHAT ARE THOSE MONSTERS DOING HERE?
KASU-KABE...
DAMN... THERE'S NO RECEPTION.

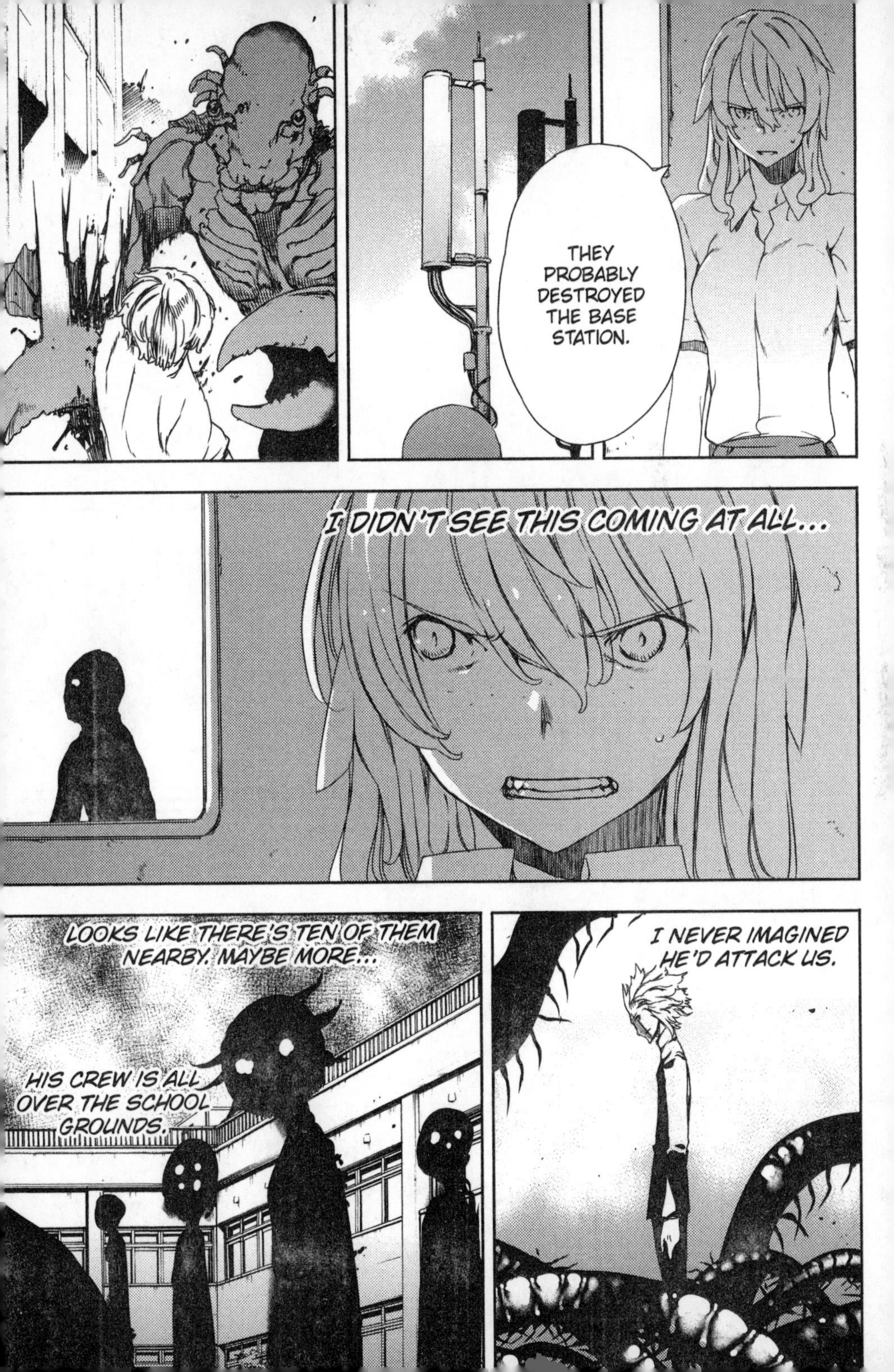
THEY PROBABLY DESTROYED THE BASE STATION.
I DIDN'T SEE THIS COMING AT ALL...
I NEVER IMAGINED HE'D ATTACK US.
LOOKS LIKE THERE'S TEN OF THEM NEARBY. MAYBE MORE...
HIS CREW IS ALL OVER THE SCHOOL GROUNDS.

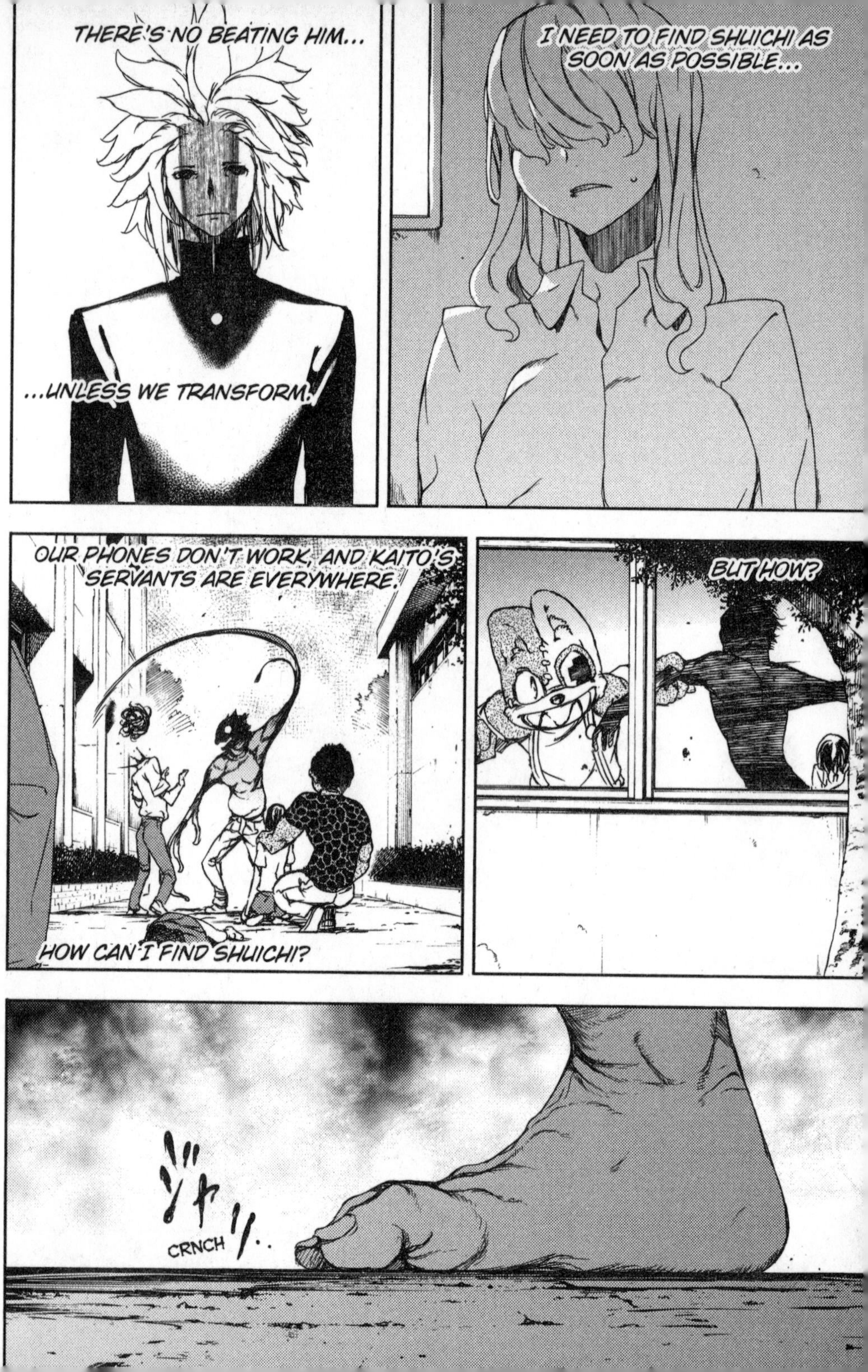
I NEED TO FIND SHUICHI AS SOON AS POSSIBLE...
THERE'S NO BEATING HIM...
...UNLESS WE TRANSFORM.
BUT HOW?
OUR PHONES DON'T WORK, AND KAITO'S SERVANTS ARE EVERYWHERE.
HOW CAN I FIND SHUICHI?
ジャリッ..
CRNCH

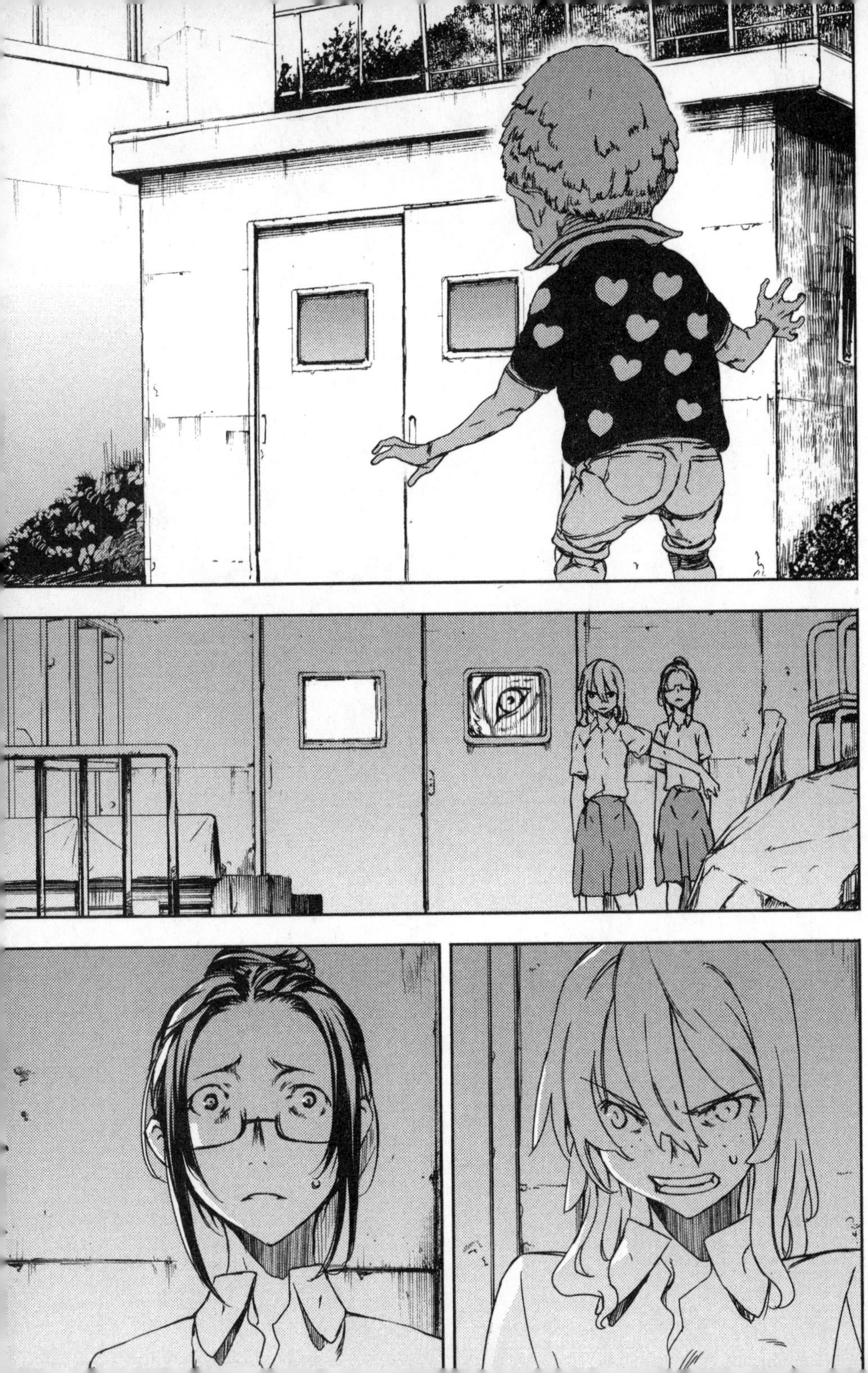

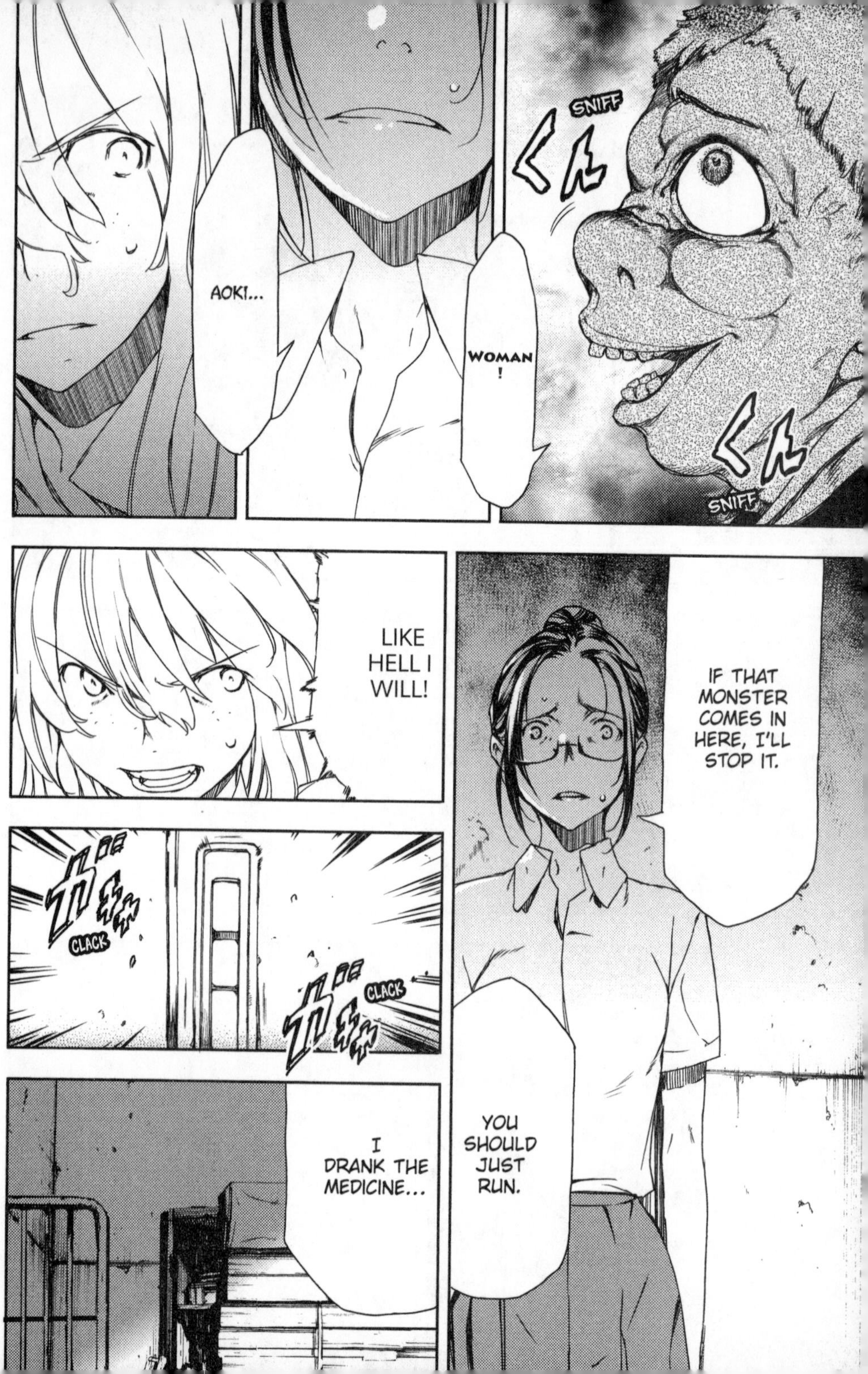
SNIFF
WOMAN!
SNIFF
AOKI...
IF THAT MONSTER COMES IN HERE, I'LL STOP IT.
YOU SHOULD JUST RUN.
LIKE HELL I WILL!
CLACK
CLACK
I DRANK THE MEDICINE...

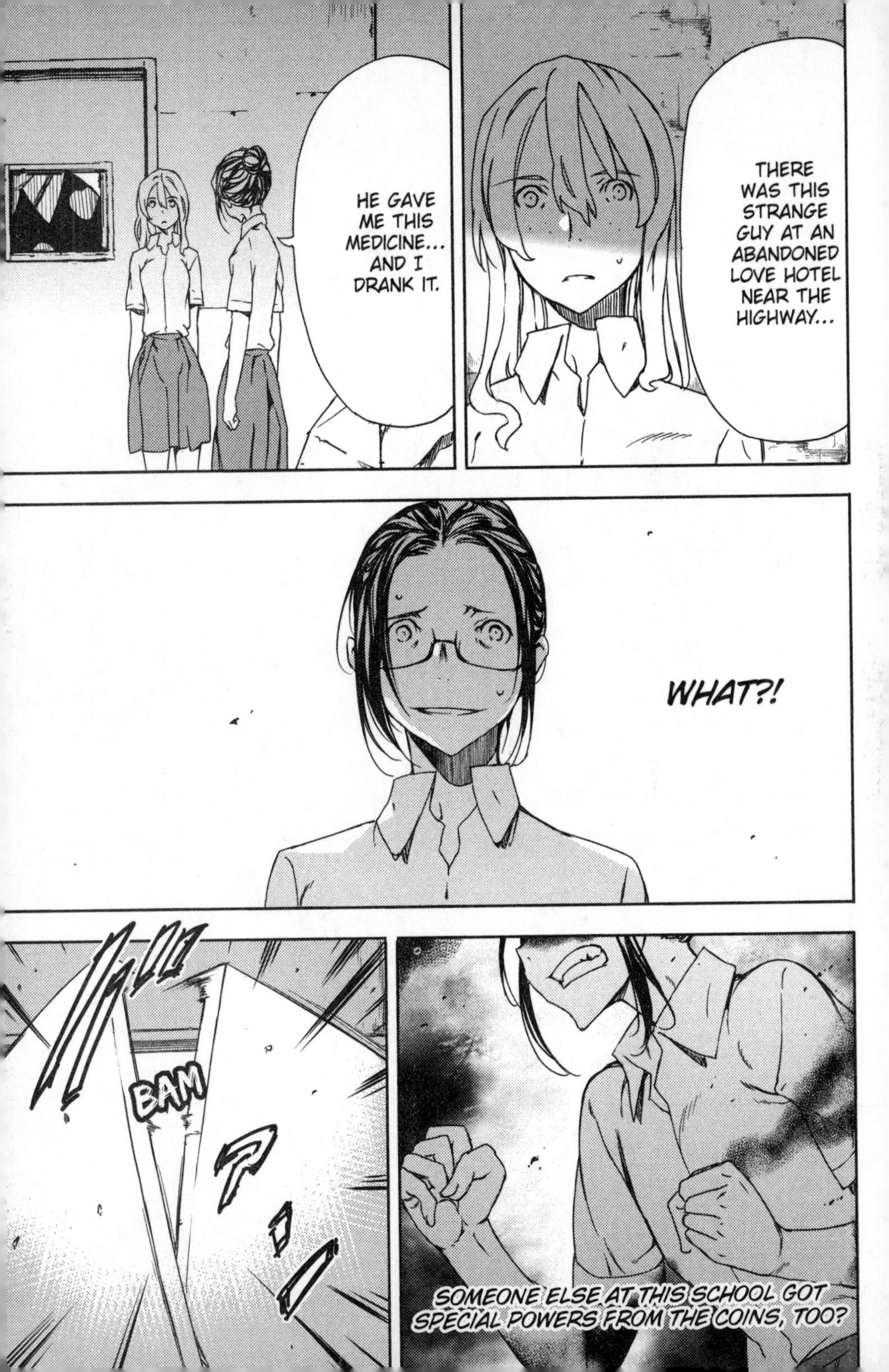
THERE WAS THIS STRANGE GUY AT AN ABANDONED LOVE HOTEL NEAR THE HIGHWAY...
HE GAVE ME THIS MEDICINE... AND I DRANK IT.
WHAT?!
SOMEONE ELSE AT THIS SCHOOL GOT SPECIAL POWERS FROM THE COINS, TOO?
BAM

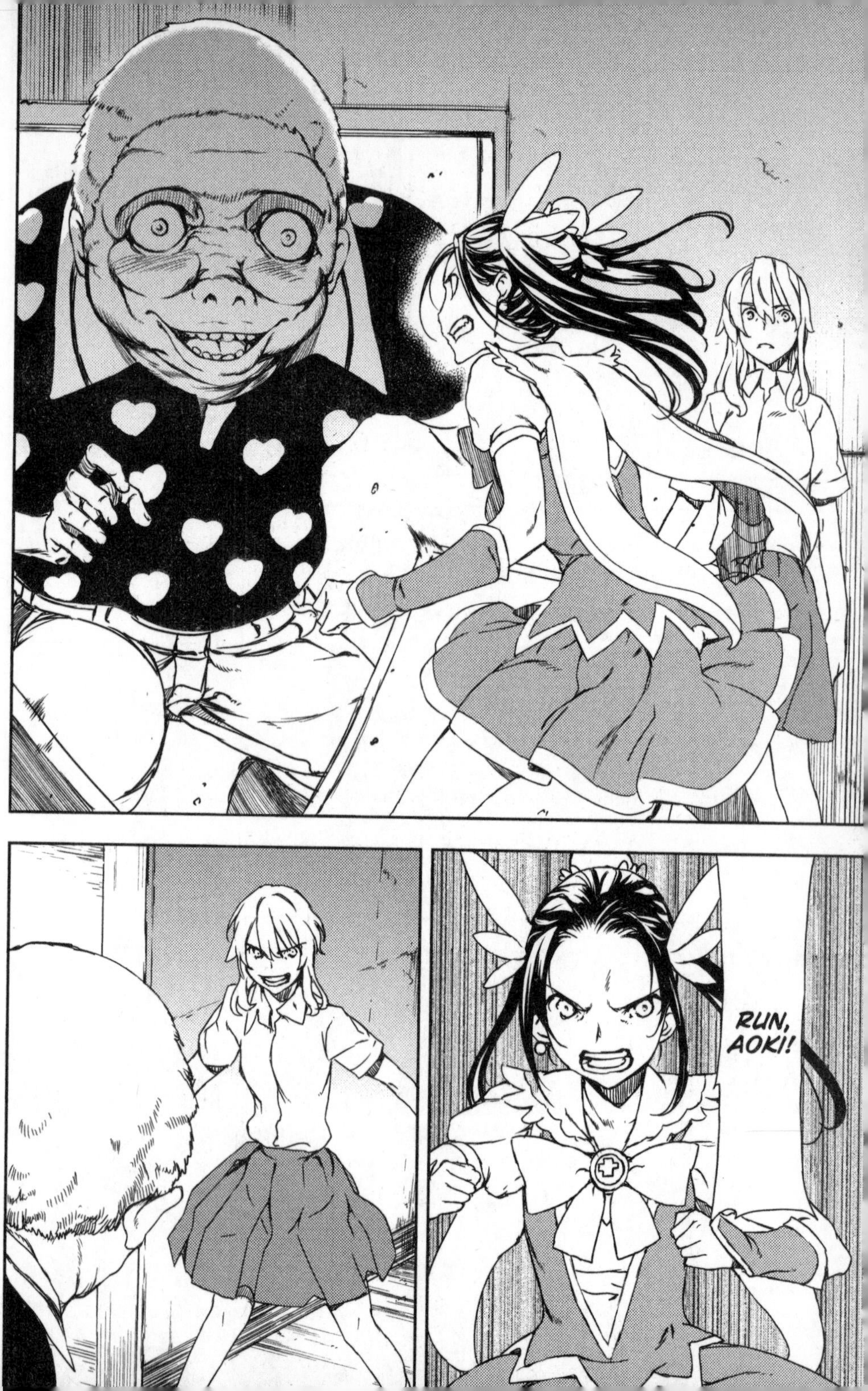
RUN, AOKI!

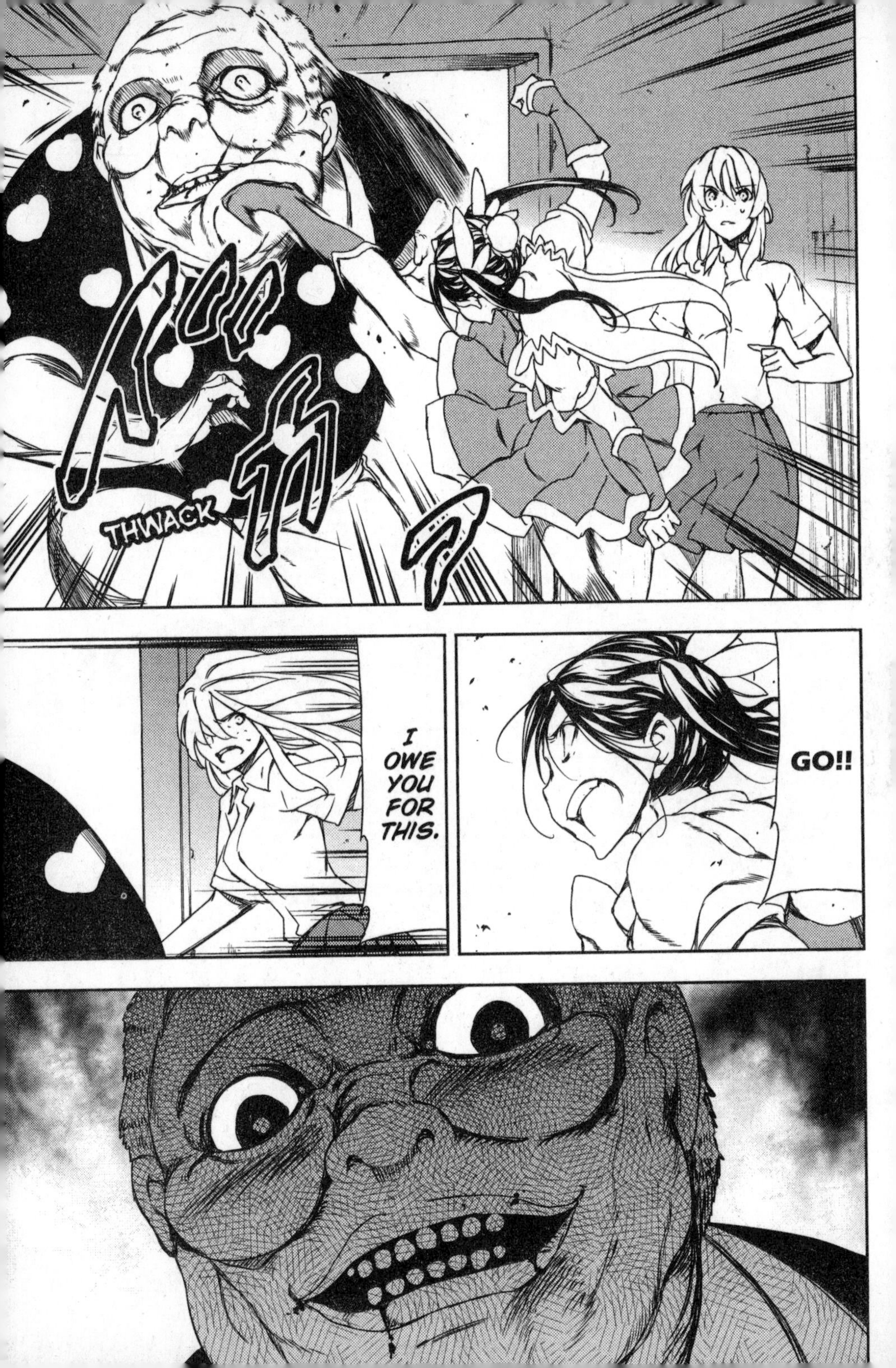
THWACK
GO!!
I OWE YOU FOR THIS.

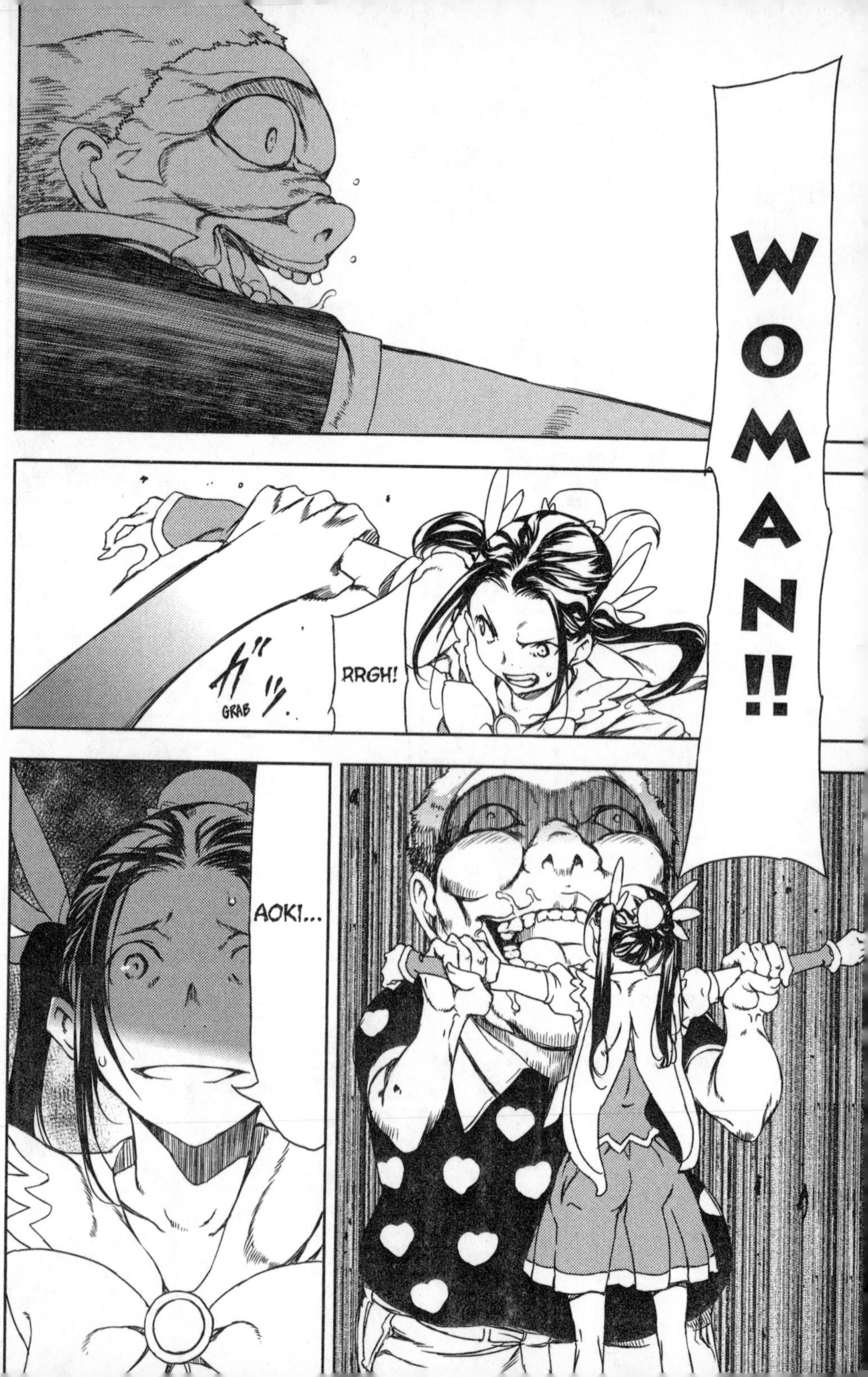
WOMAN!!
RRGH!
ガッ
GRAB
AOKI...

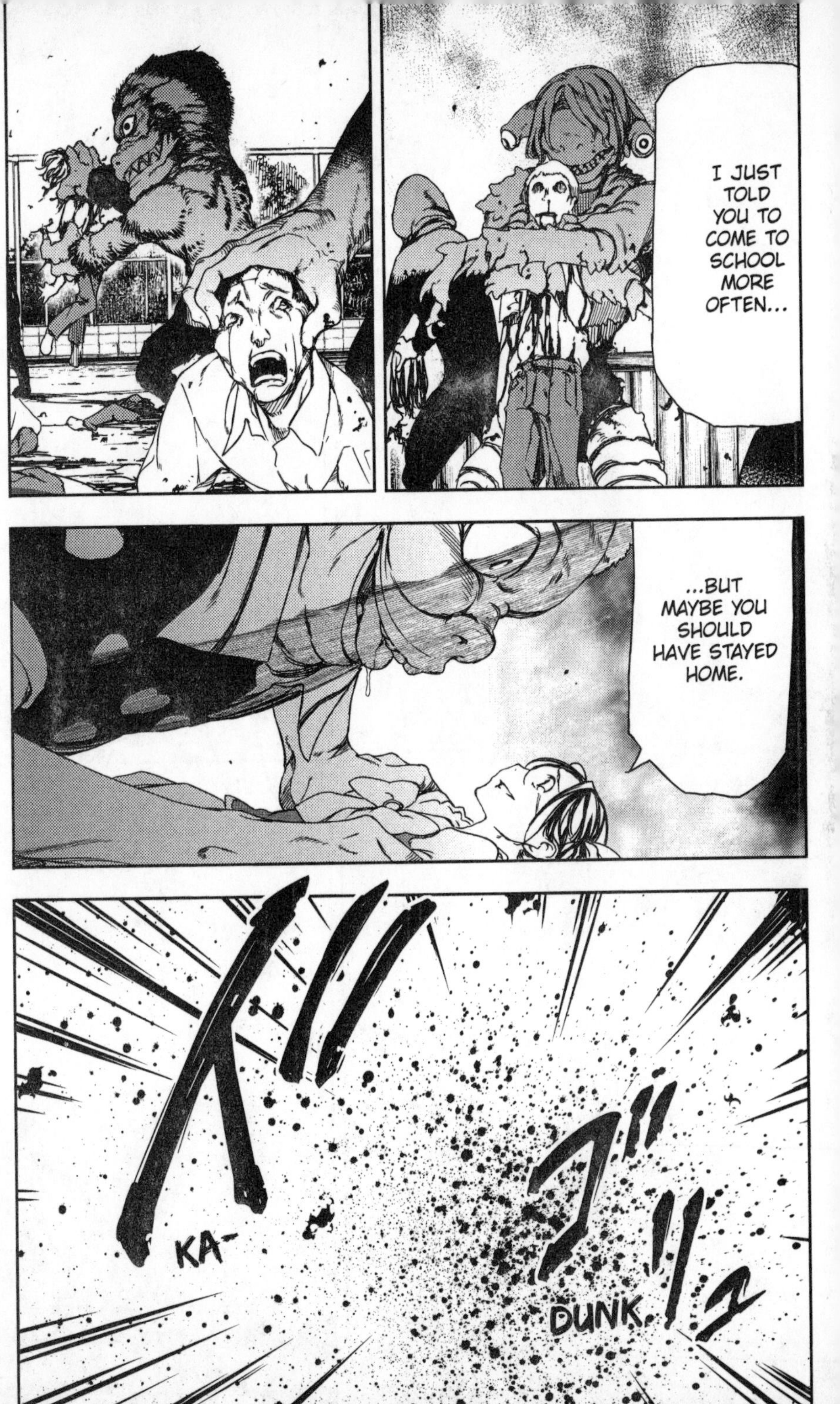
I JUST TOLD YOU TO COME TO SCHOOL MORE OFTEN...
...BUT MAYBE YOU SHOULD HAVE STAYED HOME.
KA-
DUNK

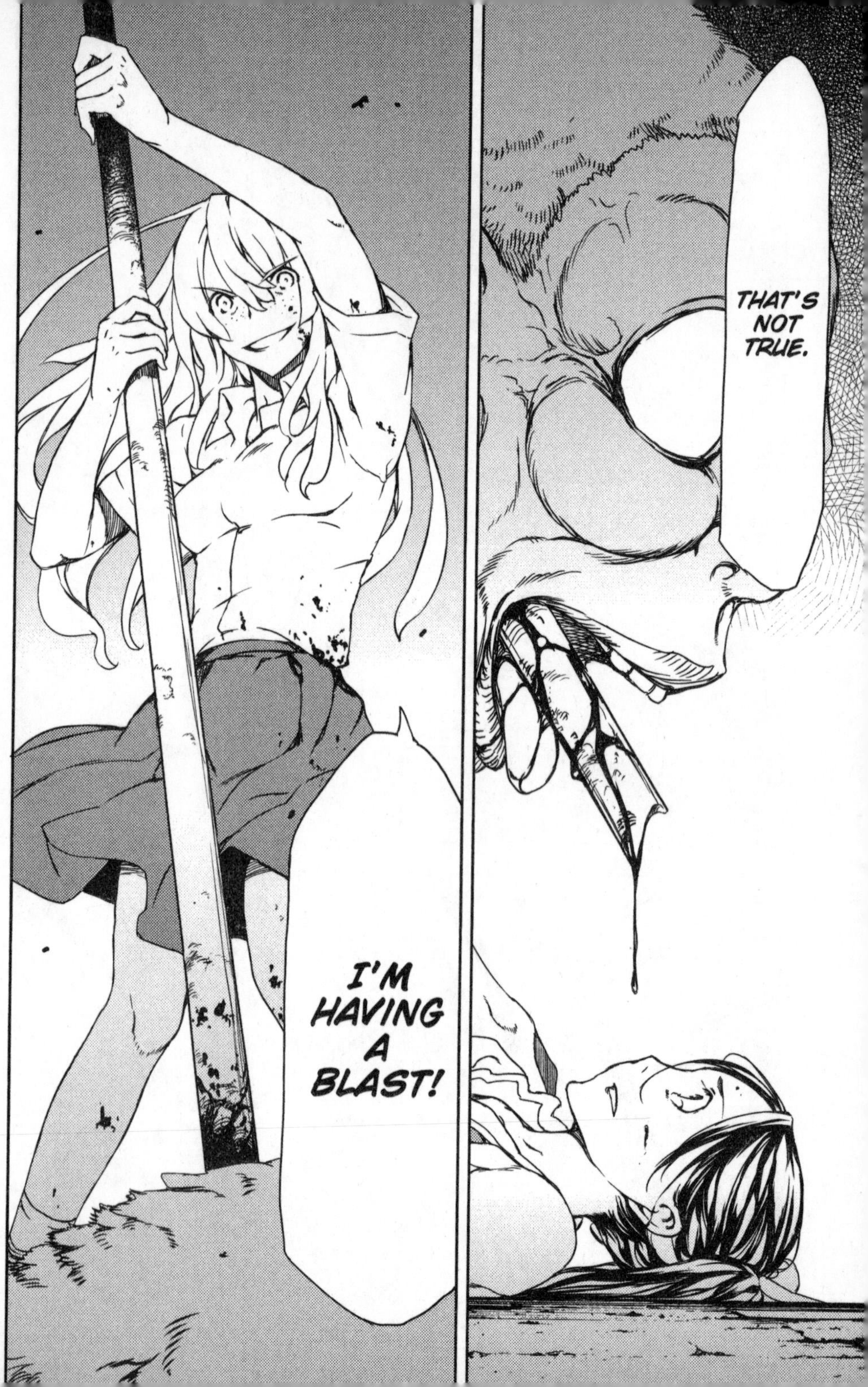
THAT'S NOT TRUE.
I'M HAVING A BLAST!

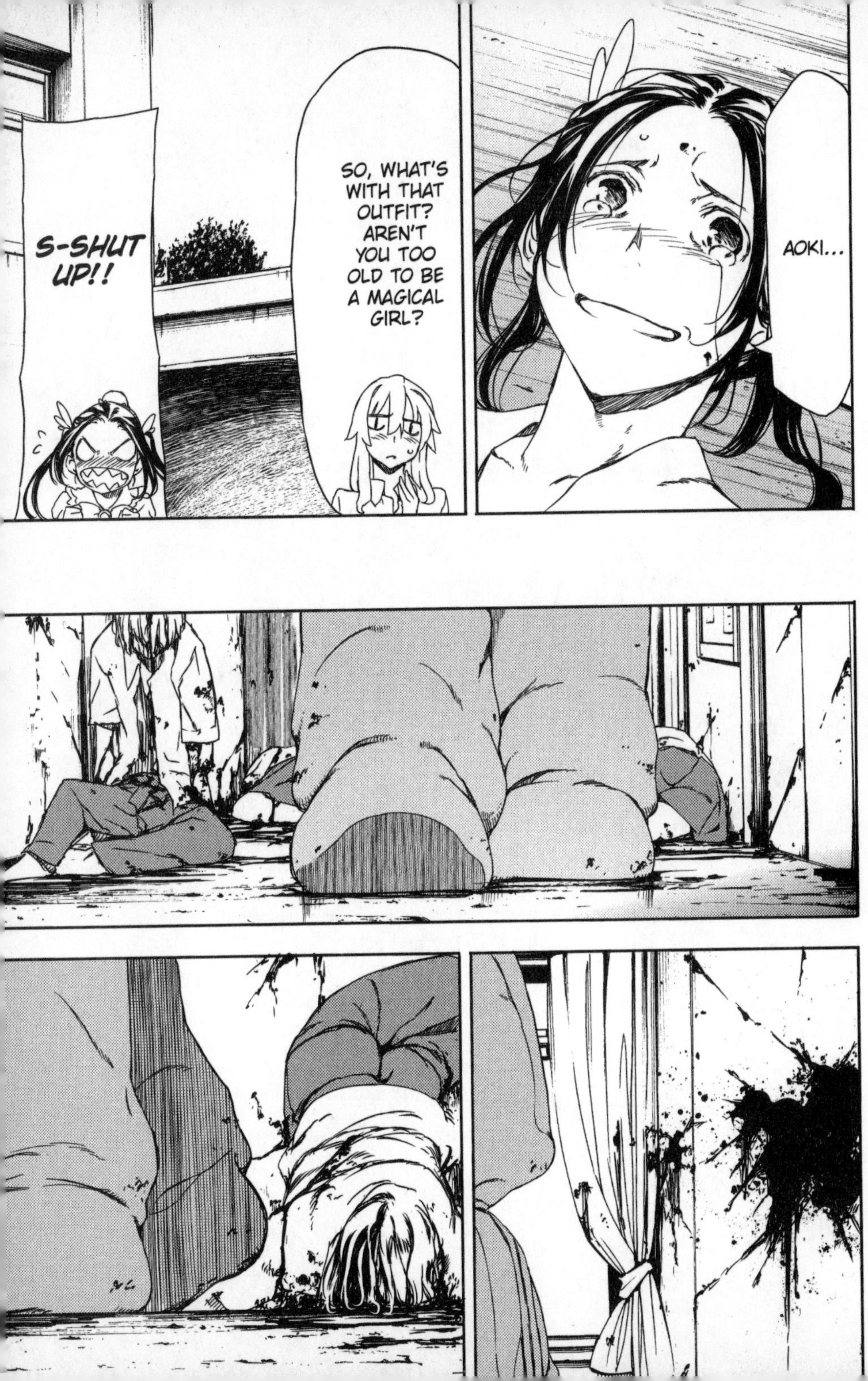
AOKI...
SO, WHAT'S WITH THAT OUTFIT? AREN'T YOU TOO OLD TO BE A MAGICAL GIRL?
S-SHUT UP!!

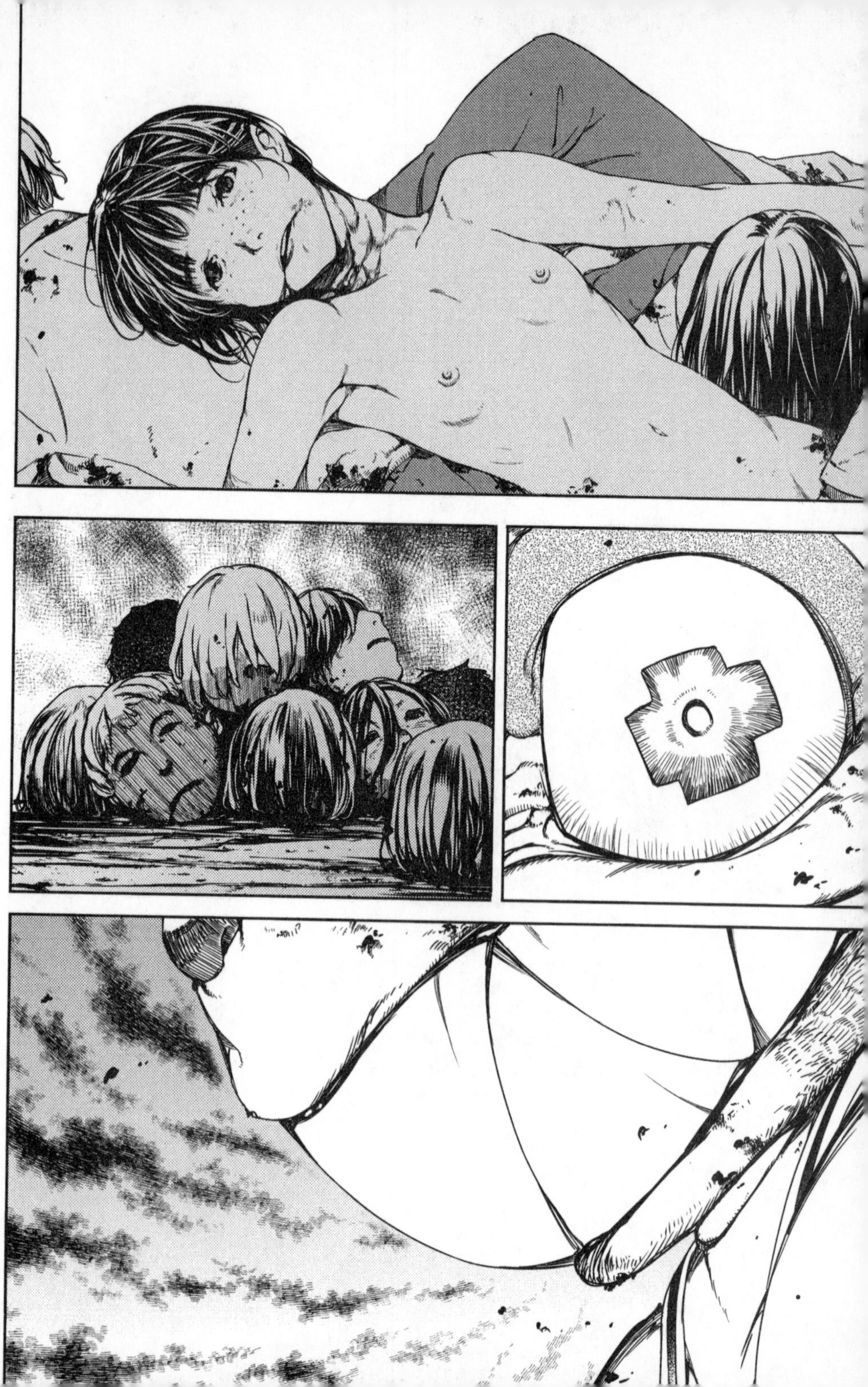

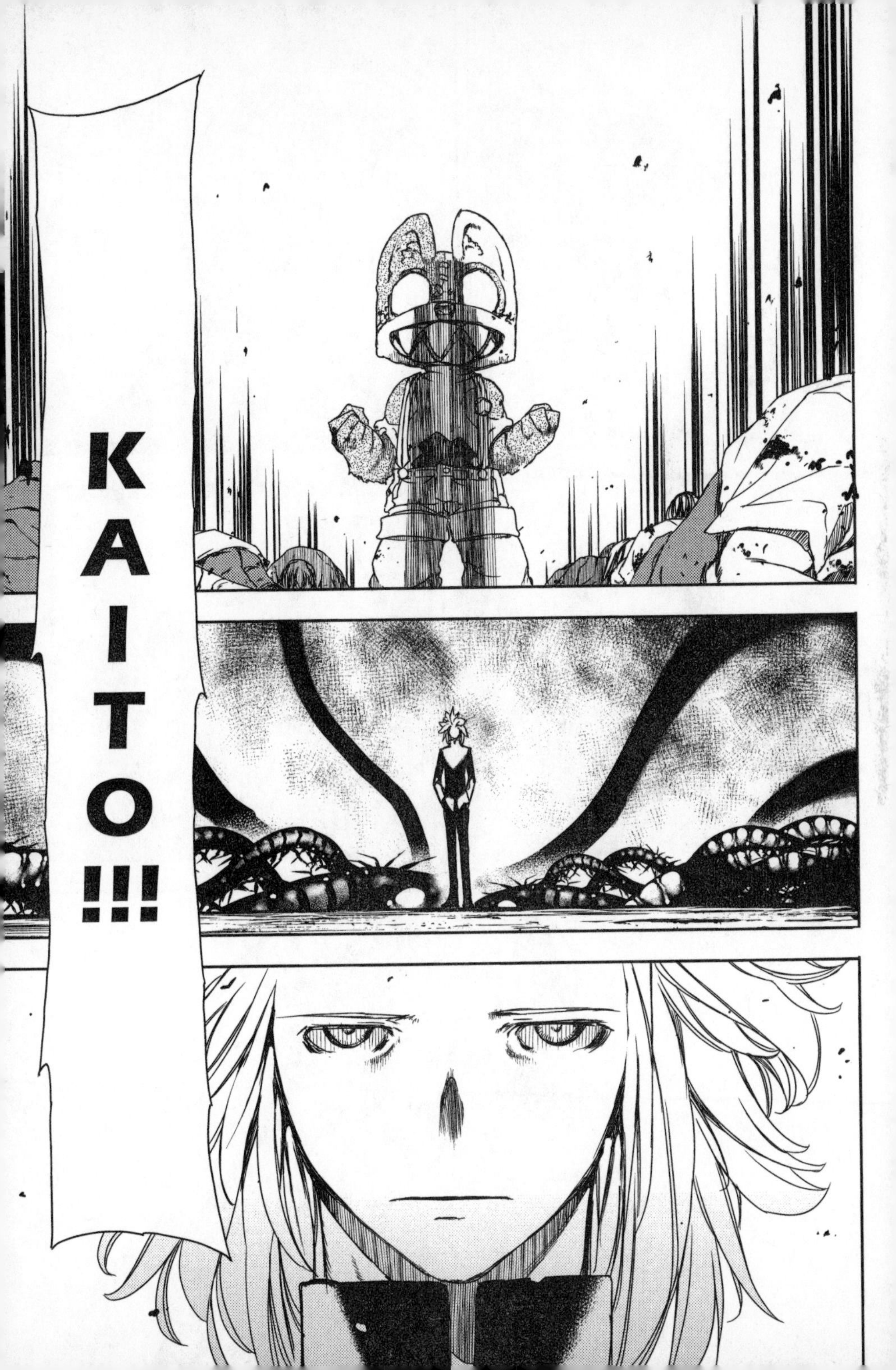
KAITO!!!

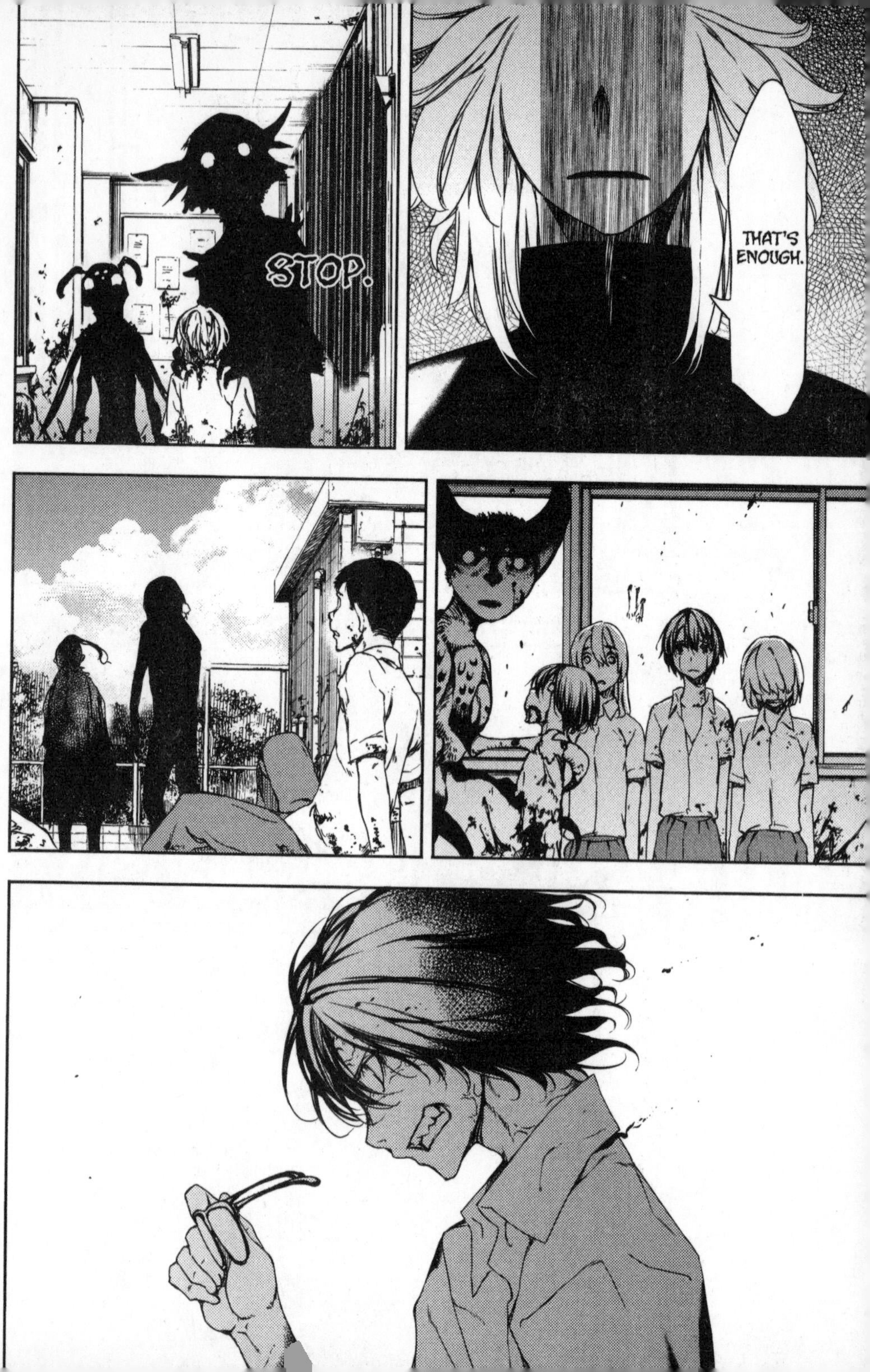
THAT'S ENOUGH.
STOP.

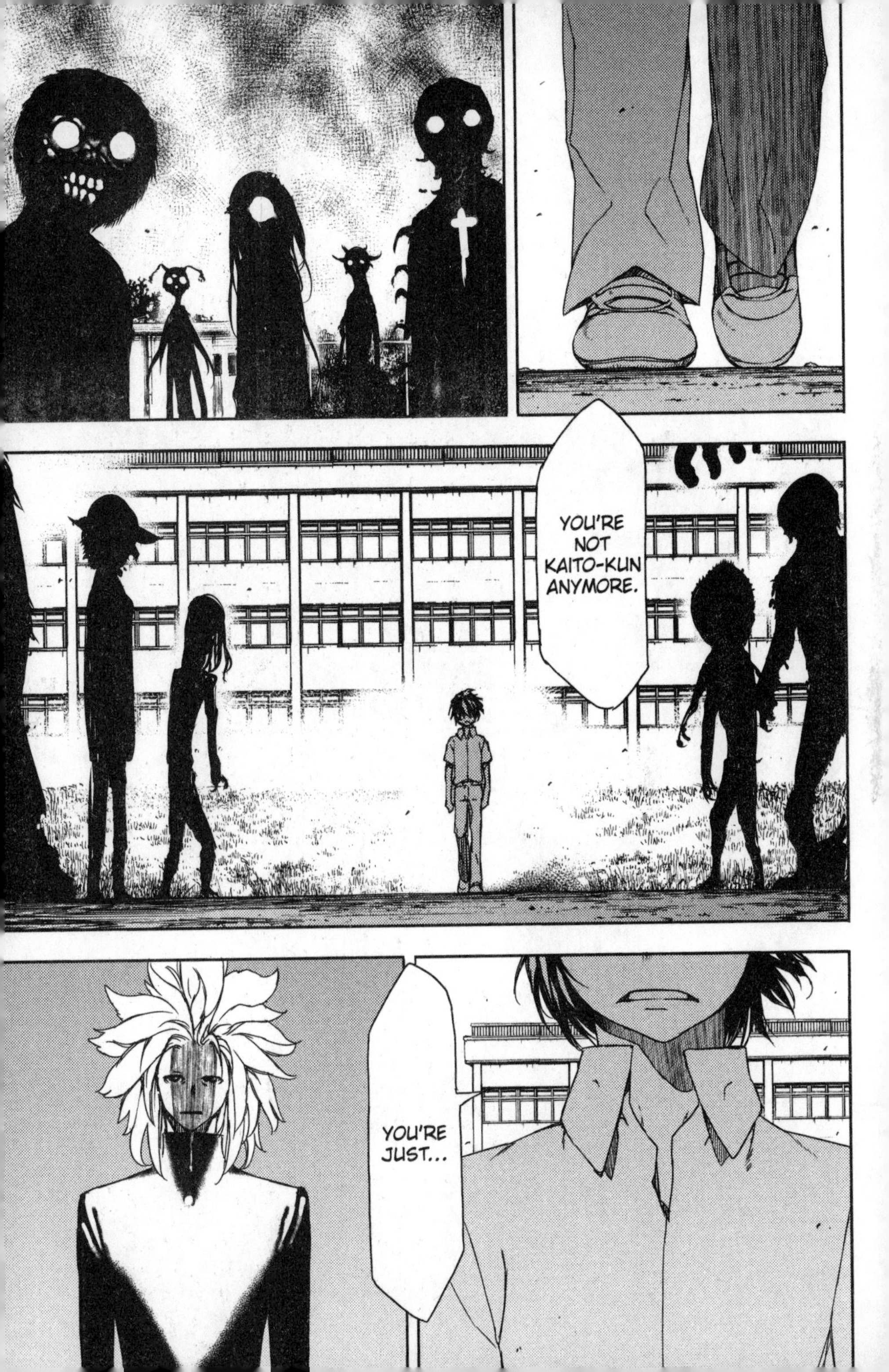
YOU'RE NOT KAITO-KUN ANYMORE.
YOU'RE JUST...

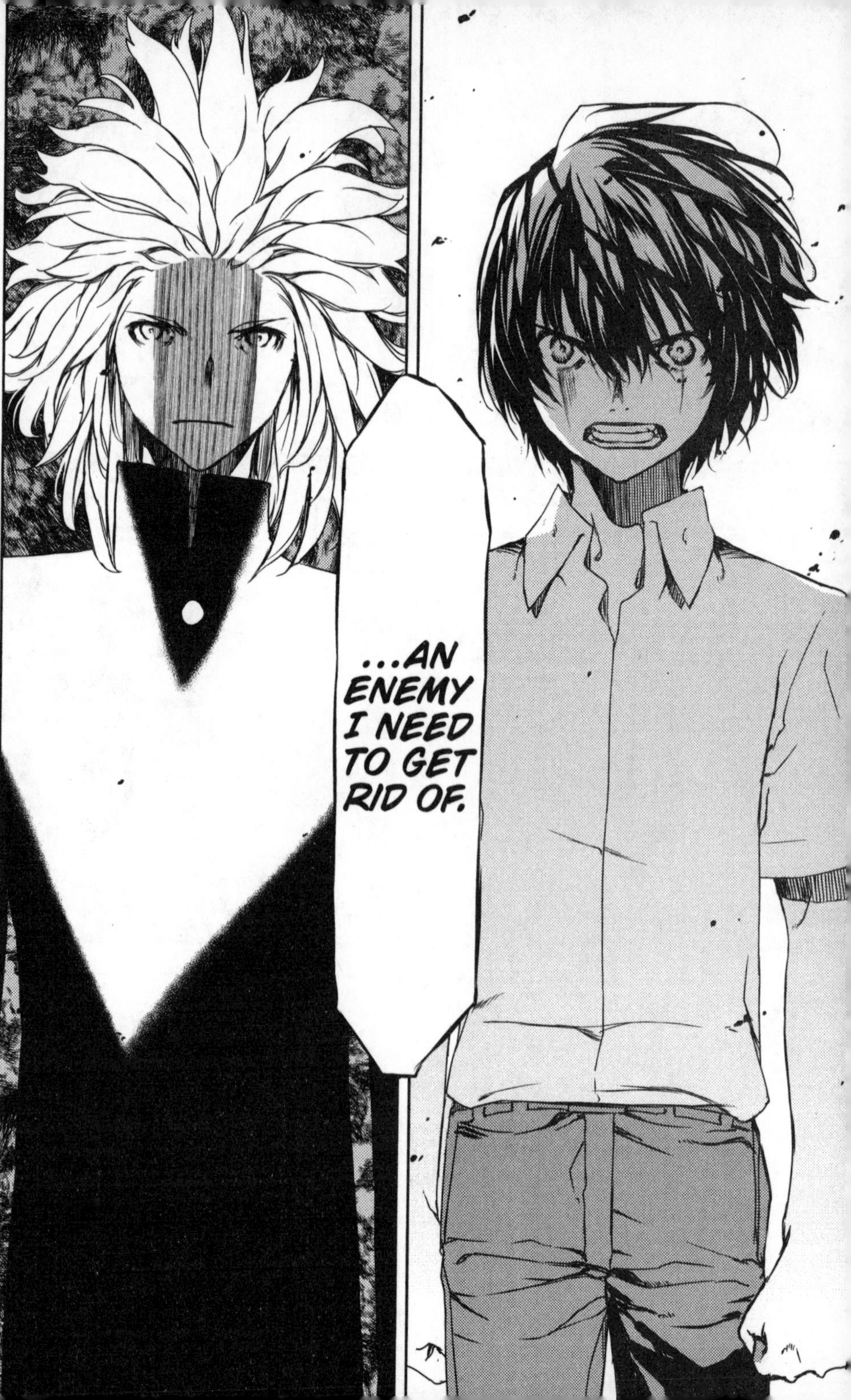
...AN ENEMY I NEED TO GET RID OF.

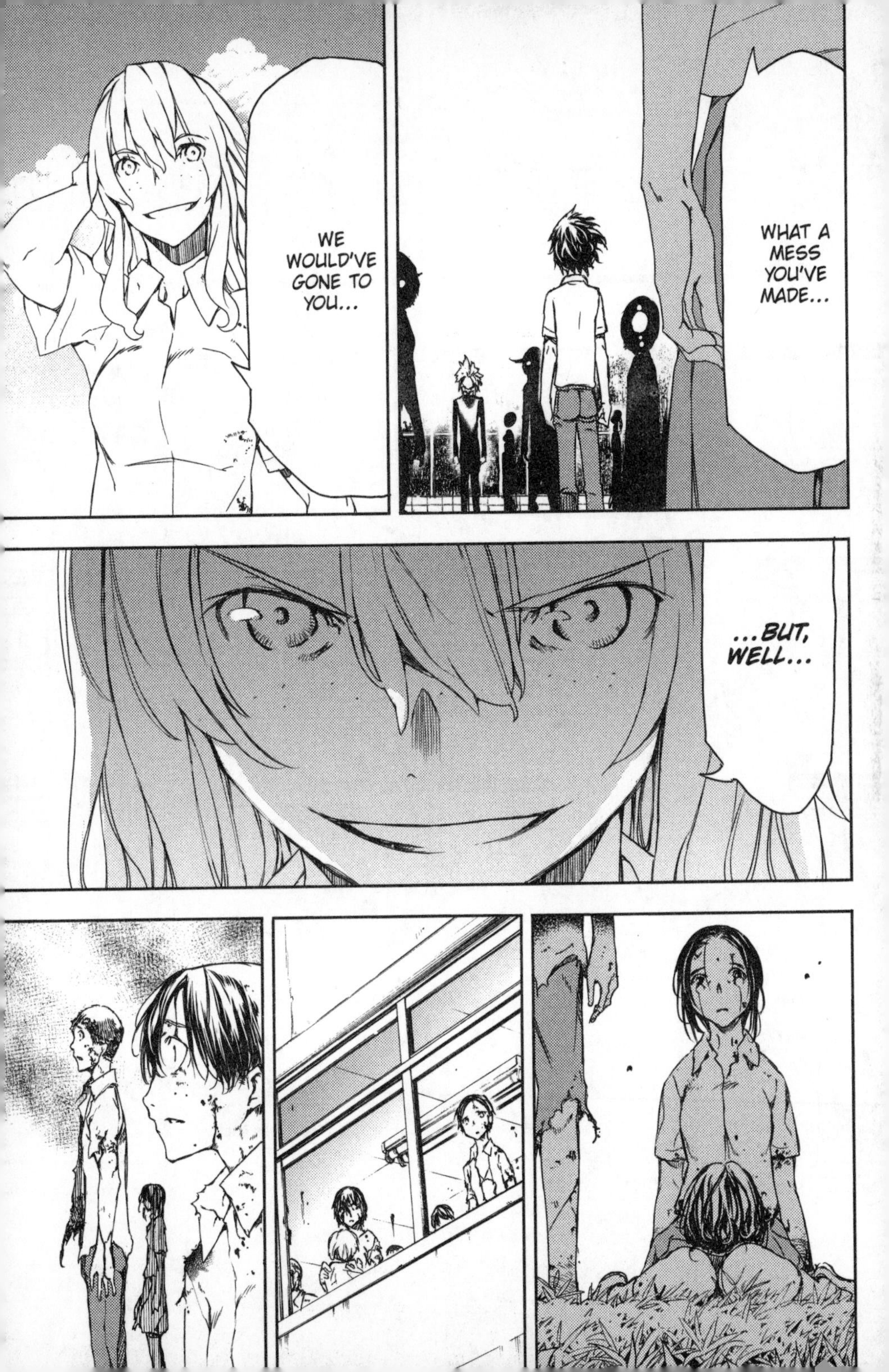
WHAT A MESS YOU'VE MADE...
WE WOULD'VE GONE TO YOU...
...BUT, WELL...

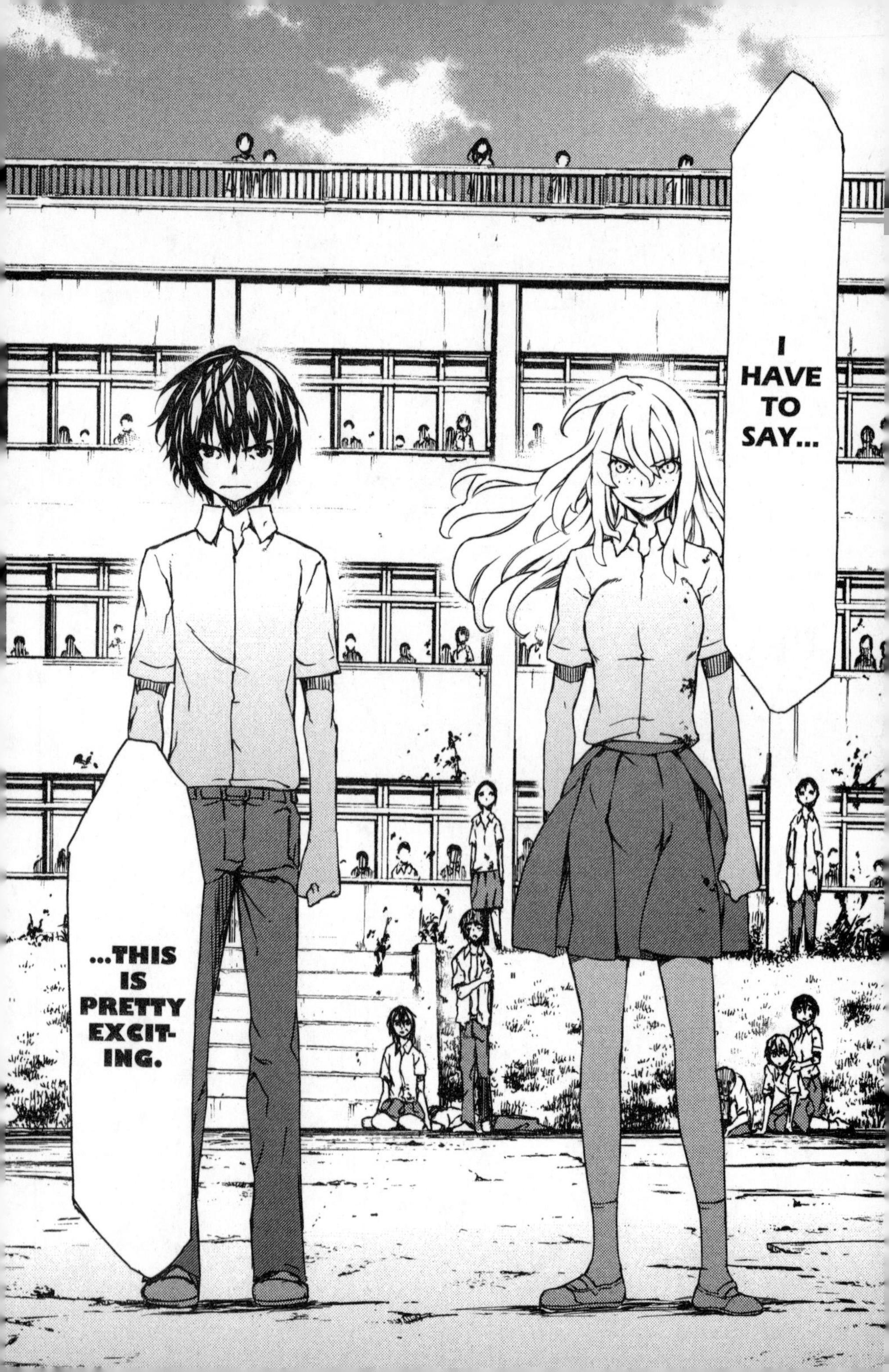
I HAVE TO SAY...
...THIS IS PRETTY EXCIT-ING.

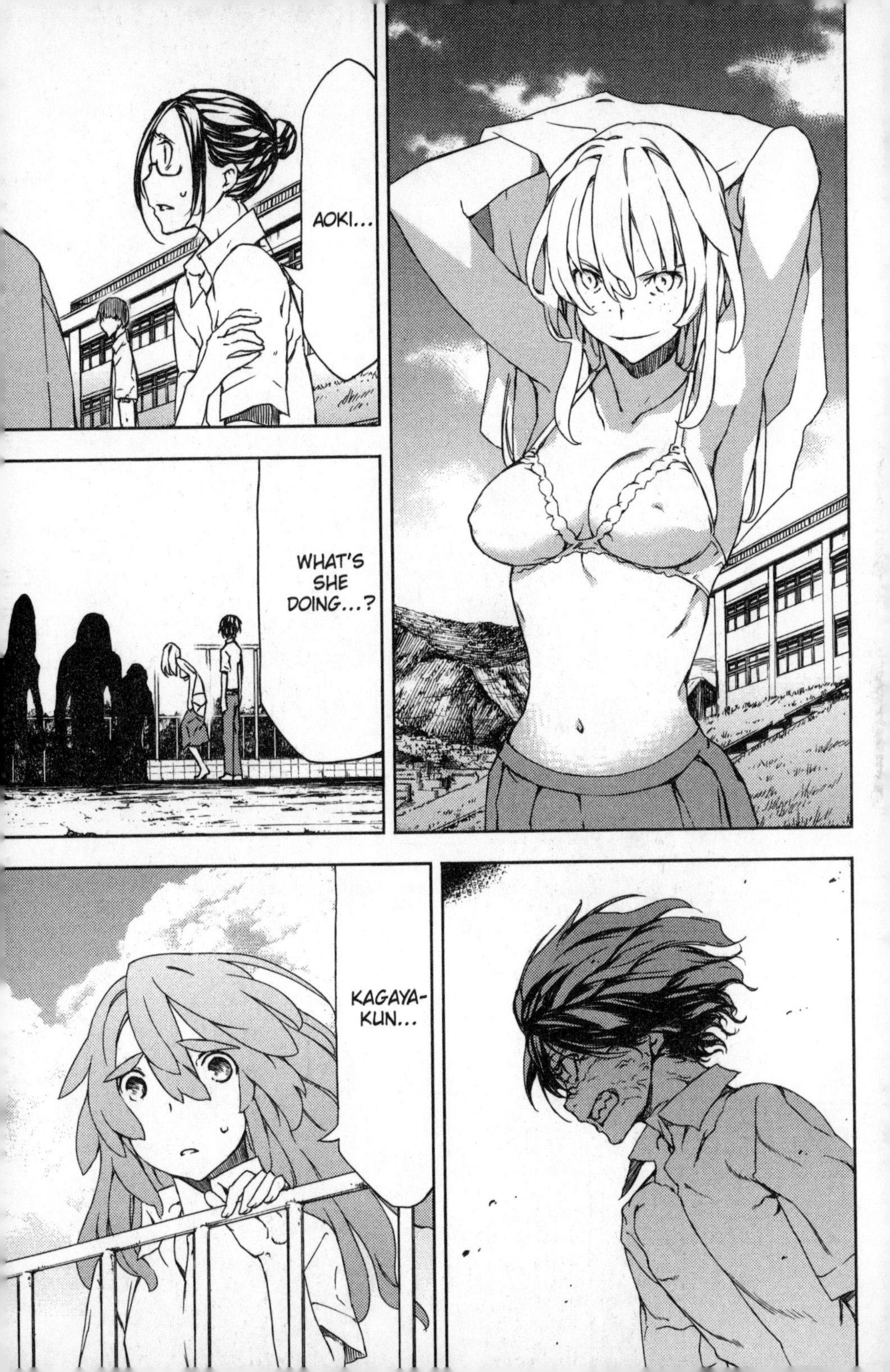
AOKI...
WHAT'S SHE DOING...?
KAGAYA-KUN...

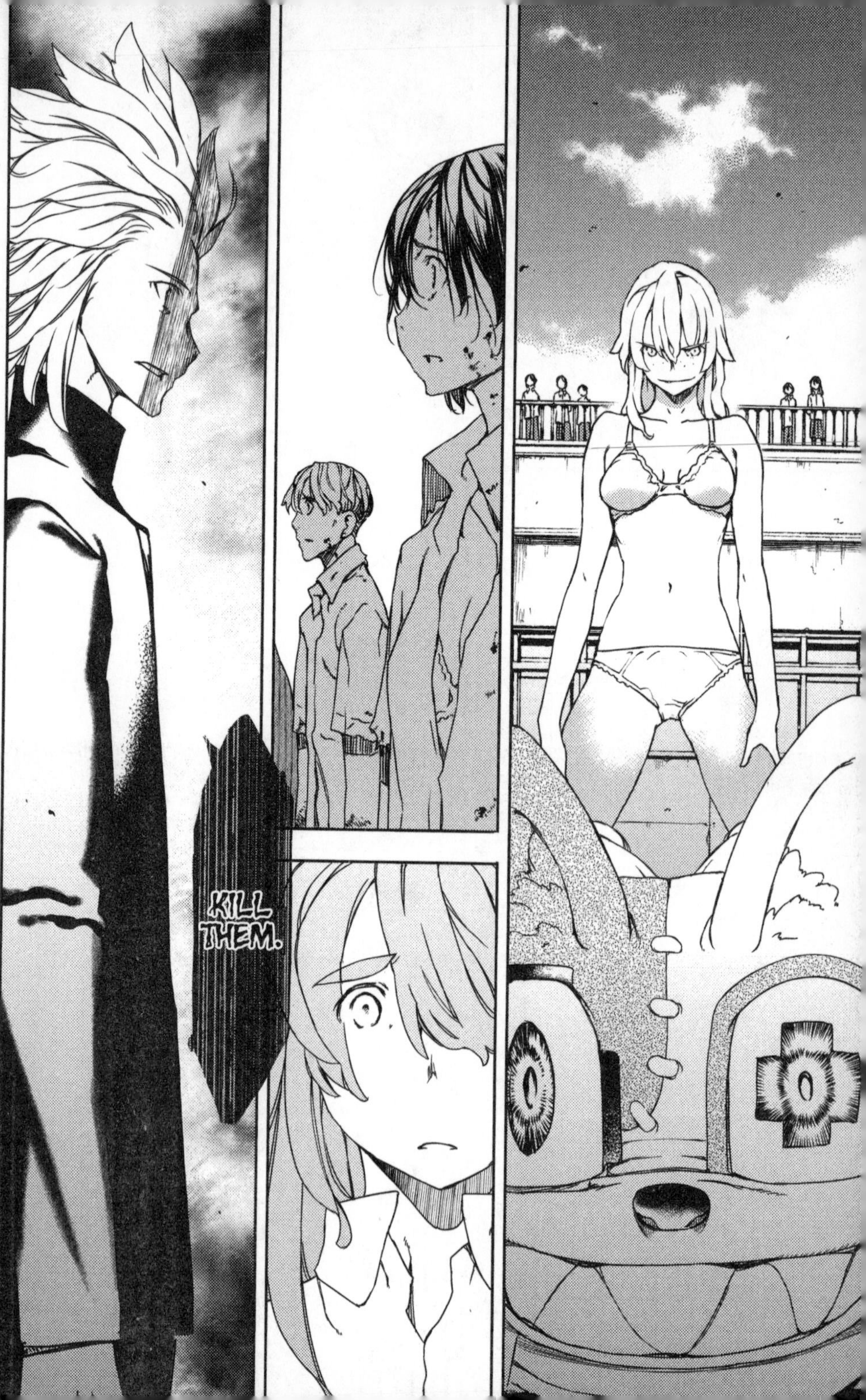
KILL THEM.

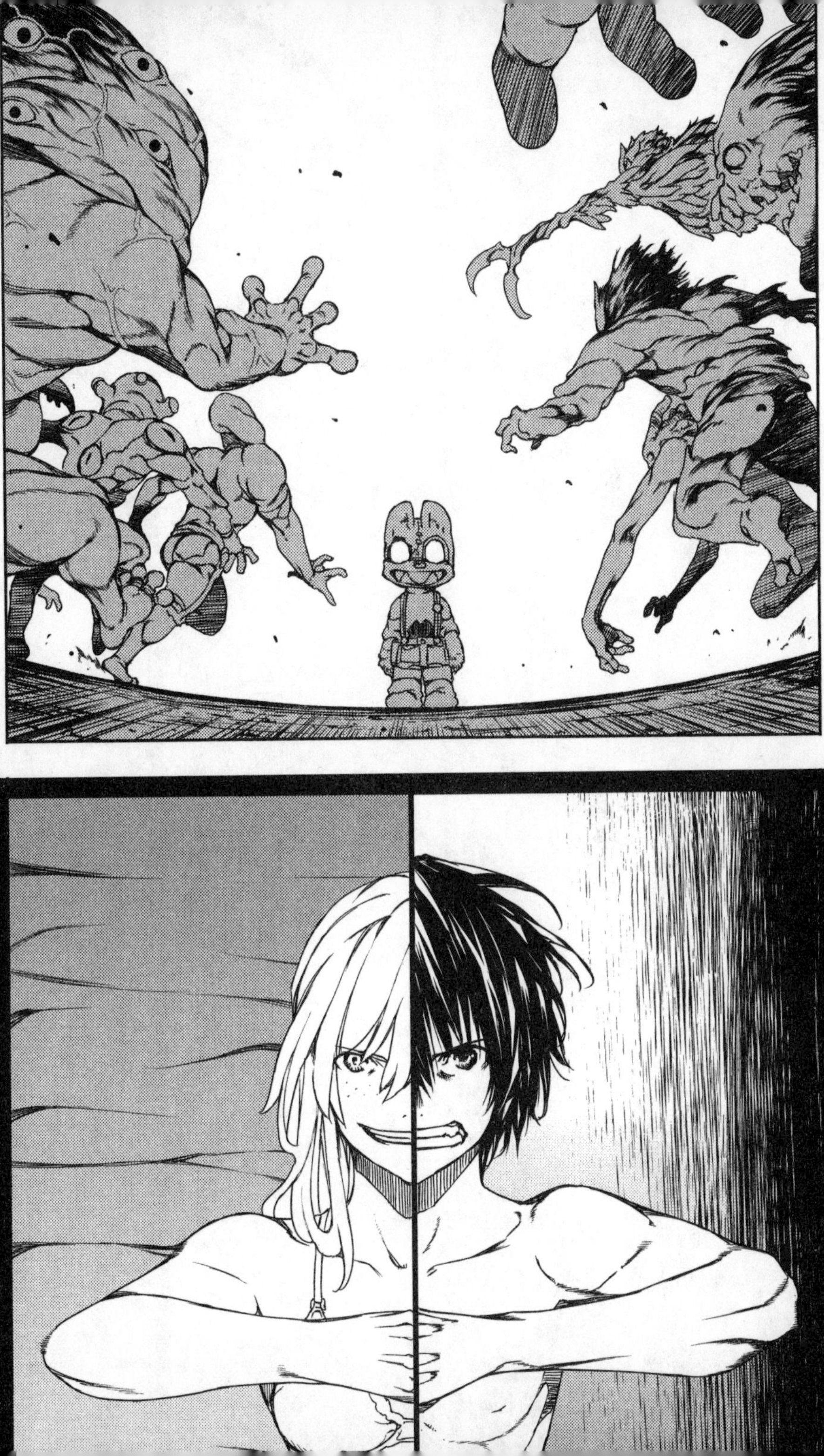

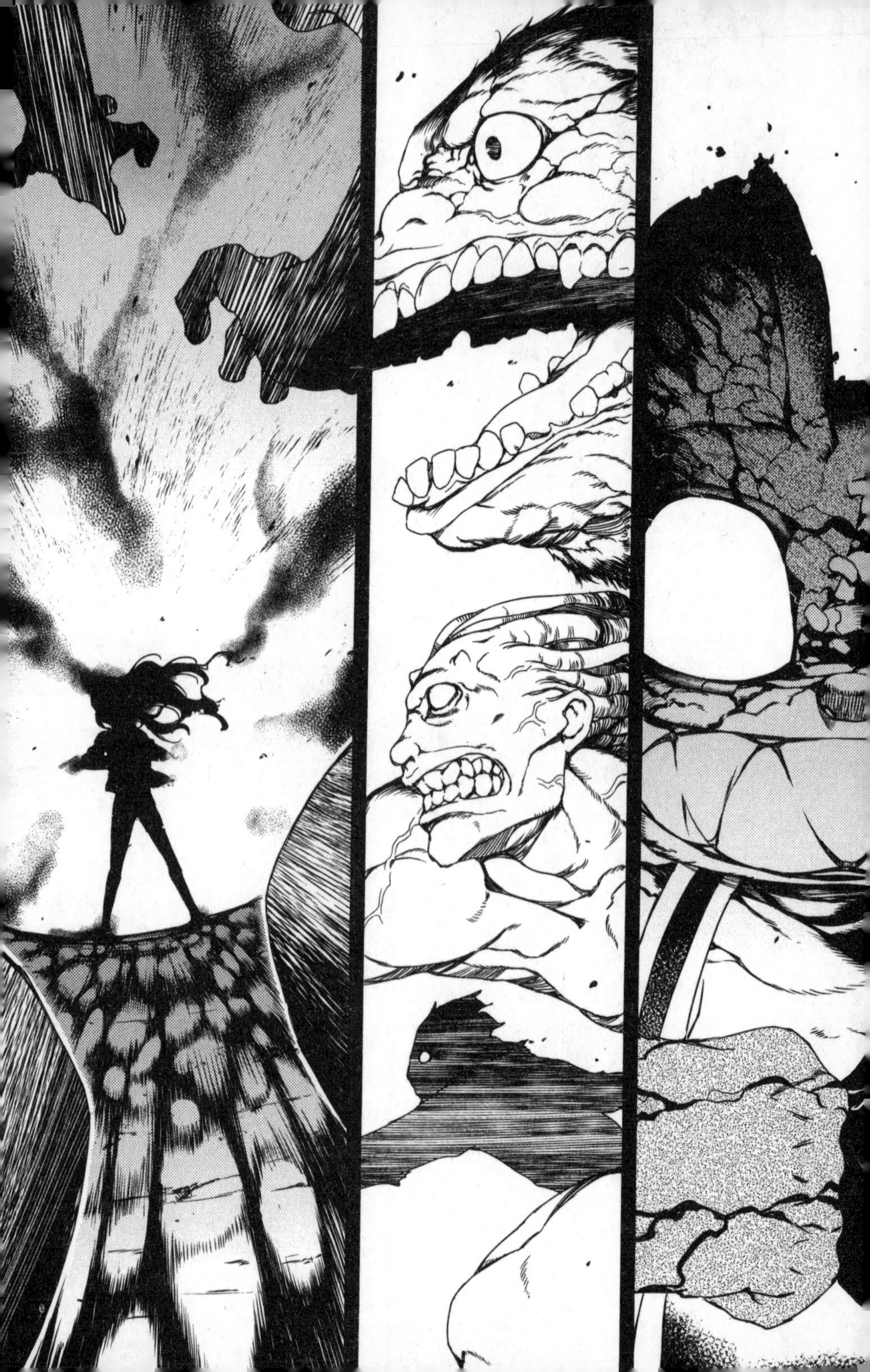

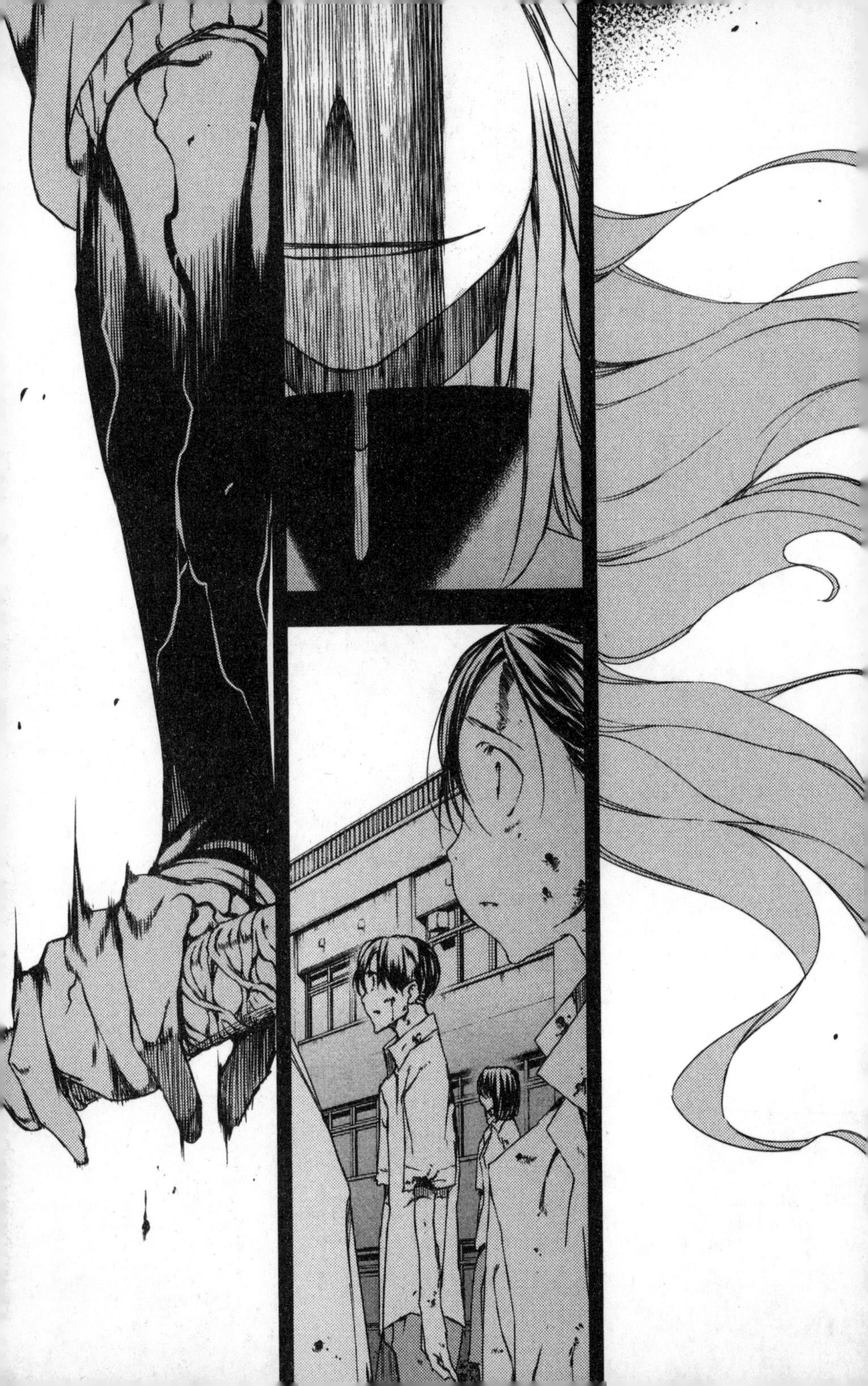

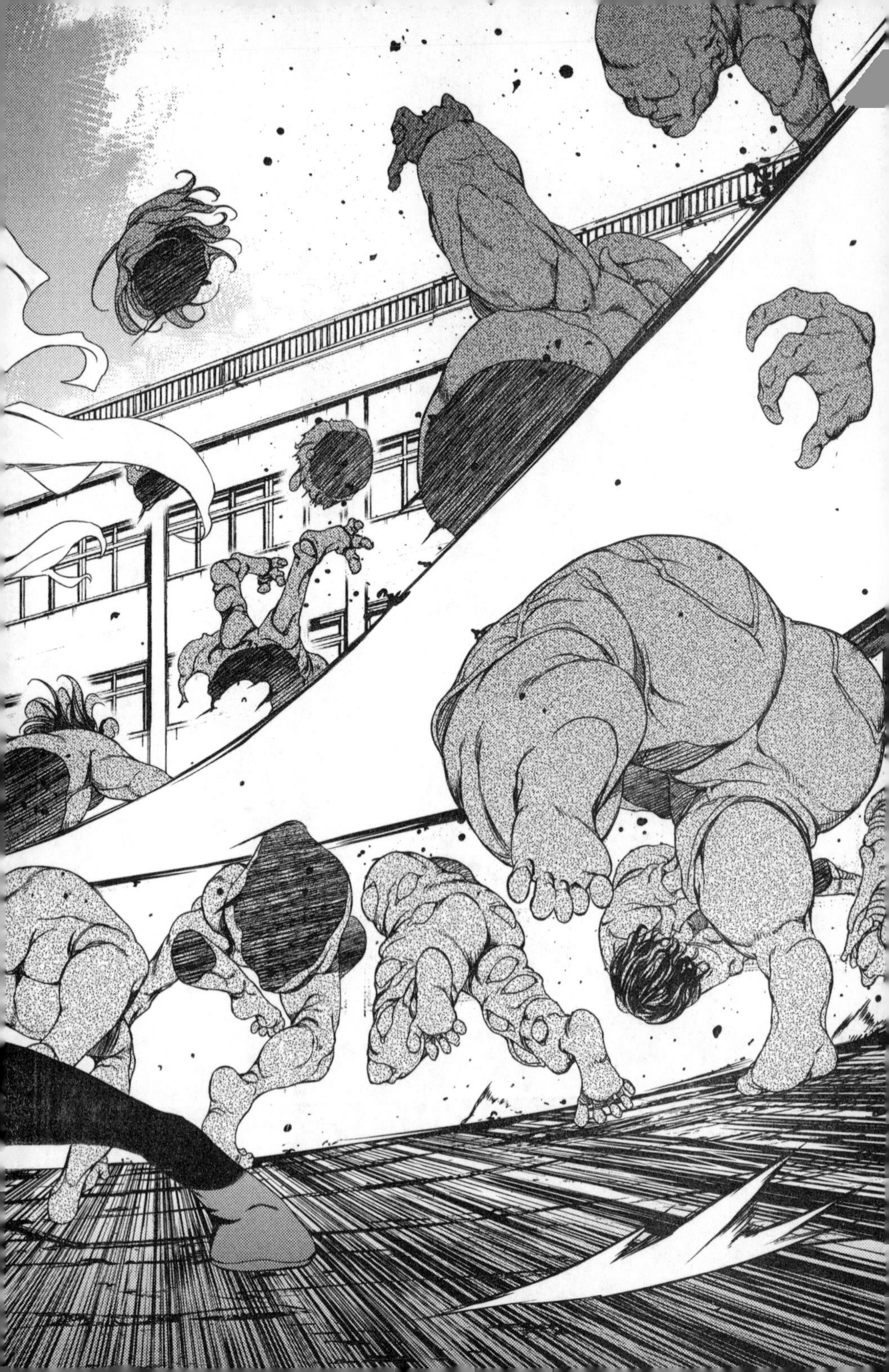

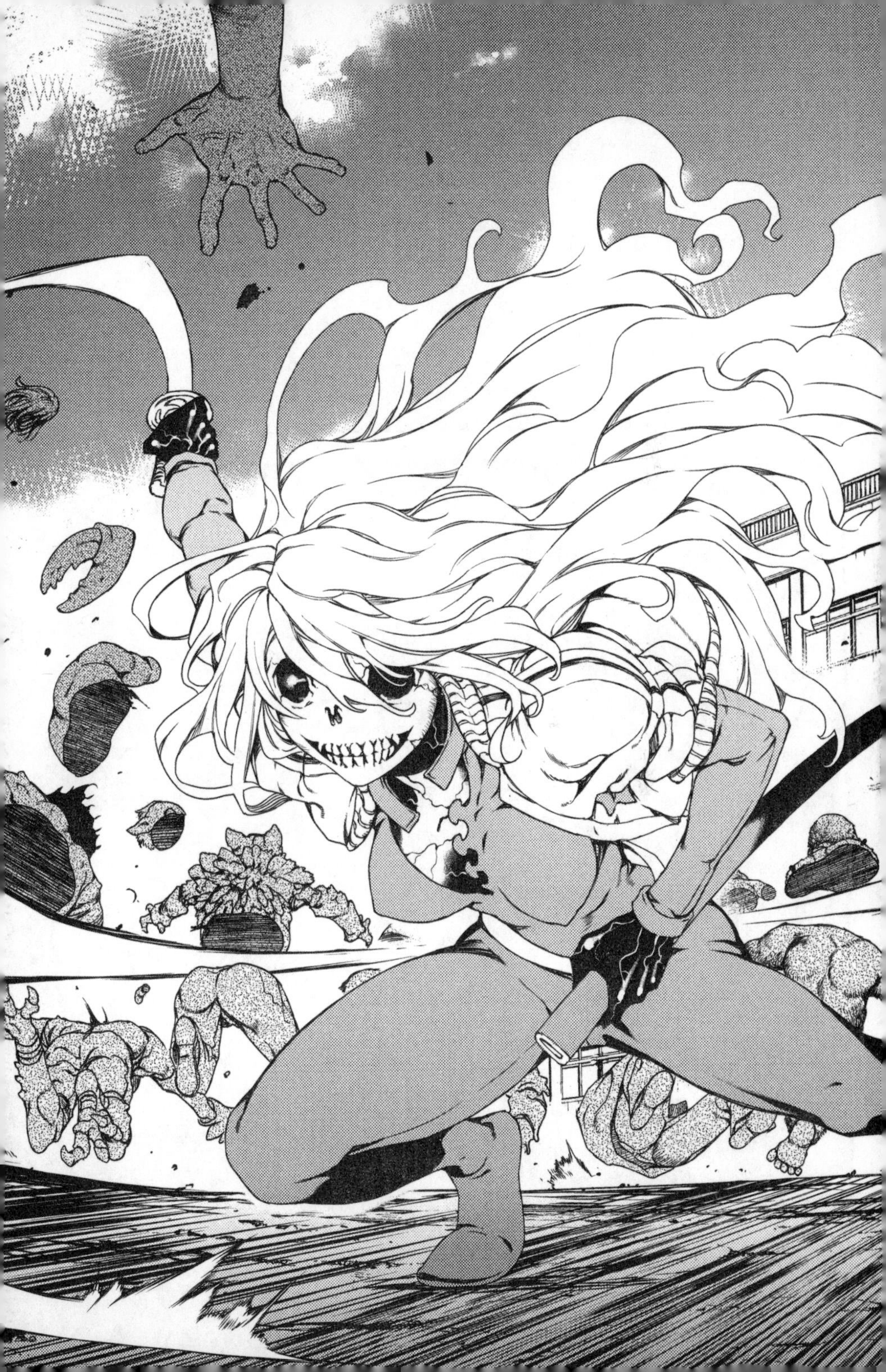

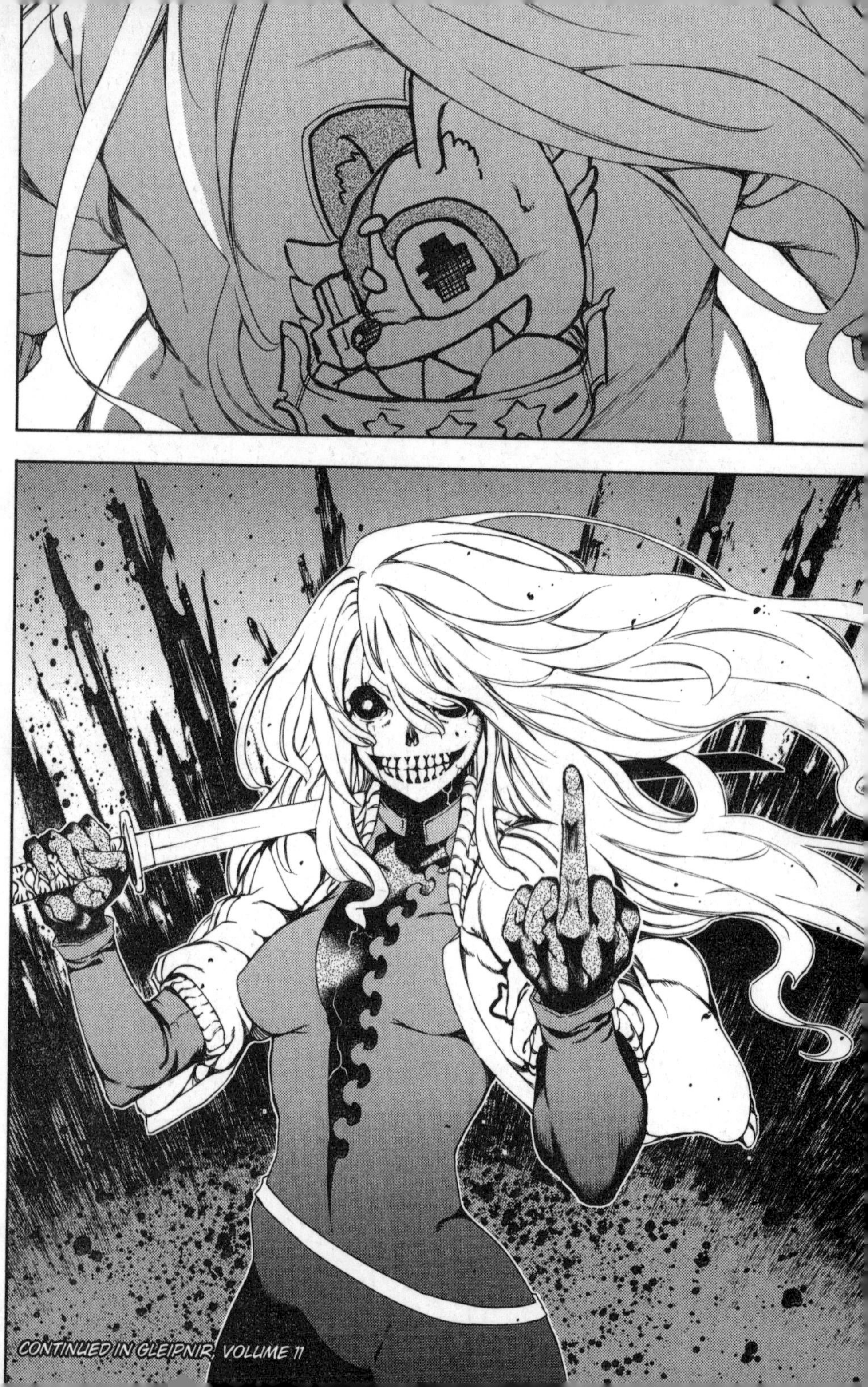
CONTINUED IN GLEIPNIR, VOLUME 11

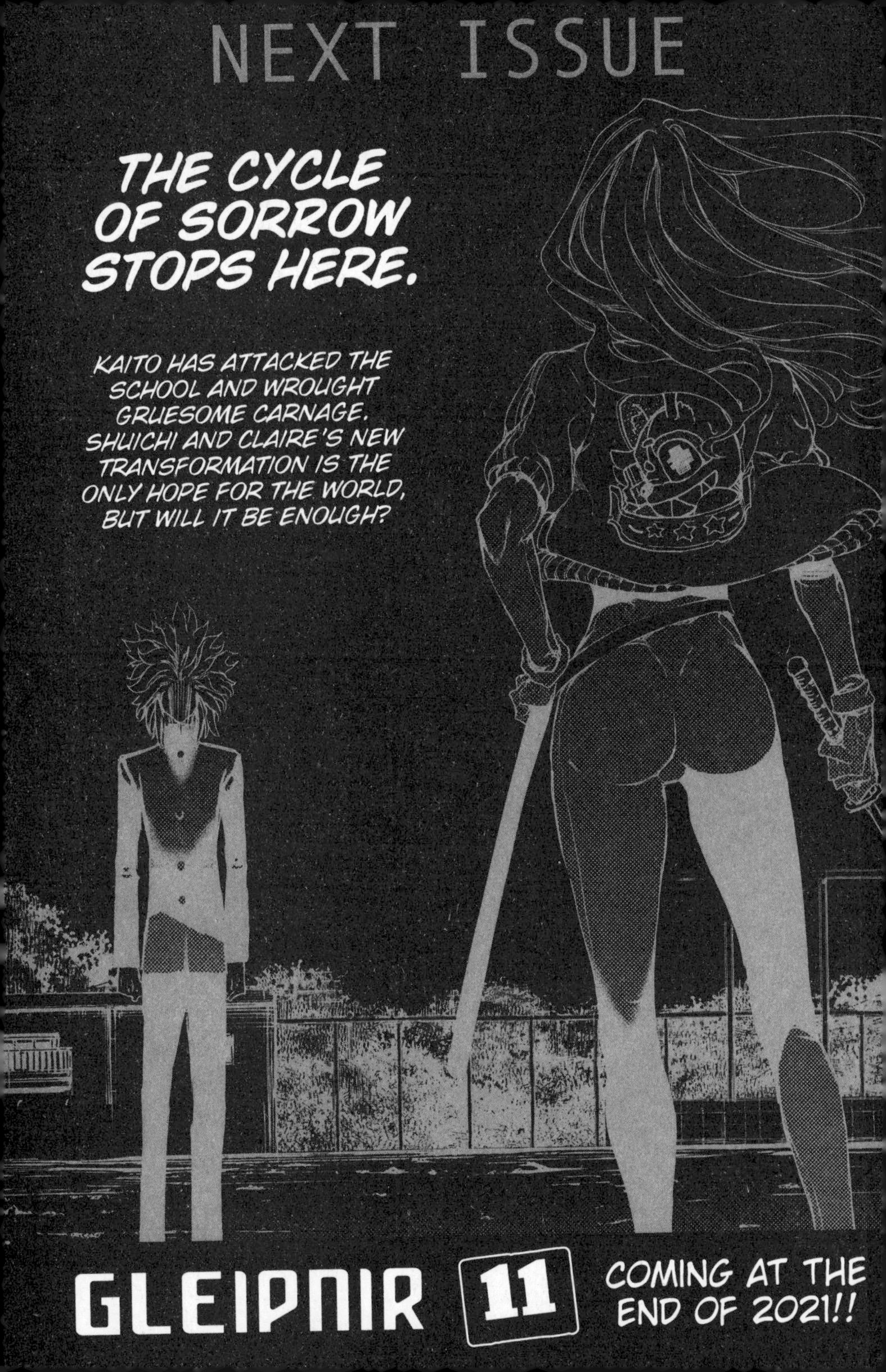
NEXT ISSUE
THE CYCLE OF SORROW STOPS HERE.
KAITO HAS ATTACKED THE SCHOOL AND WROUGHT GRUESOME CARNAGE. SHUICHI AND CLAIRE'S NEW TRANSFORMATION IS THE ONLY HOPE FOR THE WORLD, BUT WILL IT BE ENOUGH?
GLEIPNIR
11
COMING AT THE END OF 2021!!

A Kodansha Comics Trade Paperback Original
Gleipnir 10 copyright © 2021 Sun Takeda
English translation copyright © 2021 Sun Takeda

All rights reserved.

Published in the United States by Kodansha Comics, an imprint of Kodansha USA Publishing, LLC, New York.

Publication rights for this English edition arranged through Kodansha Ltd., Tokyo.

First published in Japan in 2021 by Kodansha Ltd., Tokyo. as *Gureipuniiru*, volume 10.

ISBN 978-1-64651-359-8

Printed in the United States of America.

www.kodansha.us

1st Printing
Translation: Iyasu Nagata
Lettering: Daniel Lee
Editing: Jordan Blanco
Kodansha Comics edition cover design by Phil Balsman

Publisher: Kiichiro Sugawara

Director of publishing services: Ben Applegate
Associate director, publising operations: Stephen Pakula
Publishing services managing editorial: Madison Salters, Alanna Ruse
Production managers: Emi Lotto, Angela Zurlo